Captain L. H. McNelly
—Texas Ranger —

Purchased
Fredericksburg
8/14/01

JAMES INGLIS, PHOTO.   MONTREAL.

Leander Harvey McNelly, from the original albumen print made by
Photographer James Inglis, 51 Bleury, Montreal, Canada. The image
was probably made in early 1873, but has also been dated as 1875.
Photo courtesy the Texas Ranger Hall of Fame & Museum, Waco, Texas.

CAPTAIN L. H. MCNELLY
–TEXAS RANGER –

The Life and Times of a Fighting Man

BY CHUCK PARSONS

&

MARIANNE E. HALL LITTLE

With an Introduction
by
Governor Dolph Briscoe

STATE HOUSE PRESS
AUSTIN, TX
2001

Library of Congress Cataloging-in-Publication Data

Parsons, Chuck.
Captain L.H. McNelly--Texas Ranger : the life and times
of a fighting man / by Chuck Parsons & Marianne E. Hall Little ;
introduction by Dolph Briscoe, Jr.
p. cm.
Includes bibliographical references and index.
ISBN 1-880510-75-8 (deluxe ltd. : alk. paper)
ISBN 1-880510-73-1 (alk. paper)
ISBN 1-880510-74-X (pbk. : alk. paper)
1. McNelly, Leander H., 1843 or 4 - 1877. 2. Texas Rangers--Biography.
3. Soldiers--Texas--Biography. 4. Peace officers--Texas--Biography.
5. Frontier and pioneer life--Texas. 6. Texas--History--1846-1950.
1. Hall Little, Marianne E., 1948- II. Title

F391.M5 P37 2001   .
976.4'061'092--dc21   .
[B]   00-044545

Printed in the United States of America

FIRST EDITION

cover design by David Timmons

STATE HOUSE PRESS
PO Box 15247
Austin, Texas 78761

TABLE OF CONTENTS

A Mexican guard threatening the town of Brownsville, Texas. The original caption read: "On the Rio Grande-Mexican Cannon and 'Doubled' Guard threatening the town of Brownsville, Texas, November 20th, 1875."
From Frank Leslie's *Illustrated Newspaper*, January 1, 1876.
Courtesy The Library of Congress.

LIST OF ILLUSTRATIONS

FOREWORD

It is with pleasure that I am able to contribute a word of introduction to this biography of one of the greatest of Texas Rangers — Leander Harvey McNelly. The man who survived battles of the Civil War, engaged in personal combat against outlaws and bandits, and then lost his life to an insidious disease has long been a fascinating character for me. This biography, the first full length study of the man, is an appropriate record of his contributions in the establishment of law and order in Texas.

Years ago I found George Durham's book *Taming the Nueces Strip* and read it with great interest. Although the sub-title reads *The Story of McNelly's Rangers*, the book focuses mainly on the work of McNelly and his men south of the Nueces River in the years 1875-1876. I have long hoped that some day there would be a full length biography of the man, and now what you hold in your hands represents just that — the first complete biography of McNelly.

Few men leave a legacy by which they are remembered. I feel privileged that the citizens of Texas found me worthy of being their highest elected representative. I am proud that I am in a position to help memorialize McNelly's legacy, not that he is in great need of my efforts because he so ably made his own mark. In the First State Bank of Uvalde is a conference room, appropriately designated "The McNelly Room," containing a large oil painting by artist Joe Grandee which had hung in the governor's mansion during my terms of office (1973-1979). I feel honored to have this art work now available for the public to view and admire. It is signed by the artist and is a wonderful representation of L. H. McNelly.

In addition there is a large portrait of McNelly painted by R. Sanders as well as a number of other works of art representing McNelly and other rangers. Not surprisingly, there are mounted heads of Texas longhorns. These are, in a symbolic way, representative of the livestock which McNelly recovered from bandits during his service south of the Nueces. I muse occasionally that these longhorns in the McNelly Room are descended from those cattle recovered in 1875-1876!

We remember McNelly and his rangers here in South Texas. He recovered stolen property from across the Rio Grande. He arrested many a thief and murderer. He led his men into combat rather than sending them. For this his men loved and admired him. If he had asked them, they would have followed him into Hell. The legacy he left behind is part of the history of our great state. It is only fitting that, finally, his entire life has been researched and written and made available in book form. I am proud to have been able to contribute to it in a small way with these few words.

One of McNelly's legendary exploits was the recovery of stolen cattle from the King Ranch. I would like to conclude with a few words, from the book *The King Ranch*, by which writer-artist Tom Lea aptly expressed my thoughts. "The men enlisted to follow him [McNelly] were all young men and they did not stay unless they were daring. There were only a handful of Texans; their captain preferred to recruit from backgrounds remote from any locale of ranger duty. The basic requirements for service were unflinching bravery and disregard of hardship; skill with firearms and horses came next. McNelly was a demanding master who made his demands by example. The western frontier seems not to have had at any time a more fearless band of disciplined fighters than McNelly's border company of Texas Rangers."

—Governor Dolph Briscoe, Jr.

Authors' Preface

Leander Harvey McNelly was, in the simplest terms, a lawman. His law enforcement philosophy was to some, even to some of his own men, considered terribly brutal and cruel: shoot first and ask questions later. It was nevertheless effective in the time and place in which McNelly worked. Because he was unaware of, or at least recognized, no such modern niceties as the rights of the accused, the Miranda readings, or arrests made on solid evidence rather than on suspicions or appearances, today he would have been on suspension too many times to count. In some instances McNelly was both judge and jury before turning over the accused to his own executioner.

McNelly had no special training as a lawman, and his effectiveness is based in great part upon the dedication of his men in following the orders of their captain without question. George P. Durham, who as a teenager rode with McNelly, told his biographer when in his early eighties, ready to meet his maker, "I hope to overhaul him one more time. When I get Over Yonder, as I said, I want to go back to work for Captain if he's still running an outfit."[1] After McNelly's early death his men were often termed "Little McNelly's" in honor of their deceased leader.

His ability to lead men into danger was exhibited early in the Civil War, a conflict in which he served four years. For his daring and courage he was granted the captaincy of a group of scouts assigned to hunt down deserters. Although McNelly had fought for the Confederacy, following Reconstruction in Texas former Union officer E.J. Davis, now Republican Governor of the State of Texas, remembered him and requested him to become one of the first four captains of the State Police force just then being organized. The force proved to be extremely unpopular among the rank and file Texans, who had suffered through the war, returned home to overbearing federal occupation troops, and resented what they considered an unnecessary and despotic political force. Many a young Southerner could not deal with the social climate and became an outlaw and fugitive. McNelly chose to accept Governor Davis' offer to lead men; he became an efficient captain in a most unpopular cause but earned the respect of his fellow Texans.

After the dissolution of the State Police in early 1873, McNelly returned to his Washington County farm to lead a quiet existence, but again he was called upon to serve the state. This time the call was from Democratic Governor Richard Coke, who had reorganized the Texas Rangers and formed the Frontier Battalion, made up of six companies "A" through "F", whose primary function was to defend the westward moving frontier against the Indian menace. He also created a Special Force, a company designed to deal with more internal problems, and called upon McNelly to be its captain. Thus the Washington County Volunteer Militia Company "A" was formed, although there never was but the one company. Although technically not part of the official Texas Ranger force, the McNelly company was in all aspects a Texas Ranger company except for the name. The men were paid by the state, the captain reported to the adjutant general, and McNelly as well as the ordinary Texan of the day considered the group as much Texas Rangers as the official six companies of the Frontier Battalion. To consider them anything but Texas Rangers is merely wrangling over semantics.

McNelly first attempted to quell the violent Sutton-Taylor Feud centered in the DeWitt County area. The command remained there for several months, made some arrests, fought in a shooting engagement or two, and then was called elsewhere. There was a lull in the fighting while McNelly and his men were there, but with the company's departure the feud was renewed.

Following the disappointing experience in DeWitt County, McNelly was ordered to the Rio Grande Frontier where he was looked upon as a savior by the Anglo ranchers who were incapable of preventing their herds from being stolen and carried off across the river. Their ranches were being burned and their mere existence was constantly in jeopardy. In the popular mind, the leader of all the Mexican cattle thieves was General Juan Nepomuceno Cortina.

It was on the Rio Grande Frontier that McNelly earned his greatest fame in Texas history. He focused on one aspect of the border troubles: the stealing of livestock by raiders. To do this he employed spies, used torture to gain information, lynched prisoners, raided camps of suspected cattle thieves, and invaded Mexico on at least two occasions. His techniques brought results and earned the Texas Rangers the reputation of being *diablos Tejanos* in the Nueces Strip area and south of the river. His tactics would not be tolerated today, but McNelly did recover stolen property and reduce the amount of lawlessness on the border.

Although his force was created by the state, he received considerable support in the form of provisions from cattleman Richard King. For his accomplishments on the border McNelly earned the gratitude of the Texas ranchers. His tangible recompense, other than his meager monthly salary from the state, was a bounty for his men and a monument erected over his grave by Richard King as a show of his deep appreciation.

Following the Rio Grande experience, there was but little time left for Leander H. McNelly. He did arrest a number of Anglo outlaws, the most notorious being John King Fisher of the Pendencia, only to see his prisoner released on a technicality. McNelly's tuberculosis worsened to such an extent that he was unable to stay in the field with his men; he was reduced to being a near invalid. The state ungraciously dropped his name from the rolls and replaced him with another young man, Lieutenant Jesse Leigh "Lee" Hall, who had learned many tricks of the trade under McNelly.

For all his reckless courage and indomitable spirit, McNelly has not attracted biographers, at least to the extent of other western lawmen such as Wyatt Earp and Wild Bill Hickok. The index of the authoritative bibliography *Six-Guns and Saddle Leather: A Bibliography of Books and Pamphlets on Western Outlaws and Gunmen* by Ramon F. Adams, does not even contain McNelly's name, although it does appear briefly in some of the books listed and described therein.

The earliest work dealing mainly with McNelly and his men was *A Texas Ranger* by N.A. Jennings, first published in 1899 by Charles Scribner's Sons. This work was first reprinted in 1930 by Southwest Press of Dallas with a foreword by J. Frank Dobie, reprinted again in facsimile in 1959 by the Steck Company, and reprinted yet again in 1960 by the Frontier Press of Texas. In 1992 R.R. Donnelly & Sons of Chicago published the Lakeside Classic edition with a prologue by Ben Proctor and the addition of a map and numerous illustrations not in the earlier editions. More recently in 1997, the University of Oklahoma Press reprinted the book in soft cover with the Dobie foreword and an added introduction by Dr. Stephen L. Hardin. Adams termed the first edition of Jennings' book "exceedingly scarce."

C.L. Douglas produced a history of the Texas Rangers, entitled *The Gentlemen in White Hats: Dynamic Episodes in the History of the Texas Rangers*, but devoted only little more than a chapter to McNelly. This first appeared in 1934, published by South-West Press, and was reprinted in 1992 by State House Press with an introduction by Roger Conger. There was little new in Douglas' work and it contained a number of errors.

Taming the Nueces Strip: The Story of McNelly's Rangers, by George Durham as told to Clyde Wantland, has become a very popular book. Written in 1934, this first appeared in *West* magazine in 1937 in serial form under the title of "On the Trail of 5100 Outlaws: The Inside Story of McNelly's Texas Rangers" and then in 1962 was published in book form with slight changes by the University of Texas Press of Austin. This edition contained a foreword by eminent historian Walter Prescott Webb. Adams states the book "Gives one of the best accounts of the life and work of McNelly and his Rangers and corrects some of the errors made by N.A. Jennings."[2]

McNelly ranger George Durham had obviously read Jennings' *A Texas Ranger* and faulted the work. "This Jennings . . . sure wrote. He sold stories on McNelly to a big magazine, and he put it in a book. The boy took it mostly out of his head, and it is pretty awful. . . ."[3] Jennings did telescope certain events, placed himself in other events in which historically he did not participate, and created conversations, but he did serve under McNelly and consulted with many of McNelly's men when preparing his book. Jennings' term of service was from May 26, 1876, until his honorable discharge on February 1, 1877. For all its faults, and there are many, *A Texas Ranger* remains an important contribution to Texas Ranger history because it was written by one who was there serving under McNelly.

The major source of information on the Texas Rangers in general remains Dr. Walter Prescott Webb's *The Texas Rangers: A Century of Frontier Defense* published in 1935 by the Houghton Mifflin Company and later reissued in 1977 by the University of Texas Press. Webb attempted a sincere and complete history of the ranger force from its organization on November 24, 1835, through the early 1930s. He has since been found guilty of recording only the most positive aspects of the rangers' work, ignoring their racial prejudices and frequently brutal methods to accomplish their objectives. The importance of Webb's work is that he was the first to present a serious study of the Texas Rangers, including approximately fifty pages devoted to McNelly, concentrating on his raids on the Rio Grande Frontier. Some attention is given to McNelly and his men during the State Police period and his efforts in quieting the Sutton-Taylor Feud in the 1870s.

Fortunately Dr. Webb discovered another surviving McNelly ranger during the course of researching for the book, William Crump Callicott, then a resident of Houston who had served under McNelly as well as Frontier Battalion Major John B. Jones, who was willing and enthusiastic in providing Webb with his version of the events he had lived through while serving under McNelly. Callicott provided not only a first hand account of the engagement with the raiders on the Palo Alto prairie but also a detailed account of the McNelly invasion of Mexico in November of 1875.

More recently historian Frederick Wilkins devoted an entire chapter to McNelly and his company during the 1875-76 period in his book *The Law Comes to Texas: The Texas Rangers 1870-1901* published in 1999 by State House Press. Wilkins avoided an extensive discussion of McNelly's work in DeWitt County but focused on his accomplishments on the Rio Grande Frontier. Wilkins utilized various sources not available to Webb; his work remains a significant contribution to literature dealing with the history of Texas.

In the following work we have attempted to present the first complete biography of Leander Harvey McNelly, of a first generation American whose parents were born in Ireland, of a man who survived four years of bloodshed in the New Mexico, Texas and Louisiana theaters of the Civil War, of a man who earned the respect of his former enemies as a State Police Captain, of a leader who quieted the men causing the violence of the Sutton-Taylor Feud, and of a lawman who punished raiders on the Rio Grande Frontier for the first time. He earned the respect of the state, as well as the respect of the lawless men who infested the border, and he earned the love and admiration of his men. His record, in spite of all its faults, is an admirable one.

— Chuck Parsons &
Marianne E. Hall Little

ACKNOWLEDGMENTS

There have been many individuals through the years who have helped with this biography of McNelly. The following deserve our special thanks. In Texas: Dan Alger, Curatorial Technician, Texas Ranger Hall of Fame & Museum, Waco; Annie Maud Knittel Avis, Burton; T. Lindsay Baker, Director, Texas Heritage Museum, Hillsboro; Donaly E. Brice, Supervisor, Archival Reference, the Texas State Library, Austin; Christopher M. Crain, Attorney at Law, Cuero; George Edgerton, Rio Grande City; Florentino Gonzales & Fernando Gonzales, Victoria; Casey Edward Greene, Head of Special Collections, The Rosenberg Library, Galveston; Jeff Jackson, Lampasas; C. B. "Jeff" Jeffries, Houston; Byron A. Johnson, Director, Texas Ranger Hall of Fame & Museum, Waco; Stewart Lauterbach, Texas Ranger Hall of Fame and Museum, Waco; Robert G. McCubbin, El Paso; Bert McNelly, Uvalde; the late Charles B. McNelly, Kerrville; Leon C. Metz, El Paso; Rick Miller, Harker Heights; Jo Myler and her Texana-Genealogy staff of the San Antonio Central Library; Lisa A. Neely, Archivist, The King Ranch, Kingsville; Charles M. Robinson, III, San Benito; Bill Stein, Columbus; Robert W. Stephens, Dallas; Christina Stopka, Librarian/Archivist, Moody Texas Ranger Memorial Library, Waco; Dr. Jerry Thompson, Laredo; Lawrence E. Vivian, San Antonio; Harold J. Weiss, Jr., Leander.

Others beyond the Texas border also provided assistance: Thomas Bicknell, Crystal Lake, Illinois; Barry A. Crouch, Washington, D.C.; Robert K. DeArment, Sylvania, Ohio; Gary P. Fitterer, Kirkland, Washington; Dave Johnson, Zionsville, Indiana; Elmer D. McInnes, Yorkton, Saskatchewan; Dean Prichard, Tombstone, Arizona; Chris Roberts, Brooklyn, New York; Elizabeth Shannon, Boston, Massachusetts; Lee A. Silva, Sunset Beach, California; George W. Wright, Upper Saddle River, New Jersey.

CHAPTER 1

GENESIS OF A FIGHTING MAN

Capt. McNelly . . . is of medium stature, and physically
seems the very reverse of robust . . . . He has a high fore-
head, and his head and face create the impression of
great intellectuality. His hair and whiskers are brown,
nose of medium size and somewhat curved, with steel
gray glittering eyes under closely knit eyebrows. The
careless observer would note nothing extraordinary
about them or their owner, but those who study men
and faces find no difficulty behind the quiet address
and modest demeanor the indications of inflexible
determination and untiring activity that make him the
terror of the frontier outlaws. — Correspondent "Prickly
Pear" in *The Houston Daily Telegraph*, October 19, 1876.

Leander Harvey McNelly was physically small of stature and weak
in appearance. N.A. Jennings, ranger and later an eastern newspaper
correspondent who rode with him in the mid-1870s on the Rio
Grande Frontier, described McNelly as "under the average height
and slimly built, but he sat so erect in the saddle and had such an air
of command that he seemed like a cavalry officer at the head of a
company of soldiers." Jennings recalled that, when he saw him for
the first time, McNelly was "not more than thirty years of age,
although he wore a heavy, dark brown moustache and 'goatee,'
which, at first glance, made him look slightly older."[1] Perhaps caused
by the disease which eventually killed him, he spoke in a "weak, thin
voice that didn't carry very far."[2]

George P. Durham, who also rode with McNelly on the river and
later worked on the giant King Ranch of South Texas, when seeing
McNelly for the first time in Burton, Washington County, described
him as "a man I thought was the Methodist preacher."[3] Later he
wrote that McNelly "could have been a preacher. A puny one at
that."[4]

Although unimposing in appearance he was dynamic and forceful; his leadership abilities inspired his men to risk being massacred on the battlefield for him. As for his combat ability, one of his men described him as one of "the two best pistol fighters in Texas" when he faced down and arrested the notorious John King Fisher.[5] The other pistol fighter was King Fisher himself.

Leander Harvey McNelly was physically a weakling. Having survived the Civil War, he was able to spend a few years in relative peace on his farm and then began a new career of establishing law and order in Texas, but at the same time he was slowly dying of tuberculosis. He probably would have preferred to spend his life farming in Washington County, Texas, raising sheep and putting in crops. After gaining recognition in the Civil War then receiving additional state wide publicity as a State Police Captain in the early 1870s, national attention was showered upon him when he invaded Mexico to recover a stolen herd of cattle. Although dying of lung disease at the age of thirty-three, his contribution to ridding the state of outlaws was disregarded by Texas' officials because of his expensive medical bills.

Captain Richard King, the cattle baron of Texas whose longhorns McNelly had recovered from the hands of border bandits, had a monument erected over his grave near Burton. In 1967 a state historical marker was placed there by the Texas Historical Survey Committee.[6] If officialdom did not appreciate his worth while he lived, it attempted to correct the oversight after his death.

Captain L.H. McNelly has become the embodiment of the Texas Ranger mystique, although he was never a Texas Ranger in the formal sense. His command, which quieted the Sutton and Taylor forces in DeWitt County in 1874 and later fought bandits in the Nueces Strip, was officially the Washington County Volunteer Militia Company "A", but most often his men were simply identified as Special State Troops or State Militia or rangers. Although not part of the Frontier Battalion which indeed composed the Texas Rangers of McNelly's day, McNelly thought of himself as a ranger; the public and press in general also considered him a Texas Ranger, no different from the men who were officially part of the Frontier Battalion.

Although considered puny, physically unimpressive and quiet spoken, he was strong willed and forceful. His orders were given quietly but were followed explicitly. He was not one to send his men into battle; instead he led them and was the first to receive the enemy's onslaught. McNelly was truly one who by his leadership earned the respect of his men, a devotion strong enough that they were willing to lay down their lives for him. If McNelly had said, simply, "Well, boys, we are after the devil today. If you don't want to follow me into Hell, then stay behind and draw your pay. Come on, boys, let's ride!" they would have saddled up.

The Leander Harvey McNelly family originated in Newry, County Down, in Ireland where Eoin, or Owen or John McNelly, the father of the future Texas Ranger, was born about 1810.[7] He met and then married about 1830 a young lady, born about 1815, named Katherine Killian. They would bring two children into the world prior to leaving the country of their birth to seek their fortune in America. Owen was born about 1831 and Peter followed about 1833. Shortly after Peter's birth the family emigrated to the New World; Margaret was born in America in 1835. Evidently the Atlantic crossing was about 1833 or 1834 because Peter, born in 1833, "learned to walk while on the boat." Family tradition has the voyage taking longer than customary when the boat became "lost in crossing and was months getting across." They chose to put down roots near Follansbee, in Brooke County, Virginia, intending to find success in raising sheep.[8]

In America six more children would be born to the McNellys. The Sixth United States Census of 1840 lists only the heads of household by name. In this case the head was John McNelly, and within the household were seven males ranging in age from under five years to between thirty and forty years of age. There were three females ranging in age from less than five years to between thirty and forty years of age.[9] The census does not carry the name of McNelly as owning any slaves in 1840, 1850 or 1860. Brooke County, in what was later to become West Virginia, is in the far northern part of the state, squeezed between the states of Ohio and Pennsylvania.[10] The McNellys labored in or near Follansbee, some forty miles from the heart of present day Pittsburgh.

According to Leander's great-nephew, Charles Bowman McNelly, the family left Ireland to "get away from the strife then and now existing with religious differences being at the root of various other troubles."[11] Ironically strife would be at the center of Leander's world for many of his thirty-three years.

The Seventh United States Census is more informative. Enumerated on August 17, 1850, in Brooke County was the forty-year old John McNelly and family; the head of household is listed simply as a laborer. His thirty-five year old wife has no identified occupation, but if one had been given it certainly would have been "Keeping House." Sons Owen and Peter are listed as nineteen and seventeen years old respectively, both laborers like their father. But now there are six additional children shown, all born in Virginia: Margaret, age fifteen; Clarinda (or Clorinda), age thirteen; Thomas, age eleven; Leander, age seven; James, age five, and Mary, age three years. Enumerator Thomas Kirk spelled the family name "McNulty."[12] Son Leander, born March 12, 1844, would have his family name spelled a great variety of ways during his effective career as soldier, farmer, police captain and commander of a volunteer militia company in Texas. The date is uncertain but it is believed that father John Owen McNelly died about 1859, probably in Brooke County. All the children reached adulthood except Thomas who died at the age of sixteen in 1855.[13]

Some members of the McNelly family relocated in Missouri during the mid-1850s, probably searching for better opportunities. Leander's older brother Peter with his wife Mary Ann Downey led the trek across Ohio, Indiana and Illinois before stopping in St. Louis sometime in 1854. Whether or not St. Louis was their destination is uncertain; possibly the sojourners had to stop there for Mary to give birth to a son who would be named John and who also would become a Texas Ranger. Of the Peter McNelly family only John was born in Missouri, born in St. Louis about 1855. The family tradition indicates that the McNelly group, one of whom was young Leander, spent two years in Missouri and then returned home to the Follansbee region.[14]

Thousands of men in the east were determined to seek a better fortune in the west, and many bravely brought their families with them to the new land. Among the young men in the Follansbee area was Chauncey Berkely Shepard, born in 1812 in Virginia. He ventured into the Texas landscape on a "quest for great opportunities which he felt Texas held" and returned home "with glowing tales of what he had seen in this great new State."[15] Peter McNelly had accompanied Shepard, and their enthusiasm for relocating their families resulted in Leander H. McNelly's becoming a Texan. Peter was impressed with the land in Washington County and purchased acreage to establish the McNelly Plantation between Brenham, the county seat, and what became Burton. Some family sources place this event as being 1857 or 1859; possibly both dates are correct because the relocation from Virginia to Texas could have incurred several moves over the course of two years before they felt themselves established in Washington County.

"They came down the Ohio and Mississippi on a flat boat, their household possessions and about three thousand head of fine sheep.

Negroes to care for the sheep and family; landed at Galveston, went overland to Washington County" recalled Mrs. Robert A. Newman, a family member, in an essay published in 1966.[16] McNelly's widow, corresponding with E. D. McNelly in 1937, wrote that Leander "came to Texas when a boy of 12 years of age, with a brother who died soon after."

Texas was a sharp contrast for the McNellys, especially for the women. "Some of my earliest memories are stories my grandmother [Leander's niece] told us of those days and her loneliness in this wild strange and undeveloped land. Coming from a rather thickly populated community and from a large family and being so young, I can well understand her feelings." But they were better off than some because the McNellys came "well stocked with household goods of all sorts, had bolts of material such as linen and woolen material for the family. . . . One of their Negroes was a shoe maker so he kept the family in shoes, maybe of sheep skin? This man stayed with the family for many years."[17]

Although the prospects of the McNelly family looked bright with their land and sheep raising, the "White Plague"—tuberculosis—was already evident in Leander's physique. Charles McNelly later wrote that he was already "suffering from tuberculosis. After two years of invigorating Texas air and sun, Leander became so strengthened that he joined the Confederate Army and displayed unusual courage and ability."[18]

Ironically the relocation to Texas in the 1850s may have been an attempt to avoid the social strife which even then was causing bloodshed in what was to become the border states between North and South. Leaving their established homes in Virginia to seek their fortune in the new land, floating down rivers to a port city and then again moving over land, was a great challenge. So far as known no diaries were kept, and whatever letters they may have written back home to friends and neighbors apparently have not survived.

On arriving at New Orleans the McNellys herded their flocks of sheep across land to Washington County. In the meantime Peter's wife and children had traveled by water to Galveston.[19] As neither the Peter McNelly family nor Leander's names are found on the 1860 federal census, perhaps they were still en route to Texas and, with no permanent home, were missed by the census enumerators.

Once in Texas the family would have preferred to look forward to a long and peaceful life, but war could not be avoided. Some may have abhorred the idea, but others certainly were eager to become soldiers. Some would go through the experience unscathed; others would not. Some would come home to linger and then die of wounds. Such was the case for Leander's older brother, Peter John McNelly, who died July 8, 1865. He is buried in St. Mary's Cemetery in San Antonio. His widow survived until December 11, 1889. Their son John, who began his law-enforcement career under Uncle Leander's guidance, also is buried in this family plot although there is no visible stone. Ranger John McNelly died April 22, 1919.[20]

While these changes were taking place in the immediate family of Leander, or "Lee" as some called him, great social changes were taking place all over the country. War clouds were looming, and all men of voting age would soon have to make a decision as to whether to vote to remain in the union or to secede from the union. Texas voted against remaining, and with secession it became the western-most state of the Confederate States of America.

In Texas young McNelly began tending sheep for Travis J. Burton whose father, John M. Burton, had been one of the earliest of the American settlers to come to Texas. He had helped lay out the town of Austin long before it dreamed of becoming the capital of the state. The small community of Burton, established in the western portion of Washington County in 1862, would become the only real "home town" that Lee McNelly ever knew. A post office would not be established until 1870 when A.C. Huberich became its first postmaster. Following the Civil War the Houston and Texas Central Railroad began its extension from county seat Brenham to Austin. John M. Burton sold the railroad five-hundred acres of land but generously gave land for the Oak Hill Cemetery. For his civic contributions to the area the town of Burton was named after him.[21]

The fledgling town of Burton remained only a few buildings during the initial years of existence but grew slowly. By 1870 the neighboring county seat of Brenham gave it some recognition, the *Banner* of June 7 describing it as "no longer an embryo city, but a city of much size." A reporter from the *Banner* had interviewed various Burtonites who informed him that four and one half miles of track had been laid from Brenham and was rapidly approaching Burton. Forty-five convicts had been brought in to assist in the track laying. The stone culverts were all finished and the trestle work over Indian Creek was nearly completed. The prospect for trains to run by the beginning of August was "fair to middling."

As the tracks approached people saw opportunities and began to create permanent dwellings. In Burton "substantial wooden edifices" were being erected and "almost daily a new building presents itself." Town lots were selling for $400 to $500 in gold. Soon there were

The flint lock rifle which the McNelly family brought with them from Virginia to Texas prior to the Civil War. It is unknown which member of the family claimed ownership of this weapon.
Photo courtesy Bert McNelly, Jr. and Uvalde Photo, Uvalde, Texas.

three hotels and three livery stables. Burton was described as "situated on a hill-side, a beautiful and well populated country, with fertile lands teeming with cotton and corn to back it."[22]

Here Leander H. McNelly learned to appreciate the virtues of working the land and the peacefulness of rural life close to the earth. But the tranquillity would not last long because war was about to be declared; with his health having sufficiently improved, he would answer the call. What peacefulness in his life he enjoyed just prior to the firing of the guns at Fort Sumter would not again be realized until 1865 after which he would have five years to build up his own land and holdings, marry, and think of his own family. By 1870, however, he again heard the call to a dangerous life, and his career of service to the state of Texas would begin with the creation of a State Police force. At its demise a greater arm of law enforcement would be created, the Texas Rangers, with which L.H. McNelly would earn his place in Texas history.

General Thomas Green, circa 1860, whose leadership style to a great
degree was emulated by McNelly.
Courtesy The Texas State Library & Archives Commission.

CHAPTER 2

FIRST TASTE OF WAR

As for the results of the campaign, I have only to say that
we have beaten the enemy in every encounter and against
large odds; that from being the worst armed my forces are
now the best armed in the country . . . . But, sir, I cannot
speak encouragingly for the future, my troops having
manifested a dogged, irreconcilable detestation of the
country and the people. They have endured much, suffered much, and cheerfully; but the prevailing discontent,
backed up by the distinguished valor displayed on every
field, entitles them to marked consideration and indul-
gence. — H. H. Sibley, Brigadier-General, May 4, 1862.

In spite of any intentions he may have had to live out his life in
Washington County tending sheep, the Civil War forced young
teenager Lee McNelly to change his plans just as it altered the plans
of thousands of other young men. The sparse documentation of
McNelly's war record provides only the barest essentials concerning
his contribution to the cause. He joined the 5th Texas Cavalry, a
unit which was successively designated as Captain Campbell's
Company, Captain Benton B. Seat's Company, and Company F, 5th
Regiment Texas Cavalry.

The 5th Texas Cavalry was organized with ten companies, A to
K, mustered into service between September 4 and October 26,
1861. Captain George Washington Campbell,[1] a Tennessee native
and deputy sheriff living at Longpoint, Washington County,
enrolled McNelly into his company on August 21. "L. McAnaley" is
how his name is recorded in one instance, showing him mustered in
on September 5 at San Antonio by Lieutenant Arthur Shaaff for the
duration of the war. McNelly became a private in Campbell's
Company, 2nd Regiment of the Sibley Brigade. He misrepresented
his age as eighteen years; actually he was only seventeen. His horse
was valued at eighty dollars and his equipment valued at eighteen

dollars, although elsewhere his equipment was valued at different amounts ranging from thirty-five to thirty-eight dollars. He had traveled 190 miles to the rendezvous in San Antonio.[2] During the war McNelly would see action in battles in the New Mexico Territory, then in Galveston, Texas, and then in the Louisiana campaigns. When the war finally came to a bloody end he was a captain of scouts in Texas with the mission of hunting down deserters.

When the war commenced President Jefferson Davis realized that a Confederate victory required both money to finance the war effort and the recognition of such European powers as England and France. Henry Hopkins Sibley came forward with a plan which, if successful, would guarantee these necessities.

Sibley was a native of Natchitoches, Louisiana, born May 25, 1816. He was graduated from the United States Military academy at West Point in 1838 and served in the Mexican War. His further military experience included commanding Fort Union, north of Las Vegas, New Mexico Territory. Although he was initially an adequate military leader, he was losing his battle with alcohol. Before the war ended and while serving in the West, he was reprimanded and court-martialed as a result of differences with his regimental commander; nevertheless he earned the rank of brevet major of dragoons. He also earned the uncomplimentary nickname of "the Walking Whiskey Keg." Sixteen days after the firing on Fort Sumter, on April 28 Sibley wrote out his resignation from the United States Army. He then obtained a meeting with Jefferson Davis to discuss his plans to create the Confederacy of the West. McNelly would become a member of Sibley's Brigade and follow him through the New Mexico campaign.

Sibley's plan was to organize an army of highly mobile mounted troops to march west through the Rio Grande Valley, capture Fort Craig, occupy Albuquerque and Santa Fe and then occupy Fort Union. With New Mexico under Confederate control, Sibley would then continue the march to the northwest, eventually conquering Utah, Nevada and California. With the support of the southern sympathizers he supposed to be in these territories to aid his cause, it would not be a difficult conquest, or so he believed and thus convinced President Davis. Once these territories were conquered, the army could invade the northern states of Mexico—Chihuahua and Sonora. The conquest would result both in doubling the size of the Confederacy and adding wealth to the Confederate treasury. Recognition by other countries would naturally follow. Sibley believed this all could be accomplished with an army of 3,200

Texans, all ready to fight. One of his most capable officers was Thomas Green.[3]

Talk of war had been growing since the presidential election of 1860. By the time Lincoln was inaugurated on March 4, 1861, seven of the southern states had seceded. Still, few Texans believed war was inevitable. James Harvey McLeary, a Tennessean whose family had moved to Colorado County, Texas, and who served under Sibley throughout the war, later wrote a history of Tom Green's command with information partially gathered from McNelly's widow.[4]

Even though there were many indications that war was inevitable, the fall of Fort Sumter on April 13, 1861, was far away geographically; many Texans such as McLeary, and perhaps McNelly, were not convinced that "there would be anything more than a display of an armed force, and then they thought that the government at Washington would 'bid the erring sisters depart in peace.'"[5]

Nevertheless, Texans formed themselves into companies and began drilling and preparing for war. These companies, independent of one another, all sensed a common purpose after the news of Manassas, or Bull Run, finally reached Texas. Companies which may have felt isolated now rushed to various points and organized themselves into battalions, then into regiments, and then into brigades.

Sibley, having convinced Davis of the efficacy of his plan, left the southern capitol and returned to San Antonio by mid-July 1861, sending out immediately the call for volunteers. Initial reports indicated that the brigade had been filled almost immediately, but by mid-September Colonel Thomas Green requested the newspapers to report that Sibley's Brigade was not yet filled and twenty companies were still wanted.[6] The brigade was to consist of three regiments rather than two as first reported. Companies were to report to San Antonio as quickly as possible. The request brought results; by late October the approximate 3,200-man brigade went into training. McLeary related that drilling was done at "camps of instruction" on the Leon and Salado creeks in the immediate vicinity of San Antonio. "Instruction" was greatly needed, although many of the companies had been organized for several months and had been drilling in the vicinity of their homes, waiting to be called into active service.

The Army of New Mexico, as it was to be called by some, was under the command of Sibley with Colonel James Reiley commanding the 4th Texas Cavalry, Colonel William Steele commanding the 7th Texas Cavalry and Colonel Thomas Green commanding the 5th Texas Cavalry. McNelly would serve with Green until the latter's death in Louisiana. In the 1870s McNelly would also serve the state under William Steele when he was Adjutant General.

Colonel Thomas Green was a native of Buckingham County, Virginia, born July 8, 1814. By the time Thomas was twelve the family had moved to Tennessee where he studied law with his father. Too active to spend his days with the law books, he heard the call to adventure and left home to join the Tennessee Volunteers to fight in the Texas Revolution. He joined Isaac N. Moreland's company which operated the Twin Sisters cannons at the battle of San Jacinto. Through the ensuing years Green became a county surveyor of Fayette County, an engrossing clerk for the House of Representatives of the Republic of Texas, secretary of the Senate, and was clerk of the State Supreme Court from 1841 to 1861. His military experience during these years was extensive. He fought with John H. Moore against the Comanches, recruited and commanded a company of rangers as part of the First Texas Regiment of Mounted Riflemen led by John C. Hays, and helped Zachary Taylor capture Monterrey. Following the Mexican War he returned home and married Mary Wallace Chalmers; six children were born to the couple. When the Civil War came he was elected colonel of the regiment.[7]

Regimental officers included Harry C. McNeill, lieutenant-colonel; Samuel A. Lockridge, major; Captain M.B. Wyatt, quartermaster; Captain Joseph Beck, commissary; Lieutenant Joseph D. Sayers, adjutant; Dr. Felix Bracht, surgeon; Dr. J.M. Bronaugh and Dr. J.R. McPhail, assistant surgeons.[8]

McNelly's meager war record reveals he was enrolled on August 21, 1861, in Washington County by George W. Campbell and then mustered into Captain Benton B. Seat's Company of the 5th Regiment Texas Mounted Volunteers. Those who read the San Antonio newspapers were familiar with a long letter from Captain A.J. Hatton who had just returned from service on the frontier. The editorial note accompanying the letter, printed in the *Herald* as well as other newspapers of the state, included this fateful line, "The Captain reports that between this place [San Antonio] and Fort Bliss [El Paso] there is plenty of water, grass and Indians!"[9]

On October 21 Sibley's Brigade paraded through the streets of San Antonio. The entire army did not leave for the west at the same time; traveling *en masse* would have been too much of a drain on forage for the horses and on water for both men and horses. The 5th Texas Cavalry left for El Paso on November 10. The day before, a letter was printed in the *Texas State Gazette* of Austin, written by a soldier dated November 2, in which the writer described how many companies were "almost destitute of clothing." He wrote that "many men [were] without arms, and most of them in hand requiring repairs. The men and horses cannot be beat, and the progress made in drill evinces a spirit and ambitious determination to excel, which gives me entire confidence in the successful issue of the expedition."[10]

Another young soldier, William Henry Smith, recorded almost daily events on the march westward. Although he was from Fayette County southwest of McNelly's Washington County, his experiences were no doubt very similar to those of every other young marching soldier. "When we went through San Antonio the ladies waved their white handkerchiefs, the same as to say brave boys victory awaits you. After passing through town Col. Tom Green passed by our company and said he would bet on the Fayette county boys," recorded Smith. Certainly Green felt the same towards the Washington County boys.[11]

McLeary described the more than one-thousand-mile westward trek. "The march," beyond the early settlements of Castroville and Uvalde, "lay through an unbroken wilderness, watered at long intervals by clear streams, water-holes, lakes, mountain springs, and sparsely timbered, more or less undulating, and in sections mountainous." McLeary concentrated on the positive aspects of the ordeal and the eagerness and determination of the volunteers "to meet the enemies of Texas on their own ground, and thus prevent an invasion of the Lone Star State."[12] Green's command reached the El Paso area on New Year's day 1862, having left San Antonio on November 10. One young soldier, identified only as J.F.M. in the Houston newspaper which published his letter from New Mexico, wrote, "The mountains here are full of Indians, and we dread them worse than we do the Lincolnites."[13]

The first engagement with the enemy was not until February 16 when the brigade skirmished with Federals on the right side of the Rio Grande near Fort Craig. W.C. Burton of Company F was the only Confederate casualty, being wounded. Another skirmish followed on February 20, casualties unknown. McLeary wrote:

> The country over which the troops marched was a trackless desert of sand, yet they kept toiling on hour after hour during the night through the ravines and over the hills, resting but a short time, and daylight found them on the crest of the ridge two miles from the river, overlooking a green valley with a *mesa* lying to the southwest between the Confederates and the fort. The

men and their horses were much jaded and nearly fam-
ished for want of water, but between them and the river
lay a large Federal force, and it was plainly evident to all
the Texans that if they drank water that day they would
first have to fight for it. At nine o'clock the battle
began.[14]

General Sibley, according to McLeary, was "quite unwell" and
thus remained in the rear. In all likelihood Sibley's illness was due to
his having consumed too much whiskey.

Facing Sibley's Brigade was General Edward R.S. Canby, also a
graduate of West Point, class of 1839. He had served against the
Seminoles in that war of 1839-1842, fought in the Mexican War,
held staff posts between 1848 and 1855 and, like Sibley, had taken
part in the Mormon Expedition under Colonel Albert Sidney
Johnston. Ironically he had served on the court martial of General
Sibley when Sibley was charged with insubordination. Canby was
ordered to New Mexico Territory shortly after the commencement of
the Civil War. When the Sibley Brigade entered his territory, Canby
commanded fifteen-hundred regular infantry, a battery of artillery,
and a regiment of volunteers from the Territory of New Mexico
under the famed Colonel Kit Carson. All told the Federals numbered about seven-thousand men.[15]

The first real engagement in New Mexico Territory occurred on
February 21 at Valverde Ford, a crossing seven miles north of Fort
Craig. Colonel Green's force was initially held in reserve to guard
the beef herd. The only instance during the war in which the lance
was used occurred during this engagement with disastrous results.
The "hog-poker" as it was called was a nine-foot lance with a twelve-
inch blade and a red guidon banner with white star. Captain Willis
Lang commanded the seventy lancers; their charge on Captain
Theodore Dodd and his Colorado Volunteers was met by a volley at
fifty yards of buckshot and round shot known as "buck and ball."
Those of the survivors of the initial charge who were able to continue were met by another volley and fixed bayonets. A reserve group
of lancers, seeing the carnage, threw down their lances and adopted
whatever other traditional weapon they could obtain. Towards the
end of the day the Federals requested a two-day truce to bury the
dead and care for the wounded. By day's end Canby and his army
were retreating to Fort Craig, having lost six of their eight artillery
pieces. Sibley claimed victory at the battle of Valverde, but it was a
costly affair.[16] The Confederates had suffered 186 killed and

 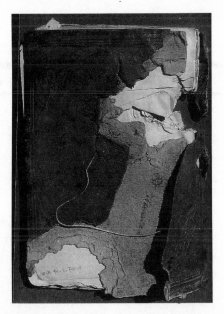

Front and back view of the blank ledger book which stopped a bullet which could have ended McNelly's life during the Civil War. *Photo courtesy T. Lindsay Baker, Director, The Harold B. Simpson Research Center, Hillsboro, Texas.*

wounded; the Federals, 260.

Back home, Texans must have felt jubilant in reading reports of this engagement. The Austin *Gazette* printed an extra on March 19 which described it as a "glorious victory!", headlining that it was a battle of five hours duration, that Green was in command, that it was an "unconditional surrender by the Lincolnites!" and that *fifteen-thousand stand of arms* had been taken! Reportedly the Confederate loss was only twenty-eight killed while the enemy suffered six hundred killed. The *Gazette* editor, no doubt anticipating that readers would wonder why Tom Green was in command, noted in the issue of March 22, taking a report from a Mesilla *Times* extra, that "Col. Green was in immediate command of our forces, but Gen. Sibley, though suffering from illness, was on the field the whole day."[17]

The retreat of the Federals was almost a rout, according to McLeary, and had it been closely followed up Fort Craig might have been captured. With a tone of regret McLeary wrote that ". . . Fort Craig was seven miles away, and the Union commander sent in a flag of truce asking leave to bury his dead, and in the mean time night came on and closed the carnage."[18]

On the first day of the truce the Confederates remained on the field of battle; on the following day they continued to bypass Fort Craig and advanced up the Rio Grande until they reached the village of Socorro where a hospital was established. The wounded who were unable to travel were left there and the march was continued on to Albuquerque.

Although tradition indicates that McNelly impressed his commanding officers in this engagement, his name does not appear among those singled out for particularly valorous action in the existing official reports. Enjoying the rush of victory, Green must have believed that all his men were among the bravest of the brave. "I cannot say enough" he wrote in his official report, "in praise of the gallantry of our surviving officers and men. It would be invidious to mention names. Were I to do so, the rolls of captains, lieutenants, and men would have to be here inserted." And later, still feeling ebullient, he wrote, "The captains, lieutenants, and men in the action displayed so much gallantry that it would be invidious to make distinctions. They fought with equal valor."[19]

N.A. Jennings, not reluctant to be so "invidious" as to mention names, wrote that at the Valverde engagement Captain Sayers, commanding the Confederate battery of light artillery, needed to know the Federals' position in order "to turn his battery loose on them." McNelly volunteered to obtain the information and "all day long was on horse-back with a few men, pressing the Federal pickets back in order to locate the forces." McNelly rode all day, exposed to "a storm of bullets. . . . In his shirt was a book he had been reading, and a bullet hit this book and tore it to pieces, but McNelly was unhurt." Later that day after performing such valuable service, wrote Jennings, carried into fanciful error by his admiration for McNelly, "when the charge was ordered he was in the front and the first of all to reach the Federal battery. The Union forces retreated across the Rio Grande and McNelly led in the pursuit." For his reward Green made McNelly an aide on his staff.[20]

If Jennings' account is accurate, then this was the first wound McNelly received during the conflict, and his life was saved by a book. In the Texas Ranger Hall of Fame and Museum of Waco is a small ledger, its pages blank, which was in McNelly's possession during the war and which stopped a bullet. According to tradition, the book saved his life. The bullet entered the front cover and its force was spent by the number of pages.

Jennings wrote that the book which saved McNelly's life was one which he had been reading; the blank ledger in the Hall of Fame could not be one that he had been reading. It is unlikely that McNelly's life was saved on two occasions by a book in his pocket; perhaps Jennings fabricated the aspect of a book he had been reading to add interest. Other sources have recorded that the book was a New Testament in McNelly's possession because he was studying to become a preacher! No solid evidence to substantiate the claim he ever intended to become a preacher has been found.

The Confederate commanders believed that the field of battle at Valverde was only the beginning of a glorious success in the west, but it was a fateful beginning. Their elation in victory was to be short-lived; Glorieta Pass was only weeks away and would be followed by a long arduous trek back to Texas.

Captain Jonathan Wainwright, killed in action at the Battle of Galveston, January 1, 1863. *Courtesy The Massachusetts Commandery Military Order of the Loyal Legion and the U.S. Army Military History Institute.*

CHAPTER 3

BACK TO TEXAS AND GALVESTON

The commanding general deems this a fitting occasion to expose publicly to the troops his high sense of the indomitable energy and chivalric heroism of the naval commander and those who so nobly supported him. The country is proud of them, and their commander will never cease to honor them. The "stormers" of the sea and the "stormers" of the land greet each other as brothers in battle, and there should be no rivalry, save as to who shall be first permitted to die for his country.— J. Bankhead Magruder, January 14, 1863.

The Texans broke camp on the field of Valverde on February 23, claiming victory over Canby's Lincolnites. McLeary recalled that six pieces of artillery and about three-hundred Minie muskets were captured or picked up on the field. These arms were naturally of great value to the rebels and were immediately reissued to the men whose weapons were useless or inadequate. Many chose the muskets, preferring them to the shotguns or hunting rifles which they had brought from home.[1]

On March 7, several weeks after bypassing Fort Craig and establishing a hospital at Socorro, Sibley's main force entered Albuquerque and then Santa Fe. Here General Sibley had planned to confiscate supplies to enable the Valverde victors to continue the conquest of New Mexico, but he was gravely disappointed to discover the retreating Federals had destroyed any supplies of real value to keep them out of rebel hands. Nevertheless, Sibley was determined to press on and divided his army into two columns headed for Fort Union, one leaving Albuquerque on March 21 and the other leaving Santa Fe on March 25.[2]

But on March 26 the rebels again engaged the enemy. Major Charles Pyron, with a small force composed of John R. Baylor's men and two pieces of artillery, halted on the road some twenty miles from Santa Fe. Here they were joined by Companies A, B, C and D of the 5th Texas Cavalry under the command of Major John Shropshire. Pyron and Shropshire's forces combined numbered approximately 250 men. About 10:00 a.m. Major John Chivington of the 1st Colorado Volunteers captured Pyron's pickets and surprised the Texans' advance troops in Apache Canyon. The rebel battery opened up on the Colorado troops and thus warned Shropshire who, dividing his men, deployed two companies as skirmishers on each side of the canyon. Some men of Company A advanced to the right well in advance of the remainder of the command. Company F of the Colorado Volunteers charged on horseback followed by infantry and cut the rebel line in two. "Thus the day was lost to the Confederates;" wrote McLeary, "being outflanked, outnumbered, and outgeneralled." Although the rebel casualties were but two men killed and three wounded, over seventy were taken as prisoners. McLeary wrote that Company A "suffered most severely," being furthest in advance.[3]

On March 28 the rebels gained a tactical victory at Glorieta Pass but had not provided adequate protection for their valuable supply train and lost it. While Colonel John P. Slough of the 1st Colorado engaged the rebels, Major Chivington with 430 men captured and destroyed the wagon train, burning some seventy wagons and killing or driving off over five-hundred mules and horses. The Confederate victory on the field meant little because of the loss of their vital supplies. The Texans were left to pillage the land and the Spanish speaking villages in order to survive.[4]

On April 15 the two armies engaged in a brief skirmish at Peralta in which the Federals emerged victorious, and the Sibley Brigade was forced to begin the long and painful retreat out of the territory. Sibley nevertheless communicated to his superiors that his army had been victorious! The defeated and demoralized Texans trudged slowly south, back to El Paso and then slowly through the West Texas frontier, arriving back in San Antonio during the summer months of 1862. Less than fifteen hundred returned of the original 2,600 men who had been filled with so much confidence months before. Once back in the relative security of South Central Texas, the soldiers of the defeated Sibley Brigade were sent home for a two-month period of rest and recuperation.[5]

McLeary, always optimistic, wrote:

> This was a wonderful retreat in more than one respect.
> The patience and fortitude of the men were as remark-

able as the misfortunes which they had to encounter. Had Canby followed up the retreat with the mounted men he had just received from Colorado, he must have succeeded in capturing the entire Confederate force, or, if he had confronted the toil-worn Confederates when they turned in to seek the Rio Grande again below Fort Craig, he could have compelled an immediate and unconditional surrender. The subordinate officers and the men among the Texans cannot be praised too highly for their courage, fidelity, patience, and fortitude, and every soldierly quality, except discipline.[6]

Sibley had convinced President Davis of his effectiveness as a leader, but for all practical purposes he proved himself incapable of carrying out his own grand plan. His absence from the field of battle, either through legitimate illness or drunkenness, proved costly, not only in terms of the leadership he should have provided for his men but for the morale of his soldiers. He left the leadership necessary for victory to his subordinates, who at times acted more on their own rather than on a concerted plan.

Major Trevanion T. Teel, who commanded the artillery during the Sibley campaign, wrote a brief essay on why it had ended in defeat. The direct cause of the "discomfiture and the failure of our campaign" was the want of supplies of all kinds for the use of the army. Canby's orders to destroy the supplies on which the Confederates depended placed Sibley in an untenable position. Teel explained that the Texans "were situated in the very heart of the enemy's country, with well-equipped forces in our front and rear" but without adequate supplies. Further, Teel provided his opinion of why the campaign would have failed even if the supplies had been provided.

General Sibley was not a good administrative officer. He did not husband his resources, and was too prone to let the morrow take care of itself. But for this the expedition never would have been undertaken, nor would he have left the enemy between him and his base of supplies, a mistake which he made at Fort Craig. The other reason for the failure of the campaign were want of supplies, ammunition, discipline, and confidence. Under such conditions failure was inevitable.[7]

Evidence suggests Sibley wasn't the only officer abusing alcohol during engagements with the enemy. Harold V. Hunter recorded in his journal on February 7, 1862, only weeks after Valverde, he "Went down to the post, don't like our staff and Gen. [Sibley] much. Too much drunkness [sic] among them."[8]

No doubt Private McNelly became aware of these administrative inadequacies early in the campaign, although no known source describes McNelly as analyzing the characteristics of his superiors. Later, in other actions against Federals as well as against outlaws and renegades on the Rio Grande Frontier and elsewhere in South Texas, McNelly's actions were virtually the opposite of Sibley, his first commander. Where Sibley remained off the field of battle, McNelly was in the midst of the fight, leading his men into battle against the enemy. Where Sibley was frequently inebriated during the battle when his alertness was needed the most, McNelly refused to allow his men to have alcohol in camp. Where Sibley tended to "let the morrow take care of itself," McNelly planned his battles carefully and gave clear and simple orders as to how they were to be carried out. Many of McNelly's personal leadership skills possibly evolved from learning what not to do in a leadership capacity by observing Sibley. It is impossible to determine just how much McNelly learned on the fields of Valverde and Peralta and Apache Canyon, but no soldiers under Leander Harvey McNelly ever complained about their leader as did the soldiers under Henry Hopkins Sibley.

Federal General Canby allowed the rebels to retreat back to Texas because he felt an effort to conquer Sibley's army would cost too many casualties and, perhaps as important, he did not have the supplies to feed that many prisoners. It was much simpler to let them march east out of the inhospitable territory of New Mexico.

The war news from New Mexico falsely reported glorious victories, and General Sibley himself may have been unable to face the realities of how disastrous his expedition had become, but at least one newspaper editor was not afraid to deal with the reality and expressed his feelings in print. John Marshall edited the State Gazette in Austin, and in the issue of Saturday, June 7, he condemned Sibley's expedition to New Mexico.

. . .a part and portion of the old deffensive [sic] policy, inaugurated by President Davis, by which he hoped to defend the Confederacy by posting a few thousand men

at every assailable point, has proven to be a grand failure. Our brave troops were sent to conquer a barren
wilderness, and after having performed prodig[i]es of
valor, and defeated the enemy in two pitched battles,
have been compelled to abandon the country from the
sheer want of something to eat.

Marshall had a reminder for his readers.

Years ago, when Mr. [Charles Magill] Conrad was
Secretary of War [under President Fillmore], he recommended in his report that the citizens of New Mexico
be paid for their property and that the country be abandoned and turned over to the Indians, [it] not being
worth the expense of holding it. We regret deeply that
the lives of so many gallant Texians, belonging to the
Sibley expedition, should have been so fruitlessly sacri-
ficed. . . . The force operating in New Mexico has been
chasing a shadow, and its flower and strength gradually
fluttered away, may the brave remnant now toiling their
way back, fighting against those worst of enemies
hunger and thirst, yet have the opportunity of meeting
and conquering them somewhere within the bounds of
civilization, where the soil is not sand, the waters the
essence of bitterness, the towns hovels of mud, the
comforts fleas and rattlesnakes, and the people *cayotes*
[*sic*].[9]

Ironically, in the same issue appeared Sibley's exhortation to
continue the struggle, stated in such terms that, without knowing
the real horrors of the expedition, the reader would think the campaign had proved to be a glorious victory. Sibley addressed the soldiers of the Army of New Mexico with "unfeigned pride and pleasure" and congratulated them upon "the successes which have
crowned its arms in every encounter with the enemy during the
short campaign which has just terminated." That Sibley was speaking to men and boys who had narrowly avoided death or a prison
camp seemingly did not temper his phrases; he reminded them how
they were called from their homes, "almost at a moment's notice,
cheerfully leaving friends, families and private affairs . . . you have
made a march, many of you over a thousand miles, before ever reach-

ing the field of active operations." He warned the young soldiers they would be called again to defend their homes after a short period of rest. One wonders how Sibley could have been so far removed from the reality of what had happened to his glorious army.[10]

In retreat the Grand Army of New Mexico was strung out for miles. Private William Randolph Howell recorded being in the hospital at Franklin (to become El Paso), Texas, from May 25 to June 9, before being well enough to obtain a horse and prepare to go home. On June 12, when he had moved on down the Rio Grande, he noted in his diary: "Colonel Green, with his regiment, arrives today from Fort Fillmore en route to San Antonio." Howell did not obtain sight of San Antonio until July 15 and did not arrive at home at Plantersville until July 23. "Once in San Antonio," he recorded, "we know it is not difficult to get home. I remain in San Antonio two days. . . . Come by way of New Braunfels, San Marcos, Bastrop, Evergreen, Union Hill, Long Point, Gay Hill, Independence and Washington and Navasota."[11]

McNelly probably traveled much the same route and, having reached Bastrop, likely proceeded nearly straight east some forty-five miles to arrive at Burton. McLeary reported the trek back with no emotion. "By the first days of August the last of the Confederates had left New Mexico and Fort Bliss, Texas, and Sibley's brigade had reached San Antonio and been furloughed to rest, recruit, and re-equip themselves with clothing, blankets, and such supplies as they could from their friends and relatives at home." The regiments, ordered to rendezvous in the vicinity of Hempstead, Waller County, on October 28, "returned to duty with renewed energy and refreshed patriotism. Most of them had been re-outfitted with arms and horses furnished by themselves or their friends at home, but they were wholly without tents or uniforms, and many of the necessary munitions of war were wholly lacking." [12]

The brigade was, nevertheless, subject to military discipline and was drilled daily in squads and companies, weekly or more often in regimental formation, and occasionally assembled for review. Through November and December the drilling continued. Meanwhile, superiors in the east were uncertain as to what to do with Sibley's Brigade. Secretary of War James A. Seddon wanted the brigade sent to New Iberia, Louisiana, to be placed under the command of General Richard Taylor, son of the late president, who was preparing to defend southern Louisiana against the Federal forces planning to push up the Mississippi and Red River from New

Orleans. Instead, an order arrived for the brigade to report to Richmond, the southern capital, as soon as possible. Possibly because its horses and mules were in poor condition and the roads were impassable, the brigade received a conflicting order to report to Vicksburg rather than Richmond to protect the city from a large Federal force under General Ulysses S. Grant.

While the men of Sibley's Brigade were enjoying their sixty days of rest and recuperation, events were taking place in the eastern theater which would effect Thomas Green's cavalry and McNelly's immediate future. On November 29 Major General John Bankhead Magruder was assigned to the command of the District of Texas, New Mexico and Arizona, relieving General Paul O. Hebert. The men of Sibley's Brigade were in camp near Hempstead, preparing to march to Louisiana, the earlier order to march to Virginia having been changed.

"Prince John" Magruder had experienced a successful career after being graduated fifteenth in the West Point class of 1830. By the end of March 1836 he had been promoted to 1st lieutenant. While with General Winfield Scott's army in Mexico he rose to the rank of captain and in 1847 was brevetted major for gallant and meritorious conduct at the battle of Cerro Gordo. On April 20, 1861, he resigned from the United States Army and was commissioned a brigadier general in the Confederate service, soon promoted to major general. Having earned the displeasure of General Robert E. Lee at the Seven Days Battle, he was reassigned to the command of the District of Texas, New Mexico and Arizona, arriving in Texas on October 10, 1862. He assumed command on November 29.[13]

Hebert had evacuated the city of Galveston, having been ordered to send all infantry stationed in Texas to Arkansas except for two regiments which were retained as a token defense. Hebert, believing the port indefensible, ordered the small forts erected at Galveston to be dismantled and their artillery to be removed to the mainland at Virginia Point.

On October 4, as part of the Union blockade of Texas ports from the Sabine to the Rio Grande, Commander William B. Renshaw steamed into the bay with virtually no resistance. Confederate Colonel Joseph J. Cook managed to delay the Federals by stating there were women and children in danger and time would be needed to remove them to the interior. The city of Galveston itself was nearly deserted; most of the civilian inhabitants had removed themselves and their belongings inland to Houston or other points in the interior of the state. The main fleet consisted of the *Harriet Lane* commanded by Captain Jonathan M. Wainwright; the *Westfield*, flagship of Captain William B. Renshaw; the *Owasco*, the *Clifton*, and the *Sachem*. In addition, two armed transports, two large barks and an armed schooner composed the Union fleet. Colonel Isaac S. Burrell of the 42nd Massachusetts Infantry occupied Kuhn's Wharf and patrolled the town.[14]

Before the men of Sibley's Brigade had started their march to the eastern theater, the order arrived to assist in recapturing Galveston. General Magruder had developed a plan to attack on New Year's day, 1863, with his small fleet consisting primarily of the *Bayou City*, commanded by Captain Leon Smith, and the *Neptune*, commanded by Captain Harry S. Lubbock. The vessels were reinforced with bales of cotton, providing cover for the men on board and resulting in the ships' being called "Cottonclads." Two other vessels, the *John F. Carr* and the *Lucy Gwinn*, were also part of the Magruder fleet. While Magruder and Brigadier General William R. Scurry led men to capture the Federals ashore, Captain Leon Smith and Colonel Tom Green commanded the troops on board the vessels. The Confederates were armed with Enfield rifles, shotguns, cutlasses and pistols. Green gave his men the following speech in an effort to obtain volunteers to act as sailors.

> SOLDIERS: You are called upon to volunteer in a dangerous expedition. I have never deceived you. I will not deceive you now. I regard this as the most desperate enterprise that men ever engaged in. I shall go, but do not know that I shall ever return. I do not know that any who go with me will, and want no man to volunteer who is not *willing* to die for his country, and to die now.[15]

McLeary wrote that every man in the 5th and 7th regiments, to whom the order was addressed, volunteered to the call (the 4th was too far away to hear of the expedition in time). Three-hundred men were selected, half from each of the two regiments, to serve as "horse-marines." The volunteers from the 5th embarked on the *Bayou City*, commanded by Green, the larger of the two vessels, while the volunteers from the 7th embarked on the *Neptune*, commanded by Colonel Arthur Bagby. As Green stepped on board he pulled out his watch and handed it to Colonel C.B. Shepard, saying, "Give this to my wife; I never expect to see her again."

On land were Joseph J. Cook's regiment of heavy artillery, six companies of Charles L. Pyron's regiment, portions of Elmore's regiment and Griffin's battalion, Reiley's regiment and "the remnants of Green's and Steele's regiments of the Sibley Brigade." McLeary recalled that the Confederate flotilla left Harrisburg in Buffalo Bayou at 2:00 p.m. on December 31. Becoming "horse-marines" was novel, but the men also realized it was extremely dangerous. Nevertheless, the Texans had such confidence in Colonel Green that the air of a "pleasure excursion" developed on board, at least until it entered Galveston Bay. At midnight the little fleet passed Half-Moon Shoals and proceeded down the bay to within five miles of the city; the signal-gun remained silent so the marines returned to the shoals and awaited the booming of Magruder's cannons.

Magruder was to give a signal from shore for the vessels to attack. When it arrived the flotilla was started for the city under a full head of steam. McLeary waxed almost poetic in describing what happened next.

> The scene. . .was magnificent. The artillery duel between land and sea in the clear starlight made an illumination superior to any other class of fireworks, rivalling in splendor the aurora borealis. Then the sound of artillery was the sweetest of music to the ears of these veteran soldiers. Their hearts beat high with patriotic impatience, and they were eager to encounter the invaders of Texas soil. They had not long to wait.[16]

The *Neptune* was the faster of the Confederate vessels and thus was the first to engage the Federal fleet. She passed the *Harriet Lane* and was struck mid-ship and sank to the bottom, but the water was so shallow that the sharpshooters on the upper deck could still engage the enemy on the deck of the *Lane*. The *Bayou City* slowly but surely entered into the fray, but Captain A.R. Weir and two others were killed in a burst of artillery. Nevertheless the vessel was maintained on course, ran her prow directly into the wheel-house of the *Harriet Lane* and stuck fast, disabling her. Then the Texans boarded, cutting away the netting as they went.[17]

Accounts disagree on the essential facts of what happened next. McLeary stated positively that a Sergeant Carson of Company A, 5th Regiment, was the first man to board the *Harriet Lane*, followed closely by Captain Leon Smith and others.[18] However, the Galveston *News* of Monday, January 5, 1863, providing details of the naval and land engagements, reported Leon Smith led the troops boarding the *Harriet Lane*.[19] Magruder, in his detailed report prepared in Galveston on February 26 for General Samuel Cooper, Adjutant and Inspector-General in Richmond, wrote, "Followed by the officers and men of the heroic volunteer corps, Commander Leon Smith leaped to the deck of the hostile ship, and after a moment of feeble resistance she was ours."[20] Captain M. McCormick, Pilot of the *Bayou City*, said, "As soon as we struck the order to board was given, which was immediately obeyed. Maj. Smith, owing to his experiences as a sailor, *being the first man on board*." [emphasis added]. Many of the boys failed in climbing the netting, and could not get over until they had cut it away, which was soon done."[21] Captain Henry Lubbock, commander of the *Bayou City*, was not quite so positive. "The vessel was then boarded without opposition and taken possession of. It is uncertain who was the first man on board. It is certain, however, that Col. Tom Green, Maj. Leon Smith, and Capt. James Martin were among the foremost, followed closely by the men. They cut the boarding nettings down with their knives, and took possession of the ship."[22] Robert Morris Franklin, who was with Smith during the battle and thus an eye-witness, delivered a lengthy speech to the Magruder Camp of the United Confederate Veterans in Galveston on April 2, 1911. He said of the boarding, "Commodore Smith appeared, cutlass in hand, climbing over the boarding netting, where it was attached to the Lane's wheel house. Half way over, he stopped and *called on the men to follow*, and was quickly joined by 15 or 20 men" [emphasis added].[23]

It is known from the record that L.H. McNelly was among Green's command participating in this battle and thus possibly among the first to board. However, Charles B. McNelly, apparently not satisfied with his great-uncle's being merely a participant, recorded that "Lee McNelly was the first Confederate Officer to board the Union Flagship, 'Harriet Lane' and accept its surrender in Galveston waters on January 2 [*sic*], 1863."[24] Further, Napoleon A. Jennings, later a McNelly ranger who interviewed surviving members of McNelly's scouts and Green's brigade in preparation of his own book *A Texas Ranger*, also believed that McNelly was first to board. "When Green returned to Texas [from New Mexico], he took his regiment to Galveston and captured the Union forces there.

McNelly was on the cotton-boat which captured the Harriet Lane, and was the first Confederate to board the Union boat."[25] However, based on the preponderance of the record indicating that Leon Smith was the first man to board, it would appear that in this case McNelly may have only been a follower.

Another important question is raised by the mementoes of Charles B. McNelly in his brief review of McNelly's Civil War experience.

> The sabre given in token of surrender was that of the squadron commander previously killed in the action, Captain Jonathan M. Wainwright I, the grandfather of the General of the same name who was second in command to McArthur in the Philippines during the early days of World War II. Incidentally, I offered this same sabre back to that illustrious family when General Wainwright had returned from the Japanese prison, and he accepted the offer very graciously, but died before we could get the return consummated; so, I have recently loaned the sabre to the Ranger Memorial Museum at Waco, Texas.[26]

Communication from Texas Ranger Hall of Fame Museum Director Byron A. Johnson indicates that their files contain no documentation on the story except for a May 1973 note from Charles B. McNelly of Kerrville, regarded as the owner of the sword, relating the fact that McNelly captured the sword on board the vessel *Harriet Lane* in Galveston harbor January 1, 1863. There was no additional information substantiating the claim. "We have the sword, a photograph of McNelly and a letter from Gen. Wainwright on an openended loan from Charles McNelly. . . . In 1990 the family requested the return of the sword and apparently changed their mind. Mr. McNelly was very elderly at that time and working through a representative."[27]

It is possible that the sword handed down through the McNelly family was indeed the property of Captain Wainwright who lost his life on the deck of the *Harriet Lane*. Assuming it was, the question remains of how McNelly acquired it since he apparently was not among the first to board. Further, and possibly more significantly, reports indicated that Leon Smith shot and killed Wainwright and thus likely would have taken the commander's sword as a trophy of war. This is almost suggested in the Houston *Telegraph* report. It was eagerly reported that the "enemy's loss is great, but not ascertained. Every officer of the *Harriet Lane* wounded, down to the master. Major Smith won the *spolia opima*, killing Captain Wainwright with his own hand."[28] To add further question, based on the Houston *Telegraph* report one assumes Wainwright was unscathed prior to the boarding and received a single shot which killed him. The Galveston *News* report of January 5 reported that Smith, on seeing Wainwright, "asked him if he commanded the boat, and on receiving an affirmative answer, Maj. Smith immediately shot him through the head, when he fell dead upon the sky light."[29] Yet the official report of Thomas N. Penrose, Assistant Surgeon, prepared for 1st Sergeant J.M. Foltz, United States Navy, dated February 26, listed the character of Wainwright's multiple wounds. "Killed instantly by musket ball through brain; had also three wounds in the left breast, and three in left thigh."[30]

Captain Leon Smith's character was later the subject of an attack in the New York *Herald* of November 30, 1864. Although the writer of the article was not identified by name, Smith learned of it and suspected it had been contributed by a Federal officer. The article accused him of being "The notorious Smith" who had "figured" in Galveston Bay in the attack on the *Harriet Lane* and "shot down Commander Wainwright after he had surrendered."[31]

Smith, writing from Havana, Cuba on December 8, 1864, explained his version of events.

> During the action of January 1, 1863, in Galveston Bay, I had the honor to command the Confederate naval forces. I made the attack on the federal fleet shortly before daylight. The Harriet Lane was the first vessel which I engaged by boarding; and it would have been impossible, owing to the darkness then prevailing, to have distinguished her commander from any of her other officers - particularly so, as he wore no uniform or ensignia [sic] of his rank. After a short struggle the ship was surrendered to me by the senior surviving officer, Acting Master Hamblin, her commander having been killed some twenty minutes previous, gallantly defending himself with his revolver and cutlass.[32]

Smith further explained how he learned that Wainwright was a

Captain Leon Smith, commander of the naval forces at
the Battle of Galveston, January 1, 1863. He led the
Confederates boarding the Union ship *Harriet Lane*.
Courtesy The Rosenberg Library, Galveston, Texas.

Mason, as he himself was, and had the commander of the *Harriet
Lane* dressed in full uniform and laid out in state. Smith ordered
"the finest coffin that could be found" and paid the expense out of
his personal funds. Smith and other Confederate officers escorted
him to his grave. "I saw to the collection and safe keeping of all of
his personal effects, including his two swords, which I placed in
charge of the senior surviving officer; but they were subsequently
sent out to Commodore Bell, at that time commanding the United
States squadron off Galveston, with the request that they should be
forwarded to his family in the North, to whom I have every reason
to suppose they were safely delivered."[33]

The informant to the *Herald* article may not have been a Federal officer as believed by Smith. The *Herald* had possibly obtained a copy of J. Bankhead Magruder's January 2 report of the affair, in which is found the following statement, "Captain Wainwright and Lieutenant Lea, executive officer of the *Harriet Lane*, were both killed, the former by Maj. Leon Smith in close quarters."[34]

Thus it remains possible that a sword was picked up on the deck of the *Harriet Lane* by McNelly, who believed it had belonged to Commander Wainwright. Smith may indeed have caused two swords to be returned through Captain Bell, but Wainwright might even have had a third which became the property of McNelly and which was then preserved by the family until his greatnephew loaned it to the Texas Ranger Hall of Fame and Museum. The weapon is thirty-two inches overall with a twenty-six inch slightly curved blade. The rack number is "M/669" and was probably made by the Ames Manufacturing Company of Chickapee, Massachusetts. There is considerable wear and pitting on the surface, so much so that what appears to be the year 1861 is partly indecipherable; the final digit is greatly obliterated by pitting and thus it is impossible to determine the earliest date of manufacture.[35] Certainly McNelly did pick up a sword from the deck of the *Harriet Lane* and told his family where he had obtained it, but through the years the story grew until it was no longer just a sabre from the deck of a Union ship but the actual sabre of Captain Wainwright himself.

CHAPTER 4

IN THE SWAMPS OF LOUISIANA

"McNally [sic] is one of the best soldiers and the most daring scout in the cavalry service." — Major General James P. Major, 28 May 1865, quoting Thomas Green.

Although there is no contemporary record detailing McNelly's actions with the Sibley Brigade in New Mexico, nor records relevant to his specific actions at Galveston, his courage and bravery in the swamps and battlefields of Louisiana is well documented by contemporary records. Various commanders, both Union and Confederate, mentioned him by name in their reports collected in the official records. Rangers who later served under him, N.A. Jennings and George P. Durham for example, also noted his Civil War experiences. Ranger Jennings, who interviewed fellow soldier W.A. Kerr and perhaps other veterans to learn of McNelly's Civil War exploits, recorded that he was commissioned in Louisiana to raise a scouting company. McNelly "gathered about him a troop of reckless young riders and fighters. His dash and daring became proverbial and his heroic exploits were the subjects of many campfire stories."[1] Durham recalled, albeit incorrectly and years after the war's end, that McNelly "served more than four years without a day's sick leave, we now know. He was made a captain and given a hundred guerrilla scouts to handle."[2]

The journal maintained by Theophilus Noel is a valuable record in which he described the campaigns of the "Old Sibley Brigade" in New Mexico, Arizona, Texas, Louisiana and Arkansas. Noel recorded that about January 16, 1863, the Sibley Brigade was sent to Hempstead and then was to move on to Louisiana. After arriving at Hempstead the men obtained additional clothing and used the time to rest and prepare for whatever their next duty might be. On January 29 they received four months pay and a fifty dollar bounty. On February 18 they headed east towards Louisiana. Even though the command was divided into smaller groups, its orders were for all to report at Cheyneyville, Louisiana, about April 1.[3]

The Sibley Brigade soon saw action in the battle of Bisland on April 13. Theophilus Noel recorded that in this engagement "Sixteen thousand live Yankees had danced to our music for two and a half long hours, and finally were compelled to retreat without accomplishing any thing," but in reality Bisland was a Confederate defeat. The day following was an all afternoon engagement at Franklin until darkness forced the end of combat for the day. Noel recorded that a mere eight hundred of the Sibley Brigade "whipped completely and drove back a 'crack army' of 9,000 under a 'gallant' General [Cuvier Grover]." Almost daily the men of the Sibley Brigade fought. There were battles or skirmishes at Jeanerette, New Iberia, Vermillionville and Grand Coteau. The Spring campaign of 1863 ended on May 24 with "a short but spirited skirmish" at Franklin.[4]

McNelly, frequently misspelled "McAnelly" in various reports, received considerable notice from Brigadier General Alfred Mouton. On June 22, an expedition numbering 325 volunteers from different regiments under his command started at 6:00 p.m. to "turn the enemy's stronghold at Brashear City." Under cover of darkness General Thomas Green, with the 5th Texas Mounted Volunteers, the 2nd Louisiana Cavalry, Edwin Waller's Texas Battalion and the Valverde and W.H. Nichols batteries, advanced opposite the Federal camp. Men of the 7th and 4th Texas and Baylor's Regiment were "thrown across" the Atchafalaya while Green attracted the Federals' attention and fire.

> Everything remained quiet, and the enemy were aware of our purpose only when awakened by the shots from the Valverde Battery. The enemy's whole attention was drawn to General Green's position, the land batteries concentrating their fire upon him, while their gunboats shamefully retreated in the beginning of the action.[5]

At 6:30 a.m. on the twenty-third the Confederates charged the enemy's guns "one after the other" and quickly the garrison surrendered without further struggle. This initial force to surrender was numbered at twelve-hundred men, "strongly posted and intrenched." Green was then ordered to move as rapidly as possible to Bayous Ramos and Boeuf to capture any of the enemy who might have escaped and also to prevent them from burning the bridges, locomotives and railroad cars. Green and his men were not quick enough to prevent destruction of the railroad and wagon bridge over the Ramos. At daylight on June 24 the enemy gave up, described by Mouton as surrendering "to a scouting party under the command of General Green's daring scout McAnelly." Mouton claimed 435 officers and men were taken prisoner and among other spoils of war were three siege guns and a 12-pounder gun. Later some twenty-five sick and wounded Federals were captured along with four pieces of light artillery.[6]

Noel devoted considerable space to young McNelly, whose name he spelled "McAnelly." In the New Mexico campaign he had observed McNelly's promotion to a captain of scouts, "For his daring gallantry on many occasions, too numerous to mention, he was promoted by the chief of chieftains, Gen. Green, to a captain of scouts. For his intrepid valor, he won the highest confidence of both soldier and officer." He also observed that McNelly, with some fifteen or twenty men, "by skillful manoeuvring," captured 380 federals at Brashear City on June 23, 1863, and that somewhere in Lafourche Parish McNelly made "another large capture in the same way."[7] The action at Lafourche Parish is one of the few which did become legendary during McNelly's own lifetime. N.A. Jennings learned of it and — while possibly adding his own "literary interpretation" — related how McNelly, with only about forty men, discovered a force of Federals numbering about eight hundred, together with nearly two-thousand Negroes.

There was a long bridge about a quarter of a mile from the Federals. Waiting until dark, McNelly began running his men back and forth over the bridge, simultaneously shouting commands to colonels and generals to make forward movements. "His men kept galloping and trotting over that bridge for an hour, and by that time the Union men were sure all the Rebs in the country were on them." At dawn McNelly took his forty men and a flag of truce and demanded an unconditional surrender from the unnamed Federal officer, who believed he was hopelessly outnumbered and easily convinced to surrender. Jennings also related that "on one or two of his spying expeditions" McNelly disguised himself as a woman, but he offered no details as to when or where.[8]

Charles Bowman McNelly also recorded an incident in which McNelly captured a much larger force by a ruse, placing the action as having taken place near Brashear City. In this version a scouting troop, numbering only about ninety men, discovered a Union force estimated to number about six hundred. There was a small creek nearby, far enough from the Federals as to be completely out of sight in darkness. When the Federals were well settled in camp, McNelly "moved his entire troop up to the bridgesite at a gallop and with orders to swing back and recross several times." In a loud voice McNelly ordered various troops to move to the right and left, "the guns to be posted on a rise near the center and supported with the remaining three troops." He then went forward and called out for the surrender of the Federals, "to avoid much bloodshed." In this version the ruse worked. Not far away was Edmund J. Davis who heard of the trickery of young McNelly; Charles McNelly wrote that it was because of this incident that Edmund J. Davis, when Governor of Texas in 1870, decided McNelly would be a good man to captain his state police force.[9]

Colonel E.J. Davis, commanding cavalry of the 19th Army Corps, was very much aware of young McNelly during the war. In his report prepared for Captain Frederic Speed, Assistant Adjutant General, he described an engagement in late May of 1864 in which Lieutenant Colonel John M. Crebs came suddenly upon a small party of fifty or sixty rebels, "being a company of scouts known as McNelly's." Crebs charged them, killing or wounding four and taking a lieutenant and seven men prisoners. Crebs lost one killed and two wounded. "His horses were so much used up by their hard service that he did not take the whole rebel party as would otherwise have been the case."[10]

Thomas Green had been promoted to brigadier general on May 20, 1863.[11] The men of the old "Sibley Brigade" had been able to spend a few weeks near the old Bisland battlefield prior to the capture of Brashear City. After the success at Brashear City Green received orders from General Alfred Mouton to take possession of the Federal fort at Donaldsonville. He left Thibodaux on June 26, marching at night, and rested the jaded troops and horses the next day. Green advanced during the night of June 27 to within less than two miles of the fort, dismounted his command and made final plans for the assault. From 2:00 a.m. until daylight they engaged the enemy, and Green reported,

> The enemy have been shown an example of desperate courage, which will not be without its effect. But for the false information in relation to that part of the

A Civil War era image of
Brigadier General E.J.
Davis, who fought against
McNelly but on the Federal
side. The original is a
mounted albumen print
made during the war. *Photo
courtesy The Texas State
Library & Archives
Commission, Austin.*

fort fronting the river, it would most certainly have
fallen into our hands. . . . our dead and wounded show
the desperation of the assault. The garrison maintained
between 500 and 600 Federals. Our assaulting party
engaged was about 800 strong.

In addition to Green's expression of regret over the loss of life
his force had experienced, he found certain men worthy of praise
and reported as such. "My own staff came fully up to my expectations. Capt. C.B. Sheppard [sic], my aide-de-camp, and my volunteer
aides, W.G. Wilkins and Leander McAnelly [sic], rendered me good
service, and behaved themselves, as they had on many former occasions done, with coolness and courage."[12] Green's report of casualties in the First and Second Brigade amounted to an aggregate of 261
with 40 killed, 114 wounded, and 107 missing.

After an assault on Fort Butler on June 28, Green was occupied
in watching the movements of Federals at Donaldsonville. McNelly
had proved his ability to work alone, and Green had great confidence in the young man. On July 5, at Assumption Church on
Lafourche, he wrote out an order which McNelly carried ready to dis-

play, addressed "To any Confederate Officer commanding on the east of the Mississippi."

> I send my young volunteer aide-de-camp, Leander McAnelly [sic], of the Fifth Texas Cavalry, to communicate with any Confederate force on the east of the Mississippi.
>
> We have a sufficient force on this side, of cavalry, infantry, and artillery, to hold it against any force the Yankees can bring against us. If a force on the east, below Donaldsonville, could hold their own on the river, we can stop the supplies to Banks' army, and force him to raise the siege of Port Hudson. We will, I am confident, be able to whip his army in the open field should he move on this side.
>
> McAnelly will give you full details.[13]

On July 11 ten transports came down the Mississippi, "crowded with troops." The next day additional enemy troops were seen coming down the river. Green ordered part of his command to withdraw from the river to Lafourche, "for the purpose of concentrating on each side of the bayou as near as possible to the enemy." On the morning of July 13 the enemy advanced down the bayou on both sides toward Thibodaux in large numbers. At 9:00 a.m. the Federals pressed with artillery and a large force of skirmishers. "The whole of this battle was a succession of charges, and I have never before witnessed such determined valor as was displayed by our troops," wrote Green. He was well aware of the disparate loss of troops between the Federals and his own, claiming over five hundred of the enemy killed and wounded. Two-hundred Federals were left dead on the field and about 250 prisoners taken. Green gave his losses at three killed and thirty wounded, six of whom were mortally wounded. One of the Federal generals was Cuvier Grover.[14]

The battles of Fordoche Bridge and Mrs. Stirling's Plantation, six miles from Morganza, occurred on September 24, and again Green was victorious, although Lieutenant W.F. Spivey of Company I was killed "while riding in the front with L.H. McNelly, who was wounded "[15] Green said of Spivey, "The lamented Lieut. W.F. Spivey, of Company I, Rountree's Battalion, was killed in the charge. We deplore his loss, he being one of the most energetic officers in the brigade, and of tried courage and discretion."[16]

In the same report Green praised the "gallant bearing and activity" of Lieutenant John B. Jones, the same Jones who would later command the Frontier Battalion of the Texas Rangers at the same time McNelly was given command of the Washington County Volunteer Militia Company. In this engagement, according to Green's report, the Federals lost 433 non-commissioned officers and privates and twenty-nine officers taken prisoner, two 10-pound Parrott guns, two new ambulances, one hospital wagon, two stands of regimental colors (the 19th Iowa and 26th Indiana Volunteers) plus many small arms. To the individual soldier who had an inferior weapon, obtaining a good and efficient one was a blessing.[17] The wounded, presumably including McNelly, were sent to the rear of the action as quickly as possible under the direction of Chief Surgeon George Cupples. Green wrote of Cupples, who would treat McNelly in Texas a decade later when he was dying of tuberculosis, "Too much praise cannot be awarded to him for his efficiency." Cupples was not the only one to receive praise, "My own personal staff, Lieutenant [E.R.] Wells, acting assistant adjutant general; Captain [C.B.] Sheppard [sic], aide-de-camp; Captains Calvitt and [Leander] McAnelly [sic], volunteer aides-de-camp, were active and efficient and rendered me excellent service."[18] Green prepared his report of this engagement on October 2 at his headquarters on the Atchafalaya in Camp McBride. He gave his own losses as twenty-six killed, eighty-five wounded and ten missing. Noel termed this engagement as "the most brilliant of all brilliant affairs."[19]

On September 1, Lieutenant General Edmund Kirby Smith, writing from Headquarters Department of the Trans-Mississippi in Shreveport, issued Special Order No. 126 authorizing the recruitment of various regiments, battalions or companies. Specifically the recruiting would "in no Case interfere with the enrolling Officer of the County or Parishes."[20] On November 25 at Vermillionville, Thomas Green again sent forward a recommendation to authorize McNelly to raise a company of scouts. Green suggested that McNelly "be authorized to raise the Company in Texas to be attached to the 1st Cavalry Brigade now commanded by [Arthur Pendleton] Bagby." Green was now lavish in his praise, "I will state that McNally [sic] has displayed more ability[,] greater activity and more daring than any officer of my command as a Scout." Green, who considered him a "Sagacious and dashing Scout," stated he had "been in the habit of entrusting him with a command equal to that of a Captain whenever in the presence of the enemy because of his superior

Qualifications." No officer in Green's division was equal to McNelly as a scout, and there was not one who did not "ardently desire" his promotion.[21]

General E. Kirby Smith did not respond until December 19 when he issued Special Orders No. 221, granting authority to McNelly due to his "gallantry and good conduct in the field" to raise, from men not otherwise subject to conscription, a company of cavalry in the district of Texas to serve as scouts with the Cavalry Division of Brigadier General Thomas Green.[22] On January 21, 1864 General Magruder, from Houston, issued Special Orders No. 21 authorizing "Private McNulty" to raise a company of cavalry in the District of Texas, New Mexico and Arizona. His authority to raise new companies would expire on February 15. Enrolling officers and other officers were ordered to furnish him "with such facilities as may be in their power." When McNelly had raised his company, he was ordered to report for duty with the Cavalry Division commanded by Green. No one would be permitted to join this elite company or any other mounted company unless he furnished his own horse and arms.[23]

Another concern for the Confederacy was the fear that General Nathaniel P. Banks was preparing an expedition to invade Texas. To meet the threat Magruder requested that General E. Kirby Smith send General Green and his brigade to Texas. On December 14, 1863, Green and his command began the march to Houston, the advance arriving there on Christmas day. "The weather," McLeary recalled, "at this time was very severe, wet and cold, and, as usual, the brigade was without tents, and sought shelter in the pine groves, where they constructed rude huts of pine boughs and such other materials as chance afforded." Ice had formed over two inches thick on all the puddles and ponds. By January 9, 1864, the brigade was in Brazoria County. Ten days later it started for Hempstead, on to Houston and then to Virginia Point where the men were able to rest for a month. By mid-February the rumor that Banks was intending to invade Texas through the Gulf was determined to be false, and Green was ordered to reinforce General Richard Taylor as quickly as possible. On February 15 the advance guard began the march back to Louisiana.[24]

On April 8 "one of the most desperate fights of the campaign, in proportion to the number engaged," as Theophilus Noel described it, took place at Mansfield, Louisiana. Here McNelly was wounded and would miss much of the action in the Louisiana swamps. Noel said that McNelly was "severely wounded" but gave no details on how he received the wound. He would be out of action until May 18.[25] Charles McNelly, in his *Mementoes* essay, wrote that his great-uncle "was hit with a rifle ball in the left chest, and but for the fact that he was carrying a small prayer book in his left shirt pocket, that may have been the first and last engagement of his life. The ball struck well toward the edge of this small booklet and did not even penetrate his skin." Unfortunately, Charles McNelly did not indicate clearly in which engagement the rifle wound was suffered.[26]

One of the most serious losses for the Confederacy occurred with the death of General Thomas Green at Blair's Landing on April 12, 1864, after being mortally wounded while leading his men against Federal gunboats patrolling the Red River. Major General Richard Taylor issued a lengthy statement informing his men of the tragedy, explaining that after having braved death a thousand times, "the destroyer found him, where he was ever wont to be, in the front line of battle." Taylor continued with his poetic praise, saying that throughout "broad Texas, throughout desolated Louisiana, mourning will sadden every hearth. . . . Moistened by the blood of Mansfield, Pleasant Hill and Blair's Landing, the tree of national independence will grow apace, and soon overshadow the land so that all may repose in peace under its grateful shade."[27] Thomas Green, idolized by his men, was replaced by Major General John A. Wharton.

Although Theophilus Noel indicated McNelly was recovering from a wound when Green was killed, a contemporary source indicates that McNelly was *standing next to Green* when his commander was killed. Austin's *Weekly Gazette* editor David Richardson wrote in the April 20 issue expressing his "word of sympathy or consolation to the bereaved family of our former friend and fellow citizen" and lined the columns of his paper with black.[28] In the May 4th issue Richardson printed an extract from a letter written by a Major Hart of Green's staff to a friend in Houston, which originally appeared in the Houston *Telegraph*.

> General Green was killed within forty yards of the gunboat that fired the fatal shot, and immediately on the bank of the river, on a bluff some forty feet high. His men were on every side of him, and attacking furiously the fleet of gunboats and transports with which

the river was filled. The transports were terribly muti-
lated by our rifles, and upon a part of our troops [cease-
less?] fire, a white flag was raised on one of them, but
the gunboats continued to pour their broadsides and
our troops opened again a murderous discharge. . . .
Our loss was about 75 killed and wounded - the
enemy's loss unknown, but must have been terrible. . . .
[Green] died, as he wished, in front of battle, with his
face to the foe. He was struck by a grapeshot in the fore-
head, and the upper part of his head carried away. . . .
Poor Chauncey [B. Shepard] was killed by my side, his
hand resting on me. Jo Sayers was struck by a shell in
the head and in the ankle. McNalley [sic], who was acting at the same time on the General's Staff, was
wounded in the thigh. Young Hays, V.A.D.C.
[Volunteer Aide-de-Camp], had 3 horses shot under
him. . . . Gen. Wharton will succeed Gen. Green in
command of the cavalry.[29]

Regardless of which wound McNelly received or when, during
his recovery period his command fell to lieutenants H.N. Stone and
T.T. Pitts, described by Noel as "men of gallantry." McNelly would
be out of action until a few days after the battle of Yellow Bayou on
May 18 during which the rebels were "badly whipped and worsted"
according to Noel's description of the defeat.[30]

Another version of McNelly's resorting to trickery, recorded less
than two years after McNelly's death, is either a reference to the
Brashear City incident or to another example of McNelly's trickery
altogether. The original appeared in the Belton, Texas, *Journal* and
then was reprinted in Brenham's *Daily Banner* February 15, 1879.
The narrator placed the incident as following the Banks Red River
campaign in which the Federals fortified themselves under the protection of their ironclads at Morganza, Louisiana.

I am fully satisfied that during its stay in that sec-
tion the [McNelly] company killed and captured more
than three times its own number of the enemy. General
M.K. Lawler, of Illinois, was then commandant at
Morganzia [sic]. He was a fat, good-natured old
Irishman, and Capt. Mac's exploits around the fort
gave him a great annoyance. Repeatedly the entire
Union force would be under arms and in battle array

on dark and rainy nights, expecting an attack, when really there were not fifty Rebs within seventy-five miles of the place, and these by firing on pickets on all the roads at once, or otherwise making a great show with but small capital, had created the impression that the whole of Dick Taylor's army had crossed the Bayou.[31]

Another incident revealed in the *Belton Journal - Brenham Banner* reminiscence of 1879 relates how on one occasion McNelly and twenty of his men observed an officer and a dozen Federals' raiding a plantation, "gathering up chickens and other small game by the haversack full." The rebels "made a dash" and killed or captured the entire group at the first pass, except for the officer, a lieutenant, who dismounted and attempted to escape in a deep ditch. McNelly himself was in close pursuit and followed the lieutenant's example by dismounting and running down the "crestfallen raider." Unfortunately, McNelly's mare broke away and galloped off to the Federal quarters at Morganza.

Having a Federal prisoner but no horse was untenable for McNelly, and again he resorted to a ruse. He released a prisoner, sending him to Morganza with a note to General Lawler saying that if he would return his mare he would release the lieutenant. But if he refused he would hang every prisoner he had by ten o'clock the next day. Early the next morning, to the amusement of McNelly's men and to the great relief of the Federal prisoners, an orderly returned with the mare and the lieutenant was released. McNelly said he could easily afford to exchange thus, for he could overhaul a prisoner every day but would have considerable difficulty in replacing such a charger![32]

Frequently McNelly and his company of scouts would aggressively harass the enemy's flanks or rear. Noel relates of the time when the company had captured a "Yankee establishment" a few miles from Plaquemine, Louisiana, and provided themselves with new clothing. While loading a mule with their plunder, they were attacked by a contingent of the "First Texas Traitors," Texas troops led by Colonel Edmund J. Davis who had opted to place their loyalty with the Federals. The looting of the "Yankee establishment" had to be forgotten and McNelly's scouts made a hasty retreat. A running fight then began which lasted ten miles; the mule carrying the loot was lost during the first mile. Before long Davis' men gave up the chase, but it was taken up by another group of Federals. "In this affair," wrote Noel, "Joe Doss was killed, a better and braver soldier than whom never shouldered a gun in any cause." Lieutenant Pitts and ten men were taken prisoner. On the Federal side eight soldiers were killed and fifteen wounded.[33]

In this engagement Corporal Joseph Doss, a married man with five children, lost his life. He had enlisted in the Confederate service on September 9, 1861, in San Antonio and had transferred to McNelly's company on February 1, 1864. He had earned the respect of the company. Upon Doss' death, with thirty-nine of the company present, Lieutenant R.J. Moore informed the men that there was a "company fund" of $500 in the hands of McNelly, and "since God has seen fit to take from them one of our best soldiers in the loss of Joe Doss" with a wife and children who would now be left destitute, did the men wish the $500 be turned over to the widow Doss? The men not only chose to turn over the money to her but took up a collection as well to increase the fund. McNelly and lieutenants Moore and H.N. Stone each contributed $200. The balance of the men present gave sums ranging from $10 to $100. With the company's individual contribution, the $500 company fund and a $100 contribution from a citizen of Point Coupee Parish, the total amount was $2,605. This amount was turned over to a Mrs. Perkins who delivered it to the widow Doss. At the request of an unidentified "N." the News printed the names and amount donated by each member of the company.[34]

Possibly this engagement in which Joe Doss was killed was the same as that described by Edmund J. Davis, writing to Captain Frederic Speed on June 5, 1864, in which Lieutenant Colonel John M. Crebs surprised a group of some fifty or sixty rebels, "being a company of scouts known as McNelly's." Davis reported that on June 4 he had sent Crebs to make the circuit of the outside of False River, and a Colonel [Morgan H.] Chrysler to make the circuit on the inside. Nothing of any importance happened to Chrysler, but Crebs had not proceeded more than six or eight miles when he came upon the McNelly scouts. Crebs charged them and succeeded in killing and wounding four and taking a lieutenant and seven men prisoners. Crebs lost one man killed and two wounded. Davis claimed that because Crebs' horses were "so much used up by their hard service that he did not take the whole rebel party, as would otherwise have been the case." This incident happened on June 4.[35]

Fortunately a lengthy report of war news was published in the Galveston Weekly News of July 5, 1864, printing a letter dated June 7 and written near West Baton Rouge. Although the contributor was identified only as "N." it does reveal a very human side to those scouts serving under McNelly during war time. The correspondent reviewed various recent actions, pointing out in particular that Captain McNelly had been operating in that section, "greatly to the inconvenience of the Yankee army, insomuch that their telegraph has been of little service to them" and suggesting that quite a few lives were lost in attempting to repair the telegraph lines. There was a force of an estimated six-thousand cavalry in pursuit of various scouting groups, but according to correspondent N. "our boys ask for nothing better in the way of a hiding place, than the swamps and cane-breaks afford them. This country has so many bayous, lakes, and lagoons, that its impossible to make a bee line in one direction without having to swim more or less every day." Only a few days before a Federal squad had "got the drop" on "our boys" leading to a running fight and "a hot cavalry encounter." After running several miles the rebels gained the swamps and "Mr. Yankee Davis did not choose to antie [sic]." Besides exchanging shots, both the pursued and the pursuers exchanged taunting words, the former being cursed as "d– d rebels" and an occasional "d– d telegraph cutters," to which the rebels would reply "come on you thieves, follow us if you dare." The Federals feared they were being led into an ambush and gave up the chase, but in retreat they were closely pursued by a few men of McNelly's company who "were so manoeuvered that the Yankee Brigade began to think themselves 'flanked' and accordingly they broke; and for two miles our Confederates found fun, in repayment for the sport the Yankees had just before enjoyed."[36]

Strangely, Theophilus Noel, after the introduction of the "Texas Traitors" under Edmund J. Davis, merely states that McNelly was "not working to suit someone" and then was ordered out and sent to hunt Jayhawkers on the Calcasieu, but this is difficult to accept.[37] Letters preserved by McNelly's widow show he received nothing but praise by his superiors for his accomplishments. A letter to McNelly, written near Alexandria, Louisiana, dated July 1, 1864, by Lieutenant and Acting Assistant Adjutant General R. Smith stated that Brigadier General B.F. Weems desired "to convey to you through me his thanks for the very able assistance which you have rendered this Brigade, and his regret that the duration of your service with it has been so short."

On April 26, 1865, Weems relayed orders for McNelly to proceed with his company of scouts to Washington County to operate there and in adjoining counties in accordance with verbal orders previously given. His orders were to arrest, and send by railroad to Hempstead under guard, all deserters and absentees without leave from whatever command and of whatever rank. County lines were not to interfere with the discharge of this duty. "Secrecy is essential to success in this undertaking, and you are enjoined to use it with celerity in carrying it out."[38]

On May 3, 1865, John G. Walker ordered McNelly to determine if one Leadbetter of Fayette County, in a recent speech, had declared himself a "reconstruction Union candidate" for the legislature. If this was so McNelly was to arrest him and to send him to Walker's headquarters at Hempstead, along with affidavits from respectable citizens as to the facts of the case. McNelly was to scout "pretty thoroughly" in Fayette and Colorado counties.[39]

The man, now identified as Ledbetter in Walker's letter written two days later, was arrested and was to be kept under guard until the affidavits were procured as to the treasonable words uttered by him. Walker had further concerns because Austin County was considered "very rotten," and he sent Lieutenant Stone and ten men of McNelly's company to investigate matters, specifically in the western part about Rador's or Roeder's Mill which was infested with deserters. If McNelly made a report of his actions it has not survived.[40]

Special orders were issued on May 23, directing McNelly to take charge of the Washington County railroad train but no details are given.[41]

Major General James P. Major prepared a letter in Houston on May 28 which contained great praise for McNelly as a soldier.

> Captain of Cavalry in the Army of the Confederate States has remained true to his colors to the very last and by his determination & other soldierly qualities, retained his company intact when those around him disbanded. In this the darkest hour of our government he has proved himself to be a true soldier. [Due to his] gallant and meritorious conduct on the principal battlefields of this department [he has earned] the commendation of his superiors, and his daring courage and consummate skill drew, from his chief the late Genl Thos Green the remark that McNally [sic] is one of the best soldiers and the most daring scout in the cavalry service. [McNelly's service under James P. Major] has been of so distinguished a character that I cheerfully

recommend him as one who will prove himself to be a
true soldier when ever & whatever he is tried.[42]

McNelly had been truly tried, having suffered the hardships of
marching across West Texas into the New Mexico territory, suffering
defeat, and then the long difficult march back home. He had been
in the thick of the action at Galveston when the Federals were driven
out of Texas. He had fought hard against the enemy in the swamps
and bayous of Louisiana. He had been wounded in action, possibly
several times. When the war was nearing its end he was given the
responsibility of tracking down deserters. In April the armies of Lee
and Johnston were surrendered, followed by those of Richard Taylor
in May and E. Kirby Smith in June. McNelly was in his home district
when he learned the war was over.

Mary Irene McNelly, only daughter of Captain McNelly, while a
student at Old Baylor, Washington, Texas.
Courtesy Elizabeth McNelly Shannon, Boston University.

CHAPTER 5

CAPTAIN - TEXAS STATE POLICE

> The war is not over yet. I tell you there is a slow civil war going on here and has been ever since the surender of the Confederate armies.— Governor E.J. Davis, 28 June 1870.

When the hostilities ended between the Union and Confederate Armies, McNelly returned to his Washington County home. He was certainly more fortunate than many returning rebels; the fields of Washington County had never been scarred by artillery shells and no armies ever had shed blood in its streams.

As a young man just entering his twenties McNelly found there was more to life than farming and raising sheep. Just when he first met Carey Cheek Matson is unknown. Born June 24, 1848, she was the daughter of John and Sarah (Hall) Cheek. When John Cheek died, somewhere in Harris County, Texas, his widow Sarah married Richard Thomas Matson. Matson, born in Missouri on September 21, 1826, died from wounds suffered during the battle of Pine Bluff, Arkansas, on October 25, 1863.[1] His body was returned to Washington County and buried in the Mount Zion Cemetery near Burton. Matson was a wealthy man; in 1860 his real estate was valued at $40,000 and he held $37,000 in his personal estate.[2] On the death of her stepfather, teen-ager Carey inherited not only eleven-hundred acres of land but the Matson home. If Leander and Carey met before the war, their feelings for each other had had an adequate test during its duration. They obtained a marriage license on October 15, 1865; two days later on October 17 they were united in marriage by teacher and minister Horace Clark.[3] The marriage took place in the Matson home, although Carey's mother had not lived to see the wedding; born December 12, 1827, she had died on January 1, 1865, barely thirty-eight years old, and was buried in the Mount Zion Cemetery adjacent to her husband.[4]

The newly married McNellys were eventually to present two children to the world: son Leander Rebel was born in 1866 followed by

daughter Irene born on April 29, 1868.[5] The children and their
mother would all outlive their father, but neither child lived to old
age. Irene, while attending Baylor College in Washington, Texas, was
the victim of a prank when someone pulled out from under her the
chair on which she was standing. She died a short time later, on May
8, 1884, of the injuries received.[6] Son L.R. McNelly died, from the
same disease which claimed his father, on January 1, 1907, in
Tombstone, Arizona, where he had gone presumably for his health.[7]

Before the war McNelly may have worked exclusively for Travis
Burton, but after his marriage he was placed in charge of consider~
able land and operations. In 1870 when the Agricultural Census was
made, he itemized an impressive list of livestock and crops. His horse
herd numbered thirty~two head; he had four mules and asses, one~
hundred milch cows and two~hundred head of cattle. The flock of
sheep numbered six hundred and he had twenty head of swine. The
value of all the livestock was $6,260.

In crops McNelly claimed production of one~thousand bushels
of Indian corn and thirty~eight bales of cotton, each weighing 450
pounds. His sheep had produced 2,700 pounds of wool. He had
raised one~hundred bushels of Irish potatoes, fifty bushels of sweet
potatoes, $200 worth of orchard products, nine~hundred pounds of
butter and ten tons of hay. The value of animals slaughtered or sold
for slaughter was $230. The value of the crops produced was $3,695.
By any standard McNelly's agricultural production was impressive.[8]

Later in 1870, while McNelly was working full time for the state
of Texas, census enumerator B.J. Arnold reported McNelly had four~
hundred improved acres and 480 unimproved acres of woodland.
The cash value of the farm at the time of enumeration, October 10,
was $12,600. The farming improvements and machinery were val~
ued at $200 while the amount of wages paid during the year, includ~
ing the value of board, was $1,615.[9] A month earlier, on September
8, 1870, Arnold had visited the McNelly family to enumerate indi~
viduals. McNelly gave his occupation as a captain in the State Police
rather than as a farmer as one might expect. His age was given as
twenty~five; his wife "Cara" was listed as twenty~two. Their son
"Rivel" was four years old and daughter Irene two years old. To help
with the duties of a plantation/farmer owner, there were two farm
laborers listed: Michael Baine, thirty years of age, born in Ireland,
and Reuben Carter, twenty~three, from Mississippi. Carter, although
listed simply as a farm laborer, was also a member of the State Police.
His commission and acceptance were both dated July 15, yet he
would not take the oath until November 22. He served until April

Edmund J. Davis as Governor of the State of Texas. *Courtesy The Western History Collections, University of Oklahoma.*

1, 1871.[10]

Following the enumeration of the L.H. McNelly family, B.J. Arnold continued on to the household of Thomas Baine, a thirty-five-year-old Irishman who gave "Farm laborer" as his occupation. Within the family household was his wife Mary Baine and six children: John, Mary A., Thomas, all attending school, and Jennie E., Chauncey (Chancy) and Rosette, all at home. The family name of the children was McNelly, ranging in age from fifteen-year-old Thomas to five-year-old Rosetta. Leander's brother Peter John had married Mary Downey, and after his death on July 8, 1865, from wounds received in the war, she had married Thomas Baine. Leander and his brother's family were now neighbors.[11]

McNelly's career as a government employee and a captain in the Texas State Police began in July of 1870. His commission was accepted on July 13; the record indicates his age was twenty-four which is incorrect because he had celebrated his twenty-sixth birthday that March. The police force was a creation of Governor Edmund J. Davis who had served in some of the same arenas as had McNelly during the war, although on the opposing side. Between the end of the war and 1870, Davis came to believe that law and order had to be the state's primary concern, characterizing lawlessness as having reached pandemic proportions. In looking for good men to serve as captains he remembered McNelly, knowing what an effective leader the young captain of scouts had been. When he requested his former enemy to serve in his police force, McNelly was at first reluctant. After consulting with other former rebels, including General Joseph Shelby and William M. "Buck" Walton,[12] McNelly accepted the position of captain in the newly formed Texas State Police. The announcement appeared in the Brenham *Banner* and other newspapers throughout the state. "Capt. L.H. McNally [sic], a gallant 'Johnny Reb,' living in this county, has received an appointment as one of the four Captains of Police under the military bill."[13]

The bill creating the special force had been passed June 23,

1870. Expectations in some corners were high, and the San Antonio *Express* of the same date predicted that the "ruffians will find Texas too hot for them and leave for parts unknown. The law abiding citizens know they have nothing to fear."[14] But there was a cry of outrage by some, a cry that Davis' new forces would turn the state into his own personal dictatorship. Five days later, on Thursday, June 28, Governor Davis made a speech to "a serenading party" in which he attempted to explain the necessity of police and militia.

> A cry of tyranny and despotism has been heaped upon me. It is said I ask a dictatorship, and have established a negro militia, and propose a secret police, and other things that I did not advocate when canvassing the State. I have always said we must have peace and quiet in Texas—that lawlessness must be suppressed or somebody would be hurt. I do not purpose [*sic*] to impose upon you a military government, and maintain it over you by force. I will establish order without regard to politics. I do not attribute lawlessness altogether to politics. A large class are not politicians. But, my friends, we have always been lawless in Texas. Twenty-five years ago, when I first came here, a man could travel from Galveston to Austin unarmed with safety, now he must needs carry his six-shooter. . . . *We are the most lawless people on the face of the earth* [emphasis added]. There are more murders and assassinations in this State than there are in the same extent of population on the American continent or in the civilized world. . . . The war is not over yet. I tell you there is a slow civil war going on here and has been ever since the surrender of the Confederate armies. This is what we propose to put an end to by means of the militia bill and police bill, the most effective of the two. We have the two forces in case of emergency.

Davis' intent may have been to convince Texans of the need for his two forces, but his choice of words in calling Texans the most lawless people on the face of the earth certainly could not have endeared him to the average law-abiding Texan!

Davis compared the homicide rate in New York City to that of Texas. In New York, "with about the same population," there were the year before last about seventy-five or eighty homicides, according to Davis. In the same period, in Texas, there were seven or eight-hundred homicides! Galveston editor Ferdinand Flake commented.

> If the Governor used this language and made these statements, he stated that which he knew to be false; for he knows that any man can travel, and that thousands of men do travel any where in the State of Texas, save on Indian ranges, without the need of arms. We do not believe that he carries them himself when he travels, and we know that it is not the habit of gentlemen traveling from Galveston to Austin to carry six-shooters or other weapons. The Governor knows this as well as we do; therefore we say that if he tells this story he lies.

Another comment in the article undoubtedly disturbed many former Confederates; with the passing of the police bill many former slaves were swarming to Austin "nearly all armed with six-shooters" looking for employment as policemen under Governor Davis.[15]

The act passed by the legislature establishing the State Police provided for a full complement composed of a chief of police, four captains, eight lieutenants, twenty sergeants and 225 privates. The captains were to receive $125 per month in salary; a lieutenant $100 per month; sergeants were to receive $75 per month and the privates to receive $60 per month. The first extant pay vouchers for McNelly, dated February 28, 1871, show he did receive the $125 per month as salary. Later pay vouchers show he received $155 for services and for horse and arms allowance. Although no uniforms were issued for policemen, in time each man was issued a silver badge on which appeared the words "State Police" and a figure denoting the number and the Lone Star of Texas "conspicuously raised in the center."[16] With a cowboy or other laborer's receiving only one dollar a day or less, it is not surprising that employment with the force seemed attractive!

The duties of the chief of police were to be performed by the adjutant general. For this position Governor Davis appointed James Davidson, a twenty-six year old native of Scotland who claimed to have served in a cavalry regiment in the British army prior to relocating in the United States. Prior to his appointment by Davis he had served in the 19th Maine Infantry Volunteers and, after being mustered out, joined the regular army where he served as a private in the Corps of Engineers. He served in other units and rose to the rank of second lieutenant. By 1869 he was in Clarksville, Texas, and assumed the duties of military commissioner for Red River County on June 18. Here Davidson earned the reputation of being a strict enforcer of military rule. The wearing of six-shooters or other weapons was prohibited. He also promoted the efforts by the Freedmen's Bureau to educate and protect freedmen. These were the qualities Governor Davis found useful in his nomination of Davidson as Adjutant General of the State of Texas.[17]

All members of the police force were to hold office for four years unless sooner removed; removal could be for malfeasance, misfeasance, incompetence or disobedience of orders. Mileage and other compensations for conveying prisoners was to be the same as for sheriffs if conveyed beyond the county lines in which the prisoner was arrested. The force was actually much larger than the potential 258 because all sheriffs, deputies, constables, marshals, police and their deputies of cities and towns were to be under the control of the governor or the chief of the State Police. Policemen would be eligible for rewards in addition to their regular salaries. Policemen had as their primary responsibility "to see that the laws of the State are observed and enforced, and use their utmost endeavors to prevent and repress crime of all kinds."[18]

Each member of the force was to swear an oath.

> I, [L.H. McNelly] do solemnly swear, or affirm, that I will faithfully and impartially discharge and perform all duties incumbent on me as [Captain], according to the best of my skill and ability, and that I will support the Constitution and laws of the United States and of this State. And I do further swear, or affirm, that since the acceptance of this Constitution by the Congress of the United States, I, being a citizen of this State, have not fought a duel with deadly weapons, or committed an assault upon any person with deadly weapons, or acted as second in fighting a duel, or knowingly aided or assisted any one thus offending, either within this State or out of it; that I am not disqualified from holding office under the Fourteenth Amendment of the Constitution of the United States; (or, as the case may be, my disability to hold office under the Fourteenth Amendment to the Constitution of the United States has been removed by an act of Congress;) and, further, that I am a qualified elector in this State.[19]

On July 3, Adjutant General and Chief of Police James Davidson wrote to McNelly asking him if he would accept a captaincy of a police company. Although McNelly's reply — he had been directed to answer by telegram — has not been preserved, it was in the affirmative because on July 21 Davidson wrote again, addressing his communication to McNelly as Captain State Police at Brenham, assigning him to the 4th Police District. This district comprised the thirty-four counties of Washington, Fayette, Austin, Gonzales, Colorado, Lavaca, Wharton, Wilson, DeWitt, Jackson, Matagorda, Victoria, Karnes, Atascosa, Frio, Zavala, Maverick, Dimmit, La Salle, McMullen, Live Oak, Bee, Goliad, Refugio, Webb, Calhoun, San Patricio, Encinal, Duval, Nueces, Zapata, Starr, Hidalgo and Cameron.[20]

McNelly, as captain, was to put himself in communication with the civil authorities of the counties comprising his command "and go to work." He was not the kind of officer who needed instructions; before he had been given any assignment he had arrested a freedman named Joe Barker in Williamson County, north of Austin. Barker was charged with the murder of Don Wallace in Bastrop County and was turned over to Bastrop County Sheriff Joseph Jung.[21]

Further initial action on his part involved searching for the murderer of John Eikel, a popular Austin business man of the firm of Kluge & Eikel. John Watson, his murderer, reportedly had been "induced" to go to Austin to obtain a position on the police force but ended up killing a man. William H. Parsons, a member of the state legislature from Houston, had recommended Watson for a position on the newly created force because he knew Watson was a brave and courageous individual — when sober. When he was in his cups he was ugly but had promised Parsons to remain temperate.[22] On the evening of July 11 Watson went to Kluge & Eikel's Restaurant for a meal but was refused service because it was after serving hours. Watson left but returned fifteen minutes later, now under the influence, and found Eikel sitting on the steps of the restaurant apparently asleep. Watson struck him violently on the head with his six-shooter, cutting his scalp to the bone. Eikel defended himself, managing to spring up and seize the pistol. The pair "closed and fell" with Watson on top, and the pistol discharged shooting Eikel in the left groin. He died in less than two hours; his killer escaped.[23]

Two days later a stage driver met Watson near Lockhart, south of Austin, and found him to be "well mounted, armed with a

Spencer rifle and two revolvers." He was using the alias of McCormick.[24] Davidson, believing McNelly would know the "renouned [sic] desperate character" since he was a Washington County resident, gave McNelly an order to "look out for Watson."[25] McNelly made no report of his efforts in locating the fugitive, but a week after the killing a Mr. Parker brought Watson into Austin, in his custody. Parker had been in pursuit of Watson since the killing and had tracked him to Milam County where Watson had traded his weapons for a horse, thus allowing Parker an easy arrest.[26] The entire episode proved to be an embarrassing experience for Senator Parsons, who had believed Watson would be a good man for the police force. Unfortunately, the man's weakness for liquor proved to be a fatal flaw.

For an unexplained reason, Davidson reassigned McNelly to the 3rd Police District. His area of the state now included the thirty-one counties of Limestone, Freestone, Anderson, Cherokee, Nacogdoches, Shelby, Robertson, Leon, Houston, Angelina, San Augustine, Sabine, Madison, Trinity, Newton, Jasper, Tyler, Polk, Walker, Brazos, Grimes, Montgomery, Liberty, Hardin, Orange, Harris, Chambers, Jefferson, Fort Bend, Brazoria and Galveston.[27]

In late July McNelly was ordered to proceed to Bastrop and obtain capiases for the arrest of "certain parties" under indictment in the district court. Once these were in his hands he was to make the arrests. Bastrop was some sixty miles directly west from Brenham; it is not known if McNelly had the opportunity to start toward Bastrop, because on August 4 he was ordered to Hempstead in nearly the opposite direction from Bastrop, another twenty miles or so, and to take with him as many policemen as he could conveniently get together and report to Justice of the Peace William S. Wright. There had been "outrages against Freedmen" by a gang of eight to ten men. Wright's letter contained no names, and perhaps McNelly was to ferret out the guilty parties based on whatever information the Freedmen could provide. Warrants would be issued; McNelly was to make the arrests and to file a written report of his actions.[28]

Just prior to the change in his district, McNelly emerged victorious in his first shooting incident since war's end. No doubt during the war he had killed, but he was now a lawman rather than a soldier. The incident reveals both that McNelly was capable of engaging in personal combat and that law breakers were able to roam the state with impunity during the Reconstruction era.

Sometime in early 1869 Mat Banks, jailed for horse theft, and

Randall Lightfoot and Charles Hine (or High or Hier), both jailed for theft and attempted murder, escaped from the Travis County jail in Austin. They evaded arrest until Davidson learned of their prob-able whereabouts and sent Captain McNelly to round them up. McNelly, presumably with some assistance, confronted the trio on the northern border of Bastrop County. The "out-lawed freedman" Charles Hine defied the officer and was shot; the other two chose to surrender. The shooting took place on Saturday, July 23. The report appearing in the Bastrop *Advertiser* described Charles Hine as an "out-lawed freedman" who was "brought to grief" by McNelly near the small community of Sand Fly on the northern border of Bastrop County. "He resisted arrest and defied authority, and was dispatched to that bourne from whence there is no return." The *Advertiser* stressed that McNelly was "doing good service in this county" but also pointed out that the murderer of Fannie on the premises of Goodloe Miller near Bastrop was still at large.[29] Later that same month McNelly made two arrests: Taylor Meyer, recently employed at or near Moss' Mills, near Houston, was arrested on suspicion of having stolen a horse; Charles Scott, one time Houston drayman, was arrested on a murder charge. Both prisoners were "sent up the country, Meyer for the purpose of identification. Scott is a colored man."[30]

One of the more notorious gangs of outlaws, in McNelly's imme-diate area, which were of great concern not only to ordinary citizens but county sheriffs as well, was the Pearce Gang. Brothers Ed and John Pearce were the recognized leaders of perhaps fifty followers and sympathizers. Some members may have been guilty of murders but others may have only provided shelter or information to them about the law's movements, either out of sympathy or fear of what would happen if they did not. Certainly the Pearce Gang's existence predates the organization of the State Police, but it was not until July 17 that Governor Davis offered a reward of $500 for the arrest of John Pearce and his delivery to McNelly's own Washington County jail. He was charged with the crime of murder, or being accessory to murder and evading arrest.[31]

On August 6, Pleasant M. Yell, a farmer of Montgomery County, wrote to General Davidson expressing his concerns about the Pearce brothers and pointing out that another Pearce brother, Benjamin, was a deputy sheriff in Grimes County![32] Two days later Austin County Sheriff William Green alerted Davidson about what he termed an "outrage" committed by Ed and John Pearce. Just exactly what the Pearce brothers did was not explained, but it was serious enough that Sheriff Green feared that there was "no use trying to catch them with a posse of citizens."[33]

By mid-August the police had worked up a plan to combat the Pearce Gang. Policeman George W. Farrow was "in pursuit" of the brothers and intended to meet up with McNelly on August 19.[34] Abner Womack, Sheriff of Montgomery County, believed that the gang had killed Goldsteen Dupree, his father and three other freedmen, and he wanted twenty policemen to help him restore order in his county.[35] McNelly may have met up with Farrow as planned, but no report was filed with the Adjutant General's office. On August 16, however, McNelly telegraphed Davidson from Hempstead informing him that there were some fifty outlaws in the Pearce camp and he wanted the authority to form his own mounted posse to run them down.[36] The next day, as reported by Brenham correspondent Dodd, McNelly was himself captured by Ed Pearce and other gang members at Cedar Bayou in Harrison County! We have only Dodd's report of this incident, but he apparently obtained his information from McNelly himself. McNelly was traveling in strange territory with a two-man squad of police and became separated from the others. He was in "a wild part of the country" and observed men approaching him from every direction. Not knowing their intentions, he dismounted and took up a defensive position in an old house, warning the men to keep away. His warnings went unheeded and in a few moments the house was surrounded by about fifty men. With at the most two sidearms, McNelly surrendered upon assurances that his life would not be taken and that he would be allowed to keep his horse and weapons. The outlaws held him a prisoner about twelve hours, several of them reading rewards that were offered for them to show the captain how little they cared for or feared the civil authorities. Later, being interviewed by a reporter from the *Weekly State Journal* of Austin, McNelly stated he thought "he would have been killed but for the fact that several of the men were only friends of some of the outlaws, who had merely turned out to prevent any violence or bloodshed."[37] What McNelly apparently didn't relate to Dodd, but did confide in his report to Davidson, was that he was captured by Ed Pearce and "placed in a position to be shot some twenty times."[38] McNelly was certainly aware that the Pearce gang had committed murders, but he remained calm in a dangerous situation which could easily have resulted in losing his life.

Once released McNelly made rapid progress in breaking up the gang. On the next day he caught up with John Pearce, but again no details have survived as to how he accomplished the feat. He reported the arrest to Davidson and informed him that he believed others of the gang were "on the coast" and that he wanted one-hundred dollars to carry his men by rail. He then must have received different information because he subsequently scoured Grimes County so thoroughly that he reported he had "exhausted" the county. By August 30 he was again ready to go to Cedar Bayou, in eastern Harris County, where he believed Ed Pearce could be found.[39]

Davidson himself may have joined McNelly on the chase after the gang because the *State Journal* reported that Davidson had "been absent for some time on an expedition to Cedar Bayou. On his arrival it was found that the birds had flown." The *Journal* omnisciently stated the "birds" had "retreated in the night to Grimes county [sic], and are now traveling fast for the Louisiana line, hotly pursued by the mounted police."[40] McNelly later learned that Ed Pearce had gone to Kansas; he offered to follow him and capture him if Davidson would give him the funds. The money was not forthcoming so McNelly had to settle for the five-hundred dollar reward for his brother John, the final payment of which was sent on September 22.[41]

Dodd, whose reports indicate he was aware of their efforts from first hand knowledge, may have accompanied McNelly or Davidson on their pursuit of the Pearce Gang. In his report headlined "The Outlaws of Cedar Bayou" he complained that outlaws "in any part of Texas, can travel where they will, and boast as they go that they cannot be taken." Citizens waited for civil authorities to act and feared molesting "these rascals." Then Dodd offered his advice as to how the state could cleanse itself of murderers and thieves.

First, the governor should order every district clerk in the state to furnish every policeman and officer a list of names of men against whom there was an indictment. Then well armed posses should be sent out to hunt down every outlaw, day and night, "until the State is thoroughly purified and made safe for law-abiding citizens and their property." Although Dodd did not itemize a second part, inference is that a part of the problem was that "a class of honest citizens" gave aid and comfort to the outlaws and a plan was needed to deal with those people. These men, first called "honest citizens" but then "spies and informers," Dodd determined "should find no mercy or favor when found, because they are the worst enemies we have among us."[42] Dodd, like many lawmen, was unable to distinguish between the outlaws themselves or those who merely assisted the outlaws.

Unlike some other newspapers which were highly critical of

Governor Davis and his police force, the official *State Journal* heaped praise on them whenever possible. The Cedar Bayou affair provided one opportunity, the *Journal* claiming that five unnamed state police-men had been shot in making arrests, and that the work of McNelly had completely broken up the Pearce Gang which for a long time had intimidated the civil authorities at Hempstead. Upon receiving "application" for assistance Davidson had ordered a detachment under McNelly to arrest those responsible for such intimidation; the gang had been "completely broken up" and soon all members would be captured.[43] Other than John and Ed Pearce, the names of other gang members remain unknown; a Bob Stephens and a Ham Hodge were accused of being gang members, and in early September Charles S. Gillespie, a twenty-one year old Express Messenger in Houston, managed to capture Hodge, stating in his notification to Davidson that Hodge had "killed two negroes and a soldier in Austin County."[44]

One of the strangest stories about McNelly was related by Texas historian Chris Emmett in his highly popular biography *Shanghai Pierce: A Fair Likeness*. Abel Head "Shanghai" Pierce, a native of Rhode Island who stowed away on a steamer and landed in Indianola, ranks high among the numerous Texas cattle kings. Following service in the Confederate Army, he established himself as a cattleman by gathering up cattle on the open range. By the early 1870s he had established a ranch in Wharton County and, during the decade, acquired some 250,000 acres.

According to Emmett's undated incident involving McNelly and Shanghai Pierce, the cattleman and his brothers had captured one of the Taylors — of the DeWitt County Taylor group with which McNelly would deal with in 1874 — and intended to hang him. Someone took word to McNelly that the lynching was about to take place; McNelly grabbed his gunbelt and headed out to prevent the lynching. But, according to Emmett, McNelly left the house so fast that he had not noticed that Mrs. McNelly "had slipped a little old two-shot derringer in his holster instead of his reliable six-gun." Thus McNelly faced the Pierce boys, intent on hanging a Taylor, with only a derringer to back up his play. In a dramatic effort to save the pris-oner McNelly offered to take Taylor's place if they would release the prisoner! The Pierce boys began to select an appropriate tree when McNelly, continuing the bluff, exclaimed, "Damit, why do you have to look for a tree when you got a man to kill? You've all got guns. I'm not fighting back. I'm your man. One of you take a gun and kill me."

At this point Shanghai Pierce himself stepped forward and

admitted that there was not a man in the crowd who could hold a gun on McNelly and pull the trigger. "You take it too easy . . . you looking us in the eye." So, according to the Emmett story, McNelly "won old Shanghai Pierce then and there." Presumably the threat of anyone's being lynched was

The Bruff single shot derringer owned by L. H. McNelly, manufactured by Bruff Brothers of New York. The weapon, an example of Bruff's work popular during the 1850s and 1860s, only 6-1/2 inches overall, is still in the McNelly family. *Photo courtesy Bert McNelly, Jr. and Uvalde Photo, Uvalde.*

over at that point, so McNelly made a promise to Pierce: he would not forget the incident, and he would never "in all his life yet coming to him, bother either Shanghai or his brothers."

So far as known no one has ever challenged this story as presented by Chris Emmett. The Pierce boys' intent to hang a cattle thief and the action of McNelly to save a prisoner by a ruse seems plausible, but for McNelly to be roused from his home to save a would-be lynch victim would place the action in Washington County, too far from the Pierce territory or the area of the Sutton-Taylor Feud to be credible. It is also inconceivable that Mrs. McNelly would tamper with her husband's weapons, and certainly if a derringer had been placed where his trusty six-gun belonged McNelly would have noticed it while buckling on the gun belt! Although Emmett presented a very readable account, it in all likelihood was his mistaken belief that what was possibly the capture of McNelly by members of the Pearce gang at Cedar Bayou was instead the Pierce brothers of Wharton County. Although Emmett's identifying the Pierce boys as a "bunch of Sutton fighters" would suggest it took place closer to the DeWitt County area, certainly this was an incident in which a respected historian confused the Pearce brothers of Cedar Bayou with the Pierce brothers of Wharton County.[45]

Correspondent Dodd had written from Brenham that "too much praise" could not be bestowed upon McNelly "for the prompt and efficient manner" in which he dealt with the lawless element. He had been on the alert day and night, and in less than ten days had captured a dozen "scoundrels and cleared four out of this county" with the aid of only two policemen. Dodd failed to identify the dozen outlaws who had been captured but did identify one who had managed to evade arrest, Benjamin Hinds whom he identified as Hines. Dodd described Hinds as a "notorious outlaw" who was chased by McNelly into Burleson County but managed to escape because he was "so thoroughly acquainted with the country."[46]

Hinds, a fugitive wanted by Caldwell County Sheriff J.S. Lane,[47] was a desperate and notorious character. Nearly a quarter of a century later John Wesley Hardin remembered him while composing his memoirs after being released from Huntsville State prison. Hardin recollected the time when he met Hinds and another notorious fugitive, William Preston Longley. Hardin described the event as occurring while he was visiting relatives in Washington County and had traveled to gamble in Evergreen, where he met Hinds as well as Longley. Hardin recalled that, when they met, Longley suspected him as being a "spy" for McNelly and said, "If you don't watch out, you will be shot all to pieces before you know it." Hardin responded saying that all he wanted was for those who were going to do the shooting to be in front of him for a fair fight. Hinds, Longley and Hardin were all in that immediate area at that point in time, but it is doubtful that the grandiose verbal exchange actually took place. What is significant is that the state's deadliest mankiller, John Wesley Hardin, years after the supposed confrontation, recalled McNelly and showed respect for the man. Further evidence of Hardin's respect for McNelly is shown in his statement, "The State Police had been organized and McAnally [sic] had been placed on the force, so on consultation with friends, it was thought best that I should leave Brenham."[48]

Longley's authoritative biographer, Rick Miller, doubts the veracity of Hardin's version of the confrontation between Hardin and Longley and suggests it did not occur at all.[49] But even if Hardin's version of events was only in his imagination, the fact remains that Hardin was impressed enough with Ben Hinds the fugitive and McNelly the lawman to recall their names more than two decades later and to indicate respect for the police captain, certainly the only policeman Hardin did respect!

Although McNelly may have had the respect of the citizens, many members of the force were detested. The Austin *Daily Republican* satirically reported that two policemen "of the loyal nigger persuasion, arrested a discharged U.S. soldier for slapping the face of an impertinent, impudent fifteenth amendment." The pair,

armed with cocked six-shooters, conducted the prisoner to jail "all the
time using very chaste and decorous
Radical language to him, such as
'strike me, you G— d d— n white son of
a b— ch!' accompanied by punching
their pistols in the face of their prisoner." Another of the "sable tools of
despotism" informed an Austinite
that he "would show the d - d white
rebels that they must obey him now"
and that they intended "to make the
d— d white rebels taste h— ll yet before
they were done with this thing."[50]

William Preston Longley, the
noted desperado who accused
John Wesley Hardin of being a
"spy" for McNelly. *Courtesy Ed
Bartholomew.*

Within the oft-criticized State
Police, no one received more criticism
than Captain Jack Helm. Among the
acts of Helm which ultimately forced
his dismissal was the killing of the
Kelly brothers, relatives of the Taylors
who were considered the leaders of
the lawless element which McNelly would later attempt to control in
DeWitt County. The four Kelly brothers — William, Henry, Wiley
and Eugene — were charged with shooting up a circus at Sweet
Home, a small community in Lavaca County, although elsewhere it
was reported that the incident was actually the occurrence of "a row"
at a camp meeting on the Cibolo which Helm attempted to suppress.[51] William and Henry had been arrested on August 25 by a
Helm posse composed of William E. Sutton, A.C. "Doc" White,
John Meador and C.C. Simmons. Reportedly the brothers
attempted to escape the posse and were killed although the several
witnesses testified that they had made no effort to escape and were
simply murdered. The other two brothers were later arrested, stood
trial and were acquitted.[52]

Ironically, the arrest of William Sutton, who would later lead the
opposition against the Taylors in what became known as The Sutton-
Taylor Feud and who had received negative publicity for his actions
involving the Kelly brothers, was reported in the pro-Davis *Daily
State Journal!* The editor reported the arrest on a murder charge of
William Sutton and Buck McCrabb in Victoria County and praised
the force. "There are but a few men in the State Police, and they
have not been at work more than three weeks, in which time

John Wesley Hardin, from the original tintype made in Abilene, Kansas in 1871. Three years later he was a fugitive from McNelly and his men in DeWitt County, Texas. *Courtesy The Robert G. McCubbin Collection.*

upwards of *fifty malefactors,* who have hitherto evaded the civil authorities, and in many instances defied them, have been arrested and turned over to the authorities. This speaks well for the State Police."[53]

Such publications as Austin's *Daily Republican* attempted to reinforce the notion that Adjutant General Davidson, as Chief of Police, was responsible for the acts of his subordinates. The citizens of Sweet Home were taxed to pay the expenses of Jack Helm while in that county.[54] Considerable printer's ink was spilled in condemning the police practice of killing prisoners under *la ley de fuga* (law of flight).[55] The *State Journal* attempted to provide praise of Davidson by reporting that on his extended tour of the state he had "dismissed over 30 of his force for inefficiency."[56] By November Helm was permanently relieved from police duty, primarily because of the notorious "Kelly affair." The *Daily News* reported his dismissal and spoke satirically of Davidson's action in removing Helm from the force "because he is a bad man. Who, then, deserves the credit for appointing him on that service? His appointment was doubtless made knowing what he was; his removal is merely a 'blind' of some sort."[57] Helm, one time police captain and sheriff of DeWitt County, had less than three years to live and would be killed by James Creed Taylor and John Wesley Hardin in 1873. Helm was replaced by a relative unknown, Robert F. Haskins.[58]

In spite of McNelly's numerous accomplishments within a short period of time, Davidson must have soon realized his captain had a streak of independence. In September McNelly was reminded that he had not yet issued any instructions to James Green, whom the governor had appointed as a police lieutenant; McNelly was expected to recognize him as such and place him on such duty as was consistent with his rank.[59] On September 17 McNelly was reprimanded; he could not receive his salary until an account in duplicate was signed and returned to Davidson's office.[60] On the next day Davidson reminded him of yet another disregarded form — the blanks furnished for the purpose of reporting names of all persons arrested had not yet been received — and questioned whether McNelly was working in other than his assigned district. As Davidson reminded him, his duties were confined to his own district. "Of course, you are supposed to travel through it but no expenses are allowed other than what is allowed in General Order No. 1."[61]

Davidson must have been becoming perturbed. His letter of September 19 referred to McNelly's "communications of the 15th inst. I wish to inform you that my telegraphic instructions did not forbid you from travelling [sic] in your District." If an arrest was to be made outside the 3rd district then "the proper way" was to inform the police officer in charge of the district where the criminal was. "If by such information it is thought the offender can not be caught, you will be ordered outside of your District for this special purpose."[62]

The next day, September 20, Davidson issued orders to select one sergeant and nine men of the force and send them to Anderson County where they were to report to District Clerk W.C. Howard. Their duties were to protect the freedmen's rights and arrest lawbreakers. Their operations were to include Anderson, Leon, Limestone and Freestone counties because complaints had come from those several counties. The sergeant was to report to Davidson's office "all matters of interest, arrests, &c &c and will take cognizance of all complaints against civil officers reporting the facts to me."[63]

On September 22 McNelly was ordered to Hurley's Mills to arrest two deserters from the United States Army, O'Neal and Webb. McNelly made the arrest, apparently without incident, and transported the pair back to Austin where they were turned over to military authorities, Department of Texas.[64]

McNelly was next ordered to direct the officer in charge of an Anderson County detachment to proceed to Kidd's Mills, a small community in Leon County some ten or twelve miles from

Centerville, and call upon a Mrs. Kiels, probably the widow of A.D. Kiels, a farmer. Her husband had reportedly been murdered on July 28 by a gang of eight or ten desperadoes.[65]

Changes were constantly being made in McNelly's rosters within the first few months of service. On September 28, Private J.W. Wade was dismissed, no reason given. Then Cyrus Shanks and Claiborne Johnson's resignations were submitted to McNelly. The captain was again derelict and was told that he had "neglected to transmit [the resignations] to this office." In spite of the apparent neglect of his paperwork, on September 29 McNelly received payment of $204.16 for his services through August 31. He also had the five-hundred dollar reward for the capture of John Pearce. On September 30 Davidson wrote to him that policeman John C. Ryan had been dismissed from the force for robbery.[66]

In mid-October McNelly had the unpleasant duty of arresting a fellow lawman! There are few details, but according to the Calvert *Tribune* Abner Womack, sheriff of Montgomery County, "was arrested last week" by McNelly and charged with the murder of Miss Lucy Russell and William Fowler. Womack was lodged in the jail at Anderson in Grimes County and afterwards admitted to bail. A Lieutenant Gilbreath was also indicted by the Grimes County grand jury for complicity with Womack in the double murder. Womack had been appointed sheriff on October 10, 1869, by General J.J. Reynolds' Special Order #233 but served only until November 1869 when the order was revoked by Special Order #246. He later was elected on December 3, 1869, and served until August 12, 1871, when he resigned.[67] State Police arrest reports record only that Womack was arrested by McNelly on a charge of murder in Montgomery County, and records of the final outcome of the murder charge or the final fate of Sheriff Womack have not been found.[68]

In correspondence with McNelly of October 27 Davidson told of complaints made by J.S. Thornton against H.S. Clark for "being principal in the organization of Ku Klux Klan." Captain Jack Helm was ordered at the time to investigate but failed to do so, and McNelly was ordered to meet with several citizens of Lavaca County, H.M. Shoemaker and state representative H.M. Youngkin among them, who had made affidavits about the Klan activities. McNelly, ordered to confer and "see what can be done in the premises," was given the names of various policemen in surrounding counties and was also reminded that local citizens would lend their assistance if needed.[69]

On November 5 McNelly received three more reprimands in the same communication! First, he had altered stations of policemen without authority to do so "except for a short time." Secondly, he was ordered to countermand his own order to take away the pistols from persons "except as provided by law." Carrying a deadly weapon was disallowed in assemblies such as balls, public meetings, elections, and so on. Thirdly, within the last month and half, "a number of communications" from Davidson addressed to McNelly had not been answered. Davidson ordered, "You will attend to this." It was as if Davidson was consciously playing the role of understanding parent, gently chastising an irresponsible son.[70]

Later that month, on November 9, a disturbance in Burleson County four miles from Caldwell took place between freedmen and whites. A Caldwell correspondent reported that some freedmen had gathered at the premises of Thomas Hudson for the purpose of forming a State Guard. Whisky was distributed among them gratuitously by certain parties opposed to the division of Burleson County, "evidently to court favor with the freedmen, and thus influence their votes in favoring anti-division." After drinking freely the freedmen started towards the residence of farmer John Gee, one who had been displaced as county registrar by a friend of Hudson's. Shots were fired into Gee's house and his nephew Newton was struck over the head with a six-shooter by mulatto Simpson King who farmed nearby when not working as a State Policeman. King was arrested on November 10 and appeared before Justice McAddison, pleading guilty to the charge of assault and battery with intent to kill. He was able to give bond of $250 to appear at the next term of District Court in December. Davidson went through Caldwell on November 20 and placed several other parties under arrest, leaving "a force of the State Police, under Capt. McNelly, to preserve order."[71] On November 11 McNelly had been ordered to go to Bryan in Brazos County to organize the police there in that city and then await Davidson's arrival![72]

On December 5 Davidson again had occasion to write to McNelly, this time pointing out that he had honored the draft of seventy-five dollars in favor of C.R. Bries, but he cautioned McNelly that "in the future you will not draw upon me without advising me of the fact and having my permission to do so." Two days later there was yet another reprimand; McNelly, as captain, was required to provide monthly reports of operations according to the policies set forth in the circular issued October 15, but yet Davidson had not received them. "It is highly important these reports be sent at the proper time as it is by them that I can judge of the efficiency individually & collectively." Further, Davidson warned, "Your neglect to comply with my Circular is detrimental to the good of the Police force and you will immediately transfer the required reports."[73]

Another reprimand followed on December 12 in which Davidson complained of not having received McNelly's written report concerning his investigation of the murder of Mr. Kiels at Kidd's Mills in Leon County. McNelly could not have received this letter before Davidson was writing about reports of lawlessness and riot in Columbus. McNelly was ordered to report what action he had taken on Davidson's telegraphic instructions of November 24 to send policemen to Columbus.[74] Perhaps Davidson himself could not keep up with his captain; the Houston *Telegraph* reported on the same date that Captain McNelly and General A.J. Burnes of the International Railway had checked into a local hotel.[75]

It is possible that Davidson was so accustomed to regular military actions that he was unable to adjust to McNelly's seemingly relaxed method of reporting his own activities to a superior. James Davidson's reputation of being a strict enforcer of discipline had preceded his arrival in Texas and influenced Governor Davis' nomination of Davidson to the position of adjutant general with the rank of colonel on June 24, 1870. His nomination was confirmed by the Texas Senate on July 6, and he quickly resigned his United States Army rank to organize the State Police. By March 15, 1871, he was promoted to major general of the State Militia. His early priorities included the suppression of outlawry and the Ku Klux Klan. He felt comfortable out of his Austin office, personally leading military operations following the declaration of martial law in several counties in 1870 and 1871. During the first month of the State Police's existence the force made 3,475 arrests.

On December 13 Davidson ordered McNelly to detail a "discreet policeman" to Palestine to arrest R.D. Hightower, a "murderer from Walker County."[76] By coincidence another brutal murder had just taken place in Walker County, one which would have far reaching consequences for McNelly. The body of old freedman Sam Jenkins had recently been found just outside Huntsville, in Walker County, where he had given testimony before the grand jury against several white men who had whipped and beaten him. He never arrived home after his moment in court.[77]

CHAPTER 6

GUNFIRE IN WALKER COUNTY

> We have always admired Capt. McNally. From a stock
> boy he became a soldier, and from a soldier in the ranks
> he worked himself up by merits to a captaincy, and
> when the late war closed, no officer in his position bore
> a prouder name[.] [W]hen we heard that he accepted a
> Captaincy in the State Police, we rejoiced because we
> believed that he loved law, the Constitution, and his
> people, and would not trample them under his feet. We
> have therefore watched his career with interest, and
> have not been disappointed in the man. But when he
> was appointed, we expressed the fear that he would not
> be subse[r]vient enough to please Davis, and we now
> expect soon to see his official head roll into the capa-
> cious basket of the Iron Hand of Texas.— J.C. Chew &
> Theo. Bering, Editors, *The Daily Telegraph*, Houston, 11
> March 1871.

As Captain of Police McNelly occasionally had to discipline
policemen under his command. One notable example was that of
policeman J.H. Patrick. Patrick, whose commission dated from
August 30, 1870, was sending reports from Madisonville, Madison
County, which were "fearful to read." One report claimed that eight
people had been killed and thirty-five wounded in a "little skirmish
between the citizens and his company of State Guards." After this
"terrible row in Madison" Patrick reported the county in a state of
insurrection. McNelly was sent to investigate, accompanied by members of the militia and police. Although he did not find any real
signs of insurrection he did find Patrick totally unfit for service.
McNelly found that only one person, a freedman named John
Copeland, had been killed,[1] and instead of insurrection McNelly
"could not hear even of a dog fight. Madisonville was as quiet as a
Quaker meeting-house." There was an election in progress but there
was no liquor to be found "on any terms or conditions." McNelly
was so dissatisfied with Patrick's conduct that he dismissed him on
the spot.[2]

McNelly expended a great amount of time traveling throughout his district. On Saturday night December 17 he arrived at Kosse in Limestone County to "close up all gambling houses and to arrest those found in the act of gambling." What exactly McNelly did has not been recorded, but it was effective; Ferdinand Flake reprinted the Kosse *Enterprise*'s jocular report that "the Captain found the Kosse 'Tiger' too wary to be caught in his toils, as he had [an] intimation of his intended visit. All the gamesters were gone a-hunting." The police did manage to arrest four men playing euchre in a saloon "across the way."[3] The Galveston *News* of December 15 reported that thirty-eight arrests had been made by the police in Kosse. The *News* shared with the rest of the state the comment of the Kosse *Enterprise* that "the police are rather arbitrary in their proceedings."[4]

McNelly, in company with Grimes County Sheriff Jephthah M. Gibbs, went from Kosse to Galveston where a *News* reporter found him. He, or perhaps McNelly himself, suggested that the "problems" in Madison County were apocryphal and made up to hide the outrages committed by the State Police. Reported the *News*, "Recollect this was not the report of a rebel, nor of a Democrat, but of his superior officer, a gentleman who bears the reputation of being fearless, zealous and incorruptible." Unfortunately the *News* edited much of their interview, explaining "[we] will not give the whole statement of the social conditions of Texas."[5] What a loss!

Newspaper editors always welcomed the opportunity to visit with McNelly, and Alfred Horatio Belo of the influential Galveston *Daily News* was no exception. Belo, five years older than McNelly and from North Carolina, had served in every major engagement of Robert E. Lee's Army of Northern Virginia and had fought a duel defending the honor of his regiment, which resulted in his being chosen as lieutenant colonel and then later colonel. Even though severely wounded at Gettysburg in 1863 he remained in the service and was again wounded at Cold Harbor, Virginia, in 1864. In 1865 he rode horseback to Texas and joined the staff of the *News* just before it relocated to Galveston from Houston. Belo and McNelly must have had similar feelings about their sacrifice in the war. Belo visited with McNelly the evening of December 14 and commented positively on his work. "We were glad to renew acquaintance with Captain McNelly of the State Police on yesterday. He has labored with zeal and energy to make the Police of this District efficient and to so direct and control them that they might prove the protectors of the public peace and good order of society."[6]

McNelly's order from Headquarters, 3rd District, State Police dated at Burton on December 13, read:

> All peace officers will make it their special duty to
> arrest any parties found playing cards in a public place,
> or gambling in any manner, time or place, except upon
> race horses.
> Officers failing to comply with the above order, will
> be immediately dismissed from their office, and other-
> wise punished in accordance with the law.[7]

The McNelly descent on Houston gambling houses began on
Monday, December 12. Fines imposed amounted to $130. But
McNelly experienced resistance from some quarters — the Galveston
police! Apparently it was easier to deal with desperadoes than with
some of his fellow lawmen, because McNelly found it necessary to
telegraph Davidson for advice. He reported to the adjutant general
on December 16 that Galveston Police Chief Thomas Smith was
refusing to cooperate with him in closing up gambling establishments. Davidson responded the next day, inquiring if McNelly had
indeed ordered the Galveston gambling houses to be closed as he
had read in the *News*. If so, Davidson pointed out, he had no right
to do so as he did not have the right to dictate to local police officers. Davidson explained that his order that "gambling establishments were to be suppressed" did not imply that McNelly himself
could give orders to any peace officer as to what to do. He felt
obliged to remind his captain that he had "no right by law to dictate
to Peace officers and that it is not in your province to issue any order
without first obtaining authority to do so from this office." Certainly
Davidson was reluctant to allow McNelly much latitude in his interpretation of orders. Davidson explained — at least in *his* mind it was
an explanation — that the order to suppress gambling establishments
did not give McNelly a free rein in the manner of closing them.
Local police officers were responsible for how the suppression was to
be accomplished. In spite of the reprimand, McNelly was to make a
full report of his activities with Chief of Police Smith. The locals may
have found some enjoyment in this conflict between the authorities,
but even so McNelly had created "quite a stir in certain circles" and
many local gamblers became more circumspect in their activities.
One of McNelly's raids upon the "Knights of the Green Cloth" at
Houston had resulted in fifteen more arrests.[8]

The editor of the Houston *Daily Telegraph* of Wednesday
December 17 reported that McNelly had left the city, probably off to

arrest more gamblers "as the Captain no doubt had other game in view besides what he bagged in Houston. He most probably had other fish to fry, and whether he has fried, or shall fry them, remains to be seen."[9]

By December 26 Davidson had received McNelly's report concerning his anti-gambling operation, and he did approve McNelly's action with the exception of the order concerning peace officers. In the future he was to sign "By order of Chief of Police" on orders issued by him. Davidson also wanted to know the names of the gamblers arrested.[10]

The State Police *Report of Arrests* shows that in December in Harris County McNelly, with the assistance of policemen James C. Keesee and J.H. Catlin, arrested a total of twenty-six for gambling, reported only as "two men" and "eight men" and "sixteen FMC" suggesting they were the results of raids on gambling houses rather than individual arrests. Also the report shows that one Moses Lewis, a former State Policeman whose appointment had been revoked on August 29, was arrested by the three for disturbing the peace and riot. W.F. Welch was arrested on the same charge, and Joe Clark, George Derrick and a man named Chilton were arrested for carrying deadly weapons and riot.[11]

By December 21 had McNelly received yet another reprimand; his account of $234.00 was disallowed "in its present shape." Accounts for mileage were to be made separately.[12] Obviously, handling paper work was not McNelly's strong suit!

A more serious matter occurred one-hundred miles north of the bothersome conflicts with Galveston police. Sam Jenkins had been found dead on December 5 with two bullet holes in him and his murderers were still at large. He had "been the cause of a good deal of trouble wherever he has lived, but we can't understand why anyone should have taken his life, thereby bringing our entire community into risk of trouble" commented the Houston *Daily Telegraph*. Even though there were indictments against Jenkins, "surely there is no occasion for individuals to constitute themselves – or himself – judge, jury and executioner." The *Telegraph* advocated that whoever the murderer was, black or white, he should be "ferreted out and properly punished."[13] Governor Davis issued a reward of $500 for the arrest and delivery of Jenkins' murderers to the Walker County sheriff, the notice stating incorrectly that the murder had taken place on or about December 9. The reward was offered to any individual providing information to the adjutant general which would lead to the arrest of same.[14]

Many perhaps felt the death of a troublesome old freedman — he was seventy years old — was of no importance, but McNelly had his orders to determine who was guilty and bring the culprit or culprits to justice. Some considered Jenkins a harmless old man whose murder was a senseless act of cruelty. Others considered him a tool of the Carpetbag rule who had made himself obnoxious to white people in general. The trouble may have begun that fall when Jenkins, working for a young farmer named Fred Parks, disagreed with Parks about dividing the crops. Parks ordered Jenkins off his place, which naturally prevented Jenkins from obtaining any settlement. Not long after this two friends of Parks, Nat Outlaw and Joe Wright, obviously aware of the dispute, met Jenkins on the road not far from town and gave him the choice of being whipped or shot. Jenkins submitted to a whipping with sticks. On December 5 the Walker County Grand Jury was impaneled. In spite of having been warned about testifying against the quartet, Jenkins testified against Outlaw, Wright, Parks and Jonathan Parrish. That afternoon, upon leaving the grand jury room, he was followed by four men; later three of them were identified as Outlaw, Parrish and Wright. On his way home that evening he was shot.[15] Although some considered the old man harmless, ex-Terry Texas Ranger H.W. Graber recalled that he was one of a "few insolent negroes who had insulted some young ladies on the street returning home from a shopping trip."[16]

Whether there were other acts of cruelty besides Jenkins' murder is unclear, but Adjutant General Davidson felt the case had to be investigated and called for McNelly. The captain, perhaps relieved to be free from dealing with Chief Thomas Smith and the gambling element, was at his home in Burton for Christmas when orders came to report to the Walker County sheriff or District Judge at Huntsville. Specifically McNelly was to work at "ferreting out the perpetrators of the recent murders."[17]

McNelly and his force of police investigated and determined that four young men were responsible for Jenkins' murder: Nathanial A. Outlaw, Joseph Wright, Fred Parks and Jonathan Parrish. The quartet was arrested and their examining trial was set for January 11, 1871, before Judge James R. Burnett, Judge of the Thirtieth Judicial District. From testimony the judge determined that Parks had nothing to do with the murder, but he refused bail for the other three, believing the proof was evident of their guilt.[18]

McNelly had three other policemen in the court room with him: Tom Keesee, William Martin and L.E. Dunn, while two others — Hugh Pennington and Val Lemmons — were stationed at the base of the stairs leading up to the second story where court was held. Even though County Sheriff Cyrus Hess was nominally in charge, subsequent actions indicate McNelly was in command in spite of the county sheriff's presence.

Judge Burnett rendered his decision and handed to McNelly the warrant of commitment, ordering the prisoners to be confined. He then left the court room "not at that time anticipating any trouble." But there *was* trouble; each of the three prisoners had a brace of concealed six-shooters. Gunfire exploded in the court room within moments after the judge had left.[19]

Before removing the prisoners from the court room to deliver them to confinement, McNelly had ordered them to be searched. He faced Nat Outlaw and said, "are you armed" more in the manner of a routine statement than a question. McNelly did not expect the prisoners to be armed but initiated the search as a precaution. Outlaw, whose degree of honesty must have been sorely tested, responded, "I am, sir" and showed a pistol. McNelly took the weapon and handed it to Defense Attorney James A. Baker. He then saw the outline of a second pistol, on Outlaw's chest, which he also confiscated.

While Outlaw was being disarmed Sheriff Cyrus Hess should have been making sure Wright and Parrish did not also have weapons; instead, the two prisoners immediately drew their pistols from concealment and began firing. Wright's first shot missed McNelly but the second shot hit him in the thigh and he went down, falling backwards. Even though wounded, McNelly managed to draw his own weapon and fired at Wright, hitting him in the arm. Parrish's shot wounded Thomas Keesee in the face and neck. Wright and Parrish escaped although both were wounded, Parrish in the right hand and Wright in the arm and perhaps in the body as well. Outlaw, his pistols having been taken away, fell upon the floor "and stayed there until after the shooting was over" as McNelly later stated.[20] Strangely, Tom Keesee testified that Hess *had* asked Wright if he had arms and told him he must give them up before Wright fired on McNelly while Parrish fired at Keesee. Keesee said about thirty shots were fired that day in the court room. "After the firing Hess was still in the court-room. He said he was pretty badly scared."[21]

With four policemen and two prisoners' firing at each other in a crowded court room it is a wonder that no one was killed. The two policemen at the base of the stairs were prevented from interfering by friends of the prisoners who threatened death to the policemen if they did interfere. Outlaw, although not wounded, was prevented from escaping.

On the street Wright and Parrish found sympathetic citizens who were willing to aid in their escape. William G. "Willie" Parrish, younger brother of the escaped prisoner, held his brother's horse and assisted him in mounting. Thomas Walker provided a horse and shotgun for Wright while someone else handed him a hat. People in the street were hollering "Go! Go!" George W. Rather, in spite of being intoxicated at the time, also assisted the prisoners in mounting. Then Wright and Parrish, mounted and well-armed, galloped out of town, firing their pistols and "yelling like savages," followed by their friends. With himself and policeman Keesee wounded, McNelly was unable to pursue the escaped prisoners. He and Sheriff Hess did manage to deliver Nat Outlaw to the penitentiary, the jail having been determined to be insecure. In spite of Hess' disappointing lack of action in the court room, McNelly took Hess along with him, thinking he might be attacked on the way by Outlaw's friends and one more gun might be needed. It was only then that McNelly sought medical attention for his and Policeman Keesee's wounds.[22]

Others had been placed in danger by this reckless escape from custody. Michael Butler, acting as a deputy, had his arm broken in the melee. In spite of his injury he was able to replace Hess as acting sheriff, serving until April 1871. District Attorney William E. Horne and Judge Burnett both believed they had also been targets for the desperate prisoners. With no weapons on their person, Horne and Burnett were unable to return the fire. Horne later wrote that he no longer believed he had been in real danger, "I have had evidence to satisfy me that a great majority and in fact the citizens generally of the county had no sympathy with the attack upon the officers of the court. . . . The excitement of the moment over I can view more calmly what really occurred."[23] Horne admitted the prisoners did shoot down the officers of the court and escape "aided and abetted by a party of desperate friends" but he now believed the populace was law-abiding. As for being shot at personally, Horne admitted that "several shots came near and while in the street but am now disposed to doubt whether they were aimed at me personally."[24]

An immediate attempt to capture the escaped prisoners was not practical. McNelly and Keesee were both wounded, and the next night was cold and sleety making pursuit difficult. Hess went through the motions of attempting to raise a posse but failed completely, later admitting to McNelly that he could obtain only two men to obey his summons. It was understood that most refused to obey because they had no respect for the sheriff,[25] who had carried a pistol in the court room that he hadn't used. Responding to a later question as to whether he drew his weapon, he said "I don't know. I was so badly frightened, I did not know what to do. I am of a nervous temperament, and was very much alarmed." No doubt everyone was "alarmed," because estimates as to the number of shots fired in less than a minute in the court room ranged from twenty to forty. Tom Keesee said thirty.[26]

During the subsequent court martial various citizens were found guilty of offenses such as aiding and abetting the prisoners to escape and refusing to respond to Hess' call for a posse. Nathaniel A. Outlaw was later found guilty of the murder of Sam Jenkins and sentenced to five years confinement in the state penitentiary. General Davidson, who had to approve the verdict as the reviewing officer of the court martial, expressed "his unqualified disapprobation of the action of the General Court Martial" and reprimanded "the uncalled for leniency of the Court, extended towards a murderer, whose hands, as proven, were red with the blood of a fellow-being." Davidson felt that when the "juries of the Country fail to punish assassins, Courts Martial must fill the full measure of their duty."[27]

Willie Parrish, brother of prisoner John Parrish, was charged with aiding Joseph Wright to escape by holding his horse and assisting him to mount. Thomas Walker was charged as well with aiding and abetting Wright to escape by handing him a shotgun. He was found guilty of the charge and fined $500, but Parrish was found not guilty.[28] George W. Rather was charged and found guilty of aiding and abetting the escape of Joseph Wright. His young son, Charles Taylor Rather, was present on the city square that day and recorded that one of the prisoners "was having difficulty in untying his horse and called on someone to cut him loose. My father chanced to be close by and performed the act. He drew a hundred-dollar fine for assisting a prisoner escape, which was sometime afterwards remitted." Besides the fine he was sentenced to thirty days in the county jail.[29] Sheriff Cyrus Hess was found not guilty of conspiracy to kill the officers of the court but was found guilty of negligence in the performance of his duties; specifically he was held responsible for the prisoners' being allowed to acquire weapons while in his custody. For his negligence he was fined $250.[30]

Although found guilty, several citizens were able to avoid paying their fines thanks to the assistance of citizens who successfully petitioned Governor Davis. George W. Rather was held not responsible because his action was determined to be "unpremeditated and committed in a moment of excitement, he being intoxicated at the time."[31] The fine would bear heavily upon his family and it was ordered to be refunded. Thomas Walker was the only support of his widowed mother and her three younger children, and his $500 fine was remitted because it "would break up the family."[32]

According to Charles Taylor Rather, after Governor E.J. Davis was out of office and replaced by Richard Coke, the prisoners, Wright and Parrish as well as ex-sheriff W.H. Stewart, returned to Huntsville and stood trial for their actions. They were all acquitted.[33]

The work of McNelly in ferreting out the murderers of Jenkins and his courageous action in the court room in preventing all the prisoners from escaping brought him considerable publicity in the area's press. A reporter of the influential *Daily News*, the journal which claimed the largest circulation in the state, found and interviewed McNelly in his room at Galveston's Washington Hotel. McNelly was by then fully recovered from his wound and gave the reporter a lengthy interview. It began with asking McNelly why no report of his actions had been published. Rather than even hinting at his verifiable deficiency in completing paper work, McNelly answered, "I made two, the first by telegraph from Navasota, the second by mail, some eight or ten days after the occurrence. I do not know why they were not published." He was then asked if he had recommended Governor Davis' declaration of martial law, to which he responded, "No, sir. There was no reason for it." McNelly felt strongly there was no need for the declaration of martial law. "The evidence is that Gen. Davidson, with eight or ten men, and he has not more, is collecting that tax. If the people of Walker county were lawless, they would show it now. . .", in other words, with force of arms.

And why, asked the reporter, was martial law declared? McNelly answered he did not know. "Was it for money?" McNelly's straightforward answer was simply, "Possibly." And what about the rumors that the Ku Klux Klan was active?

> There is no such thing in my district. In the year 1867 some of the most respectable Texans were alarmed lest the Negroes would rise rob and murder them. They formed a society for protection. It died out in a few months. There is no secret political society in Texas but the Loyal League. There may be young men in neigh-

borhoods who have signs and calls by which they communicate with each other, just as thieves, gamblers and
prostitutes do, but there is nothing more than this.

He then gave in detail the facts of "this much magnified occurrence," recorded by the reporter in the third person.

> The three young men, Wright, Par[r]ish and
> Outlaw, were accused of the murder of Sam Jenkins.
> McNelly was ordered to arrest them. He did so. He
> turned them over to Sheriff Hess.
> He was ordered by telegraph to put them in the
> penitentiary for safe keeping; but he had already turned
> them over to the Sheriff to be confined in the county
> jail. Still, the fact of the telegram was known on the
> street, it having "leaked out" of the telegram office.
> Capt. McNally [sic] had reason to expect that if they
> were held to answer, that his progress with the prison-
> ers on their return to jail would be interrupted by their
> friends; but he believed, and still believes, that his
> expostulations would have been heeded, and his deter-
> mination respected — that he could have carried his
> prisoners to jail without firing a shot. He had six police-
> men. Three good men on whom he could depend, one
> a good man connected by friendship with the prisoner,
> and two good for nothing. The trial ended, the mitti-
> mum was filled out, read by the Judge, and handed to
> McNally, who stepped up to the prisoners, and said to
> Outlaw, "are you armed." This was not said because he
> thought they had arms, knowing it was the Sheriff's
> duty to have disarmed them when first arrested.
> Outlaw replied, "I am, sir," and showed a pistol, which
> McNally at once took from him and handed to Judge
> Baker, that was taken also. Wright then fired at
> McNally, the first shot missing, the second shot striking
> in the thigh. McNally returned the fire, wounding his
> assailant in the arm. The other officers drew their pis-
> tols, and about thirty shots were fired, filling the room
> with smoke. Wright and Par[r]ish escaped to their
> horses, though both were wounded. Outlaw remained,
> and was taken to jail. McNally, having found that the
> jail was insecure, took the prisoner to the penitentiary,

and sought surgical aid for his wound, after giving orders for a pursuit in which he was too weak to participate.

The succeeding night was cold and sleety, a vigorous pursuit was impossible. The Sheriff, Mr. Hess, was ordered to summon a posse, but after some twenty-four hours reported that the citizens would not obey his summons. He was ordered to make a list of their names, and Capt. McNally asserts that he could have had them punished for disobeying the command by the civil courts without the necessity of a court martial intervening. The suppressed report expressed the opinion that citizens refused to serve because they were unwilling to act under the command of "an old woman like the Sheriff," and that he, Capt. McNally, would not be willing to engage in a dangerous expedition under such a leader. As soon as his wound permitted, the Captain went to Navasota and reported in writing, as he had previously done by telegraph, that there was no disturbance, that he believed the wounded fugitives were still in the vicinity, and that if permitted to take some twenty-five men from the State militia, that he would capture them. He was ordered to take the necessary force — did take sixteen men — and would have captured Wright and Parrish had they been in the State.

The *News* reporter then asked on whom the blame of the disturbance rested. McNelly answered that the blame lay on the sheriff because it was his business to have disarmed the prisoners when they came into his custody. McNelly claimed that, had Hess actually disarmed the prisoners, he could have taken them to jail without firing a shot. "I would have been stopped outside, but I could have overcome the friends of the young men by fair expostulation and reason." Concerning Hess' failure to raise a posse, McNelly, perhaps in a mild boast, said, "After their escape, I could, had it not been for my wound, have got a hundred citizens to volunteer for the pursuit."

The final question was whether there was a determination on the part of the Austin authorities to force the people of Texas into resisting authority. The captain prudently declined to answer, and the interview closed.[34]

A.H. Belo, who probably was the unidentified reporter, regarded McNelly's explanation "as one of our most important elucidations of affairs in the State that has been given to the public." The Huntsville affair had been the "theme of comment" not only in Texas but "by the press of the entire United States."

> Reverend Senators have dwelt upon it. It has received Presidential consideration. It has been used as an argument for additional burthens upon the whole South. And yet here we find the trusted officer of the State Police, the next in rank, for he commands the most important district, to Gen. Davidson himself. The cool, calm tried officer who was in command the day when the outrage occurred, who was wounded and who has, if any man has, cause to speak harshly of the people of Walker, saying that there was no cause for martial law — no reason in the world for it. That commanding as he does the obnoxious State Police, he can procure the aid of the best citizens (old rebels, at that), in repressing lawlessness.

The *News* demanded the publication of McNelly's report, and "if there is a particle of justice in Gov. Davis he will give them to the public."[35]

McNelly's remarks appeared in the *News* of Wednesday, March 8, 1871. When the candid remarks of McNelly appeared in the highest circulating publication in Texas, other members of the newspaper community feared he would be punished. Houston's *Daily Telegraph* commented, "The best evidence of the total depravity of the declaration of martial law in Walker county, is what Capt. McNally [sic] says as to the very small force used by Davidson to *grind out* the military tax, and being collected in that county by *force*. Davidson has gone, and yet the grinding goes on by his underlings." It was a "disgusting picture" which McNelly gave.[36]

McNelly's superiors instructed him to recant his statements that martial law had been declared in an effort to "grind out" money from the citizens of Walker County. His "apology," actually in no sense of the word a real apology, included the line, "[Davis and Davidson] have ever cautioned me to be prudent and courteous in the discharge of my duties as policeman, and have promptly dismissed all officers that I have reported for doing otherwise."[37]

McNelly's remarks regarding the declaration of martial law may have resulted in some embarrassment in the governor's office, and rumors that McNelly would be appointed assistant adjutant general did gain some plausibility. The *News* stated that the rumor was that the post was to be created, that McNelly was to fill the post, and "generally he is to have power, place and emoul[e]ment." The *News* commented further on the character of the captain, "Of course we know nothing of the facts, but we do not believe that Captain McNelly can be bought. He is a brave man, and brave men are seldom mercinary. We esteem him to be a truthful and honest gentleman, and we shall not believe any reports to the contrary."[38] Possibly Davidson indeed had suggested to Davis to create such a position in order to obtain tighter control over their independent captain, but the position was never created.

Charles B. McKinney (left) and George W. Farrow during their ranger days after the McNelly era. Farrow earlier had been a Captain in the Texas State Police force but had problems with McNelly. *Courtesy C. Fred Meyer, Houston, Texas.*

CHAPTER 7

AFTER THE WALKER COUNTY AFFAIR

> It appears the king Edmund Davis and his party are
> determined to effect the ruin of Bastrop County. Her
> people are declared "disloyal," "not in favor of law and
> order," and denounced as being altogether a "lawless
> set." — Thomas C. Cain, Editor of the *Bastrop
> Advertiser*, 12 August 1871.

Reports of lawlessness in Walker County, as well as in other parts
of the state, reached the collective ear of the Texas Senate. On
February 7 the Senate passed a resolution calling for information in
possession of the governor respecting acts of lawlessness and crime,
and what action had been taken, if any. Davis quickly responded and
had printed a twenty-seven page pamphlet containing documents
dealing not only with the Huntsville troubles but also the events
leading up to his declaring martial law in Walker County and in Hill
County. After a brief synopsis of the Huntsville shooting Davis
added,

> I am not aware that the history of the United
> States, or in fact of any country where the English lan-
> guage is spoken, presents a parallel to this Walker
> county affair, for overbearing lawlessness. While,
> doubtless, many of the citizens of that county deprecate
> the act, they all stood by supinely, or actively aided the
> attack upon the judge and officers of the law, while
> engaged in the exercise of their legitimate authority and
> sworn duty. It is greatly to be regretted that the people
> of any part of our State, do not see that it is [in] their
> true interest, without regard to the question of duty, to
> put a stop to such lawlessness.[1]

During the days following the court room shootout and escape of the prisoners, Attorney Horne had time to ponder the events which he had witnessed. He and McNelly had left Huntsville together and arrived at Navasota on January 19. The *State Journal* reported, although almost certainly an exaggeration, that a full *fifty* shots had been fired in the court room melee, that friends of the prisoners had formed a plot to assassinate Judge Burnett, McNelly and other court officers, but it had been "frustrated by the coolness and nerve" of the captain.[2] Horne traveled to Austin where on January 26 he had prepared a report giving a summary of the events in which he named the ex-sheriff, William H. Stewart, as an "active aider and abettor" in the attempt to assassinate Judge Burnett! Stewart had been appointed sheriff on March 1,1869, then was elected on December 3 and had served until December 19, 1870, when he was removed from office by the district judge.[3] He was charged with embezzlement of public money, committed October 1, 1870, although he would not be indicted until April 15, 1871. He was still wanted as late as 1878 when a list of fugitives from justice, printed and distributed throughout the state, listed him as being in his late thirties, of light complexion, light hair inclined to curl, heavy set, about five feet ten inches tall and weighing about 170 pounds. He spoke with an Irish accent.[4] Certainly there may have been some animosities within Stewart which explained his actions against the judge.

When Horne left Huntsville he had learned that the prisoners were guarded by about forty well-armed friends who defied arrest and threatened death to Captain McNelly "at all hazards." There were so many sympathizers and others actually helping them to escape that Horne found it easier to give the names of those who did not in any way give aid or comfort; he was able to name only eight individuals, a judge, six attorneys and a county commissioner! Yet Horne was able to conclude his report on the optimistic note that "even now public opinion, slowly forming, points to McParrish [sic], Wright and Outlaw as the murderers and assassins of Sam Jenkins."[5]

On February 15 Governor Davis ordered Adjutant General James Davidson to Walker County with three objectives: he was to cause to be published an order declaring martial law (to be dated as of January 20); he was to assess the amount of expenses incurred, either upon the county or upon the parties implicated in the "recent outrages, as may be deemed most expedient," and he was to convene a General Court Martial for the trial of the offenders. In addition a strong squad of State Police was to be left in Walker County, and if such a squad was not available then a detachment of the State Militia or State Guard was to hunt down and bring to justice all offenders.[6]

Bringing men to justice was easier to order than to accomplish. Henry W. Graber recorded, nearly five decades later, that Judge Burnett suspected the prisoners to be armed, and it was for that reason that he left the court room to hide in his hotel room! After Burnett's exit McNelly ordered the prisoners to hold up their hands but they immediately drew their six-shooters and "commenced shooting at him and his gang of police." Graber incorrectly recalled that McNelly was wounded in the arm and then dropped down between some benches, pretending to be dead. Burnett, upon hearing the gunfire, broke into a run and crawled under the hotel. Graber recalled that the prisoners, Wright and Parrish, headed north to the Indian Territory, "by way of Rusk and Paris, with McAnally [sic] and his police in close pursuit."[7]

While the court martial was taking place in Walker County, McNelly continued his work elsewhere. Apparently Davidson was still concerned about the Cedar Bayou affair; on February 21 he wrote to McNelly mentioning James and Ed Stevenson, two men Davidson suspected were involved in that unlawful "arrest" of McNelly back in 1870. It took until March 15 for McNelly to respond to this letter, but he responded by writing from Burton that he did not think any of those involved in the Cedar Bayou affair were named Stevenson.[8]

On February 27 another reprimand was issued: on January 26 McNelly, utilizing the steamer *T. M. Bagby*, had moved nine men and seven horses from Lynchburg to Houston, leaving the $46 bill for the state to pay. McNelly believed that, since he was working for the state, the state should pay the transportation bill. But Davidson felt otherwise, informing McNelly that the amount would be deducted from the monthly pay of those nine policemen! He indicated that the state was not responsible for transportation and that mileage was paid only for conveying prisoners from one point to another. McNelly was told to report the names of the nine men so that stoppages could be made against their pay and the money reimbursed to the steamer operator.[9] This had not been the first time the State Police had created a problem with transportation officials. In early January a policeman at Navasota had become intoxicated and endeavored to force the conductor to take him and his horse to

Bryan, some thirty miles north of Navasota, in a passenger car. The conductor was "threatened with the vengeance of Gov. Davis and the whole radical party, but still declined to carry the horse" as the Galveston *Daily News* humorously reported the incident.[10] The transportation dilemma was ultimately resolved in the form of a circular issued from Davidson on March 20, "Captains of State Police will not hereafter transport their detachment by rail road or Steamboats except under written authority from this office." [11]

The efforts to suppress gambling, except on horse races, occasionally resulted in humorous situations. Although McNelly was not personally involved in an incident at Crockett in Houston County, his name was brought in as authority! As the San Antonio *Daily Herald* reported the incident, a "posse of the Davis bodyguard, or Police" arrested several of the "most respectable citizens" for indulging in playing the game of nine pins. The reporter wrote that remonstrations were of no avail, that processes of law were laughed to scorn by policemen, that the police held warrants in "profound contempt" and that "the only authority they would deign to acknowledge was that Capt. McNally [sic] had ordered them to arrest all persons found gambling, except on a horse race." The *Herald* accused the police of being "ignorant and brutal."[12]

The results of the Walker County affair brought further condemnation of Davis and the State Police by the *Herald*. An article appeared in the March 1 issue headlined "Reign of Force in Texas" and stated that with the "ravages and executions of Davis and his Police force" Texas and her millions of people were likely "to be smashed in the earth." The grave results of this conduct should cause the most thoughtless to pause and seek shelter from "the absolute despotism" engulfing Texans. The report of the court martial at Huntsville that a tax of fifty cents on each one-hundred dollars of property was intended to illustrate further the "tyranny of Davis" in subjecting the people of Walker County to martial law, to fines and imprisonment.[13] Reports of police misconduct, including drunkenness on duty and other abuses of the rights of Texans, were frequently published in the newspapers, bringing further condemnation in many quarters against Governor Davis and his police force.

Besides the frequent condemnation of the police for which McNelly served, his wound which must have caused him some difficulty at least temporarily, and the matter of such bothersome things as transportation of men and mounts, McNelly now learned that the governor wanted information on the interview published in the Galveston *News* in which his declaration of martial law had been criticized.[14] With McNelly's not having been enthusiastic about being interviewed in the first place, and then having his comments challenged by his superiors, it is no wonder that he preferred to avoid publicity, choosing instead to let the results of his actions speak for themselves.

But McNelly continued to concentrate on the work he perceived to be important — that of enforcing the law as he understood it to be. In early March he was still on the warpath against gamblers. He arrested Moore, Monell and Jones on the Galveston, Houston and Henderson Railroad, the trio having indulged in that "seductive amusement" best known as "three card" or "French monte." Charged with playing cards in a public place, they were found guilty by a jury of six and fined ten dollars each. They paid their fines and then were again arrested on the charge of "exhibiting or dealing" and held to answer in the next term of district court. Commented the Galveston *News*, "We trust that the actions of Capt. McNally [*sic*]. . .will put an end to that practice, not that people foolish enough to be trapped into such a foolish swindle are much to be pitied, but because such doings ought not to be permitted."[15]

Another transportation problem occurred in April. Although McNelly's request has not been preserved, it dealt with the railroad's providing transportation to policemen. Davidson's reply, dating McNelly's request at April 12, disapproved the request, explaining that every policeman was expected to keep himself "properly mounted and ready to proceed at a moment's notice to any point of the State, and authority will not be granted except in special cases . . . for the transportation of men of the force by railroad."[16] One of McNelly's policeman may have disobeyed or ignored an order from McNelly, for in the same communication Davidson pointed out that any policeman failing to comply with an order "will be immediately dropped from the rolls and will not be allowed pay from the date of disobedience." The next day Davidson, having received a document "purporting to be [a] copy of a capias," sent another communication to McNelly describing the copy as being "utterly worthless and illegal." Not satisfied, Davidson continued to castigate the captain. "The manner in which this paper is prepared is careless and not to be repeated from a police officer. The original capias against Harris will be forwarded at once to the Headquarters."[17]

Nat Outlaw's name surfaced again in April when Governor

Davis published a statement that the evidence condemning Outlaw was "altogether circumstantial in its character," but even so he believed Outlaw should have been found guilty of murder and sentenced to receive the extreme penalty of the law. But the testimony had been "disbelieved," and as governor he had remitted the sentence passed upon Outlaw and discharged the prisoner from Huntsville. The order releasing Outlaw was dated March 11, but Galveston *News* editor A.H. Belo did not learn of it until their issue of April 3 and commented on the governor's remarks. "Such a state paper as that would consign the Governor to an asylum for idiots, if presented to any disinterested jury. Such a piece of reasoning is entirely unique."[18]

On April 26 Davidson inquired as to what action McNelly had taken to arrest and bring to trial the parties who had killed the son of Navasota newspaper editor Joseph Lancaster; if he had neglected the matter he was to report there and investigate. McNelly had done some work on the Lancaster case; his letter to Davidson of the same date recommends that Frank Lancaster, the deceased William's older brother, be discharged from the police force, he being "recognized as a thief and gambler."[19]

Two days later McNelly was ordered to Hearne in Robertson County![20] If McNelly did go to Navasota to investigate the killing there, he could hardly have accomplished much prior to being ordered to go to Hearne, forty miles away. There are few details dealing with the troubles at Hearne; the Kosse *Enterprise* reported that on Thursday and Friday nights, April 20 and 21, "the city of Hearne became the theatre of a general shooting and cutting row, in which two persons were killed, and two or three others slightly damaged. As the fuss was confined to the roughs few tears will be shed over the affair." This item from the Kosse newspaper was reprinted in the Galveston *Weekly News* without further comment and with no indication that one of the two "roughs" was a policeman! Later, the *News* reprinted an item from the Houston *Union* which provided additional details and identifying the State Policeman killed as Robert Stern, although both the police force roster as well as the census spelled his name "Steen." The man identified as his slayer was Code Brown, son of Green Brown of the firm of Brown & Wilkerson. If the *Union*'s report was correct, then the "fuss" began as a bar-room brawl when Brown, drinking and firing his pistol, was interrupted by Stern. What Stern said was not disclosed, but Brown responded by shooting Stern and shooting him again on the floor. Brown then fled. McNelly did "investigate" this killing, either directly or else by learning of the details from other policeman, because by May 3 he was able to write a full report to Adjutant General Davidson. He identified the slayer as T.C. Brown, alias Code, and requested permission to go to Hearne to pursue the murderer. Unfortunately McNelly's report of this incident has not survived, but he had learned through communication with Hearne's mayor that policemen Merrick and Giles Trammel were guilty of "cowardly conduct." The names of the Trammell brothers frequently appear in police records, and apparently in this instance their conduct was not suitable in McNelly's view. He made remarks which reached the ears of Adjutant General Davidson who, on May 29, ordered McNelly to explain how he learned of the apparent cowardliness of the Trammells.[21] No reply from McNelly has survived.

On May 1 Davidson found reason to reprimand McNelly yet again, reacting to a letter apparently written by McNelly to Governor Davis himself concerning the appointment of certain men to the police force. Wrote Davidson, "You have been a member of the force sufficiently long enough to be aware that you have been guilty of a serious breach of discipline in addressing the Governor upon a matter referring solely to the Department, and in the future address all such communication to the Chief of Police."[22] Davidson did not appreciate being skipped over in the chain of command.

Back on July 21, 1870, McNelly had been placed in command of the 4th Police District, then on July 25 placed in command of the 3rd Police District to which Washington County was attached. Now on May 5, 1871, he was once again placed in command of the 4th Police District; no explanation was given by Davidson as to why the change was made. The district now included the twenty-two counties of Brown, Comanche, San Saba, Lampasas, Hamilton, Coryell, Hays, Travis, Williamson, Bell, Falls, McLennan, Limestone, Freestone, Leon, Robertson, Milam, Brazos, Burleson, Bastrop, Fayette and Washington. Brazos County would be removed on August 9 from the district. McNelly's headquarters would be in Burton. He was to go to each station in his district and "make a thorough inspection of each man" and was to be held to a strict accountability for the peace and good order of his district, arresting all criminals and so on. What Davidson meant — apparently not clear in McNelly's mind — was that he didn't need to inspect each man personally but to write to them and order them "to properly perform their duties without unnecessary delay."[23] Now that he was again in charge of the 4th district, he was ordered to Houston to be there during the fair "on official duty."[24]

Another reprimand followed on May 29. While at Houston he had made "several arrests" instead of keeping himself to "the special duty" to which he had been ordered. Davidson was fearful that the arrests were "calculated to cause ill feeling" between himself and Captain George W. Farrow, commander of that police district. McNelly's action was "disapproved."[25]

On May 30 Davidson communicated to McNelly that Fisher, who had killed a freedman, was reported to be in Washington County, in the Travis settlement nine miles from Brenham. McNelly was to bring about his arrest.[26]

On June 6 it was Captain Farrow's turn to be the recipient of Davidson's irritation instead of McNelly. Farrow was reprimanded for repeatedly being negligent in not arresting parties accused of gambling within the limits of his command. "Had you properly dis-charged your duty in regard to this matter, it would not have been necessary for Captain McNelly to make the arrest of gamblers when in Houston attending the fair." Davidson was certainly adamant in this matter; he further stated to Farrow that the "negligence or col-lusion (it is difficult to say which) on your part must be stopped at once," and if another failure to arrest a party accused of gambling occurred he would receive a "summary instant dismissal from the police force."[27]

On June 12, less than two months after Davidson's first inquiry concerning the matter, McNelly was again ordered to report what action he had taken to arrest the murderers of young William Lancaster. Davidson expressed great concern over the killing of this son of the noted editor. The matter "should have received your attention long since," fumed Davidson.[28] It is unknown what efforts had been made prior to the State Police's being organized to solve this murder, and it is unknown when Davidson first decided to renew efforts regarding the old crime. Undoubtedly the Lancaster case received special attention because Joseph and Mary Lancaster, the parents of William, were close friends of Governor and Mrs. Davis, and the killing of their youngest son was especially brutal. On the night of September 12, 1868, the eighteen-year-old was returning to his parents' home at Navasota from the west. About dark he arrived at the house of a freedman near Washington, Washington County, where he spent the night. The following day he again was in the saddle and when fatigued stopped at the house of another freedman where young Lancaster's "second mother" lived, a former slave who had helped raise William. Young William Lancaster understandably felt secure in stopping there to spend the night, but a group of armed and disguised white men forcibly entered the house at midnight, pointed six-shooters at Lancaster's head and breast, and took him to a secluded spot where he was tortured and then left hanging from a tree limb.[29]

Joseph Lancaster was convinced that the Ku Klux Klan was to blame for his son's brutal murder. In the columns of his *Navasota Ranger* he thanked friends who had gone to Washington "to seek for the body of an unfortunate son and brethren," and explained that his son had "been foully murdered, at the hour of midnight . . . by a party in disguise."[30] Washington County Justice of the Peace J.W. McCown, Sr. provided to Davidson a list of murders in his precinct since the war, writing that young Lancaster, whom he incorrectly identified as Frank, "was found hung near Washington by unknown parties — crime — Supposed horse stealing."[31] In 1868 — and certainly young Lancaster must have known this — the Klan's unwritten rules forbade a white person from spending the night in a black family's house, regardless of the "relationship." It is also possible, however, that William Lancaster had been suspected of horse stealing, and his choice of where to spend the night provided a vigilante group the opportunity to cover their action in the guise of a racial act.

What effort was made immediately to apprehend the mob is unknown. By the time Governor Davis was in office and the State Police organized, perhaps Lancaster felt justified in pressuring his friend to place extra emphasis on bringing someone to justice. Davis naturally turned the matter over to his adjutant, who assigned the matter to McNelly because the killing had occurred in his district.

In an effort to exert additional pressure, Lancaster wrote a letter to fellow newspaper editor Horace Greeley who published it in his New York *Tribune*, headlined "Ku-Klux in Texas." In this letter Lancaster described the murder as he had learned of it and wrote, "the assassins of my son are well known; but because they have money and thereby influence they are not molested, notwithstanding the proclamation of the Governor and the offer of $1,000 reward." Lancaster further stressed that there were many other instances of murder committed in Texas "at night, by men in disguise" which created the conditions which prevented "many a good emigrant from settling among us." Lancaster explained how he had arrived in Texas in 1835, had suffered and survived the massacre of Fannin at Goliad and served at San Jacinto. "Whenever we are rid of these midnight murderers and assassins, Texas will be blessed with an immigration that will make her rich indeed."[32]

Certainly some in Texas, although they empathized with Lancaster in the loss of his son three years earlier, resented Lancaster's statements. Ferdinand Flake printed in his *Bulletin* of July 18, "We deprecate mob law, and have no apology for these unwarrantable executions. But Parson Lancaster does wrong to class this unfortunate affair as a Kuklux outrage, and we apprehend his family pride will be worsted in the ventilation of this letter." Flake stated categorically the hanging of the Lancaster boy was not an act generated "from political causes." Flake concluded his remarks accusing Lancaster of attempting "to make political Kuklux capital out of the hanging of his unfortunate son of an unfortunate father."[33]

Davidson's attention was diverted from the Lancaster investigation when he learned — not from McNelly but from Captain George W. Farrow — the details of a confrontation between McNelly and the gate keeper at the Houston fair. According to Farrow, the "most serious difficulty that occurred during the entire Fair" was between McNelly and a fair employee, Adolph Cramer. On the evening of May 24 McNelly and a friend rode out to the fairgrounds in a buggy and attempted to drive through the gate without showing proper identification. Cramer halted McNelly and demanded to know by what authority he could enter. McNelly, without any explanation or show of official authority, told Cramer "he had a right to go in and intended to." When Cramer grabbed the bridle, McNelly struck him "over the back and shoulders with his whip several times and finally succeeded in riding over Mr. Cramer and passed in." Farrow stated that Cramer was obeying his orders not to pass in any persons without proper authority and especially "not to pass any buggies or carriages in."[34]

Davidson also learned further details of the arrest of the Houston gamblers. According to Farrow, Captain McNelly may have indeed arrested twenty-four men for gambling but, if so, not more than a half dozen were convicted and fined. Whatever explanation McNelly may have written to his superior has not been preserved, and we have only Farrow's version of events. Davidson thus had three serious matters on his mind in regards to McNelly and the Houston business: the apparent assault on Mr. Cramer; the questionable arrests of alleged gamblers; and the report of a statement supposedly made by McNelly to a young attorney from Bryan, a Mr. A.B. Cunningham, insinuating that McNelly had been sent to the frontier because Davidson was fearful that McNelly would replace him as adjutant general! Davidson's concerns were so serious that he suspended McNelly from all rank and pay as Captain of Police until he had made satisfactory explanations of all three matters.[35] Either McNelly's "explanation" satisfied Davidson or the suspension was temporarily overlooked, because on June 15 Sergeant Samuel D. Harn was ordered to report to McNelly for duty. Further, existing pay vouchers show that McNelly was not reduced in pay during this time period.[36]

On June 28, after receiving a letter from Mrs. Lancaster, Adjutant General Davidson found it necessary to communicate directly with the grieving Lancaster about the unresolved murder of his son. He wrote that McNelly had been ordered to "take immediate steps to thoroughly investigate the murder of your son with the view of bringing the guilty parties to justice." He again ordered McNelly to "take steps to arrest the murderers," but in frustration Davidson eventually gave up on McNelly and assigned Sergeant S. D. Harn to the duty of "ferreting out and arresting the guilty parties." McNelly had been told twice to investigate the murder, and now it became the responsibility of Sergeant Harn.[37]

By the end of June McNelly was reinstated as captain although he had not yet explained the nature of his remarks to Cunningham. Davidson was willing to overlook the slight and suggested that in the future he should "talk less and devote your time to your police duties. Nothing detracts more from the dignity of an officer than meaningless bragadocess [sic], forgotten as soon as uttered."[38]

On June 30 Davidson wrote again, including another reprimand for authorizing Private Charles Langhammer of the State Police to sign an order; this was disapproved and not to be repeated.[39] Although Sergeant S.D. Harn had been assigned to the Lancaster murder case, he apparently was not working satisfactorily and Davidson assigned it back to McNelly. But now he was ordered "to give this matter your *personal* and immediate attention. Go in person to the scene of the murder and take the steps to bring the guilty to justice." Ultimately one Andrew Holliday was arrested for the killing of William Lancaster.[40]

On August 8 McNelly received another reprimand for not having made any reports "for some time past."[41] The next day Davidson removed Brazos County from his district with no explanation.[42] On August 14 McNelly was ordered to go to the western counties to "make a thorough examination of Indian depredations in that locality, especially the number of murders committed, number of horses stolen, houses destroyed &c, together with all other information in regard to this matter."[43]

Again there was trouble in Bastrop County, so close to the capital city itself. The initial reports indicated that, following the election on Monday, August 14, there had been a drunken row in Bastrop and three men had been shot, one a policeman. Citizens of Bastrop, the county seat only some thirty miles from Austin itself, had complained of being "outraged and imposed upon" by policemen, one of whom had only recently beaten an unarmed citizen. The shooting affray on August 14 had started between Ben Yoast, also known as "Bird," and a freedman. During the course of the argument Ben's father Frank Yoast rode up, drew his revolver, and demanded that no one interfere, threatening to shoot anyone who did. Nevertheless, two citizens named Green and Burleson did interfere and separated the two fighting men. Sheriff Joseph Jung[44] and a policeman then attempted to arrest Frank Yoast, but State Policeman August Werner and another man fired their pistols at the senior Yoast who turned and emptied his pistol, containing three shots, into policeman Werner, mortally wounding him. Before Werner died he was able to fire his pistol, unfortunately wounding a Mr. Procop and a machinist. At this point a Mrs. Holter came out from a house near by. She became excited in seeing the difficulty — some reports contend that her children were close by which caused her to become frightened for their safety — and collapsed and died of fright within a half hour. Commented the *Statesman*, "Politics as far as we can learn had but nothing to do with the occurrance [sic] which was caused by mean whisky, and is to be regretted by all."[45] In a remark revealing the callous attitude of some towards the State Police as an organization, the San Antonio *Herald* commented about the incident that the "Davis police were drunk, as usual, and fired several shots at Mr. Yoast. He returned the fire and the Police was reduced one."[46]

Strangely enough the election in Bastrop had to do with the question of declaring martial law. Existing records are very sparse, but the Bastrop *Advertiser* had been claiming the alleged lawlessness in the county was not as widespread as some claimed. In fact, editor Thomas C. Cain had published two letters from Governor Davis himself which stated that because the Grand Jury had found no one to blame for "recent flagrant cases of violation of law," and because the parties charged with Ku Klux Klan activities and house burning had been discharged, perhaps declaring martial law would assist the grand jury in carrying out its rightful duties. Cain suggested that perhaps "king Edmund Davis and his party" were determined to ruin the county. If the grand jury indeed brought forth indictments against unnamed parties who were responsible for a number of murders within the past year and more, then that would be satisfactory to the governor. Editor Cain on August 14 sent a special to the Galveston *News* in which he declared the vote on martial law had been taken with the count being six to one against its being declared, all the white men voting against it. His report, ending with an optimistic "All quiet," was obviously telegraphed before the gunfight in which policeman Werner lost his life. The next issues of the *Advertiser* are no longer extant, and one can only speculate as to how Editor Cain reported the news of the riot and killing and death in the streets of Bastrop.[47]

McNelly did learn of the affray and sent his interpretation to Adjutant General Davidson, but only a summary of his report survives. Writing from Burton on Friday, September 1, McNelly wrote "in relation to the Bastrop riot and murder of August Werner" but explained that he had not had the time to pursue Yoast "as a cold blooded murder was committed near Bastrop, and he left in pursuit of [the] murderer the day after the crime was committed but failed to arrest him."[48]

Although we do not know what role McNelly may have had in bringing the slayer of Policeman Werner to justice, in April of the following year Ben Yoast appeared in District Court in Bastrop, charged with two counts of carrying deadly weapons and assault to kill and murder. No existing court record carries the name of Frank Yoast who, according to contemporary reports, was the actual slayer of Werner.[49] On August 7 the cases were called again; Yoast pled guilty to the charge of carrying deadly weapon and paid a fine of $25 and the cost of prosecution. His father, as surety, probably paid the fine so that his son would not have to sit in jail. The assault to kill and murder charge was dismissed, probably because it could not be determined who fired the fatal bullets. If indeed Werner was firing as well, the authorities might have considered the killing to be a case of self defense.[50]

Ironically, on the same day that Policeman August Werner was killed in Bastrop, the attorneys for James "Coon" Taylor, William Sutton and others stood before Judge W.B. McFarland's bench in Bastrop. They were charged with the killing of Charley Taylor, whose death provided one more determining factor in the violence which led to the Sutton-Taylor Feud which McNelly would enter into in mid-1874 in DeWitt County. The motion to quash the indictment was sustained and the defendants were told to go henceforth without delay.[51] Four days later C.C. McGinnis and other lawyers expressed their faith in Judge McFarland, in spite of Governor Davis' inept criticism of the judicial activities in Bastrop, with three resolutions stating that the Bastrop Bar members recognized the good conduct of McFarland on the bench, that he should receive the respect of all members of the legal profession, and that the resolutions be entered into the official minutes.[52]

Frequently McNelly was able to accomplish uncontroversial arrests which were nearly overlooked in the records. On September 23 he arrested one Alexander Thomas for theft of a horse, undoubtedly a peaceful arrest because the *Report of Arrests* provides no details or remarks, not even giving the location of the arrest or what McNelly did with his prisoner.[53]

McNelly's arrest on October 24 of William Forrest, charged with the murder of James Holt at Vine Grove in Washington County in the fall of 1858, did attract attention because Forrest had been a fugitive for thirteen years! It is not known how McNelly discovered the whereabouts of Forrest, but he singlehandedly made the arrest in Gonzales County and then delivered him to the county jail in Brenham, heavily ironed.[54]

The Brenham *Banner* also reported that McNelly had arrested freedman Bob Layton while he was serving on a jury. He was charged with the theft of a trunk, the property of Mrs. Hugh Lewis, containing a lot of fine clothing, all of which was found in the possession of Layton's wife. Commented the *Banner*, "Bob is a devout member of the God and morality party, and attaches a great deal of importance to himself, and as a matter of course feels highly indignant at the idea of being arrested upon such a frivolous charge of *theft* and that too while sitting in the jury box for the trial of criminals."[55] Only a few weeks before Layton had received dubious recognition in the columns of the Brenham *Banner*.

On Saturday last [September 17], in the heat of the day, a nigger company of Davis' "meelish," [militia]

under command of a big, black rascal, calling himself
Bob Layton, formed a black streak on Court house
square. There they stood for two hours in the broiling
sun marking time. Our farmers are offering fifty cents
and upwards per hundred pounds to have their cotton
picked, but some of these niggers, "case why dey hab
jined de meelish and is gwine to git a gun wid a bagonet
on it," and ain't got time to pick cotton. Again, the sun
is too hot; and we heard one say he would "catch the
yaller janders shore, if he went into the cotton
patch."[56]

Some used only ridicule against Davis and his police, but in
other places deadly force was used. In Gonzales County on October
19, 1871, two State Policemen, Green Paramore and John Lackey,
had a difficulty with John Wesley Hardin. In his autobiography
Hardin claimed the pair had attempted to arrest him, but he resisted
and gunplay erupted. When the policemen, in that portion of the
county intending to arrest a freedman on an unspecified charge,
stopped at a country store, a group of DeWitt County's white men
led by Hardin rode up and ordered them to lay down their arms
then commenced firing on them. Paramore was killed instantly and
Lackey was wounded in four places. The wounded Lackey walked
into town where he was able to alert authorities. Other freedmen
grabbed their weapons intending to capture young Hardin, but the
county sheriff and the Gonzales mayor managed to prevent this
undertaking, one which no doubt would have produced further
killings. Serious consideration was given to declaring martial law in
Gonzales County, but matters did not develop to that point.[57]
Although McNelly was not sent to Gonzales County in 1871 to track
down Hardin, he would later have the opportunity to capture him
in adjacent DeWitt County after the young desperado had developed a formidable reputation as a man-killer.

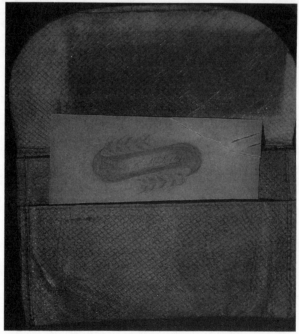

McNelly's wallet which held his business cards, probably from the early 1870s as a Captain of the State Police. The wallet was from the Baltimore & Ohio Rail Road. *Photo courtesy T. Lindsay Baker, The Harold B. Simpson Research Center, Hillsboro, Texas.*

CHAPTER 8

A DEATH WARRANT AND A TRIP

TO THE RIO GRANDE

"[T]he frontier needs protection is a melancholy fact, written in deeds of blood, robbery and murder. That the United States has failed to protect that frontier is a disgraceful fact — a fact which should cause the President to blush with shame." — The Galveston *Daily News*, July 16, 1872.

The year 1872 began with McNelly still in command of his district in spite of one suspension and the many reprimands from Adjutant General Davidson. The year would find him in many different situations, arresting a senator in the state's capital, capturing a fugitive sheriff, keeping the peace during a railroad strike, leading an expedition to the Rio Grande frontier against border marauders, and unsuccessfully pursuing Adjutant General Davidson for embezzlement of state funds. In addition to these major actions McNelly continued to provide leadership in the police force.

One of the most notable actions during his police career involved Senator Matthew Gaines, a noted black politician from McNelly's own Washington County. Gaines was born August 4, 1840, near Alexandria, Louisiana, to a slave mother. He learned to read by candlelight from books brought to him by a white boy who lived on the same plantation. From youth to the end of the Civil War, Gaines attempted several escapes from slavery, only to be recaptured each time. After Emancipation, Gaines settled in Burton in Washington County where he established himself as a minister and a leading politician in the black community. During Reconstruction he was elected as a senator to represent the Sixteenth District in the Texas legislature.[1]

Gaines might have had an extremely successful career in politics had he not been charged with bigamy. The details have not been preserved, but he was indicted on December 9, 1871, by the grand jury at La Grange, Fayette County. Naturally the press treated the matter lightly, the prestigious Galveston *Daily News* reporting that on January 31, 1872, Captain McNelly had come up from Washington County in pursuit of a fugitive "who had been prowling about Austin for some time." The reporter observed McNelly's making for the railroad depot "in possession of his prize" — Senator Matt Gaines — "the black leader of Radicalism, a prisoner, charged with the high crime of bigamy."[2] McNelly delivered Gaines to Fayette County where he eventually stood trial and was convicted of bigamy, forcing him to relinquish his senate seat. Although the conviction was overturned on appeal and he was reelected, he had lost much of his influence. Gaines died in Giddings, Lee County, on June 11, 1900.[3] Among Gaines' accomplishments, other than working for education, prison reform and the protection of blacks at voting places, was the passage of a bill which authorized his district to levy a special tax for construction of a new jail.[4]

On April 24 the first report from Corsicana told of the disappearance of the Navarro County Sheriff, James A. Nelms, who was reported to be a "defaulter to the amount of sixteen hundred dollars."[5] Governor Davis issued a proclamation stating that it had been made known to him about April 13 that Sheriff Nelms did leave the state for parts unknown, having in his possession a considerable amount of money, "the property of the State, and is still at large and a fugitive from justice." On April 23 Davis offered a reward of $500 for the arrest and delivery of James A. Nelms to the proper Navarro County authorities, "inside the jail door."[6]

A year earlier Nelms must have been considered a trustworthy official among the paradigms of law officers. He had written to Governor Davis giving a statement of affairs in Navarro County and inferentially asking for approval of how he had handled certain affairs in his county, not discussed in his letter. Davis responded on January 13 that Nelms' course of action had been "very satisfactory to me since your appointment as Sheriff of Navarro County, and I recommend that you hold to your office and enforce the laws. I will endeavor to sustain you from here." Nelms had been appointed sheriff by Governor Davis on July 16, 1870, with Jacob Eliot and O.M. Airheart's signing his $30,000 bond. He now was experiencing difficulties at the professional level.[7]

Within days of the governor's reward offer, Captain McNelly had him in custody. Immediately there were rumors that there was more involved than just a sheriff who had absconded with county funds. The Galveston *News* suggested as much, saying that Nelms would be "a valuable witness for the State at Governor Davis' trial."

The *News* reporter, probably A.H. Belo, went to the Washington Hotel in Galveston to interview McNelly, but he found his old army friend "particularly reticent in regard to the matter, stating as a reason that he did not wish by any publication to prejudice the case of either the accused or his accusers." McNelly undoubtedly remembered the problems he had encountered with his interview dealing with the Walker County affair. Whereas "mum was the word" with the captain, the same was not true with Sheriff Nelms, who offered a full explanation of his departure from Texas and his arrest.

Nelms claimed that he had started for Austin, presumably with the intention of turning in collected tax monies, but while at Houston learned that a man by the name of Harry Sinclair, whose bond he had guaranteed for a considerable sum of money, was in New Orleans, spending money very freely. Since Nelms felt he had been "left in the lurch" he decided to go to New Orleans and see the man, hoping to obtain from him a collateral in money equal to the amount for which he had become responsible. He still had Navarro County tax monies in his possession. Nowhere in the available record is there an explanation as to why Nelms did not go directly to Austin — if he actually intended to deposit tax monies with the state as he claimed — since Austin is approximately 130 miles *southwest* from Navarro County while Houston is approximately 180 miles *southeast.*

At New Orleans he learned that a man by the name of Nolen, who had some time before stolen over $3,000 from him, was in Memphis, Tennessee, and was "flush with money." When he arrived in Jackson he ascertained that Nolen had not been flush with money but in reality had been for weeks "strapped." He decided it would be a waste of time and effort to attempt to locate Nolen so he went to his sister who lived near Mobile, Alabama. She had recently lost her husband and Nelms planned to bring her back to Texas, or so he said.

But while still in New Orleans he learned Governor Davis had offered a reward for his arrest. He at once went to Captain Cad. Hite, formerly of Galveston, told him of the circumstances, and surrendered to him. A short time later the local police took charge of him, put him in jail and treated him very roughly. He sent word, via his sister to Governor Davis, that "when thieves fall out honest men would get their dues."

Soon after he received a telegram from his sister that Governor Davis had instructed her to tell him it *would be all right*, and to come to Austin because Governor Davis wished to see him. McNelly by then was at Memphis, where he had gone in search of Nelms. Apparently authorities at Austin telegraphed to him that Nelms was in New Orleans. Returning there, McNelly took him out of prison and transported him to Galveston on a steamer.

Nelms was described as a handsome young man of about twenty-seven years of age, intelligent and "of a pleasing address." He claimed the entire affair was "malicious from beginning to end" and that he was worth $25,000 in good property in and about Corsicana, sufficient to cover all the taxes he had ever collected. He concluded his remarks "with a peculiar twinkle in his eye" saying, "They must not push this thing, or I will make it too hot for the whole of them."[8]

By Tuesday April 30 McNelly was back in Austin with prisoner Nelms. They left for Corsicana on Thursday May 2; McNelly intended to collect the $500 reward by delivering the fugitive within the jail door at Corsicana. The Nelms case occasionally made head-lines for several months during 1872. McNelly made a report but unfortunately it has not survived. Reference is made to it in an arti-cle appearing in the Austin *Democratic Statesman* in which McNelly reported finding several thousand dollars in Nelms' possession when arrested. No such amount of money was paid to the state when Nelms arrived in Austin. "Where is it, and why is it that Nelms, after all the blow made about his absconding and stealing money belong-ing to the State, is still occupying the position of sheriff in his county?" This statement from a leading newspaper certainly demanded a response from the governor, but no such response is known to have been made. Supposedly Nelms had all the money he was accused of stealing.[9] To the further irritation of the *Statesman*, the reward offered by the state was paid to an officer of the state. The Galveston *News*, always supportive of McNelly, again took up this item by the *Statesman*. The *News* did not make clear what it was hinting at but printed, "So! So! Nelms did hold the whip in his hand, and Davis dare not punish him. The irons were all a pretext — bracelets worn a few hours in public and removed when out of sight. We are at least glad of this. Davis has found a master — one that can hold the rod in *terrorem* over him."[10]

But the difficulties did not end there. As late as mid-August there were claimants over the division of the reward. When Nelms surrendered to Captain Hite in New Orleans he had $4,600 on his person. After New Orleans Police Chief A.S. Badger took Nelms in custody, he took the $4,600. Nelms had to employ A.A. Atocha, Esq., for a fee of $600, to recover the money. Badger claimed $500 for his services and also, before he returned the money, retained

$500 to secure the payment of the Texas reward. When McNelly returned Nelms to Corsicana he, of course, claimed the same $500 reward because he was the one delivering the prisoner to within the county jail as prescribed by the reward notice. With both McNelly and Badger's claiming the reward, the matter was turned over to Colonel John D. Elliott of Austin for arbitration. Elliott decided McNelly would receive $400 and Badger $100. Badger did not accept the terms of the arbitration and retained the $500 he had originally taken from Nelms. Badger's letter of rejection, in part, stated,

> It was well understood by all parties interested that the $500 was left in my hands to guarantee the amount of reward offered by the State of Texas to my officers. . . . It was well understood that my sole object in retaining the $500 was solely to preclude the possibility of being, by any hocus pocus, defrauded of the whole or any part of the reward . . . since I had never agreed to the appointment of Colonel Elliott as arbitrator, I therefore decline to abide by this decision or award, and reiterate my demand for the full reward.[11]

Governor Davis, on August 5, wrote that the reward had already been paid according to the decision of the arbitrator, and in his opinion Badger was not authorized to keep the $500 he had retained. James A. Nelms also made a sworn statement that when he was captured by Colonel Badger in New Orleans after having surrendered to Colonel Hite, he was searched and $4,600 was taken from him. He was thrown in prison and was able to obtain meals only upon paying three dollars for each meal. The record does not show if the various amounts of state money taken by the various officials, Atocha, Hite and Badger, were returned totally or in part, but by early June Nelms was able to execute a new bond for the sum of twenty thousand dollars, dated May 30 and approved by F.P. Wood, judge of the Twenty-fifth judicial district. This was shown to be "worthless," and enough pressure was exerted on officials to disallow Nelms from continuing to hold office. Efforts were made for E. Sheldon Bell to take the position of sheriff, but he failed to qualify. The *Daily State Journal*, usually very supportive of Governor Davis and his actions, found fault with the entire affair, claiming that "the people of Texas have had a surfeit of straw bonds and straw sheriffs" and further expected the judicial officers of the state to "render proper and prompt assistance to the fiscal department in this essential matter."[12]

Exactly how the money question was ultimately settled is unknown, except that McNelly did receive $500 reward for the delivery of Nelms to the Navarro County jail as well as $451 mileage for his apprehension. Bell apparently was able to serve until August, but on August 3 he surrendered the office to James H. Brent who had been elected to fill out the term. After Nelms' disgraceful end as county sheriff, he served as a policeman in Corsicana, then as a cotton gin repairman, farmed, and perhaps concurrently served as an auctioneer and a merchant.[13]

With the expansion of the railroad in Central Texas a different type of problem arose, one which McNelly certainly could never have envisioned — the railroad strike. When the Civil War began there were less than four-hundred miles of track in Texas; the number of miles by 1870 was less than eight hundred; by the time of the 1872 strike there were barely a thousand miles of track. A work stoppage by the engineers on the Houston & Texas Central Railroad (H. & T.C.) was the result of a new policy issued to railroad employees in early June, stipulating as a condition of employment that if an employee of the railroad was injured due to fault or neglect of another employee then the company would not be held liable for that fault or neglect. Engineers called this new policy a "death warrant" and struck.[14]

In Houston on Tuesday, June 4, some engineers, conductors, firemen and train hands of the H. & T.C. Railway met and issued certain resolutions in protest. Their primary concern was that they felt the act requiring them to sign an agreement "refusing to claim compensation for ourselves or families . . . in case of loss of life or limb in their employ" was "unjust and uncalled for." Secondly, those who signed the resolution believed that they were held in "utter abhorrence" by their choosing to do so either from lack of judgment or through fear of losing their job.

The employees meeting at Hempstead resented the threat of any violence being used against them or railroad machinery. They equally resented being called "strikers," reasoning that they did not strike for back pay or pay increases but only "stopped from our work to bid defiance to a law, or order, of the said company for the benefit of their own pockets and the starvation of our families in case of the death or injury to us in the faithful discharge of our several duties."

In spite of their grievances, the strikers wisely resolved not to interfere with the passage of the United States mail. They even agreed to detail a "responsible and competent engineer to carry said mail," and only the mail, until the company withdrew the policy. The strikers resolved that the "Death Warrant" as well as their resolutions be sent to the Houston newspapers "so the citizens at large can see for themselves what the said Company wishes to do."[15]

The strike did create great excitement along the road. Correspondent "D.R." at Hearne reported that on June 5 there were many passengers left at all stations.[16] At Hempstead there was "intense excitement" with seven trains and about fifty men lying idle. Some forty passengers were delayed there. Correspondent "L." reported that one employee had been "maltreated last night by unknown parties" but the strikers were "orderly and determined."[17] Delays had become expected and no passengers were being taken on. At Hempstead the strikers detached all cars except the mail car and placed them on a side track, allowing only the mail car to continue.

At 2:00 p.m. on June 5 a town magistrate and deputies appeared at the Hempstead depot, but they did nothing and there was no disturbance. Three hours later Captain McNelly arrived from Navasota but made no arrests. Whether McNelly was acting alone or had a detachment of police with him at this point is uncertain. Surviving documents in the adjutant general's correspondence suggest he may have had up to two dozen policemen under his command. Correspondent "L." concluded his dispatch by saying the strikers seemed determined to hold their own, while on the other hand the company seemed fully determined to yield nothing. "It is thought that McNelly will make arrests to-morrow, and it is probable the passenger trains will resume regular trips to-morrow. About one hundred passengers are detained at Hempstead. The excitement is calming down. No trains to-night."[18]

To add something of a bit of morbid humor to the entire strike, on the same day that McNelly arrived, June 5, the train going to Hempstead from Austin ran off the track near McNelly's home with a squad of police aboard. This accident occurred about 10:00 p.m., caused by the Austin train's hitting a cow on the tracks near Burton and derailing two cars. Reports of the number injured ranged from several to as many as ten. Donovan, Bitter, Kuhln and Kenna were the most seriously injured.[19] Donovan and Bitter both died from their injuries.[20]

While crews had to contend with overturned cars and a dead cow near Burton, ten engines at Hempstead were left immobile after strikers removed portions of their works to render them unfit for immediate use. Correspondent "S." reported that although there was intense excitement no hostile demonstrations were expected. Further, Captain McNelly with some policemen remained on the grounds. The strikers were "still very determined and defiant," while the railroad company showed strength and would "yield under no circumstances."[21]

On Thursday June 6, the railroad company discharged all employees who had signed the declaration against the so-called "Death Warrant." One employee, August Becker, who had signed the agreement and then offered to work, was taken out and tarred and feathered "by unknown parties."[22]

Apparently the maltreatment of Becker was the only act of violence although there was great apprehension experienced by some. William N. Haupt, a farmer and leading citizen of the community of Kyle in Hays County south of Austin, did take the time to record the efforts of some policemen to ensure the safety of all passengers. Haupt had placed his wife and children on the Central Railroad going to Houston on June 5. At Hempstead the train was met by "the mob" and stopped, as were all trains, "creating intense excitement, badly frightening the ladies and forcing them as prisoners to an unknown detention." Police Lieutenant Thomas G. Martin, who lived near Haupt and knew the family, attempted to persuade the rioters to permit Mrs. Haupt and the other ladies and children to pass on through but was unsuccessful. He was unable to do anything until Captain McNelly and Sheriff Asher B. Hall of Harris County arrived. With their assistance, Haupt reported, the cars were re-coupled and someone was found who would take the train on through. Haupt wrote, "By the combined efforts of Capt. McNelly and Lieutenant Martin, they succeeded, the next morning, in getting off the train for Corsicana, with three coaches, loaded with passengers, the rear coach being filled with ladies and children. Lieutenant Martin taking possession of this train to conduct it through." At Hearne the "mob" attempted to detach the coaches but the policemen prevented anyone from touching the coupling.

Fortunately Lieutenant Martin did observe that "at a very high and dangerous point on the road" he discovered that "the mob" had securely bolted ties, with wedge shaped ends on each side of the track, in such a way as to "throw the train off the track, to wreck and smash at the bottom of the steep embankment with its load of innocent women and children, and to send a shock of horror to every mind except the . . . mob." Martin managed to see what had been done to the tracks and was able to slow down the engine enough so that only the front wheels were thrown off the track. He jumped off the tender and was uninjured, but those who could not jump off, perhaps McNelly himself, were bruised by falling wood. No passengers were injured.[23]

The June work stoppage was not the first strike in Texas, but it was the first involving a significant number of people. Some 80 percent of operating employees walked out, effectively stopping all trains for several days. The trains were then manned by supervisors and new employees. Ultimately the "Death Warrant" was withdrawn as policy, but most of those who had struck were not rehired.

With the ending of the strike McNelly had little time to rest as there was another call from Austin which would place him on the Rio Grande Frontier in an element potentially more suitable to his leadership abilities.

The genesis for what was known as the "Rio Grande Expedition" came from Dimmit County deep in South Texas. Influential rancher Levi English, Sr., had suffered raids on his herds and probably exerted enough influence to cause Adjutant General Davidson to send a special group to that area to provide assistance to him and other ranchers. English had been raising stock since 1860 between the Nueces and the Rio Grande, the area popularly known as "the Nueces Strip" into which, especially since 1864, armed Mexicans had been making incursions and driving off cattle to Mexico. According to his own reckoning English had lost most of the cattle he owned. Further, William C. Dickens, Edward English, John R. Burleson, William V. Bell and Rafael Rellas, neighboring ranchers, had also lost much of their herds. On more than one occasion Levi English followed the raiders; in 1862 he had followed the trail made by about two hundred of his cattle to the Rio Grande but failed to recover any of them. Four years later he followed another herd of stolen cattle and found them in Guerrero, Mexico, but the authorities refused to surrender them. He had suffered losses many times, and once in 1870 he and his employees had been attacked in Texas by a band of Indians and Mexicans disguised as Indians, losing thirteen head of horses and camp equipage. With some friends he managed to overtake them on the banks of the Rio Grande, killed one of the marauders, and recovered a horse and saddle from the dead raider. On June 15, 1870, a party of ten attacked a small party of his "Cowdrivers" engaged in gathering up his horses and cattle. English gathered up some neighbors and pursued the thieves to the Rio Grande; after a short engagement the thieves abandoned the cattle but English was unable to recover the stolen horses.

In 1872 he managed to obtain the state's assistance in the form of McNelly and a group of policemen. All that English revealed in a report to the House of Representatives was expressed in two terse sentences, "In 1872 [I] followed several trails of these marauders, and on one occasion was accompanied by thirty State police under Captain McNally [sic]. The trail followed on this occasion was that of about one thousand cattle; this trail was followed to the river, where the cattle had been crossed into Mexico."[24]

By mid-July McNelly essentially had his command ready for the expedition. His orders, dated July 9, were clear: he and his detachment were to proceed to Brownsville, Texas, scout between that point on the Rio Grande to Eagle Pass, Texas, "for the purpose of arresting criminals and breaking up the cattle and horse stealing prevalent in that locality." Any parties arrested for violations of the law were to be turned over to the civil authorities.

McNelly's orders also included the statement that, in the execution of these duties, he was to see that his detachment was "kept under control, orderly & active, and that persons engaged in Legitimate business are not molested." On the road between Austin and Brownsville he was to "render any assistance required by civil authorities in the apprehension of Murderers & other criminals evading arrest."[25]

In its Sunday, July 14 issue, the Galveston *Daily News*, possibly suggesting much stronger action should be taken by the state authorities, headlined Davidson's order in bold print with "Does This Mean a War With Mexico?" By Tuesday the editor had had time to reflect upon the order and wrote, "[that] the frontier needs protection is a melancholy fact, written in deeds of blood, robbery and murder. That the United States has failed to protect that frontier is a disgraceful fact — a fact which should cause the President to blush with shame." Editor Belo pointed out that it was not the business of Governor Davis to make war on Mexico, but it was clear that the president was using McNelly to "bring on an engagement." The troops sent to the frontier would want neither opportunity nor pretext to get into a brush with Mexican troops, and then President Grant would conclude that a state of war existed and would "go for 'em." The *News* editor stated there was no objection to the president's doing this, but he did not like the manner or the timing of the supposed affront. It was simply not right to bring on a war with Mexico on the eve of an election.[26]

Talk of war between the United States and Mexico frequently appeared in the press, perhaps reflecting the feeling of Texans, remembering San Jacinto but forgetting the Alamo and Goliad, that a conflict would not be a difficult undertaking. It was generally understood by Texans that another war with Mexico would result in victory and the southern border of the United States would be extended still further below the Rio Grande. The lawlessness then existing in the Nueces Strip between the Nueces River and the Rio Grande would be eradicated. But war did not come, and the raiding of Texas ranches and lawlessness continued. The intent of many of the men sent to the Rio Grande with McNelly may have been to whip the marauders once and for all.

There is but one muster roll extant of the police serving with McNelly: J.J. Bozarth, E.S. Gantt, T.C. Lusk, J.W. Hackworth, B.E. Bedell, J.S. Chapman, R.C. Wood, Robert E. Hamney, H.B. Waller, P.W. Sapp, J.M.H. Young, B.F. Early, F.M. Griffin, Christopher Geesenchslag, Joseph L. Priestly, C.S. Bell, J.T. Bozarth, J.B. Fauntleroy, J.E. Kirby, J.W. Haley, L.G. Gatlin, John K. Dorman, M. Arnel, R.C. Brown, E.H. Armstrong, Alexander L. Roy, John Tom, J.C. Beck and Pablo Escamina. Dates of qualification ranged from June 1 through August 2. Escamina signed on at Laredo on August 2, presumably to act as a guide and translator.[27]

McNelly knew them as dependable fighting men, some of whom had served with him during the war. The roster shows they were mainly from the Brenham, Burton, Giddings and Hempstead area; one was from Hockley, Harris County, one from Long Point, Fort Bend County, one from Austin, one from Fayetteville, one from San Antonio, and the guide from Laredo. By Tuesday July 9, McNelly and his command were in Austin and were described as "thoroughly armed and equipped."[28] The next day at about 4:00 p.m., they were in the yard of the capital building where they were addressed by Governor Davis. A reporter from Austin's *State Journal* was there taking notes. "Boys, I authorized Capt. McNally [*sic*] to select thirty good, honorable, brave men, as policemen, for the purpose of sending them out upon the Rio Grande frontier to chastise and bring to justice the numerous horse thieves and outlaws that are depredating upon the good citizens of that portion of our State," said the governor.

Davis continued praising McNelly for his bravery, saying that he was satisfied that McNelly had chosen men for the expedition who were good, honorable and brave, men "upon whom he can rely in all respects."

Davis was concerned about the possible racial friction which might lead to trouble. He reminded the policemen that the citizens of that section of the country into which they were to enter did not speak "our language" because they were Mexicans. But Davis reiterated that just because of the language barrier they were not enemies. The Mexicans "are your fellow citizens and as such must be treated by you as friends." None was to be interfered with except those who were violating the law. "I do not send you out to make war upon Mexico, but to preserve citizens in their rights and to bring to justice as may be in your power, under the direction of your captain, the scoundrels of whatever nationality they may be, who are now infesting that section." But where Davis seemingly wanted to provide protection to Mexican citizens, the same argument was not made for Indians. "Should you come across or encounter any of the Indians, you need not stop to ask whether they will surrender, but bring them down by the shortest means." This may have seemed like a difficult distinction to make, as it was a well known fact, at least in the mind of many Texans, that the Mexicans and the Indians often combined forces to raid and plunder white settlements or ranches.

Davis should have ended his "pep talk" at that point but instead continued, reminding the audience that most of them had fought on the side of the Confederacy against him. He wanted their allegiances during the war to make no difference now, seven years after the surrender. "I have long since found it to be a fact that the brave and honorable soldier, Federal or Confederate, of the late war has proven himself the honorable, law-abiding citizen since the war." He continued his praise of the bravery and good judgment of Captain McNelly and expressed confidence that the men would conduct themselves as brave and obedient policemen in their mission.[29] Davis issued his capital grounds speech on July 10, and three days later a Special Order was issued by General Davidson for the benefit of all officials.

> As Capt. L.H. McNelly State Police, is to proceed to the Rio Grande, for the purpose of arresting criminals, breaking up horse & cattle stealing & restoring & enforcing the laws in that Section of the State, all sheriffs & other civil officers, policemen & other persons are hereby directed to assist Capt. McNelly & his detachment in the discharge of the duties instructed to him.[30]

On the same day Governor Davis sent a gently expressed request to the Commanding Officer of United States troops of the Rio Grande district at Brownsville, "Any assistance you can render Capt.

McNelly in the way of information or detail of troops when this assistance of such is required will be thankfully appreciated."[31]

Due to undisclosed reasons the departure was delayed following the Davis speech on July 10. The group did not arrive in San Antonio, less than one-hundred miles to the southeast, until a week later. There the *Herald* made note of their passing on July 16. "They are a stout, hearty looking set of men, raised in Washington and Austin counties, and are most all ex-Confederates." The *State Journal* reprinted the article and commented, "We respect and honor the brave soldier and endorse all the Herald says, only Mr. Herald, had they been ex-Federals would you have been so complimentary in your remarks[?]"[32]

Indications are that the McNelly company became an annoyance in San Antonio. The *Herald* reported on July 17 that the company did not get off on the evening of Monday, July 15, as originally planned, but were still "sloshing round" San Antonio Tuesday morning. The editor "stumbled on our good looking friend John Beck who it seems didn't get enough of soldiering during the war" and thus joined McNelly. The men were "well armed and mounted" and appeared to be able to give a good account of themselves should the occasion arise. "From all accounts they will find plenty to do along the Rio Grande."[33]

McNelly and his command finally did start en route to the Rio Grande Frontier, not to Brownsville as originally planned but to Eagle Pass, the seat of recently organized Maverick County. The village had a history rich with Confederate lore; during the war it was one of the ports of entry which had remained open for the export of Confederate cotton. At the close of the war General J.O. Shelby bivouacked five-hundred Confederate soldiers of the Trans-Mississippi Department in the immediate area, and on July 4, 1865, he and his men crossed the river to offer their services to the Emperor Maximilian. Midway across the river Shelby stopped to bury the last Confederate flag to fly over his troops. During the war Indians had gradually increased their influence and then began a period of raiding against white settlers as well as Mexican. In addition to the problems with outlaws, McNelly knew he could anticipate trouble with Indians; the last raid did not occur until 1877.[34]

McNelly and his force possessed the potential for creating havoc among the rustling bands, but McNelly made no dramatic moves. At this point in his career there were no gun battles with raiders, either Anglos or Mexicans, nor were there any engagements with Indians. Three years later in 1875 he would again be on the Rio Grande, with different men and orders that gave him virtual free rein, and would cause an international sensation with his treatment of rustlers. Three years later he would have significant support from Nueces County rancher Richard King, and it is possible that McNelly met King during this 1872 expedition. If so, perhaps the cattle king told McNelly just how dangerous the border country was; on July 31 King, his driver George Evans and Franz Specht, a traveler who had asked to ride with him from Corpus Christi to Brownsville, were attacked by a band of eight to ten Mexicans only six miles from the King Ranch. Traveler Specht was killed. Governor Davis offered a reward of $600 for information to identify the assassins, who undoubtedly had intended to rob King and possibly kill him. Police Sergeant Fred Bader with eight policemen and a posse of twenty citizens scoured the country side and arrested six persons, "against whom there is proof positive of complicity."[35]

McNelly's expedition did not result in significant actions against Indians or stock thieves. His July 25 report of operations only mentioned Indian raids along the line of march. The actual report does not survive, only the summary, so it is not clear if he actually engaged any Indians or merely described the damage inflicted by Indians. Perhaps he was only able to collect information as to the number of raids, casualties among the settlers, children kidnapped, and damage suffered. At this stage of his career, he likely realized that if his actions brought results then the paper work was not all that important. He also realized that if his meager written report was unsatisfactory then he could amplify it in person in Austin. Scarcely had he arrived on the river than he had to dismiss some of his men, discharging brothers Jonathan J. and Joseph T. Bozarth, J.M.H. Young, J.B. Fauntleroy and John K. Dorman. On August 2 McNelly reported his action; Davidson's response on August 12, addressed to McNelly at Laredo, expressed his approval of what McNelly had done. McNelly gave no reason for the men's dismissal except that Dorman had been discharged for "drunkenness and absence without leave" from the command.[36]

Perhaps the only real action in which this command participated was assisting Levi English. English's deposition gave no details, not even enough to determine if the group did any more than merely follow a trail. No mention of any action on the line of march has been located in the contemporary press, and the single surviving official document giving evidence that the group did arrive at the river is Davidson's letter addressed to McNelly at Laredo. Davidson had not received a report of the actions after weeks of waiting; as late as

September 27 McNelly was being reminded to provide a report![37]

The expedition could not have lasted more than a few weeks. Having left San Antonio by mid-July and arriving in Laredo by mid-August, McNelly was back in Burton by the end of August! On August 30 Davidson telegraphed to policeman Ryan at Navasota, George W. Farrow at Galveston and McNelly at Burton, directing each of them to proceed by the first train to Millican, in southern Brazos County, to protect Policeman Myers accused of murder.[38] However, Davidson must have reconsidered his order because another communication was directed to McNelly on August 31, addressed to him at Burton, ordering him to proceed to Wood County with a twenty-man detachment. He was to report to the sheriff, J.T. Holbert, and arrest the murderers of J.M. Brock, described as a "notorious disturber of the peace in that county", and "Such other criminals and violators of law that may be found in that County." Davidson ordered him to not return "until you are satisfied that the desperadoes in the County have all been arrested."[39] Perhaps McNelly himself questioned these orders, because a follow-up communication stated, "Pursuant to instructions already Sent you[,] you will immediately proceed to Quitman, Wood County with your detachment of twenty (20) State Policemen & assist the sheriff in restoring order in the County."[40] This must have been one of his more unusual orders!

Again one is left to wonder what transpired to force Davidson to order McNelly and a detachment of twenty men to Wood County. No report filed by McNelly has been found. A Mr. Luckey of Tyler wrote that the Wood County jail at Quitman had been broken open and "some prisoners released" and that "great excitement prevails in Wood county." By September 12 the Canton *News* reported that the "entire force of the State Police" had been ordered to Quitman. Mr. Luckey apparently observed McNelly on his way through Tyler, but he reported that there were but fifteen policemen with him.[41] Davidson had written to Sheriff J.T. Holbert (who would soon be replaced as he failed to qualify) on August 23 advising him to call a public meeting and alert the citizens to the monetary cost which would be charged to them if martial law was declared, urging them to cooperate with the civil authorities in putting down lawlessness and crime "so prevalent" in Wood County. Davidson alerted Holbert that the cost of maintaining a force in Wood County would cost $30,000 a month![42] McNelly and his force of fifteen men were apparently able to establish order in Wood County, because martial law was not declared. It is unknown whether the killing of Brock and the release of jailed prisoners were connected events, or whether there were other serious concerns not identified in existing documents. A later report from Quitman indicated that about 150 citizens of Wood County had been arrested and bound to appear at the next term of United District Court at Tyler. Their charge was "conspiracy against the United States Government and other offenses."[43] Eventually Davidson became tired of waiting for reports and ordered McNelly, "You will make a written report to this office, of your Expeditions to the Rio Grande & Wood County, giving full particulars of your action in each case."[44]

But McNelly didn't have the time to make a written report with "full particulars" because on September 27 he was ordered to detail six men "immediately" to proceed "without delay" to Woodville in Tyler County, some thirty miles west of the Louisiana line. He was to report to Police Sergeant W.S. Durham, stationed there for duty, until further orders arrived.[45] One wonders why a captain of the State Police was ordered to report to a sergeant.

Six days later, on October 3, Davidson issued further orders which seemingly asked McNelly to do the impossible. On September 27 he was ordered to proceed immediately with a six-man detachment to Woodville and await further orders. Six days later Davidson sent orders, addressed to McNelly at Burton, to report to Round Top in Fayette County and inquire into the difficulty between State Policeman Nathan Busby and W.G. Blanchette, the Mayor of Round Top. Again he was to make "a full and detailed report of the whole affair" to Davidson, who added, "These difficulties between Peace officers must not be allowed."[46] If McNelly made any reports of these various actions, covering the many miles from Laredo to Woodville to Round Top, they unfortunately have not been preserved.

In October McNelly did report that at Burton on the night of October 3 William Neese was murdered and recommended a reward be offered. Neese operated a general store in Fayette County; about 3:00 a.m. he discovered a burglar in his store. Neese struggled with the burglar who shot him in the breast with a derringer, mortally wounding him. Neese's clerk, also in the store at the time, fought back, striking him on the head with a pistol, but the burglar managed to escape. Seen on the train that night, his wound obviously causing suspicion, he was arrested and turned over to a policeman by Herman Knittel, Sr., a Washington County merchant, but the prisoner escaped. His identity was not provided to the press,[47] but perhaps McNelly suspected the identity of the murderer and requested a reward to cover his expenses on the trail. Friends of the victim did offer a $500 reward for the murderer.[48]

Although McNelly must have been too busy with his travels and keeping control of his men to concern himself with individual goals, he may have nursed a strong desire to capture the young Gonzales County desperado John Wesley Hardin. A year earlier Hardin had confronted policemen Green Paramore and John Lackey, killing the former and severely wounding the latter. This action prompted Governor Davis to offer a $400 reward for Hardin's arrest and delivery to the sheriff of Gonzales County. While McNelly was following orders to quell disturbances miles apart, Cherokee County Sheriff Richard Reagan did capture Hardin. Editor Joseph Lancaster, who had lost a son to frontier violence, described the arrest in his *Lone Star Ranger*, which was then reprinted in the Galveston *News* of November 21. The murderous son of a Methodist minister was credited with having killed two dozen men in Texas and four in Kansas. The *Ranger* called him "the most bloody desperado we ever heard of."[49]

But McNelly could only read about the capture, and another lawman would claim the $400 reward this time. On October 8 Davidson transmitted a clipping from the Houston *Telegraph* "relative to apprehension of J. Hardin by Sheriff Reagan." Hardin, however, would evade justice; placed in the Gonzales County jail to await trial for the Paramore killing, he escaped from custody on November 19, 1872. Gonzales County Sheriff William E. Jones offered his own reward of $100 for the fugitive's capture and delivery to the jail door. As the months went by Hardin continued his killing ways and McNelly, as perhaps every other lawman, must have dreamed of capturing him and gathering in the rewards which continued to grow. But McNelly would never see Hardin, although he would be the object of at least one scout in DeWitt County in 1874; the bloody desperado would finally be run to earth in 1877 by one of McNelly's own men, John B. Armstrong.[50]

Ed Pearce, who had been involved with his brother in "arresting" McNelly during the Cedar Bayou campaign, was now himself arrested, although the details of who accomplished this and how have not survived. Pearce had been charged with the murder of an old freedman, Paul Sante,[51] and stood trial on October 10 in Anderson, Grimes County. The jury was out for only ten minutes and returned with a verdict of acquittal.[52] According to one telegram announcing the acquittal, Pearce had prevented the other Cedar Bayou outlaws from killing McNelly when they had the chance!

Adjutant General Davidson, while outwardly showing great concern for the law-abiding citizens of Texas in sending McNelly hither
and yon to enforce the law, had his own inner torments to deal with.
Rather than focus on his position's requirements, he chose to flee
them. In late 1872 he accompanied Secretary of State James P.
Newcomb to New York where he had gone to sell bonds. While they
were in New York, Frank L. Britton, acting adjutant general, discovered that there were serious shortages in Davidson's accounts.
"Dame Rumor," according to the *Statesman*,

> had much to whisper in regard to him and his absence.
> The idea prevails that he will not return to Texas, and
> there are some broad hints, which we will not give pub-
> licity to yet, about the shortcomings of his office. Gen.
> Davidson was one of the tools of the Davis administra-
> tion, and when the veil is drawn from its hidden
> scenes, a tale will, we doubt not, be unfolded which,
> though not startling to the public, will be a copious
> record of crime.[53]

Davidson had drawn warrants on the treasury for payment of
State Police officers, which the comptroller had allowed without
requiring vouchers showing legal services to be filed, and had pock-
eted the funds. The state immediately ceased payment on the warrants and seized Davidson's property. It was ultimately determined
that Davidson was responsible for a loss of $37,434.67. Governor
Davis offered a reward of $1,000 for his former adjutant general.[54]

Rather than depending on New York authorities, Governor
Davis ordered Captain McNelly to take up the pursuit, and by late
December McNelly was in New York. Here again McNelly apparently failed to make any report of what he did, but a few documents
have survived. A letter dated December 24 from Governor Davis to
S.M. Swanson of No. 80 Wall Street, relates that "Brevet Capt. L.H.
McNelly of the State Police" had been sent to New York "about a
matter of considerable importance to the administration of the criminal laws of Texas." Due to the possibility of McNelly's requiring
more funds than he had taken with him, Governor Davis was asking Swanson to allow him money up to the amount of $500 "or so
much of that sum as he may require."[55]

Few other details have surfaced concerning the matter. On
December 26 Britton informed his boss that a "considerable
amount" in state warrants, drawn for disbursements through his

office in payment of State Police, issued by Davidson since July 1872, had "been disposed of without warrant of law." Britton felt obligated to request that no warrants issued for police pay be paid unless presented by the policemen to whom they were issued.[56]

The *Galveston Daily News* readily suggested that things were not right, stating the "intimations are pretty strong against General Davidson."[57] Closer to home, the *Statesman* reported with deep irony that it was "pretty well understood that James Davidson . . . is largely behind in his accounts" and that it was "highly improbable that the 'General' will ever voluntarily return to the scene of his late brilliant military operations."[58]

In New York McNelly stayed at the St. Nicholas Hotel; a letter from Frank Britton, written on January 20, 1873, was addressed to him there and referred to McNelly's telegram to Governor Davis received that very morning. Davis had followed by instructing McNelly, presumably by telegram, to send photographs of Davidson with description to various points in Canada, "where he would likely to be found, and not go yourself, as that will require too much time and expense." Britton pointed out that by writing to the different places at the same time, he would "disseminate the information" much more rapidly than going in person. Britton further noted that no more money could be advanced to McNelly, and that after sending the necessary information to the various points in Canada he should return home unless something definite was learned. Britton further noted that he had written yesterday at Governor Davis' direction "cautioning you against extravagance in money matters, and directing that you keep an itemized account of your expenses, else they could not be audited on your return." Britton concluded by saying that McNelly should inform the police of New York, Boston and other cities that the $1,000 reward had been increased to $3,000.[59]

During this December-January period McNelly did go to Canada, perhaps to investigate "something definite." The single known formal portrait of him was made by a Montreal photographer, James Inglis, who kept a studio at 51 Bleury Street, Montreal. Although some have dated this image as being made in 1875, it is just as likely that it was made when McNelly was in that area of the country in 1872-73 in pursuit of the Adjutant General of the State of Texas![60]

During the same period, on January 30, 1873, M.P. Hunnicutt, former State Police captain who had been dismissed for malfeasance in office, wrote to Governor Davis offering his sleuthing abilities to "hunt and capture" Davidson. Davis, wary of giving money for work not yet performed, assured Hunnicutt that if he should find and bring Davidson to Austin, presumably meaning within the doors of the Travis County jail, only then would the state pay him the $3,000 reward, "but I cannot advance anything."[61]

McNelly did report his actions to his superior in at least one report received by Britton on February 12; unfortunately only the report's summary is available. The prediction of the *Statesman* did prove to be true. Davidson never returned to Texas, and it was believed, probably based on evidence unearthed by McNelly in New York or Canada, that he had fled the United States to Belgium. W.D. Wood, a quarter of a century later, recorded his reminiscences of the Reconstruction days in Texas, and described how Davidson had "proved unfaithful to his trust" and did indeed flee to Belgium, "a country with which the United States had no extradition treaty, to save himself from the effect of his defalcation."[62]

While McNelly was scouring the eastern coast for his former superior officer, Carey McNelly was attempting to keep his finances secure at home. On January 10, 1873, newly appointed Adjutant General Britton received a request from her that money due the captain be sent to her at Burton. The following day Britton forwarded her $155, and on January 12 he sent $25 for McNelly's arrest of Peter Bostic, convicted of carrying a deadly weapon, and also for the arrest of Gus Affleck.[63]

CHAPTER 9

1873 - FOLLOWING THE STATE

POLICE EXPERIENCE

I think I am justified, from the information before me
in stating that to-day not less than one hundred men,
many of whom are charged with the highest crimes
known to our law, are prowling about the State in gangs
of twelve to twenty, murdering and robbing almost
without restraint. — Adjutant General Frank L. Britton
to Governor E.J. Davis, April 18, 1873, reporting on
"Conditions of the State."

The year 1873, the year the State Police force was terminated, was
one of those years in which very few of McNelly's activities were
recorded. Vague references are found but little concrete information
has been discovered. Part of February was taken up with settling
accounts from the trip to New York in pursuit of James Davidson; in
communications on February 12 and February 20 and again on
March 5, Adjutant General Britton ordered McNelly to report to
Austin for that purpose and for "other matters outstanding, con-
nected with your recent trip north."[1]

In late February the Brenham *Banner* informed its readers that
McNelly had been ordered to investigate and arrest parties in the
"late disturbance in Bastrop County."[2] The Bastrop County problems had been fired by rumor and appeared much greater than reality. The *Daily State Journal* of October 11, 1872, had printed a lengthy
article, based on information provided by a Mr. O.H.P. Cole,
described as a native Texan, forty-seven years of age and a resident of
Bastrop County for over twenty years, a "gentleman of wealth and
high standards," who related that there was a "formidable force . . .
of blood-thirsty desperadoes" who most recently had fired into the
Cole home, injuring several of the occupants. The gang was led by
the Cattinghams and G.W. Gray. Other notable exploits of the gang
included forcing W.C. Lanhon, Justice of the Peace of Precinct #4,
to stand on a stump and publicly acknowledge himself a "liar,

scoundrel, and villain generally" because he had earlier spoken ill of the gang. In addition several citizens had been murdered, one only a few days before, and no one had been allowed to perform an inquest or even bury the corpse. The *Journal* headlined its article "A Reign of Terror in Bastrop County" and "White Desperadoes Murdering Old Citizens — Men Fleeing to the Capital for Protection, from the Scene of Outrage."[3]

The *Journal* article was followed by a letter to the *Statesman*, printed in its issue of November 14 above the signatures of four of Bastrop's citizens: Sam Sheasby, Ben Duckworth, D.V. Spring and J.W. Allen, contradicting much of the earlier report. These four claimed the statements allegedly from O.H.P. Cole were "so far from the truth that we cannot bring ourselves to credit the editorial state-ment that Mr. Cole gave them as they appear in the Journal." The Bastrop citizens even suggested that the editor of the *Journal* himself created much if not all of the report, "to prepare the public mind for a declaration of martial law over Bastrop county." The writers felt that if Mr. Cole indeed was suffering from difficulties with his neigh-bors that was unfortunate, but it was necessary to speak out when hearing of "our neighborhood represented as terror stricken by an organized band of desperadoes and afraid to discharge the common duties of humanity." It was time to report the facts.

The "Cattinghams" and "G.W. Gray" were now identified as the Cottinghams and J.W. Gray, and as far as known they had never had any trouble with the law. Further, no one had heard of Justice Lawhorn's having to stand on a stump and declare anything. What was most irksome was the statement that several unoffending citi-zens had been murdered in the last few days; the only homicide com-mitted within the previous ten months was "the unfortunate killing of young Oscar Cottingham by young Richard Litton in Perryville, about 2 months since." This was not a cold-blooded murder but one arising from "sudden passion." In short, the letter writers declared, there was not "a particle of truth" in the *Journal*'s report. As for the dead man who was not allowed to be buried, there was the body of old Dr. Dorn whose body was discovered but on whose body no sign of violence had been found. The report was termed "all humbug," prepared purely for political purposes, possibly creating the atmos-phere necessary for Governor Davis to declare martial law in Bastrop county, or preventing immigrants from settling within its borders.[4]

But the reported difficulties were not entirely humbug, although few details have emerged from existing records. The *State Journal* in its issue of November 20, 1872, headlined an article "Desperadoism in Hog Eye" and told how a resident from that section had that morning informed them of the "very bad state of affairs" existing there in that section of Bastrop County. Bands of armed men were riding about and through the country, "threatening death and extermination to any State policeman they may come across." These "scoundrels" reportedly shot into the houses of the respectable peace-loving citizens. Concluded the *Journal*, in a near humorous tone, "We think that the new Adjutant General has now an excellent opportunity of putting a handsome feather in his hat by sending a competent force down to classic Hog Eye and arresting the outlaws, who are reported to be residents in and around the picturesque hominy associate." The new adjutant general was a nephew of Governor Davis' wife and had formerly served as an Austin city attorney. He began his adjutant general duties officially on November 15, 1872, and served until January 15, 1874. He failed to put "a handsome feather in his hat" on this occasion, or any other occasion.[5]

McNelly proved to be the "competent force" sent to Bastrop to investigate the "late disturbance," but he apparently determined rather quickly that there was no cause for alarm and returned to other duties. However, McNelly's interpretation of need followed his own definitions. Earlier that year, in January, William Cottingham had been killed by unidentified Mexicans and no one had yet been arrested for this crime. Although there are no details of exactly what he personally did there, McNelly ordered policemen T.C. Lusk, who had served with him on the Rio Grande expedition, and J.W.H. Harris to report, possibly to make sure that any minor problems did not become serious.

McNelly may have been too ill to do much because, in the same communication telling Britton he had sent the two policemen to Hog Eye, he requested to be excused from going to Jacksonville in Cherokee County due to illness in the family.[6] Although the Bastrop citizens claimed the Cottinghams had not been troublemakers, on April 10, not long after McNelly's "investigation" of affairs there, John Cottingham had a difficulty with a man identified only as Newton, in Bastrop, which resulted in Newton's being shot and killed.[7] Racial difficulties may have been part of the problems; Green Harris of Hog Eye later requested permission to carry weapons because he was "teaching a colored school in the district."[8] Hog Eye as a community did not long survive the problems of the 1870s. It had flourished from 1855 to 1872, according to ghost town historian Ed Bartholomew, but only a cemetery remains today to mark its brief existence.[9]

In late November McNelly took into the police force a young man who later would prove invaluable as a ranger serving on the Rio Grande Frontier. George A. Hall was selected as a private and swore his oath of office before McNelly. About November 24 McNelly forwarded the oath and a recommendation that Hall be issued a regular appointment as private in the State Police.[10] Hall then was a twenty-five year old man, son of A.C. and Anna Hall. Prior to the Civil War, A.C. Hall was one of the more successful farmers of Washington County, claiming $20,000 in real estate and $17,000 in personal estate. In 1860 he owned sixteen slaves.[11] McNelly had met George through family ties; his mother-in-law was sister to A.C. Hall.[12]

On March 14, four State Policemen were gunned down by Lampasas desperadoes, members of the Horrell clan. Complaints of lawlessness in Lampasas and the authorities' inability to control the situation resulted in Lieutenant Thomas Williams' being sent there to preserve order. Williams walked into a trap which resulted in his death and that of three of his men, J.M. Daniels, Wesley Cherry and Andrew Melville. It was the worst disaster to befall the police force diring its brief existence.[13]

Among the scant police correspondence concerning the catastrophe in Lampasas is a letter from William D. Shepherd who, writing from Austin on March 18, 1873, informed Adjutant General Frank Britton, then at Lampasas, of the incident. Shepherd noted that three policemen who were to report to Lampasas would not be able to; Peter Stein, Clabe Hankins and Jacob Ward had returned because their horses gave out. Policeman Ferdinand Marechal returned as well, no reason given. McNelly's men had not yet arrived as of that morning. Shepherd wrote that Lieutenant J.H. Adams' men had arrived on the train the night previous and were to start for Lampasas that morning with Lieutenant Madison Wear. He ended his note stating that when McNelly's men arrived he would send them on, presumably to Lampasas. He ended his note with a pleasant "Hoping you are meeting with abundant success."[14]

On March 24 Britton, still in Lampasas and accompanied by a dozen State Policemen, detailed Lieutenant Madison Wear and ten men of the force to be stationed there and deliver prisoners Jerry Scott, Martin Horrell, Allen Whitecraft and James Grizzell, the four Horrell gang members accused of the killings, to the Travis County jail in Austin for safe keeping until the next term of district court. Britton was apprehensive that friends of the prisoners would liberate them if they were kept in Lampasas.[15]

But McNelly never arrived in Lampasas County; he was needed elsewhere. On March 10 while at Burton he received orders to report to Austin with seven or eight men "without delay."[16] Three days later Britton wrote another letter, addressed to him at Burton, to send a detachment of police to Milam to arrest the murderers of one J.D. Kitching. This was an old murder which had occurred in September 1869; there was obviously a delay in the indictment of the men accused of the killing. Britton enclosed a description of the wanted men.[17] Two days later Britton again wrote to McNelly, still addressed to him at Burton, suggesting he had not left "without delay" as the March 10 communication had ordered, and now was ordering McNelly to Bastrop because four prisoners had escaped from the jail on March 7 and Sheriff John A. Kohler needed assistance in recapturing the quartet.[18]

Three days later yet another communication came from the adjutant general's office, still addressed to McNelly at Burton, which must have amused McNelly because now the important news from the capitol was that someone had stolen the governor's horse! It was described as sixteen hands high, a light bay with white face and seven years old. A $25 reward was offered, and suspicions rested on a Mexican as being the thief.[19] No further information was provided. Perhaps Britton suspected that McNelly would recognize Governor Davis' horse!

Certainly the recovery of the governor's horse was not a high priority, at least in McNelly's mind. He had just received additional orders to report to Navasota and report to the mayor, Allen D. Harn, for duty during the municipal election.[20]

Apparently the five communications from Britton to McNelly at Burton did not bring about the desired response; on March 31 another terse order arrived to "Report in person at this office immediately."[21] Possibly the order had to do with his "inaction," or possibly it had to do with payments for his service to the state. On April 4 McNelly received payment of $150 for services rendered from March 15 to March 31, 1873.[22]

Further orders came on April 17 when he was ordered to report to Waco with one private, to execute his orders and then return to Burton. No further explanation was provided.[23] The state of Texas was indebted to McNelly for $75.67 for services from April 1-22, 1873.[24]

Another tantalizing document shows that at one point McNelly was appointed a deputy United States Marshal in 1873! No records seem to have survived except the name of L.N. McNelly [sic] on

Emolument Returns for the State of Texas.[25] Only one incident of McNelly's acting as a deputy U.S. Marshal is known; in April he traveled to Hill County to arrest two postal officials for stealing from the United States mail. The details are sparse but McNelly, acting in his capacity of deputy marshal, arrested ex-postmaster Booth and ex-deputy postmaster Doss from Hill County. McNelly returned to Austin with his prisoners on April 30 and placed Doss in the Travis County jail and turned Booth over to a United States Marshal. Booth stood trial on the charge of extracting money from registered letters while acting as postmaster, but neither the verdict nor the fate of Doss is known.[26]

McNelly was certainly shrewd enough to know that the legislation authorizing the State Police was soon to be repealed, and with the disbanding of the force he would be unemployed. McNelly possibly considered working for the Austin newspaper, the *Daily Democratic Statesman,* because a notice appeared in late 1872 listing him as a traveling agent who could take subscriptions and receive payment for any sums due. The notice could possibly have been a serious consideration on McNelly's part to become a traveling salesman, but it also might have been a cover for McNelly while acting as a detective.[27] At any rate McNelly must have welcomed the end of his police duties as he now had the opportunity to return to his family and agricultural interests near Burton. He was less than thirty years old, had served four years in the Confederate Army and then served his state almost three years as captain of the State Police, a position he had not sought but had accepted upon the advice of people whom he respected.

Frank L. Britton, Davidson's replacement, in preparing his annual report for the year of 1873, reported that as of the year's beginning there were four captains, eight lieutenants, fifteen sergeants and 156 privates. He perhaps felt some pride in writing that the force had continued to perform its duty until the date of the police legislation's repeal, April 22. During the first four months of the year the State Police had made 403 arrests for crimes ranging from murder (twenty-seven cases), attempts to kill (twenty-five cases), rape, swindling, theft and "Miscellaneous offenses." Of the sixteen different categories, the most frequent was disturbing the peace (sixty-seven cases).

Although Governor Davis had certainly intended to have only the highest quality of men serving in the State Police, thirty-five policemen had been discharged for neglect of duty. In addition numerous policemen had been killed or wounded; most recently the four killed in Lampasas. Although Williams had acted with bad judgment in attempting to arrest the Horrells on their own ground, Britton nevertheless noted that these "men died bravely while attempting to execute the laws."[28]

Even though the State Police law was expected to be repealed, some members of the press still championed its cause. James P. Newcomb, proprietor of Austin's *Daily State Journal*, in concluding a lengthy report on lawlessness in Kerr County, editorialized, "To-day hundreds of murderers, thieves and rogues, who, before the passage of the police law claimed Texas as their own, sit upon the borders of Mexico and the territories patiently awaiting the repeal of this law so that they can return to their old haunts and ply their fiendish avocations."[29]

Newcomb prepared for publication a lengthy article in which he attempted to persuade the legislature to continue its support of the State Police by enumerating how lawlessness had caused the death and wounding of many policemen. It was headlined "The Roll of Honor - State Police Who Have Fallen in the Line of Duty." The list identified a dozen policemen who had been killed between January 22, 1871, and March 11, 1873. Newcomb called for members of the legislature, who in opposing the police law "became the champions of the murderer and thief," to take note of the roll of honor. When the State Police was organized statistics showed that there were seven-hundred murderers in the state and several thousand other criminals. Many of them were in organized bands and "defied the officers of the law, and rode rough-shod over the community." Newcomb reminded his readers that when the police force was being organized, "the desperadoes whet[t]ed their knives and cleaned up their pistols for the encounter. A desperate struggle arose between the officers of the law and the violators of the law," but the law was triumphant. Proud of the policemen who had died in the line of duty and of those who had been wounded in enforcing Texas law, Newcomb proposed that above the grave of Thomas Williams "a monument should be erected inscribed with the names of all who have thus died."[30] No monument was ever erected over Williams' grave, but it was marked with a small stone in the State Cemetery in Austin. Only a few feet away stands the huge monument erected to the memory of Governor E.J. Davis.

In response to Newcomb's article, Austin's *Daily Democratic Statesman* printed a letter from Davis M. Prendergast which questioned whether all of those named did indeed fall "in the line of duty." He reminded his readers that every question has two sides and stressed that the policemen had "been a constant source of irritation wherever they have been" not to mention "the many minor offenses of which they have been guilty." Prendergast pointed out that it was "well known" that they had "brutally murdered quite a number of the quiet and peaceable citizens of the State" and listed seventeen men from nearly as many counties who "have been murdered." He concluded his "roll of horror" by stating that the "list might be greatly extended with but little trouble."[31]

Governor Davis vetoed the bill repealing the law which had established the State Police, but on April 22 his veto was overruled fifty-eight to eighteen in the House and eighteen to seven in the Senate. Reported the *Statesman*, "And so the obnoxious Police Law stands repealed in spite of the obstinate opposition of the Governor. Republican aid was necessary to procure its repeal, and three Senators, who had the manhood to throw off party allegiance in this matter, will receive the grateful acknowledgment of the intelligent public of Texas."[32]

Although we have no indication of how McNelly himself felt about the repeal — and the elimination of his position as captain — nor how the public in his area reacted to it, Lieutenant John M. Redmon did write a letter to General Britton expressing how the news was received in Denton County. Although Redmon had learned from various reports that the law had been repealed, nevertheless, in his May 1 report written at Denton, he described both his continued fruitless efforts to capture Hardin and his gang and the public's reaction to the repeal.

> I reached Denton on the 29th Inst where I find *greate* rejoiceing [sic] over the repeal of the Police Law, by the Ku Klucks, murder[er]s & thieves. When the news was received here the people of this place fired Anvils from 2 oclock in the evening till 3 or 4 oclock. I am told by Sergt. [G.W.] Davis that the citizens of this place threaten to mob Capt [A.C.] Hill on his return from Austin, though while I fully believe they (Some of them) have it in their hearts to do so I think they will be afraid to do it. Yet I do believe there is men in this County if they had the power and it would not be found out on them [they] would murder ev[e]ry Republican in it, but thank God they are afraid to do the crime they So much desire."[33]

Thus, in spite of such communications as the letter from Prendergast, which seemingly condemned the entire police force as a unit, there were obviously policemen such as Redmon who were conscientious and willing to perform their duty, even after the police bill was repealed.

No doubt many feared that with the end of the State Police there would be an increase in lawlessness and crime; others felt that it had not come too soon. Editor A.B. Norton reported his joy in the *Union Intelligencer*, albeit with a mixed metaphor, "The People of the State of Texas are today delivered of as infernal an engine of oppression as ever crushed any people beneath the heel of God's sunlight. The damnable Police Bill is ground beneath the heel of an indignant Legislature." John Henry Brown telegraphed from Austin, "The Police Law is abolished over the Governor's veto. 'Glory to God in the highest, and on earth, peace, good will towards men.'"[34] Editor D. McCaleb of the *Dallas Weekly Herald* headlined his editorial "Glad Tidings." He stressed that the "solicitous and anxious constituents of a well chosen Legislature have great cause to rejoice," and triumphed "that the roar of Edmund I. [E.J. Davis] has been hushed, and the loud voice of the friends of the plundered and oppressed tax-payers strikes terror to the foul hearts of his police pets, and proclaims their doom above the trembling whine of their keeper."[35]

James W. Cox, one time state policeman at Clinton, and
ambush victim of John Wesley Hardin in 1873.
Courtesy Ed P. Cox and Dr. C.L. Sonnichsen.

CHAPTER 10

AN INTERLUDE FOR MCNELLY

Had not the State Police fallen into the hands of bad
men, it would to-day have been a popular and useful
institution. — San Antonio *Daily Express*, June 9, 1873.

Although there is virtually no documentation of McNelly's activities following the end of the State Police, it is probable that he spent some time in Austin finishing up the paper work and reports required of his rank of captain. He must have been very anxious to return to Washington County, his wife and two children, and his farming interests. He was responsible for some 880 acres of taxable land; in 1872 and 1873 the land had a value of $7,000.[1] The family had been without him frequently during his trips to various counties in the eastern portion of the state as well as during the expedition to the Rio Grande. There must have been deep concern about his safety during the potentially violent situations which might have exploded during the railroad strike, while scouting on the Rio Grande, and while chasing outlaws and malefactors of all types. The family certainly knew of his confrontation with Charles Hine, in which the fugitive was killed. Furthermore, his health had never been robust.

Assuming the above scenario is accurate he could not have totally ignored what was happening elsewhere. Although he could not anticipate being called back into service for the state, he certainly was aware of such problem areas as the conflict in DeWitt County between the Sutton and Taylor forces; their deadly confrontations were gaining greater and greater recognition. Furthermore he certainly could not have been unaware of the continued and growing problems of cattle rustling on the Rio Grande. He had met some of the ranchers who had lost livestock to raiders while there in 1872, and such ranchers as Richard King and Levi English may have continued to express their concerns to McNelly directly, as well as to the governor's office.

While McNelly was resting in Washington County, many of the violent acts which were occurring in DeWitt County involved former state policemen and would ultimately draw McNelly back into service. If McNelly read the Austin *Statesman* he learned that in late

July 1873 two men identified only as Cox and Chrisman had been ambushed and killed.[2] Although the report did not identify them with more than their surnames, the unfortunate two were James W. Cox and John W.S. "Jake" Christman. Reportedly the pair were killed between Helena and Yorktown, DeWitt County, while returning from court in Helena, then county seat of neighboring Karnes County. There were others in the group including "Captain Joe" Tumlinson, a man identified as H. Ragland, a William Wells, and possibly others. The *Statesman* reported they had been waylaid by a party of sixteen men, but no members of the ambushing party were identified by name. Tumlinson and Ragland were in the rear when the shooting started, thus it was only by chance that they escaped with their lives. Victor M. Rose, who authored the first serious study of the Sutton-Taylor Feud, quoted an article from the Victoria *Advocate* which reported that Cox's body was found to have nineteen buckshot and his throat cut "from ear to ear." The report pointed out that Cox had worked with Jack Helm in his "Regulator depredations, and no doubt he was killed to avenge some injury inflicted then." Christman was not nearly as well known and the *Advocate*, identifying him as Cresman, reported him as "a stranger in this section, and not a party to the feud."[3] Jake Christman may not have participated in any battles of the feud but he was certainly a close associate of Cox, who had been a witness to Christman's marriage in August 1867.[4] Cox and Tumlinson had both served with the State Police stationed at Clinton, DeWitt County. Cox had been a private in the force, having taken his oath on July 13, 1870.[5] Among other actions of Joe Tumlinson to earn the enmity of the Taylors, in the summer of 1871 he had arrested one of their close associates, George Culver Tennille, charged with horse theft.[6]

John Wesley Hardin never claimed participation in the Cox-Christman killing, but he did note in his autobiography that he had "at this time little to say except that Jim Cox and Jake Chrisman [sic] met their deaths from the Taylor party about the 15th of May, 1873."[7] Although he was wrong on the date, he certainly had a hand in planning the ambush even if he wasn't there physically.

The same issue of the *Statesman* reported the death of Jack Helm. Word had come to Austin via a private letter identifying his slayer as "another desperate character of the name of Harden [sic]."[8] Hardin *did* claim responsibility for this killing, although he credited Jim Taylor as being there and participating. Of interest is that Hardin recalled using a shotgun to dispatch Helm; he had also used a shotgun to dispatch Jim Cox.

Certainly the increased violence of DeWitt County could not have escaped McNelly's notice, even if he was tending to his other interests in Washington County. James W. Cox and Joseph Tumlinson both had been members of the State Police. John Marshall Jackson "Jack" Helm had been one of the first four captains. Other State Police members who had been active in the area and who had been involved in bloody encounters with fighting adherents of the Hardin-Taylor faction included A.C. "Doc" White, John Meador, C.C. Simmons and William Sutton himself.

William E. Sutton and wife. His followers waged war for years with the Taylor family, bringing McNelly and his company to DeWitt County in 1874.
Courtesy Cynthia Salm.

Close friends or relatives of the Taylors had been killed by members of the police force, most notably the Kelly boys, their lives taken by a posse after being placed under arrest. Witnesses claimed that William Sutton shot William Kelly, while Doc White shot his brother Henry P. Kelly. C.C. Simmons and John Meador were the other two members of the posse. Brothers Eugene and Wiley Kelly were also arrested but for some reason were not killed. The notation made in the *Report of Arrests* indicated the Kelly brothers were "Killed in attempt to escape — by guard charge of C.C. Simmons." The two surviving brothers were turned over to the Lavaca County sheriff, charged with "Disturbing performance of Smith Circus at Sweet Home." Eugene and Wiley Kelly were acquitted of the charges brought against them.[9]

Much of the violence in this period involved former police members. Following the Kelly murders Pitkin B. Taylor, attempting to prosecute the Sutton posse members, was lured from his house and ambushed, allegedly by Sutton. His son James Creed Taylor then became the titular head of the Taylor clan. A squad in command of

A youthful James C. Taylor, killed
along with ex-McNelly Ranger A.R.
Hendricks and Mason Arnold.
*Courtesy the University of Southwest
Texas at San Marcos.*

William R. Taylor, nephew of John
Milam Taylor, who was never punished
for the killing of Gabriel Slaughter in
1874. *Courtesy the Eddie Day Truitt
Collection.*

Policeman Charles S. Bell killed Hays Taylor, and Sutton himself was
responsible for the death of Buck Taylor as well as Charles Taylor, who
may or may not have been related to the DeWitt County Taylor family.
The series of killings and murdering prisoners who allegedly were trying to escape brought a great amount of negative publicity to the
DeWitt County area, but it was the double killing of Sutton and his
friend Gabriel Webster Slaughter which brought statewide attention to
the feud. The killers were William Riley Taylor and his cousin James
Creed Taylor, two young men who had learned Sutton and Slaughter
intended to leave Texas for Kansas via steamer and were ready to depart
from Indianola on March 11, 1874. Exactly how the Taylors learned of
this is not known, but it involved members of the Taylor-Hardin gang.
Their efforts to locate Sutton paid off for the Taylor purposes; when
Sutton and his wife, who was pregnant at the time, and Slaughter
arrived at the Indianola dock, the two Taylors were waiting. The deck
of the steamer *Clinton* became the battleground, although only the
Taylors fired their weapons. Jim Taylor claimed the right of first shots
at Sutton because he believed Sutton had killed his father. Bill Taylor

killed Slaughter, who had only a very limited involvement in the feud.[10]

Richard Coke, having defeated Governor Davis by a two-to-one majority, took office in January 1874. The Sutton-Slaughter killing was another act which would facilitate his decision to send a force to DeWitt County; the newspapers gave much greater coverage to the feud after the double killing. Because Sutton had an uncle living in Dallas, the news of the killing was reported as far north as that metropolitan area. Sutton, explained the Dallas *Daily Commercial* of March 13, had sent four-thousand head of cattle to Kansas, but apparently had chosen to travel with his wife over a totally different route, possibly going up the Mississippi River and then overland to the Kansas markets.[11]

Although the principal leader of one of the two warring factions was dead, the feuding continued. Less than a month later a petition was prepared and delivered to the *Galveston Daily News* as "the most powerful advocate" obtainable. "Many Citizens" signed the petition, which described the situation.

> The country is infested with a band of very bad people; they are so extensive as to render life and property insecure. Legitimate business is almost suspended entirely, even in this city [Cuero], on account of it. These outlaws do not hesitate to take the life of any citizen who favors law and order, when an opportunity to assassinate presents itself. . . . A continuance of the present state of affairs is disgraceful to the State, as well as ruinous to business.

The "Many Citizens" suggested as a remedy "for this evil" that a company of United States Troops be stationed "without delay, to aid the Sheriff in the execution of the laws, and to preserve order."[12]

The petition was published elsewhere; the San Antonio *Daily Express* added an editorial note requesting Governor Coke to take notice of the appeal to help preserve the lives of peaceable citizens. The *Express* reminded its readers that if the unpopular State Police force had not been abolished, then perhaps many peaceable citizens would not have lost their lives.[13]

Governor Davis and his police never had gained popular support, but in some quarters his failure was preferable to what was happening under Governor Coke. Commented the *Express*:

> Lawlessness, violence, and murder hold high carnival in Texas. Murder and lynch law prevail in many

counties in the State. Things are worse now than when Governor Davis had to crush public disorder by the State Police and martial law. Had not the State Police fallen into the hands of bad men, it would to-day have been a popular and useful institution. But it seemed to be the fate of the late administration to employ worth-less or villainous men to execute good measures. Instead of 150 State Police, we now have 500 State troops, to do virtually the same duty at five times the expense to the State.

Coke was accused of doing his utmost to "denounce, defame, belie, and bring odium upon what he knew to be the honest efforts of Davis to preserve order; now the avenging Nemesis is rewarding him as he deserves. His administration this day has not the respect that Davis, had, party prejudice aside."[14]

Violence continued to increase in DeWitt County. By mid-1874 some felt such an aversion towards the sheriff and local officials that mob law was becoming excusable. Some hoped the sheriff, William J. Weisiger, would resign, explaining he "has had his pockets full of writs for the past three months, and had he executed them, the state of things which now exist in DeWitt county would not be heard of." This was the voice of one signing himself simply "DeWitt." He complained that the officers had failed to execute the laws and there was but one thing left to do, "the suppression of crime by the most speedy means." Although the remedy was severe, the facts of the case "fully warranted the sum-mary proceedings resorted to. . . ," i.e., the lynching of wanted men.[15]

By late June a group of seven prisoners had been escorted to the jail in Clinton, delivered there by Texas Ranger Captain John R. Waller who left them in the hands of the sheriff. They and the others had been rounded up in Brown and Comanche counties after Hardin killed Brown County deputy sheriff Charles M. Webb. Three of them, Rufus P. "Scrap" Taylor, John Alfred "Kute" Tuggle and James White, were taken out and lynched. Correspondent DeWitt described these three as "notorious criminals," identifying White as the leader and claiming he was "a bad man — a refugee from justice from Mississippi." Further, the "hands of two of them, at least, had been stained by the blood of inno-cent men, and theft had been their occupation for the past year."[16] It is unfortunate that correspondent DeWitt did not amplify his claims; other feud historians have maintained that Taylor, with no specific crimes laid to his door, was lynched because his name was Taylor.

Tuggle and White have been designated as having the misfortune of working as cowboys for John Wesley Hardin and were simply in the wrong place at the wrong time.

Whereas the killing of Sutton and Slaughter in March had brought statewide attention to the feud, this triple lynching brought additional pressure to bear on the state authorities to do *something*. Governor Richard Coke realized he was ultimately responsible and had to quell the disturbances in DeWitt County. With the six companies of the Frontier Battalion spread thin from the Red River to the Rio Grande, hunting Indians as well as all types of lawbreakers, Coke knew he had few options. McNelly would be called again into the service of the state.

While the violence was increasing in the DeWitt County area, lawlessness seemed to be on the increase on the Rio Grande Frontier as well. Washington had sent a committee to study the troubles on the border between Mexico and the United States. By mid-1873 the Mexican Border Commissioner's report had been made available and showed to national authorities what every Texan knew or at least believed: a fortune was being driven across the border, either by Mexican thieves or renegade Indians. The report showed that over a thousand petitions had been received, representing an aggregate claim of loss in the amount of $27,859,363. Over three-thousand petitions supported these claims; in addition to the amount of actual stock stolen, there was also the amount of natural increase, termed "consequential loss." Besides the stolen livestock, there was the human loss; the commissioners found it impossible to estimate the number of the killed, wounded, and kidnapped. Further, the commissioners stated that "the Mexican raids cannot be entirely stopped by the United States or the regiment of Texan volunteers, unless Mexico determines to destroy the banditti."[17] Readers of such reports probably smiled in derision, knowing there was little chance of that happening.[18]

View of Congress Avenue, Austin, Texas in the early 1870s. At left is Bullock's Hotel with outside stairway and flag pole. It was at this corner of Congress and Pecan (today 6th) that young men of Austin wanting to join McNelly met to leave together for Burton in July 1874. *Courtesy The Austin History Center, Austin Public Library.*

CHAPTER 11

MCNELLY AND THE SUTTON–TAYLOR FEUD

[The] reign of lawlessness and terrorism at Cuero continues unabated, and desperodism [*sic*] rules the county, trampling law and order under foot. – J.G. Rankin, Editor and Proprietor, The Brenham Banner, April 16, 1874.

It was but a short time before the announcement came of the formation of various companies to protect peaceable citizens. Besides the six companies of the Frontier Battalion, the legislative bill authorized the governor to organize, where there might be needed, county companies to suppress lawlessness and invasion. It was not until July that a company would be organized in Washington County, whose stated objective was "to assist the civil officers of DeWitt county in enforcing quiet and obedience to law in that desperado ridden section." Commented the Austin *Statesman*, "This is a move in the right direction."[1]

As the month ended the *Statesman* could report that a group of Austin's young men had left for Burton the night of July 24 to report to McNelly. They were C.B. Cook, C.C. Carrington, H.G. Rector, Horace Mabin, J.W. Thompson, O.G. Balemon, A.C. Tumey, E.A. Northington, and T.C. Robinson, generally known in Austin as "T. Chanders" who had developed a reputation for his ability to write interesting and humorous letters which were published in the *Statesman* under the pen name of "Pidge." Pidge was a twenty-six-year-old Virginia native who had a greater than average knowledge of literature and human nature. More importantly, he was talented with a pen; his letters written about ranger life are a joy to read. He began as a private identified on the muster rolls as "T. Chanders" but quickly rose to the rank of lieutenant and was utilized by McNelly to handle the paper work until he took leave to return to his home state of Virginia to fight a duel. Pidge provided a valuable commentary on the work of McNelly's State Troops while

This tintype was among the papers of William C. Callicott given to Dr. W.P. Webb. Although they are not identified the ranger at the left is possibly T.C. "Pidge" Robinson who served as McNelly's 2nd lieutenant in 1875-76. *Courtesy The W.P. Webb Collection, University of Texas, Austin.*

in DeWitt County and later on the Rio Grande Frontier.[2]

The *Statesman*, knowing that its one-time type-setter Pidge now had joined up with McNelly, commented,

> Captain McNally [*sic*] ought to hurry up his company if he has not already gone, and take position in DeWitt county with the sheriff, so as to be ready to turn the tide of battle in favor of law and order. Some effectual disposition ought to be made of the factions who now keep the good people of that country in constant dread, and retard the suppression of crime and the enforcement of the laws. Can it be possible that there are not enough good men in that section to put them down and restore order? We sincerely hope that the present state of affairs may not long continue, and that before long we can announce that both parties have made a final end of the matter.[3]

A notice appeared in the *Statesman* which reflected the warlike atmosphere, possibly submitted by Pidge himself. "FOR THE SEAT OF WAR.– The members of Captain McNally's [sic] company now in the city intend leaving for DeWitt county immediately upon the receipt of orders from the Captain, which are expected daily."[4]

By the 4th of July editor Rudolph Kleberg of the Cuero *Weekly Star*, knowing that McNelly would soon be there, expressed some confidence that the presence of troops would "prejudice no good man, and will nerve the officers of the law to arrest notorious outlaws and bring them to justice, give the good citizens of this county a nucleus of justice, around which they may rally, and law

Adjutant General William Steele whose investigation resulted in McNelly and his troop being sent to DeWitt County and later to the Nueces Strip.
Courtesy The Library of Congress.

and order will soon be restored."[5] Things were indeed looking optimistic with the anticipation of McNelly's arrival.

Even with the organization of McNelly's Washington County Volunteer Militia Company "A," violence increased in DeWitt County. The Austin men were aware of the mob action resulting in the lynching of three prisoners only weeks earlier. Editor Kleberg reported how the three were taken near the Clinton cemetery to be killed, their corpses left hanging until the next morning when relatives took them down for burial. Commented the Cuero *Weekly Star*, "while public opinion condemns the manner of their execution, it does not deplore their fate."[6]

The executive office received official notice of the triple lynching and almost immediately the order was given to Adjutant General Steele "to repair to Clinton and to report whether he would be justified in calling out the militia to preserve the peace and to arrest lawbreakers. The Sheriff, it is thought, will resign unless aid is furnished him by the State Government. His force is utterly inadequate to the emergency."[7] Sheriff William J. Weisiger did receive severe criticism; correspondent DeWitt claimed that the problems which now drew the attention of the governor would not even exist if he had acted on the writs. DeWitt believed the sheriff should be replaced, even though the victims of the lynch mob were "notorious criminals" and the lynch mob was not composed of DeWitt County citizens.[8] Governor Coke issued the order to Steele to examine the situation which allowed the feuding to continue.

Adjutant General William Steele arrived in Cuero by stage on Thursday, July 2. He was to investigate thoroughly the conditions of affairs then existing in DeWitt County. In order to get a true expression of public opinion he interviewed citizens of Cuero and Clinton and other parts of the county, also citizens in Victoria in Victoria County and Indianola, in Calhoun County, where the killing of Sutton and Slaughter had occurred four months earlier. The Cuero *Star* praised Steele as having "made a favorable impression so far, and it is generally presumed that he will pursue a judicious and effectual course in the premises."[9] DeWitt County was beginning to assume that a company of State Troops would be stationed there to establish peace and assist the local authorities in preserving order.

By July 10 Steele was back in Austin and reported unfavorably on the condition of affairs in DeWitt County to Governor Coke. Steele's written report has survived and is most revealing. Among other important statements is that, in his opinion from talking with people who had witnessed many acts of the feud and who were acquainted with many of the participants, the cause of the feud could be traced back to State Police Captain Jack Helm! Steele reported that the "*present state of violence had its origin in the operations of Jack Helm, a sheriff appointed by Gen'l. J.J. Reynolds, and afterward made Capt. of State Police under Gov. Davis.* [emphasis added]" Steele explained that it was only necessary for a man to be pointed out as a cattle thief or a "bad man" and he would be arrested and started off to Helena, then the county seat of neighboring Karnes County, "for trial by Court Martial; but the greater portion of those who started for Helena never reached that point but were reported as escaped, though never heard of since." [10]

Steele related the case of the Kelly boys, killed by their guard on the way to Lavaca County, one member of the guard's being William Sutton. Sutton and the others were tried and acquitted because the jurors were afraid to bring about any other verdict. Pitkin Taylor, whose daughter had married one of the Kelly boys, was murdered not long after because he had employed counsel to prosecute Sutton and the others. In an effort to quell the murderous acts within the

THE PRESENT GOVERNOR AND PUBLIC OFFICERS OF TEXAS.

Texas officials during McNelly's service as a Texas Ranger. Prominently displayed are the portraits of Governor Richard Coke and his successor Richard B. Hubbard. *Courtesy The Texas State Archives & Archives Commission.*

county, citizens managed to have the parties sign a treaty of peace. This agreement was kept until the double killing of Sutton and Slaughter. Further, Steele continued, the citizens of the towns along the railroad were "much in favor of the Sutton party, as I suppose from the fact as stated to me that their conduct had genuinely been orderly during their visits to towns, whilst the Taylor party was given to drunkenness and riotous behavior; shooting pistols & threatening policemen & in one case, shooting one." This was a reference to the killing in Cuero of J.B. Morgan by Hardin who was still enjoying his freedom.[11] Steele's conclusion was that,

> nothing short of an armed force from Some other local-
> ity & having no interest in the feuds or quarrels of that
> county, and of sufficient strength (not less than 50) to
> ensure the safety of prisoners against mob violence and
> to aid in making arrests, will put a stop to the existing
> state of violence in DeWitt County. At present the
> courts are powerless against these armed & organized
> parties. Indeed so great is the fear of assassination that
> was stated to me, that no information on which to base
> an indictment could be found in the case of a murder
> to which there was not less than forty witnesses.[12]

Between Steele's return to Austin and the end of the month L.H. McNelly was busy recruiting men for the company. There were men already reporting to Burton to join up as early as late June. McNelly must have had some type of verbal orders to begin recruit-ing, because the written order was not dated until July 14. He received the appointment as captain and was to "immediately pro-ceed to organize his Company with a strength of fifty non-commis-sioned offficer]s and privates." As soon as organized he was to muster into the service the men for a period of six months, unless sooner discharged. After muster he and the company were to pro-ceed to Clinton and report to the sheriff, to "aid him in the enforce-ment of the law and to Act in all Cases in strict Subordination to the civil authorities."[13] McNelly had definite and clear-cut orders to fol-low during his assignment in DeWitt County. The essential points were: (1) that he would act at all times in "strict subordination" to the sheriff and civil authorities. He should be accompanied by the sheriff or some other peace officer and have a legal warrant or capias from the proper authority; (2) in making arrests McNelly was to take care not to transgress the limits of the law. "The reckless taking of human life must be avoided. Homicide by an officer in the execution of the lawful orders of the magistrate and courts is justifiable only when the officer is violently resisted, and has just ground to fear danger to his own life in executing the order." Force should be used only when a prisoner attempted to escape or when the life of the officer was endangered; (3) the commanding officer and his men had to remember that "the purpose and object of their mission, is to preserve the public peace and tranquillity in that Section of Country to which they are ordered." McNelly was reminded that "the most rigid discipline" should be maintained.[14]

These specific orders from Adjutant General Steele and the governor certainly were to counteract the harm done by such men as Jack Helm whose reputation for killing prisoners in their custody had brought about such censure for the state police.

On July 18, with McNelly still at Burton, Steele telegraphed an order to hurry up, that his presence was "needed now in DeWitt County." He was to organize his company at the "earliest possible moment" and proceed directly to DeWitt County. He was authorized to draw $250 to defray expenses in organizing and conducting the company there.[15]

John Wesley Hardin, while a fugitive from Texas lawmen in 1875, who in the mid-1890s recalled the effectiveness of McNelly as a State Policeman. *Courtesy The Robert G. McCubbin Collection.*

Four days later, rumors having reached the ear of the governor, Steele telegraphed to McNelly that Governor Coke had been informed that he was enlisting "Some boys" in the company! If this was the case he was to discharge all who were not of age. "It is desirable that you should have discreet men; boys are too likely to be unduly excited for the duty you will have."[16] Two days later Steele gave the order to Captain J.H. Wells of Austin to issue to McNelly fifty Sharps carbines, fifty cartridge belts, waist belts, slings, swivels and three-thousand rounds of carbine ammunition.[17]

On August 1 McNelly and his forty-member troop arrived in DeWitt County and made camp close to Clinton on the banks of the Guadalupe River. He dutifully reported his arrival to Sheriff William J. Weisiger, the successor of Jack Helm. McNelly wrote to Steele that he could increase the number to fifty men "at any time" if necessary. "The citizens," he wrote, "seem to be very much pleased with our presence & I will see that they are satisfied with our conduct while here." McNelly was concerned, however, that his men had no pistol ammunition and they would soon be out of money. With cash the company could purchase necessities 30 percent cheaper than with warrants or on time. McNelly requested a month's payment for his men.[18]

During that first month of McNelly's stay in DeWitt County, he sent out scouting parties "in pursuit of notorious criminals" and made the county jail more secure by establishing "sentinels whose duty consisted in preventing a repetition of the effects of mob law" such as the lynching of three of the Taylor party in June, "under the eyes of the guardians of the public peace." Several arrests had been made and the prisoners delivered to the county jail or delivered to officers from other counties; long and arduous scouts had been made but often without any tangible result. However, McNelly was showing to all his "utmost willingness to suppress disorder wherever it might exist." He could boast of having successfully prevented several "commencements of the old vendetta . . . without bloodshed." Any show of favoritism to either party had been "studiously avoided," and his strict orders to his men to avoid giving cause of offense to members of either party whatsoever had been observed. Even the most vindictive of the Sutton party tolerated the presence of McNelly and his men. They would have attacked the ranger force "but for fear of immediate consequences."[19]

Victor M. Rose, Civil War veteran, historian and recently coeditor and publisher of the influential Victoria *Advocate*, compared the feuding factions to the wars in the days when knighthood was in flower. Of McNelly's arrival in DeWitt he wrote, "In conformity to the provisions of the law, Captain McNally [sic], formerly a policeman under the Davis regime, organized a company of soldiers, and repaired to the distracted kingdom of DeWitt, where the houses of York and Lancaster were struggling for the supremacy."[20]

McNelly established a system of his men spying upon the "leading spirits" in the feud to gain a knowledge of their plans. He bragged that they could make "no plot of which I will be ignorant," and his scouting parties kept continually on the move prevented a gathering of the people for any unlawful purposes.[21] He had learned that John Wesley Hardin and Jim Taylor planned to be in the country and he resolved he would get them even if it meant killing all his horses running them down.[22] McNelly would later utilize an effective spy system while on the Rio Grande Frontier, one based on the system in use here, but more dangerous for the spies and with results far more dramatic.

John Wesley Hardin had a wide reputation by this time, even though the man killer was just turning twenty-one years of age. He had killed his first man as a teenager and continued killing former slaves, United States soldiers, State Policemen, and anyone else who displeased him. He added more victims while driving cattle up the trail in 1871 to Kansas. The Sutton-Taylor Feud was a situation clearly made for the expert gun handling abilities of a Hardin. Wrote Pidge,

> we received advices as to where we could find Wes. Hardin. This has cooled me down considerably, for I had heard of him before I ever came to Texas. He kills men just to see them kick, and on one occasion charged Cuero alone with a yell of "rats to your holes!" and such a shutting up of shops has not been seen since the panic! He can take two six-shooters and turn them like wheels in his hands and fire a shot from each at every revolution. There is a reward of eighteen hundred dollars for him, and it will be well earned when he is captured. He is said to have killed thirty men and is a dead shot.[23]

Although McNelly made no mention of sending his men after Hardin, Pidge wrote of a rumor that Hardin was in a certain settlement and a scout was attempting to arrest him, McNelly of course leading the squad rather than sending his men on such a dangerous mission. Wrote Pidge,

> About daylight we arrived at our destination, where Capt. McNelly divided the party, giving your correspondent one-half, with orders to surround a certain house, while he, with the other half, surrounded another. The two were situated about the distance of a

mile from each other, and Wes. Hardin was said to be in one or the other certain. It was the first time I ever made a call so early in the morning, and a long ride to pay a visit; but I would not have been offended in the least if he had not been at home — in fact, I believe I would have preferred his absence, for I did not wish to see him particularly . . . . We drew near the silent house; the ghostly looking moss, trailing from the trees, swept across my head, making me think of Wes. reaching for my scalp. We dismounted and cautiously approached the building . . . . Sending part of the men to the rear of the house, I advanced in front. I had orders to wait until nearly sunrise before making myself known, and to fire a gun if I saw Mr. Hardin, in which case the Captain could come down from the other station.[24]

But Hardin was not at either house, and Pidge made light of his being mobbed by a large number of barking dogs who resented their territory being invaded.

The leaders of the feuding parties "are men long accustomed to doing as they please regardless of consequences and have never experienced restraint upon their movements until now," wrote McNelly. To the law-abiding the presence of McNelly's men was of incalculable value.

The intimidation of the weak, by armed bodies of lawless men has ceased and a feeling of Security unknown until recently, prevails. Numbers of both factions would willingly witness a renewal of hostilities as peace leaves them out of employment. These have nothing to lose and everything to gain by a return to open warfare and will do all in their power to promote discord. A strict watch is Kept upon these characters and they are beginning to learn that they can no longer persist in their lawless course with impunity.[25]

Pidge, who began as a private, was advanced to sergeant and then was promoted to lieutenant, handled much of McNelly's paper work and wrote his first letter from DeWitt County on August 4. He described Cuero, which later would become the county seat, as a town situated almost in the centre of the county, near the banks of the beautiful Guadalupe river, as pretty a stream as there is in Texas. DeWitt county, as everybody knows, is bounded on the north by Gonzales, on the east by some county the name of which I do not remember, on the south by one which I do not recollect, and on the west by another, the name of which I have since forgotten. Clinton, near which we are at present encamped, is the county seat, and contains about 400 inhabitants when they are all at home from "out of the hurly-burly." They have a cute way of carrying their six-shooters around here without breaking the law. Every man carries his coat tied behind his saddle, and in its folds is a peace preserver of the Smith & Wesson persuasion, ready at all times to demonstrate to any officious individual that his views on certain questions are not sound, and his argumentative position untenable unless he is behind a tree. Reports from here, however, have been much exaggerated; the citizens seem to be anxious for peace and quietness, and some are ready to fight for both at any time.[26]

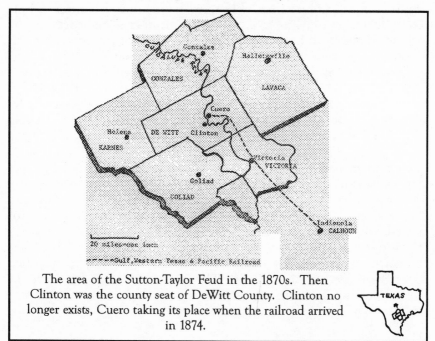

The area of the Sutton-Taylor Feud in the 1870s. Then Clinton was the county seat of DeWitt County. Clinton no longer exists, Cuero taking its place when the railroad arrived in 1874.

Pidge could find humor in almost any situation, and he later added to his remarks about DeWitt County and its location. "When I first wrote to you from here, I was not acquainted with the geography of the country; I have since been told by an old citizen of Clinton that it takes five large counties to bound DeWitt, and it is an awful strain on them to hold it all."[27]

McNelly, upon his arrival in the turbulence, had found "a perfect reign of terror existed" not only in DeWitt but adjoining counties as well. He described the men who composed the fighting forces as "armed bands of men" who made "predatory excursions through the country, overawing the law-abiding citizens." The civil authorities either were unable or unwilling to enforce the laws framed for their protection. Those who wished to remain neutral "were considered obnoxious to both parties." The several treaties of peace made between the contending parties were easily broken so that no one had confidence in the promises of either party.

The Sutton force, McNelly estimated, numbered about one-hundred men, although they claimed 150 sympathizers. McNelly could not determine the power of the Taylor party because their main strength lay in the neighboring counties of Gonzales and Lavaca and kept no regularly organized force. He estimated that the Taylors could gather one-hundred well armed men to their banner as well, so both sides were close to equal in the number of fighting men.[28]

The feudists did not fear McNelly in spite of his forty-man force. District Attorney P.B. Word requested that McNelly have a subpoena served on John Milam Taylor of Yorktown. On the night of August 6 he sent out a squad of four men — Privates J.T. Irvin, J.F. Turner and John W. Chalk under command of Sergeant C.M. Middleton — to deliver Taylor to court. After securing the witness, the squad returned towards Clinton when, about eight miles from their destination, "they were suddenly met in the road by about fifteen armed men who demanded 'Who are you[?]" Middleton may have been surprised but flung back the same question to the fifteen! The would-be attackers yelled a "Que dow!" [Look out!] "Here they are boys give em hell," as McNelly later reported. A rifle volley followed whereupon Middleton ordered his men to dismount and take their stand behind a fence bordering the road. Private Chalk had already received a bullet wound in the shoulder. From behind their cover the rangers fired upon the attackers who were sheltered behind trees. The fire fight lasted about fifteen minutes. During a lull the attackers decided to be coy; they "pretended to discover that

Left: John Milam Taylor, uncle of William R. Taylor and subject of Sutton ambush when in McNelly's custody. Right: James Creed Taylor, head of the Taylor faction after the murder of Pitkin B. Taylor.
Courtesy The Robert G. McCubbin Collection.

it was my men and at once stopped, offering assistance to the wounded man and loaning my men three horses (two of our horses being shot)." This was Middleton's initial encounter with either of the feuding parties, and the rangers showed they were willing to fight. McNelly added, "The Company will have hot work for awhile."[29]

The fight impressed not only McNelly but two of his rangers; both Private E.A. Northington and Pidge wrote of it to the *Statesman*. Northington dated the action as having taken place on August 6 and estimated that the Sutton party numbered "about twenty men." Northington wrote, "We rather expect hot times down here, as the Sutton men say they intend to have the Taylor men we are protecting."[30]

Pidge provided a short letter to the Austin *Statesman* but only one paragraph appeared in print. He wrote that while the squad, "in command of a sergeant were escorting John Taylor from his home, they were fired into by about twenty or thirty of the Sutton party, who claim to have mistaken them for the Taylors; one of the men from Bastrop, named Turner, is missing, and another named Chalk, from Lampasas, shot through the shoulder. Two of the men's horses were shot and left on the field."[31] McNelly estimated the Tumlinson attacking party at fifteen; Northington gave the number as about twenty and Pidge, who obviously enjoyed the use of hyperbole in his correspondence, stated the number was about twenty or thirty!

The attacking party was commanded by "Captain Joe" Tumlinson, formerly of the State Police. McNelly, knowing that Tumlinson would not surrender, assured Adjutant General Steele that capiases would be issued for Tumlinson the next week and their work would commence. All of the feuding parties were willing to come into court but would not surrender their arms! He described the feudists as being "all alike [with] Taylor & Sutton equally turbulent and reckless." McNelly complained to Steele that he needed Winchester rifles because "these people are all armed with them and Tumlinson has from 40 to 75 armed men in town (Clinton) every day and if I am compelled to fight I don't want to get whipped."[32] McNelly's men were furnished with Sharps carbines, but apparently McNelly determined he needed weapons which would give faster fire power than the single shot Sharps. Later on the Rio Grande border he would specify the Sharps as the weapon of choice.

Tumlinson, as McNelly discovered, was a fighting man who could command great loyalty and a large force. He was a man who had earned the right to lead, and one who was long used to being, in effect, his own law. In 1823 he had been one of the group who tracked down his father's murderers. He lived with his mother until her death in 1829 and then received his own headright. Tumlinson's land adjoined that of the widow Hephzibeth Taylor, and in 1834 Joe Tumlinson married the widow's daughter, Johanna. Tumlinson served under Captain Robert M. Coleman in his ranger force, fought at the battle of San Jacinto and continued to serve under other commanders. After the Civil War, having settled down on a ranch near Yorktown, DeWitt County, he became embroiled in the difficulties with the Taylors. By 1874, when McNelly entered the conflict, Captain Joe was living on a pension he had earned for his military service to the state of Texas.[33] McNelly may have been aware somewhat of Tumlinson's record. Although he did not so indicate, he and Tumlinson must have had some sort of meeting to discuss matters.

> I saw him at the head of seventy five well armed
> men, & men who have no interest but in obeying his

orders; he is a man who has always righted his own
wrongs, & he tells me that the only way for this county
to have peace is to allow him to kill off the Taylor party.
He has never been made to feel that this civil law could
& should be the supreme arbiter between man & man
& I am satisfied that when the sheriff calls upon me to
aid him in serving papers on Tumlinson that he will
resist or at least refuse to go into Court without his
arms & men as he has done heretofore . . . . I feel
entirely able to whip "Tumlinson" with the men I have
if it must be a fight but will need more men, fifty men
cannot over awe these people; they have been in the
habit of overriding the officers of the law so long that
it will require more force than I have, to "bluff"
them.[34]

McNelly concluded his letter to Steele explaining that the
Tumlinson party had wanted to kill John M. Taylor, because Taylor
could have provided damaging evidence to convict them of the murder of Senator Bolivar J. Pridgen's former slave, Abram Bryant, identified as Abraham Pickins as well as "Old Uncle Abraham," whose
death "would relieve them of many fears." [35]

Pidge was also impressed with "Captain Joe," as he was known
to many.

Tumlinson goes about like Robinson Cruso[e] with
a gun on each shoulder and two Smith & Wesson's No.
3 in his belt. I had the pleasure of seeing this gentleman
a few days since; he has the frosts of sixty winters on his
head, and green spectacles on his nose, and, it is said,
can see with his naked eye farther than any hawk this
side the Rio Grande; when he gets on his spectacles
there is no telling what he can see, as he magnified five
of the company who were traveling the road into an
ambuscade of the Taylor party. The Cuero Star termed
it the first fair fight, which was all right, as they were
four to one.[36]

Here Pidge unwittingly expressed the concept that a single well-
armed ranger was superior in fighting ability to a greater force. The
incident may have caused McNelly some embarrassment when the

Victoria *Advocate* reported, "McNally's [sic] men have already had an engagement with the *Chevaliers d'Encinal*, in which it appears that the soldiers came out second best. Call up the reserve!"[37] Of course there was no reserve.

McNelly realized fairly quickly that the authorities in DeWitt County were in sympathy with the Tumlinson-Sutton forces. This should not have come as a surprise to McNelly; some of the officials had been members of the State Police force. A number of the Taylor adherents, most notably John Wesley Hardin, were recognized fugitives. McNelly observed that during the court term, "subsistence" was furnished by the sheriff "under the plea of being prisoners, but they were never disarmed." Neither the district judge nor the state attorney attempted to have them dispersed or disarmed, even though McNelly "told them that orders to that effect would be gladly received & promptly executed." Here McNelly observed that the reason the feud was able to continue was because civil authorities simply did not perform the duties for which they were responsible. "In a country of such strong prejudices much has been accomplished by the good conduct of the State troops, which has been most exemplary. No sympathy with, or favoritism to either party has been shown by the men of this command, and our presence here is favorably looked on by all peaceful citizens and is considered by them to be an absolute necessity for their protection and for the welfare of the country."[38] Some rangers were even stationed in the homes of certain citizens, perhaps as much to protect them as to learn about the movements of the feuding parties. William Lawrence Rudd for example, who began his ranger service with McNelly and later served as sheriff of Karnes County from September 1886 until November 1888, was at first stationed in the home of Captain Joe Tumlinson and later in the home of Senator Bolivar Jackson Pridgen, men on opposing sides of the feud.[39]

During the next few months McNelly had concerns other than dealing with feuding families. In addition to his receipts and vouchers, the trial of William Riley "Bill" Taylor was scheduled and McNelly was told that "in case you should be suddenly called upon to take your Company to Indianola that you be prepared to leave your horses and take the Rail Road to that place." On September 13 Steele telegraphed him that he had not heard from him and he should now go to Indianola and report to him at the Cosmopolitan Hotel at Galveston.[40] Anticipating mob action either to kill Taylor, or to have his friends attempt a rescue, Steele had requested McNelly to be present as well. This McNelly did not do. The trial began on Thursday, September 24, with Adjutant General Steele himself being present. McNelly, however, had been in Burton for a visit with his wife and children and did not leave there until September 21. The excessive rains and high water delayed travel and he did not reach Clinton until September 28, four days after the trial was scheduled to begin, having killed one horse by driving through the muddy roads. Unable to find a place to leave his family while he could hasten on to Indianola via train, McNelly remained with them. He did notify Sergeant "Pidge" Robinson to take the company on to Indianola, but Robinson did not receive the telegram until the 28th.[41]

Senator William H. Crain whose life was saved by fugitive Bill Taylor. *Courtesy Texas State Library & Archives Comission.*

Authorities wanted to try both William and James Taylor for the double killing, but James was still a fugitive and would remain a fugitive until his death. In an effort to involve the entire state in the pursuit of James Taylor, District Attorney William H. Crain asked for an *alias capias* to every county in the state.[42] Bill Taylor, who denied even being present at the Sutton-Slaughter killings, submitted an application for continuance due to several important witnesses' being absent, and the case was postponed. A holiday atmosphere surrounded the trial of such a noted individual as Bill Taylor. The Lone Star Rifles and Washington Guards were there to surround the prisoner for his own protection whenever he was moved; the Indianola brass band and a large group of citizens "escorted" the prisoner along with the guards from the court room to the steamer which would take them to Galveston where the jail was more secure.[43] Due to the severe weather conditions McNelly was unable to be at Indianola for the Taylor trial. He was able to spend some time with his family in Burton and also was developing a plan to capture James Taylor. McNelly communicated to Governor Coke why he was absent from Indianola and gave only a hint that he had a plan to capture Taylor. His communication to Steele written from

Clinton indicated he was "*well* Satisfied that I can catch Jim Taylor" but gave no indication as to where Taylor was or how he proposed to accomplish the arrest. He did admit that it would be "a long trip" and with at least a portion of the company escorting him and "it would cost something more than our ordinary rations." There is no further mention of the plan to capture Jim Taylor in the existing records.[44]

As a further indication that McNelly anticipated battles with the feuding parties, he asked Adjutant General Steele for a personal revolver and ammunition. On September 18 Steele notified Captain Wells to issue to him one Colts nickel plated pistol and fifty rounds of ammunition.[45] Apparently McNelly did not have his own personal weapon prior to this! A further matter unanticipated by the captain had to be attended to; several of his company were fugitives! On September 28 Steele ordered McNelly to arrest and turn over to Bastrop County Deputy Sheriff Oscar F. Nash any members of the company for whom he had capiases; three members of the company apparently were wanted by Bastrop County authorities. How Sheriff John A. Kohler learned of these wanted men having enlisted in McNelly's company is unknown.[46]

In October McNelly was feeling the pressure from Austin to provide "complete reports." Further, it was important for the office to have receipts in order to insure the annual message of the governor to the legislature was accurate. McNelly's company "with the Services it has rendered, and its expense form" was considered "an important item." The report was to be completed at once up through August 31, the end of the fiscal year. By October 20 McNelly had found a solution to his problem with submitting reports: he wrote to Steele stating he found it difficult to get along without the assistance of a commissioned officer. After "due trial" he felt satisfied that T.C. "Pidge" Robinson, his 2nd Sergeant, would "fill the position with credit to himself & honor to the State."[47] Robinson's nomination was approved by Adjutant General Steele.

McNelly did include the description of one near-shooting affray in his letter dated September 30. On September 25 Corporal L.P. Ellis and a squad were escorting John M. Taylor from Indianola when several members of the Tumlinson party, headed by Cuero City Marshal R.H. "Rube" Brown, attempted to board the train threatening to kill Taylor. McNelly reported that the killing was prevented only because his men guarding Taylor drew their pistols and threatened to shoot anyone that attempted to enter the caboose car which Taylor and the rangers occupied by McNelly's order. The Brown party later apologized to McNelly for the incident and said they were drunk, but McNelly constantly feared a "reancountre [sic] under just some like circumstance."[48]

A year later Bill Taylor was back at Indianola standing trial for the Sutton killing, but this time the catastrophic hurricane of September 15-16 struck the city. Attorney William H. Crain was the first to express grave concern about the prisoners confined in the jail, fearing that the rising waters would drown them. The jailer refused to release the prisoners, fearing they would escape, so Crain himself obtained the keys and took responsibility. Seeking safety, Crain and the prisoners headed for the new courthouse, a concrete structure built on higher ground. They all made it, but the wind had blown Crain's hat away so Bill Taylor took his own hat and put it on Crain's head, saying as he laughed, "Bill Crain will never prosecute me." Another version of the incident had Crain's falling into the treacherous water and being saved by Taylor. When the waters began to recede there were about a hundred people on the courthouse hill, many of whom owed their lives to Bill Taylor who had entered the rising waters to save them from drowning.[49] Taylor's prophecy proved to be correct; he escaped and Crain never saw him again. Cousin Jim Taylor eluded capture until December 27, 1875, when he and two companions, Mason "Winchester Smith" Arnold and A.R. Hendricks, a former McNelly ranger who had left the militia and married into the Taylor party, were surrounded in Clinton and killed by a group of Sutton sympathizers.[50]

The court matters of William Taylor received wide publicity in Texas newspapers. A correspondent provided a lengthy article in the Galveston News which was published in its issue of September 27, 1874, in which a brief history of the feud and items of interest about the trial were provided. The article complimented the militia captain even in his absence, "I hear only the most flattering reports as to the conduct of Captain L.H. McNelly and his command, and would suggest that by some means he be appointed Sheriff of the county [DeWitt], and allowed to retain his command to enforce the law, which he would do if the Legislature would enlarge his powers. I believe it would break up both gangs, or at least their carrying weapons."[51] It is not believed that any serious effort was made by DeWitt authorities to nominate McNelly as sheriff.

McNelly found the inaction of the present district judge and state's attorney "the cause of trouble which might other wise have

been nipped in the bud." He was satisfied that if a judge and attorney of probity, ability and nerve were sent to hold court at the next
term, in December, "they could effectually prevent a continuation of
disgraceful Scenes in and out of the halls of Justice. With the present incumbents there is no hope; fearful of giving offense they have
passed over in silence infringements on the law which have transpired under their immediate observation, and have given just cause
for bringing the majesty of the law into contempt among a class of
men who at best have had a slight regard for it."[52]

The feuding forces did quiet themselves down but it was only
because of the constant patrols sent out to prevent mob associations.
After three and one-half months in the county, on October 18,
McNelly wrote to Steele that "Everything seems very quiet at present," certainly a feeling of peacefulness which could only have been
accomplished by his practice of having his men seemingly ubiqui-
tous. McNelly believed that his sending out four or five squads at a
time with instructions to ride a certain "course," allowing him to
communicate with them if necessary, and ordering his squads to
approach towns and country stores in the most unexpected manner
possible, did a great deal of good as it dispersed "congregations of
these parties that usual[l]y meet at 'grog shops' to have dif[f]iculties
or concoct devilment." Many of these men were under indictment
in other areas of the State, and in constant expectation of some officer. McNelly could brag, "when they hear of my men coming they
scatter."[53]

McNelly expressed his concerns for the law-abiding and analyzed
the situation so as to identify at least one reason why the hostilities
would continue. Although his purpose was to restore law and order,
he may have actually welcomed a fight. With the December term of
court coming, members of both parties would be in town and "a difficulty between them may be expected, but if prudence & circum-
spection can prevent it, shall not occur; but if it does take place you
may rest assured that I will have my men in such a position as will
render the escape of the survivors impossible, and they will be held
to answer on account for their offenses."[54]

McNelly's presence established a quiet atmosphere in DeWitt
County. He was at his best when dealing with potential combat and
arresting fugitives, thus such mundane things as pay vouchers and
other paper work were frequently neglected. By not checking into
the background of his recruits sufficiently he had to see members of
his troop occasionally taken from him by other law officers. He may

have been not only surprised but disappointed as well that J.F. Turner had to be turned over to the sheriff of Bastrop County. He had already learned that Turner was wanted, but McNelly waited for a capias to deliver him to the county jail there. Pidge wrote of having the duty of arresting Turner.

> I was at [John] Taylor's yesterday; went there to arrest a young man from Bastrop named Turner, charged with serious crimes. He was a member of this company, and has acted in it so as to win the respect and admiration of all his comrades. This was my first experience in getting the "drop" on a man, and I have not the highest respect for the practice. . . . We finally arrived at Taylor's where this young man was on duty as a guard, and as I introduced the sheriff, I pulled my pistol, and the men under my command did the same. Twice he attempted to draw his weapon with our leveled six-shooters cocked in his face.[55]

Another, Private O.G. Balemon, had been discharged for drunkenness and disobedience, having refused an order from Corporal R.P. Orrell. McNelly reported to Steele that this was the third offense of "this Kind he has committed."[56] And Private John W. Chalk, wounded in the ambush by the Tumlinson party, requested a discharge, no reason given. McNelly pointed out that Chalk had provided "unusual good conduct."[57] Private G.H. Chilton had been discharged August 10,[58] and ten days later C.B. Cook requested to be discharged.[59]

By mid-November McNelly felt things were quieted down sufficiently to ask for some time at home. Steele answered that he could return "for the time requested" on condition that a "discreet officer is left in Command." In the same communication Steele returned the commission for T.C. Robinson's promotion to lieutenant. Steele presumed Robinson was "discreet," as well as "politically with the administration."[60]

In spite of his best efforts McNelly did nothing more than establish a measure of tranquillity in DeWitt County during his presence there. He did not capture John Wesley Hardin nor James Creed Taylor, the two leaders of the Taylor faction, nor make any significant change in the attitudes of the feuding parties. He did prevent mob actions against prisoners, however. Court was held but none of the leading feudists stood trial. The arrest of Bill Taylor was not accomplished by his men. Basically the DeWitt County experience of dealing with feuding parties was only a hiatus before his second mission to the Rio Grande Frontier where he would be in an element more similar to that of the Civil War in which his objectives were clear. He was to end cattle raiding and he did not need to consider making friends with anyone. Killing the enemy was clearly an understood part of the equation on the border, whereas in DeWitt he was somehow expected to make the Suttons and Taylors cease hating each other and become friendly and law-abiding. an unpractical assignment.

McNelly's departure was not brought about because he had ended the feud but because the company had to be disbanded. No doubt many DeWitt County residents resented seeing McNelly and his troop depart, knowing that it had only been his presence there which had brought about that peace and quiet. Governor Coke had to go before the legislature to explain that more money was needed to support such special forces as McNelly's. Having to make the expenditure to guard Bill Taylor during his trial was a significant factor. Coke anticipated the need of keeping McNelly and his company in DeWitt for about another year, although at the time the funds for such an expenditure were not readily available.[61]

Editor Kleberg, when learning his comrade from the Civil War days was to be sent elsewhere, provided a brief resume of the period when the rangers were there, paying a "high" and "deserved compliment" to the captain and his men. "We know Capt. McNally [sic] well as a gallant, enterprising and accomplished Confederate officer, while he served on the staff of the heroic Green; and we know that no change of circumstances could make of him, anything but a gallant soldier, and a most notorious and accomplished gentleman."[62]

No doubt McNelly felt some satisfaction with what he had accomplished while in DeWitt County, for he was an individual who cared deeply for the safety of his fellow citizens. In early 1875 he was in Austin and stated to a reporter that he feared the violence would again flare up, that the disturbances in DeWitt County were only "temporarily allayed." [63]

CHAPTER 12

MCNELLY – ON THE BORDER

There is a considerable element in the country bordering on the Nueces and west, that think the killing
of a Mexican no crime. . . .
The thieves and cut-throats, who have collected on
the border, think the killing of a Texan something to be
proud of. . . .— William Steele to Governor Coke, July
1, 1875.

Little is known of the activities of McNelly or the Washington
County Volunteer Militia during the winter months of 1874-75. The
experience in DeWitt County must have been discouraging for
McNelly, because the reign of lawlessness and terrorism at Clinton
and Cuero which had caused Governor Coke to order McNelly and
his men there in the first place, although somewhat abated, was only
quieted by the rangers' high visibility. There had been only minor
skirmishes with the feuding parties, and no real results had been
accomplished. With the exception of the Tumlinson attack on John
Taylor and the ranger escort and the attempted attack on the train,
the feudists had avoided confrontations with McNelly and his men.
It was as if everyone realized that the Washington County Volunteer
Militia would not be there for long, and the violence could be held
in check until they departed.

Even with the violence held in abeyance, merchants realized that
the acts of terrorism brought unwanted publicity to the area; it dis-
couraged people from moving into the community which in turn
affected economic growth. Many considered McNelly as having
failed in his mission, even though the fighting had essentially been
stopped. McNelly's "failure" still received considerable publicity. His
own county seat newspaper, the Brenham *Banner*, reprinted a report
first published in the *Daily State Gazette* which all Austin and central
Texas had read, that there was "no real solution to the difficulties in
DeWitt county." The report stated that offenders were arrested,
tried and acquitted from a sense of fear on the part of members of

the jury. The *Banner* recommended that, since the State of Texas had the authority to determine in which county the offenders could be tried, a change of venue to other counties for the trial of such cases was in order.[1] This was done on occasion, but for the most part the feud between the followers of the late William E. Sutton and the Taylors would continue for several more years, finally being brought to a conclusion after more deaths and more trials in the court sys-tem.

During January the concern was how to keep the company together. McNelly did not want to release the men, knowing full well that in their absence the feudists would start the shooting war again. Many citizens wished the company to be retained in DeWitt. In McNelly's letter to Steele on January 8, 1875, he reminded the adju-tant general of his promise to allow him to go to Austin that month. "I am anxious to start by the fifteenth. There will be a number of the best citizens (monyied [sic] citizens) [who will] accompany me to Austin to try to have my company retained here."[2] In a letter written two days later he informed Steele he would start to Austin on the 16th or 17th, "that is if everything is perfectly quiet & I can Settle my bills for company expense."[3]

Considerable concern was felt by many peace loving citizens, fearing that if the company was disbanded or greatly reduced there would be a return to lawlessness. At the year's beginning McNelly was ordered to keep his company at Clinton for thirty days until the legislature had time to act on appropriations.[4] The month of February passed with no decision in the capital. The legislature was scheduled to adjourn on March 15, and on March 9 Steele directed McNelly to buy only the supplies absolutely necessary for immediate use "as in the event the Legislature refuses to make any appropria-tion for the purpose of keeping your Co[mpany] in service it will be disbanded at once. No appropriation of any kind has yet been made. . . ."[5] On March 17 Steele had to order McNelly to have Lieutenant Robinson return the company to its place of organization immedi-ately and muster out the men. McNelly was to report to Austin "to arrange for a final settlement."[6] But no sooner had this order been issued than funds were allocated by the legislature, still in session, to keep the company in the field. But instead of being retained in DeWitt County, McNelly would be sent to the Rio Grande Frontier.

For the first time in McNelly's career there are extensive reports of his operations in addition to the numerous reminiscences pro-vided by his rangers in their later years. Lieutenant T.C. "Pidge"

Robinson provided accounts of many of the actions within days of their occurrence, no longer to the Austin *Daily Democratic Statesman* but now to its rival, the *Daily State Gazette*, for the benefit of Austinites and for posterity. Robinson intended to be accurate, but due to his sense of humor he occasionally exaggerated for humorous or dramatic effect. Whereas others, such as rangers Callicott, Durham and Jennings, recorded their experiences decades later, Robinson wrote his letters within days of the occurrence and was thus extremely accurate.

The initial report that McNelly's company was to be disbanded resulted in immediate criticism of the decision by some. The *Express* of San Antonio, critical of Governor Coke's policies but never of McNelly himself, headlined one article, "Frontier Protection Fallen Through" and claimed the state troops, having been

> organized with such a flourish at the beginning of Coke's reign, are to be withdrawn soon and disbanded. The Legislature gets the credit of doing it, because they failed to make the requisite appropriation to keep these troops in the field. During the winter there was little use for these troops on the frontier, and Coke used them as a kind of state police force to regulate some of his unruly partisans in DeWitt county and elsewhere.[7]

McNelly must have believed that he was severely hampered by the orders from Austin. He had entered the warfare of DeWitt County with orders to bring about an end of the violence and create a semblance of friendship between the feuding parties. McNelly himself felt the continued violence happened because of the weaknesses of the local authorities; however, in some quarters the opinion was expressed that some of McNelly's men actually contributed to the lawlessness! Richard B. Hudson, a DeWitt County farmer and deputy under Sheriff William J. Weisiger, wrote a lengthy letter to the Austin *Statesman* describing certain events of the Taylor-Sutton feud. Hudson wrote how horse thieves and outlaws of other states and counties "once annoyed" the people of DeWitt County. Hudson expressed his belief that the Suttons were honest, hard working men who acted against a band of thieves who "overran the country and stole thousands of head of cattle and murdered whom they pleased." Hudson explained that the one party took the name of Sutton because Bill Sutton had been the first man to resist the

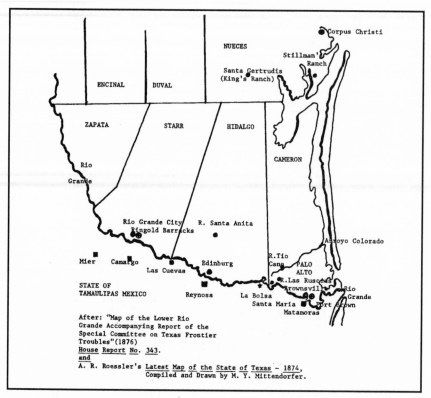

The Nueces Strip and area of McNelly's border war against mobs,
Cortina's raiders and outlaws.

thieves, whose leaders were Jim Taylor and Wes Hardin. Sutton may
indeed have been among the first to "resist the thieves," but Hardin
did not enter into the picture until 1872, several years after the commencement of the hostilities. After the killing of Sutton the thieves
went to Comanche County, killed Charles Webb, and then returned
to DeWitt County. Hudson concluded that after Jim Taylor and two
of his associates were killed and Wes Hardin and others had left the
country "we have not been troubled with outlaws since; but we are
under no obligation to anyone but the good citizens or the so-called
Sutton party for getting rid of them; but *indebted to Capt. L. H.
McNelly's company for many recruits to the thieving party* [emphasis
added]."[8]

This is a strange communication to a major newspaper. It
accuses McNelly of allowing members of his company to contribute

to the lawlessness, yet McNelly prided himself in insisting his company be impartial to the feuding parties and in allowing no favoritism. Granted, several members of the company did become involved with DeWitt County women, several marrying there, but with the exception of A.R. Hendricks, killed with Jim Taylor and Mace Arnold in December 1875, none became allied with either side of the feuding forces so far as known. In spite of the absence of McNelly, 1875 would be a relatively peaceful year in DeWitt County.

McNelly would have free rein on the Rio Grande Frontier, however, and the results would be dramatically different. His service on the Rio Grande elevated the McNelly star to the heights of hero worship in the mind and heart of many a Texan. But on the other side of the river, his actions gave cause for Mexicans to believe the Texas Rangers were the devil incarnate, *los diablos tejanos*.

The "Nueces Strip," that area between the Nueces River on the north and the Rio Grande on the south, between Corpus Christi, Nueces County on the east and Laredo, Webb County, on the west, had long been a controversial ground between Mexico and the United States. Mexico had claimed that the Nueces was its northern boundary; the United States claimed the border was the Rio Grande, and from the U.S. point of view the defeat of the Mexican Army and the occupation of Mexico City, ending the war with Mexico in 1848, resolved the question. Yet even then the Nueces Strip remained a no man's land, a dangerous area where every man had to be a law unto himself, whether he be *greaser* desperado or *gringo* outlaw or law-abiding citizen. The area was sparsely populated, and only the bravest ranchers attempted to establish themselves in this country. Richard King developed his holdings into an empire but maintained a private army to defend his property.

The wild untamed country below the Nueces was McNelly's new assignment. Governor Coke issued orders for him to begin organizing a company of forty men for service in what would become known as the Rio Grande Frontier. The news was reported over the entire state, and newspapers as far north as Dallas carried the announcement that McNelly and his men were to see service on the Mexican border, their "range" being from Corpus Christi to Laredo.

Although never proved in a court of law, U.S. authorities generally considered that the principal leader of the raiding Mexican bands was General Juan Nepomuceno Cortina. Born May 16, 1824, at Camargo, Tamaulipas, Cortina spent his life fighting in one cause or another. He had been a soldier opposing the United States dur-

Juan Nepomuceno Cortina, from the original portrait. *Courtesy The Robert G. McCubbin Collection.*

ing the Mexican War and had served on the battlefields of Resaca de la Palma and Palo Alto in 1846. Thirteen years later he raided the city of Brownsville, shooting the town marshal and liberating prisoners. Later he raided Brownsville again, taking over the city and hoisting the Mexican flag over the city square. A ranger group led by William G. Tobin failed to defeat Cortina, and it was not until the renowned John S. "Rip" Ford with Major Samuel P. Heintzelman and a force of 165 regulars engaged Cortina that he experienced defeat. Cortina's fame south of the Rio Grande grew until he could command a huge number of followers who raided across the river almost at will. He supported the Union during the American Civil War and was considered by Texans to be the leading force behind all organized gangs of thieves from south of the border through the 1870s.[9]

As early as 1871, a year before McNelly's first expedition to the Rio Grande with a squad of State Police, Texas ranchers were suffering severe losses from Cortina's raiders. The San Antonio *Express* was fearless in condemning Cortina, saying he had "sworn undying hostility to the Americans, and has let no opportunity pass to give vent to his hate. He boasted then that he had never signed the treaty of Guadalupe-Hidalgo, and his sentiments then, as now, are 'eternal hatred to the Americans.'" Concluded the *Express*: "Cannot the American Eagle at least *show* the Mexican Buzzard his talons?"[10]

The United States House of Representatives Report on *Texas Frontier Troubles* had this to say of him:

> Cortina, the old robber chief, had obtained the rank of brigadier-general in the Mexican army, and had

risen to power and distinction. From that time forth he was the central figure of the robbing population which established itself on the Mexican side of the Rio Bravo. His power was despotic. The lawless men who, through him, enjoyed the advantages of organization and political power on their own soil, and unlimited license to plunder on the Texas side, supported him with enthusiasm and devotion, and in turn gave him the power and position which, in such a country, naturally falls to the leader who can command the unhesitating services of a large body of warlike followers. He became individually far more powerful than any other power — national or state.[11]

The Brownsville *Sentinel* early expressed the feelings of the people in the Nueces Strip when it reported in 1871 that the people had "become so accustomed to being robbed, that they hardly consider it worth while to say anything about it."[12] A late 1872 report originally appearing in the New Orleans *Republican* and then again in the Austin *Daily State Journal* described the situation as "deplorable." Instead of rivaling the Mississippi or the Nile, the delta of the Rio Grande supported "a vagabond population, inured to rapine and violence, and who make it the theater of incessant lawlessness." Even though "commerce languishes and profitable industry is unknown," the Rio Grande attracted the attention of the public because of the repeated raids. "Such bandits as Cortina . . . stimulated by their dislike of the Americans and the rich booty represented by numberless herds roving on the vast prairies of Texas," was the source of the problems. The suggested remedy, the only "reasonable conclusion," was that if the violence within the Nueces Strip could not be stopped by local officials, then more drastic measures such as another war with Mexico would be taken.[13]

More recently, in October 1874, word from Brownsville was that the bandit organization's preparations to invade Texas had been delayed only because of high water in the river and the almost impossible traveling conditions of the country. The reported plan was to strike soldiers who were guarding the border, then "to murder and rob generally. Gen. Cortina heads the movement, he will not probably cross in person but will send some one else." The Galveston *News*, naturally concerned about the potential for conflict on the river, concluded that Americans on the north side were organizing to defend themselves, for when the river fell sufficiently to enable an easy crossing, "look for trouble . . . . The mounted men are held ready to move at short notice. A border war has never been more imminent."[14]

A month later another Brownsville special reported a raid in Los Almos which caused great excitement and again suggested war was imminent. The raid proved the existence of organized bands of marauders. Ricardo Flores, mentioned by name as one who prac-ticed the trade of stealing cattle, would later be a target for the fight-ing men of McNelly's company. The dispatch concluded, "These events speak for themselves. They show whether the reported raids were fabrications or well grounded warnings. The party which robbed Los Almos intended to have gone to Corpus Christi if they had a sufficient force. This was divulged by a man who overheard a conversation in Matamoras. The cloud of border war is more lower-ing."[15]

And in December, while McNelly was concluding his work in DeWitt County, José María Olguín, *alias* El Aguja (The Needle), escaped from the Brownsville jail after having been sentenced to fif-teen years in prison for theft. Perhaps to celebrate his new found freedom Olguín led a raid into Cameron County and stole one-hundred head of cattle belonging to James G. Browne, the county sheriff! About the same time that El Aguja was stealing Sheriff Browne's cattle, Ricardo Flores, having been arrested for murdering a Frenchman but then escaping from the authorities, was reported to be back "in the cattle business." Flores made a raid into Cameron County with some followers, gathered up a drove of cattle and crossed back into Mexico about two miles below Brownsville.[16] Both these fugitives had escaped from custody at about the same time and immediately returned to their chosen profession of theft. McNelly would encounter both El Aguja and Ricardo Flores on the border in 1875.

Sheriff Browne was not the only lawman having problems with raiders from across the Rio Grande. Hidalgo County Sheriff Alexander J. Leo notified Governor Coke on March 4 of various depredations committed on the border, explaining that he was "entirely helpless in executing the laws in regard to criminals."[17] Naturally Adjutant General Steele was informed of Sheriff Leo's concerns, and he presented his opinion as to the serious state of affairs to the governor later that month, suggesting that a call for "decided action" should be taken. He described the conditions as being in a "state of war" between the Mexican bandits and the people of Texas living between the Rio Grande and the Nueces rivers. Even the military posts in operation appeared to have "little or no effect on preventing the incursions of bands who come singly or in small parties and unite at a distance from the border. . . ." Steele had to admit that the U.S. military forces on the border were totally inadequate to cope with the problem. He recommended the calling out of at least six mounted companies to be stationed outside the "dense thickets of chapperal [sic]" and that they be kept in constant movement. Steele theorized this action would cause a suspension of the depredations, and if it did not, then the raiders "should be followed to their asylum."[18]

As Texas officials pondered the border situation, a raiding party was approaching the community of Nuecestown, located some thirteen miles southwest of Corpus Christi. They struck on Good Friday March 26, 1875, and although Cortina was not physically present it was the general belief that he was the leading spirit behind it. A large group of raiders had intended initially to attack the town of Corpus Christi, but due to internal arguments the majority of the band retreated.[19] One group, numbering about thirty armed and mounted Mexicans, did continue their way towards Corpus Christi. At San Fernando Creek two Anglos were stabbed to death. At a place called Chocolate, twenty miles from Corpus Christi, two Hispanics were left hanging, apparently refusing to join the raiding party.[20] About noon on March 26 the raiders appeared at the ranch of Samuel H. Page where they looted the house and took the men prisoners. One old Hispanic refused to join them and was hanged for his obstinacy. Continuing towards Corpus Christi the band robbed any traveler who happened to have the misfortune of being in their way. At Nuecestown they met the first real resistance in the form of Thomas John Noakes.

Noakes had been a pioneer merchant in Nueces County, his store having become a landmark of sorts as travelers going east or west, north or south, stopped there for provisions and news. "Old Man" Noakes, also known equally well as Tom or John, an Englishman born in 1829, had come to America at the age of sixteen, landed at Corpus Christi, liked what he saw and stayed. He soon became known by everyone in the region. Noakes' Store was recognized as a border outpost for Anglo civilization on the edge of the Nueces Strip.[21]

When the raiders arrived Noakes was well prepared to defend his

Thomas John Noakes, who suffered severe losses at the hands of Cortina's raiders in the Nuecestown Raid, Good Friday, 1875. *From the New Encyclopedia of Texas.*

property; in anticipation of just such an emergency he had designed and built his home with trap door and trenches dug beneath the floor in order to escape unseen if the situation ever demanded it. Immediately aware of the bandits' purpose, Noakes shot one, Godina, before he realized the size of the raiding party and had to retreat, not only for his own safety but for the safety of his family. He availed himself of the trap door in the floor and escaped to the outside. For some reason unknown to Noakes, his wife was still in the house, surrounded by several raiders who were setting fires. She bravely put them out until it was impossible to continue to do so, then she managed to gather her children and a few personal items and escape to safety. No member of the Noakes family was physically injured, but the raid was a tremendous monetary loss because all their possessions had been in the combination store and home which was burned to the ground.[22]

During the confrontation at the Noakes store, groups of men in Corpus Christi were organizing to defend their homes and the town. Nueces County Sheriff John McClane commanded one company, Pat Whelan another. After a brief skirmish between Whelan's group and the raiders, which cost the life of John Swanks, Whelan retreated back to Corpus Christi after having run out of ammunition. The raiders were able to hasten back to relative safety in Mexico.[23]

The raider which Noakes had shot did not fare so well. Wounded, he was abandoned by his comrades who apparently believed he would not long survive and would slow down their retreat. Angry citizens quickly found him and took him into Corpus Christi intending to lynch him. Sheriff McClane managed to avert the lynching but only for a while. A Dr. Spohn was allowed to treat his wounds, then he was tied up again in the two-wheeled cart which would become his tumbrel.

Initially the townspeople intent on lynching the raider were frustrated by their inability to find a suitable gallows. With no scaffold available for that purpose, the mob found a *zapatería* [shoe store] with a sign supported by two posts. The tumbrel was backed up under the sign but it was quickly determined to be too low for a lynching. Then someone thought of the church steeple, and several men clambered upon the roof and began looping the rope to the steeple. This plan was frustrated because no one could agree on the proper way to make a hangman's noose!

At this point cattleman Martin S. Culver came into town after being out for hours searching for the raider group. In spite of any personal feelings he may have had towards the raider, as he had undoubtedly lost cattle to thieves, Culver put an abrupt end to any further thoughts of hanging the man from the church steeple. But the determined mob found a field not far away where a new gate had been recently erected. A heavy cross pole from gatepost to gatepost was high enough to make an adequate scaffold, and the wretch was forced to stand on the cart with one end of the rope around his neck and the other tied over the cross pole. Then the cart was slapped away and the dying raider left hanging. He was buried the next day after a local priest and a local official cut him down.[24]

Governor Coke received news of the raid and felt such concern that he telegraphed President Grant, stating that the "depredations of organized bands of robbers from the Republic of Mexico have of late increased in frequency and atrocity, to an extent which threatens the depopulation of the lower Rio Grande country. . . . [O]ur people are ruthlessly murdered and their property forcibly taken by these foreign desperadoes. . . . [these invasions] have been of almost weekly occurrence for several months past, and are increasing in their force and boldness." President Grant was absent from Washington and the telegram was turned over to Secretary of War William W. Belknap, who responded by ordering the commanding officer of the Department of Texas "to distribute troops along the Rio Grande to prevent further outrages by Mexicans."[25]

Rancher Martin S. Culver, certainly aggrieved with losses to the raiders, requested Governor Coke to commission him with authority to organize companies of mounted militia men. Culver may have intended to create his own Nueces County Volunteer Militia Company, similar to McNelly's. Various Corpus Christi merchants met on March 31 to discuss their situation; they requested Governor Coke to commission Culver and to "furnish immediate relief." Coke replied that McNelly and his company would be starting from Austin within the week, and that his company "is already organized and armed," thereby notifying the Corpus Christi merchants that there was no need for them to consider backing Culver or any one else. Certainly the Anglo ranchers felt they were suffering the most, but incidents of mob law against innocent Hispanics were also occurring. In mid-January word had been brought to the *Valley Times* of Corpus Christi that five "Mexicans," hanging from a tree, "some distance beyond King's Ranch," were "supposed to belong to a gang of thieves and cut-throats." On the return trip to Mexico the gang had stabbed two Anglos to death and lynched two Hispanics, "evidently the work of the raiders."

Ironically, at the same time the Nuecestown raid was taking place McNelly was in Austin, his ranger force reportedly having been disbanded, worrying that the DeWitt County disturbances would flare up again in the absence of his troops. Although McNelly had forced a degree of peace upon the Cuero-Clinton communities, McNelly received criticism from a Taylor adherent, the senator of the 12th Legislative District, Bolivar J. Pridgen! Pridgen had been highly critical of the Davis administration and became a Taylor sympathizer after his brother Wiley had been murdered. He may have been instrumental in alerting the Taylors that Sutton and Slaughter would be in Indianola on March 11, where both were killed. Pridgen wrote a letter to Attorney General Williams complaining that McNelly had refused protection in his camp to certain parties, presumably Taylor adherents. The letter was published in the Pittsburg (Camp County) *Dispatch*. In addition Pridgen had written Governor Coke complaining that McNelly had failed to establish a guard he had requested around the Pridgen home in Galveston. The newspaper clipping as well as the letter to Coke were both provided to McNelly. Upon reading these accusations McNelly demanded Pridgen write to the *Dispatch* stating that the accusations were not true, that he had not refused protection for Pridgen and naturally resented the implication that he was derelict in his duties. He further corrected Pridgen on the matter of his home's being guarded. McNelly told him he had had a guard at his home since the previous August and he would continue to provide a guard to protect the family.[26]

As the files of the *Dispatch* are no longer available, it is uncertain if indeed the second Pridgen letter was published or exactly what the original published letter had said. In spite of these nuisances, McNelly had his force together and left for the Rio Grande Frontier on Saturday, April 10. One of the new recruits was Oscar F. Pridgen, the son of the senator; he would serve under McNelly from April 1 to August 31, 1875.[27]

George P. Durham was also a young ranger in McNelly's company and later wrote an account of his experiences with the company. His book, *Taming the Nueces Strip*, as told to Clyde Wantland, has remained popular and provides a reasonably accurate history of McNelly's rangers. Prior to the 1962 publication in book form, the story had been serialized in *West* magazine in 1937 under the title "On the Trail of 5100 Outlaws." Durham recalled marching during the night and, an hour or so before daybreak, seeing water off to the left and knowing they were on the coast.

> As we rode into Corpus Christi that morning, I wouldn't have known that it was Corpus unless someone had told me. I recollect the town seemed mighty quiet for a settlement its size. There were no women or children on the street. And mighty few men . . . . [T]hey were ready for a bandit raid. They were forted as best they could be — had their window shutters drawn close and all hands inside.[28]

Durham later learned that the Nuecestown raid was significant for several reasons: it was the farthest inland the raiders had yet struck in force; it had occurred on a religious holiday, and the raiders had stolen eighteen new Dick Heye saddles from Noakes' store which caused McNelly to give a deadly order which later caused great problems for him. His reference to the saddles has caused doubt to be cast on the accuracy of much of Durham's recollections.

The Dick Heye saddles, which he described as the "Cadillacs of the saddle world," were new to the Nueces Strip. Anyone who had one—in McNelly's way of thinking, according to Durham—was automatically guilty of belonging to the gang which had raided the Noakes store. Durham recalled that McNelly's order was to shoot down any rider on a Dick Heye saddle on sight. He had a detailed description of the saddles given to all the rangers, a description which Durham recalled as being "heavily studded with silver conchos in a pattern you could tell half a mile away, a fact that proved

Left: George P. Durham who served with McNelly on the Rio Grande Frontier.
He later became a long-time foreman on the King Ranch. Right: Senator
Bolivar J. Pridgen, a leader of the Taylor faction who found fault with McNelly.
Photos courtesy The Western History Collection, University of Oklahoma.

to be the death warrant for many a man."[29] When a man was seen riding a Dick Heye saddle, the rider was to be shot, left where he fell, and the saddle brought into camp. Durham wrote that Captain McNelly was later in trouble in Austin for this order, "and it was talked about a whole lot in the governor's campaign. But I can say for sure, after all these years, there wasn't a man shot out of a Dick Heye saddle who wasn't down in The Book."[30]

Durham's mention of a book, a published list of fugitives from justice consisting of 227 pages "about the size of a novel" and containing the names and descriptions of wanted men, also poses a problem in substantiation. McNelly had supposedly received enough copies to give one to each man in the company and told them it contained the names of *fifty-one hundred* outlaws "that we know are in this vicinity."[31] The earliest known published lists of fugitives is dated 1878, and it is believed this recitation of the company's receiving a book listing 5,100 fugitives is a figment of Durham's, or his co-author Wantland's, imagination. There may have been some other form of fugitives list, but McNelly would not have had a copy for each man in the company, and no list was available this early in book form. And certainly McNelly himself did not believe there were 5,100 fugitives "in this vicinity!"

In addition to the fugitives book being a reminiscence problem of an old-timer, efforts to learn more about the Dick Heye "Cadillacs of the saddle world" have proved disappointing. There was a merchant in San Antonio in the mid-1870s, Diedrich Heye, who dealt in leather goods and undoubtedly saddle, harness and tack, but nothing in his advertisement in the city directory indicates his saddles were different from those of any other dealer.[32]

Since the Noakes store was a general merchandise establishment, there naturally was a supply of saddles and other tack. Coleman McCampbell published a history, *Saga of a Frontier Seaport*, in which a half-dozen pages were devoted to the raid. McCampbell stated that Noakes' loss from the theft and fire was estimated at $20,000 and the loot included twenty-five new saddles. For months afterwards the area was "a hot place for Mexicans. On the least provocation, the innocent along with the guilty, are shot or strung up to a mesquite limb. On glimpsing a Mexican riding new leather, a Texan was wont to say, 'Yonder goes a Noakes.' Unless a quick and satisfactory explanation could be furnished, good-bye to the Mexican."[33] This suggests that the raiders had stolen some new saddles, but there was nothing special about them.

Further, Ruth Dodson, born in South Texas a year and a half after the raid and knowing of it from her early years, did considerable research on the raid and published her findings in the popular periodical *Frontier Times*. She also mentioned saddles. At the S.H. Page home the raiders had left "old saddles" which were "exchanged for better ones." Further, Dodson wrote, the raiders "plundered the store of whatever they wanted, especially of the stock of saddles, which Noakes himself had made, he being a saddle-maker."[34] Dodson here verifies that new saddles were taken, but now they are a product of Noakes himself!

It thus appears that among the loot the raiders obtained there were new saddles, possibly made by Thomas J. Noakes himself. If this was indeed a fact then it would be easy for Noakes or others who had suffered losses from Mexican raiders to spread the word that any Mexican riding a new saddle was automatically one of the Noakes' store raiders. With the racial hatred of the time and place, it is probable that an Anglo, possibly having lost stock to raiders, would shoot any Hispanic riding in a new saddle if the opportunity presented itself to do so. However, no contemporary evidence yet uncovered suggests the saddles were so ornamental that they could be distinguished from any other new saddle *from a half mile away*. It is possible that McNelly give verbal orders to shoot anyone riding in a so-called Dick Heye saddle, but in all probability this is yet another myth created about the man.

Another ranger, Napoleon Augustus Jennings, published an account of his service with McNelly in 1899. A *Texas Ranger*[35] has also proved to be very popular throughout the decades and has been kept in print by different publishers even though Jennings was guilty of telescoping events in his narrative and placing himself in actions which the record shows he could not have been in. Jennings had to have been aware of the Noakes Raid and yet found no need to mention the Noakes store by name, made no mention of saddles, and made no mention of an order given by McNelly to shoot any man riding the Heye or any other saddle. Jennings was in communication with rangers who had served much longer than he and was certainly in a position to learn of such an extraordinary order if it existed. Neither did Jennings mention a "Fugitives Book" similar to that described by Durham.

William Crump Callicott served eight months with McNelly from April 1 through November 30, 1875. He had earlier gained valuable ranger experience under the command of John R. Waller of Company A of the Frontier Battalion, the same Waller who had unsuccessfully pursued Wes Hardin and Jim Taylor in Comanche and Brown counties. In 1921, while researching for what became *The Texas Rangers*, Dr. Walter Prescott Webb located Callicott and convinced him to write down his recollections. Callicott, in a definite position to know of such things because he was with McNelly during the entire Rio Grande Frontier experience, made no mention of the Dick Heye saddles, made no mention of a fugitives book, and made no mention of an order to shoot any one on sight if riding in a particular saddle. One is forced to believe that the account of the 1875 fugitives list in book form and the Dick Heye saddles as recounted by Durham are apocryphal.[36]

CHAPTER 13

THE LAW WEST OF THE NUECES

> The Brownsville *Sentinel* says the people between the Nueces and the Rio Grande have become so accustomed to being robbed, that they hardly consider it worth while to say anything about it. — The *Democratic Statesman*, Austin, September 9, 1871.

With dissatisfaction of the military expressed openly, and with county sheriffs admitting helplessness, it is not surprising that some persons believed it was time for Texas ranchers to take the law into their own hands. Brownsville Attorney William H. Russell went so far as to recommend to Governor Coke that he issue a proclamation to Texas citizens authorizing them "to band together and defend themselves and pursue the raiders and murderers. This would be a recognition which would add much to the effectiveness and moral forces of any body of men which might take the field."[1]

In early April William Steele sent a lengthy communication to McNelly. He first complimented him on his work, saying that in the new field of operations much would necessarily be left to his discretion, a discretion which now was greatly trusted due to his satisfactory handling of the troubles in DeWitt County. Steele issued instructions which must have reminded McNelly of E.J. Davis' "pep talk" on the lawn of the capital building prior to taking his squad of men to Laredo for the 1872 Rio Grande Expedition. Wrote Steele,

> As you are doubtless aware the Country bordering on the Rio Grande has been subjected to frequent raids of armed robbers who crossing from Mexico in small numbers elude observation until gathering in the interior, [where] they carry destruction to isolated ranchers and small villages. Your object will be to get as early information as possible of such gatherings, and to destroy any and every such band of freebooters. At the same time be careful not to disturb innocent people, who speak the same language with robbers. You will

doubtless find that in every town, ranch or village, the inhabitants will strive to convince you that their own particular locality is the one that especially requires pro~ tection[.] — Of that you must be the judge; recollecting that the best way to protect all is to find the robbers and make them harmless.

Steele stated his expectations clearly. McNelly was to be "gener~ ally" on the move and when at a ranch to take note of the residents and employees in order to determine if they were legitimate or if waiting for an opportunity to plunder. Many of the bandits, Steele advised, "have pretended employment with those who are afraid to inform on them, until the opportunity serves to show them in their true colors."[2]

McNelly and his company headed for the Rio Grande on Saturday, April 10, 1875.[3] In spite of the threatening reports in the press there may have been justification for a delay in sending McNelly south. Neal Coldwell, Captain of Company F of the Frontier Battalion, had been stationed there. In his report to Major John B. Jones of February 28, 1875, less than a month before the Nuecestown Raid, he wrote that everything seemed "to be quiet in this part of the Country at present. The people think that the Robbers will Keep clear of the country as long as we are here." Coldwell believed the conditions on that part of the frontier had been greatly exaggerated to Governor Coke. He ventured the asser~ tion that it was better protected than any other part of the frontier because of the troops stationed at Brownsville, Edinburg, Rio Grande City, Roma and Laredo. "With these patrols on this side of the River," Coldwell wrote, "and the vigillance [sic] of the authorities on the other Side, it Seems that there is little left for this company to do."[4] As late as April 30 Coldwell had "nothing of interest to report." He only could repeat a rumor that "a crowd of Americans from the vicinity of Corpus Christi had burned Some ranches in Cameron Co."[5]

The vengeance of Anglo ranchers following the Nuecestown Raid, swift and sweeping, spread as much terror in the Nueces Strip as the raiders had previously done. Not only were Mexicans gener~ ally believed to be outlaws to be hunted down, but peaceful rancheros and even Hispanic merchants paid dearly in the Anglo vengeance. The *jacales* of many Hispanics were burned at La Parra in Encinal County. In Kenedy County, at La Atravesada Ranch, adult

Hispanic males were shot.[6] Killings and burnings also occurred at El Penascal, Corral de Piedra and El Mesquite. Lieutenant B.M. Custer of the 24th Infantry telegraphed from Corpus Christi that "armed Mexicans" had cut the wires on April 18 and that three days earlier the operator at La Parra had been "chased off." On the same day, April 15, five ranches had been burned, the Prieto, La Rabasoda, Mosa, Bareto and the Mesquito. Richard King was asking for assistance because an armed party of thirty-five men was "near them with firing going on." There were rumors that the banditti were threatening to destroy Banquete, just outside Corpus Christi. Brigadier General E.O.C. Ord had ordered

Richard King, cattle king of Texas and the most influential stock raiser in the Nueces Strip. King exerted pressure on Governor Coke to send a force of special rangers to the Rio Grande Frontier. *Courtesy The Texas State Library & Archives Commission, Austin.*

mounted troops out from Fort Brown and Ringgold Barracks, and Colonel J.H. Potter of the 24th Infantry was readying a "disposable mounted force" as well.[7]

By now many men had decided to band together to protect their lives and property. Two of the groups were under the leadership of ranchers Martin S. Culver and T. Hynes Clark. Not knowing if the increasing destruction was being done by raiders from across the river or by Texas ranchers — Culver, Clark or even Richard King — Nueces County Sheriff John McClane begged Austin for official assistance, specifically McNelly. He now telegraphed to Adjutant General Steele a confusing call for help, "Is Capt McNelly coming[?] Five ranches burned last week by Mexicans disguised."[8] Were they Anglos disguised as Mexicans or were they Mexicans disguised as Indians? Steele responded by informing Sheriff McClane that the company had started for Corpus Christi ten days previously, or April 9.[9]

Although Captain Coldwell may have had good intentions for the work on the border, events proved he was better suited elsewhere. On April 24, when reports reached him of ranches being burned, he sent a scout under Lieutenant William K. Jones to investigate in the vicinity of La Parra. Jones' report sent to Major John B. Jones indicated that a party of Americans had indeed been responsible for the burning, that they were from the vicinity of Banquete, Nueces County, and hinted that this was an act of reprisal for the Nuecestown raid. Jones also reported that one of Captain Richard King's "corporals" was "concerned" in the affair. After the numerous burnings and killings of "Mexicans," nearly all of the ranchos in that vicinity were deserted by "Mexicans" for fear of further outrages. Lieutenant Jones' report to Coldwell apparently has not survived, but evidently his investigation ended when facts pointed to Anglo ranchers as the guilty parties. Coldwell wrote that Jones returned to camp on May 3, because the "burning party" had left the country. He concluded his report, "Everything in this vicinity quiet as usual. There has been no stealing since we have been here." Coldwell further implicated Anglos by repeating a statement from Justice of the Peace John Burbons who said, "the American Stock men from the Nueces country do more Stealing here than any one else."

Coldwell had further problems on the border. In his May Report of Operations he complained about the problem of reenlistments. If his men were given the opportunity to serve on the "upper frontier," twenty-five or thirty would reenlist; but only three or four of the company would want to continue to serve in the Rio Grande area. The reason, Coldwell offered, was that "there is no excitement and *apparently* nothing to be done." He further complained of how discouraging it was to hear of the activity of thieves at a given place, then after hard riding to that point named be told by some *caballero* in breach cloth and sandals that there was nothing going on and the long hard trip and been made for nothing, everything being "muy Silencio."[10]

Coldwell and McNelly met at Edinburg on May 13. Four days later Coldwell wrote to Major Jones that there was "nothing for us to do here, unless we are permitted to cross the Rio Grande." Coldwell indicated he would like to cross over "and beat them at their own game," as there was "a Splendid field of operations just across the river for a Ranger company. If I could only find a trail of the thieves going across I would Soon be on the other Side."[11]

Although Coldwell and McNelly had spent some time together and presumably had discussed the possibility of crossing over, McNelly wrote that he felt Coldwell was "disinclined to take chances in cross-ing the river. . . ." Perhaps to impress Steele with the deadly situation on the border, McNelly told of how on the day previous Cortina had "hung an Alcalde & another mexican [sic], for killing one of his cat-tle thieves."[12]

Just as Adjutant General Steele had ventured into DeWitt County to make observations personally, he now went to the border to conduct his own investigation. In company with the Honorable Joseph E. Dwyer, who was fluent in the language and whose late father had had extensive business relations in Mexico, Steele first vis-ited Corpus Christi, a few miles from Nuecestown.

Their first subject of investigation was the recent Nuecestown Raid. Among others with whom they conversed were Mr. and Mrs. Thomas J. Noakes, George Franks and Sidney G. Borden, who had all suffered during the Good Friday Raid. From these and other wit-nesses Steele learned that the raiders were all Mexicans and were not known to any of the citizens who lived there, suggesting they had crossed over from the other side. Noakes, one of the most successful merchants in the area and who had lost everything, had wounded one of the raiders, Godina, who then was abandoned by his com-rades because he could not travel and was then lynched by irate townspeople. From the victims of the raiders Steele learned addi-tional details. Those who had raided Nuecestown were but a part of a much larger group whose ultimate objective had been to raid Corpus Christi itself, but a disagreement in the group concerning who should assume command so reduced the numbers that the orig-inal idea of attacking Corpus Christi was abandoned.

Adjutant General Steele did draw some conclusions from his investigation on the border. First, there was a "considerable element in the country bordering on the Nueces and west, that think the killing of a Mexican no crime" and that this attitude had created such a fear that much of the trade between Laredo and Corpus Christi had been stopped. Further, the killing of cattle for their hides had much to do with the situation, and "some of the merchants of Corpus Christi are much to blame for their encouragement of this illegal traffic." And the thieves and cut-throats who had collected on the border "think the killing [of] a Texan something to be proud of, and they will kill anyone, even of their own nationality, should he happen to encounter them with stolen cattle, unless they have con-

fidence in his discretion." But, more importantly, Steele was con~
vinced that the single most important influence in encouraging the
brigandage was General Juan N. Cortina.

> Cortina is the recognized head and protector of all
> of the cattle thieves and murderers, from Camargo to
> the mouth of the Rio Grande. He takes them from the
> hands of any officer who is bold enough to arrest them;
> they, in turn, support him against all powers that may
> be brought against him. It is impossible to conceive . . .
> of the extent of the power of this great robber chief. It
> is a well known fact, that not only Cortina himself, but
> even his mistress, gives orders to judges, as to their deci~
> sions in cases, either civil or criminal, and such orders
> are obeyed. His armed adherents are said to number
> over two thousand.

Steele believed that the raids into Texas would continue "until
this man is removed entirely from our frontier." He continued that
raiding parties were "still being organized on Mexican soil for the
purpose of plundering ranches, stores and individuals, [and] these
acts are committed with the knowledge and connivance of Mexican
officials," that parties of Americans living near the Nueces had
banded together in order to stop the practice of killing cattle for
their hides, but these Americans had committed "the greater crimes
of murder and arson," that many merchants in Corpus Christi and
elsewhere had aided and abetted the hide peeling by knowingly buy~
ing stolen hides; that the country near the Rio Grande was being
rapidly depopulated of good citizens on account of the "insecurity of
life and property"; that the "negro U.S. soldiery give no sense of
security to citizens outside of towns, but on the contrary, are
regarded with fear"; that there was an intelligent and industrious
population on the Texas border who only needed security from for~
eign incursions, to make them "valuable, law~abiding citizens, whose
flocks and herds will add very largely to the wealth of the State."
    To prevent the "irritating causes, which, if allowed to continue,
will sooner or later involve the two countries in war" Steele con~
cluded that the "despotic power" of Cortina had to be removed; fur~
ther, officers on both sides of the border had to agree not to allow
criminals to find safety on the opposing side of the border. "Failing
in such peaceable measures, it is necessary that there should be a

large force, under one head, on the Rio Grande, with orders to pursue and capture felons into Mexico, if necessary."[13]

With orders to pursue and capture felons into Mexico, if necessary.

Joseph E. Dwyer, Steele's traveling companion, was later to
report that he was informed by a lawyer and "man of standing at
Matamoros, Mexico" that Cortina had organized and encouraged
the Nuecestown Raid. In spite of Cortina's apparently being instrumental in organizing the raid, eight of the raiders, on their return
from Texas, were arrested in Camargo and Mier, every one of them
mounted on horses bearing American brands. Dwyer did not
address this question of these raiders' arrest. From all accounts the
raiders came from Las Cuevas, Reynosa, La Bolsa and Matamoros,
communities close to the river.[14] Although Texans in general and
the press in particular cast Mexicans from below the Rio Grande as
being the criminals, Dwyer expressed the belief that the reports of
raiding were much exaggerated and thought that the Americans were
as much to blame as the Mexicans.

McNelly's arrival in the Nueces country was at first welcomed by
Texans. Durham wrote that the command, numbering forty-two
men, stopped at outfitter Sol Lichenstein where they obtained single
shot Sharps carbines. As to why the captain selected Sharps when
Winchesters were available, McNelly is quoted as saying, "If a man
misses the first shot, reloading kinda gives him time to think why'n
hell he missed the first shot. And if he didn't get his man in two
shots, dam[n] it, he ain't got no business in this outfit." Durham said
that was about the longest "speech" he ever heard McNelly make,
"but he packed into it his entire idea of fighting; and we took single
shot carbines there and we never had nothing else."[15]

After he noticed that Lina Saldana and Jesús Sandoval,
strangers, had been brought into the company, Durham noted that
McNelly already had implemented a sort of "spy system." That
McNelly had initiated a system of scouts this early can be substanti-
ated by a letter of Adjutant General Steele's to Governor Coke during Steele's trip to investigate the condition of affairs along the river.
Writing from Corpus Christi at the end of May, Steele noted that
McNelly was there "with a small party" and had been "active in getting information of the State of the other Side of the Rio Grande
which we will verify as we go along if his information is accurate."
Steele did not explain what he was referring to, but he was
impressed, writing that McNelly had "done wonders but I fear that
he has been misinformed. But I have seen and heard enough of the

Strength of the freebooters to authorize McNelly to raise his company to 75." Steele stipulated that McNelly was not to enlist from along the river, and McNelly in turn proposed that they be drawn "from the parties in Dewitt [sic] County which may have a good effect upon the troubles there[.]" McNelly's suggestion is certainly noteworthy; the fighting men of DeWitt County who would not give up their arms to the law the year before were now being considered by McNelly as worthy of serving with the ranger company!

Steele further noted that on the way from Austin to Corpus Christi they had met with Judge Sidney G. Borden and District Attorney William H. Crain. Judge Borden prom-

William Woodson Wright, rancher of the Nueces Strip who assisted McNelly in April 1875.
Photo courtesy C.B. Jefferies.

ised to call the attention of the grand jury to the raids "and have an examination under oath." It was the belief of some that the raiding parties were encouraged because Corpus Christi merchants profited from their raids. "I believe," Steele continued, "that the largest merchants here are not blameless in the matters of hide stealing at least such is the information given me."[16]

According to Durham, McNelly and his command spent that night in Corpus Christi and then went on to Banquete where they met up with William Woodson "Old W6" Wright, a prominent farmer and stock raiser from Georgia whose brand presumably reflected his name's initial and number of children. To Durham's young teenaged eyes, no doubt W.W. Wright, born on January 26, 1818, did appear "old." Durham also recalled him as "quite a character, and a good stockman," and wrote that he had made "quite a bit of money in the last ten years running a book on travelers into the Nueces Strip." Wright would "look over" a party as they prepared to venture further into the Nueces Strip and lay money on whether or not they would make Brownsville. He even made bets on whether all of McNelly's company would "stick." Wright bet that nine of the company didn't have what it took to stick it out with McNelly. Durham related that "old W6 won all these bets."[17]

From Wright's ranch they progressed on to Captain Richard King's Santa Gertrudis Ranch where they met the cattle king, "then in his prime and a dead ringer for Captain McNelly."[18] King and McNelly, besides having a common interest in protecting Texas cattle and horses, may have found an additional reason to work well together: King was a native of Ireland, fifty-years-old in 1875 when McNelly met him, probably for the first time although they had possibly met when McNelly was in the Rio Grande area in 1872. When the 1870 Nueces County census was recorded King gave real estate value at $200,000 and personal estate value at $362,000.[19]

Durham suggested King knew McNelly only by reputation and was "plenty glad to see him and see that he had come down to clean up the Nueces country." He claimed that in the previous ten years King and other cattle barons had lost nearly 900,000 head of cattle to the raiders. To protect himself from total destruction King had turned his home into a fortress, had eighty stands of Henry rifles, and had two-hundred "hard boiled vaqueros fighting for him and his stock."[20]

McNelly obtained good fresh mounts from Captain King. The

W.W. Wright with sons and cowboys at his Rancho Seco holding. The young ranger recruits who were with McNelly on the border probably looked little different from these young men on horseback. *Photo courtesy C.B. Jefferies.*

Martin S. Culver, Nueces County
rancher whose unofficial posse was
disbanded by McNelly in 1875.
*Courtesy the Western History
Collection, University of Oklahoma.*

ranchman and his partner Mifflin Kenedy brought in two-hundred horses and offered McNelly and his men the pick of the lot, furnishing McNelly and his men with dependable mounts as good as any available in the United States. With fresh horses, new Sharps carbines and their belts filled with ammunition, they were ready to head into the bandit chieftain's territory.[21]

But prior to any confrontation with marauders, McNelly met with the groups of Texans who were nothing more than mobs looking for raiders. Durham placed the meeting at La Parra where they met the "posses" of Martin S. Culver and T. Hynes Clark. Culver was a thirty-eight-year-old stock raiser from Louisiana but had lived in Texas since at least his early teens. Clark was in his mid-thirties, also born in Louisiana, and also a long time Texan, having lived in Texas since before the Civil War.[22]

Durham recalled that when they met Clark and Culver "and their hundred men," McNelly faced them down with "You damn fellows have been doing more mischief than the bandits themselves." Challenged to either disband and go home or fight, the mob disbanded. Durham remained convinced that had the mob not disbanded McNelly would have ordered his men to fire into them. Of this initial peaceful engagement he wrote, "McNelly met the volunteers there on the sands and he had it out with them in less than five minutes. And from that moment on, Captain McNelly was the law west of the Nueces — backed by the state of Texas like no other man ever was backed. And Texas made no mistake that time."[23]

A much less dramatic, but probably much more accurate, account was prepared by a reporter of *The Valley Times* who had accompanied Captain Culver and his posse. On Sunday morning, April 25, the group left Corpus Christi for the La Parra region. The first day's ride to the Gorrillas rancho, about sixty-five miles from

Corpus Christi, was so hard that the feet of some of the men were blistered by the stirrups! The countryside was nearly deserted because the rancheros had fled to the river. "Desolation" in the region "reigns supreme. It is almost impossible to meet a Mexican or induce him to stop to be interrogated."

At the Scott Creek crossing, three miles from La Parra, they met McNelly and his command. The two groups joined forces and proceeded together to the Bovido rancho. Soon others joined until there were about 125 armed men under the command of McNelly, Martin S. Culver, T. Hynes Clark, Sidney G. Borden and one Hunter. At Bovida Rancho McNelly called captains Clark and Culver and the correspondent to a council and announced that he intended to disband all armed groups except his own. McNelly further promised that a "searching and thorough examination" would be made into the La Parra affair and that the men who were responsible would be brought to justice. By taking away the power of the vigilante groups McNelly promised he would give "full security, and restore peace to the distracted section." Culver and Clark promised to cooperate and provide any assistance they could offer. The reporter's account, published within days of its occurrence, is dramatically different from the accounts provided years later by men such as Durham. The reporter concluded by stating that McNelly and his company then returned to Santa Gertrudis to obtain provisions. "The Captain himself left on Tuesday with two or three men and a guide for Brownsville, going by La Par[r]a and El Sauz, and reassuring and inviting all Mexicans who have fled from their homes to return under full assurance of protection. When he returns he will keep a portion of his command constantly in the saddle, looking for thieves and raiders. He will not remain inactive, but will thoroughly scour the country."[24]

Shortly after his arrival at Corpus Christi McNelly had clearly established that he was going to be the man in charge with no room for vigilante groups. He published an order in the Corpus Christi newspaper, written on April 27 from the "Headquarters Co. A. Volunteer Militia" at the Gorillas Ranch. Reprinted by several other papers, the order clearly established his authority.

> In consequence of the most recent outrages committed in this portion of the country by armed bands of men acting without authority of law, I find it necessary to notify all such organizations that after the pub-

lication of this order I will arrest all such bands and turn them over to the civil authorities of the counties where they are arrested, and nothing but the actual presence of some duly accredited officer of the county or State will protect them from arrest.[25]

Surprisingly this edict met with anger in some quarters! San Antonio's *Daily Express* published the order with an editorial comment.

This is an extraordinary proclamation emanating from a Captain of a Corporal's guard sent by the so-called Governor of the State to the Rio Grande to extinguish the Mexican raiders. It seems to be directed, not against the Mexicans, but against the Americans, who are characterized as "armed bodies of men acting without authority of law." He also threatens to arrest the offenders if found with arms in their hands. This high handed way of ordering citizens to disband by a Captain of police, exceeds anything that ever happened under the Davis Police; martial law had some semblance of authority; but McNelly issues his orders like an Emperor."[26]

Residents of McNelly's home county learned of the incident. The Brenham *Banner* of May 7 noted that McNelly was "doing good service upon the frontier." Further, a letter from Corpus Christi published in the Galveston *Daily News* under date of April 28, stated that McNelly had instructed the commanders of "irregular bands to take their men home and disperse them, or else be would have them all arrested." McNelly told them he would do this even "if it cost him the life of every man in his company. These men did not wait for any further orders to go, but they went at once."[27]

But Clark and Culver held no personal grudge against McNelly. In fact at a meeting in April citizens, stock raisers and tax-payers of Nueces County had met and raised a fund for the support of a forty-man company to repel Mexican raids. Richard King promised $1,000; T. Hynes Clark promised $300; Alice Clark promised $200; Martin S. Culver promised $150 and W.W. "W6" Wright promised $200. There is no indication that any of these monetary supporters ever withdrew that support.[28]

In an apparent effort to bring some type of confidence and feeling of security to the area, the press indicated things were peaceful thanks to McNelly. A Corpus Christi correspondent reported that with McNelly's approach the "Mexican army of invasion" had "melted away" and that the only army of invasion McNelly saw was from the Nueces, indicating the Nueces County posses. "Many of these were reported to be Indians in disguise. If they were not Indians in color, they surpassed any of the Indian tribes in barbarity. The scene at and around La Parra will bear testimony to this."[29] Captain King was taking no chances; after he and neighboring ranchers had lost an additional three-hundred head of cattle in early May he purchased four brass twelve-pounders for protection. A Captain Foster delivered four boxes of arms and seven cases of ammunition.[30]

Durham was beginning to admire his commander more and more. An incident reported first in the Corpus Christi *Times*, and then reprinted in Norton's *Union Intelligencer* published in Dallas could only have strengthened the admiration of all the young recruits for their leader. Desiring to visit the ranches in the La Parra neighborhood, McNelly called for three or four volunteers to go with him. "Mounted on his fine six hundred dollar horse, he heard some of the men say he could get away if pursued by an overpowering force, and they couldn't. Quietly dismounting he sent back to the Bovido Rancho and borrowed a horse that couldn't run faster, if so fast, as those of the men. He had no difficulty then in procuring volunteers, and made the visit."[31]

Although Durham made no mention of this specific incident, he did give his readers another explanation as to why his men were so devoted to the captain. Prior to going deeper into bandit territory, several young rangers, Durham among them, contemplated resigning until the captain made a little speech. Durham recalled it as follows:

> Boys, I may lead you into hell; but I'll get you out if you do exactly as I tell you to do. I'll never send you into a battle, I'll lead you. All I ask any man to do is follow me.
>
> After that only death could prevent my following Captain McNelly.[32]

William Crump Callicott as a young ranger recruit. Callicott dated this as
"1875." The image, originally a tintype, has not been reversed.
Courtesy The W.P. Webb Collection, University of Texas, Austin.

CHAPTER 14

A CHALLENGE TO CORTINA

He has sworn undying hostility to the Americans, and has let no opportunity pass to give vent to his hate. He boasted then that he has never signed the treaty of Guadaloupe-Hidalgo, and his sentiments then, as now, are "eternal hatred to the Americans." . . . Cannot the American Eagle at least *show* the Mexican Buzzard his talons? — The San Antonio *Daily Express*, 11 August 1871.

McNelly had made an excellent impression on the Texas ranchers during his first month on the border. He had established without gunplay that he was the man in charge, convincing Culver, Clark and the other leaders to disband their mobs. His action garnered considerable notice in the press of South Texas; the Galveston *Daily News* of May 4, 1875, for example, had printed a lengthy contribution from a Corpus Christi resident, which included relevant news items from the *Daily Valley Times* as well as publishing McNelly's order to disband. Although this publicity may have caused Culver, Clark and the others some embarrassment, reportedly they were satisfied with McNelly's intentions, and "promised all the co-operation and assistance they could render."

After the members of the mobs had left for their respective homes McNelly returned with his company to Santa Gertrudis, the nearest point to obtain provisions. On Tuesday, April 27, McNelly, with two or three men and a guide, left for Brownsville, going by La Parra and El Sauz, along the way reassuring and inviting all Mexicans who had fled from their homes to return under full assurance of protection. McNelly intended to keep a portion of his command in the saddle at all times, scouting for thieves and raiders.[1]

His young rangers could expect to be active, continually scouring the country. George P. Durham, only eighteen years of age and among the youngest in McNelly's command and who had just been mustered into Company A on April 1, was beginning to realize the character of the dangerous country into which the command was

entering. He recalled the country vividly when writing his reminiscences years later; he also recalled that there were five members of
the company who had decided the dangerous men they would be
fighting were too much for them. McNelly wrote out the quintet's
discharge papers with somewhat of a sneer, "he never said anything
when a man 'couldn't take it' as they say" unless they turned their
backs on the command, being fearful of such men as King Fisher,
Frank Porter and Cortina, and "hundred of others . . . known to be
dangerous; known to be deadly." Durham, who may have actually
believed there were more than five-thousand outlaws in the Nueces
Strip, suddenly realized that he was in a position where deadly situations could arise at any time. He wrote that McNelly "meant to
lead, not send, but lead them right up to these lead flingers and hold
them there until one side or the other won." Durham had to be
aware not only of the presence of such notorious figures as King
Fisher, Porter and Cortina, but of the many nameless desperadoes
who would cut the telegraph wires between Corpus Christi and
Brownsville, who would chase off the telegraph operator at La Parra,
and who would murder and mutilate helpless travelers for a small
amount of money — all recent actions which caused the Nueces Strip
to become a land of terrorized citizens, Anglos and Mexicans alike.
If Captain Richard King had to make his home into a fortress to protect his life and property, were the McNelly men capable of defending themselves?[2]

The *Express* of San Antonio continued to belittle Governor Coke
using McNelly as the means. It reprinted an article from the *Valley
Times* relating that a "contribution" had been taken up the previous
week by retired merchant Perry Doddridge[3] and others to obtain
money enough to buy a team of mules for McNelly so he could transport provisions for his company from point to point. McNelly had
acquired the mules at King's ranch. Commented the *Valley Times*,
"We should think the State could afford that much aid to our
already over-burdened citizens, and not compel us to bear the whole
burden of protecting the frontier." To this the *Express* satirically
added, "So Coke sent McNelly to the Rio Grande without anything
to eat. Just like him."[4]

The question of war and also the leadership in Mexico was continually raised. General Edward Hatch returned from the border
region describing the condition of affairs on the Mexican side of the
river as "decidedly hostile." According to Hatch, Juan Cortina was
master of the situation and had twelve-hundred men as a regular

force besides thousands of guerrilla followers on both sides of the Rio Grande. Mexicans openly boasted that they intended to take back from Texas all the land south of the Nueces. There was a "system of deliberate assassination" being carried on and if successful "every American on the river will eventually be killed." Cortina was "practically independent of all control by the Federal Government of Mexico, and is determined to kick up a row," so Hatch predicted.[5]

San Antonio could anticipate many refugees from the border, predicted the *Express*. It reported that the border situation was growing more serious every day and that, although McNelly and a few men were dispatched there, "not a single American citizen living in that region feels the least security, and they are either preparing for war or leaving their homes and coming into the posts." Captain Richard King was fortifying and installing cannons to defend his ranch. To the *Express* it seemed almost inevitable that a serious outbreak would soon occur. Although it was not stated perhaps the *Express* actually wanted a war![6]

While McNelly was gathering mules and developing a spy system, Cortina was not idle. He, or a group of his men, stole cattle from one Señor Treviño, living near Reynosa. Treviño sought out the thieves, recognized them as Cortina's men, and challenged them. In the ensuing exchange he killed one, wounded another, and captured a third. When Cortina learned of this act of defiance he gathered a force of 135 men, certainly as much for show as for effect, and headed to Reynosa. He demanded the alcalde release the prisoner. The alcalde refused, and both he and Treviño were shot and the prisoner released. It was apparent that Cortina was acting without fear of retribution. While Cortina and his friends had a "jollification" that morning, May 19, McNelly, in Brownsville, learned of the crossing of three droves of stolen cattle just that week. The theft of horses, cattle and oxen was occurring from Fort Ringgold to Fort Brown.[7]

McNelly now replaced Captain Coldwell on the border. George Durham, aware of at least several meetings between the two officers, later reflected on the change of command and recorded that Coldwell failed on the border because he had no reliable spies. By contrast McNelly, who believed in the necessity of a good spy system, had started developing his system from the time the command had left Burton. Durham began to realize changes within the command over the next few days as it approached Rancho Las Rucias, a few miles below the present town of Mercedes. There, "things began

happening in a way that made it look like hell was due to pop."
Durham identified the "strange man riding with McNelly" as "Old
Rock", but in reality he was Herman S. Rock from Brownsville. Rock
soon brought two others scouts into camp, Lina Saldana, a deputy
sheriff of Cameron County, and Jesús Sandoval, described by
Durham as "the most vicious, merciless killer that ever has come to
my notice."[8]

Sandoval had been a successful rancher in his younger years but
when his wife and daughter were ravished by raiders, his horse herd
stolen and his ranch burned, he became a maniacal avenger. From
that point on, according to how Durham remembered him, he went
"crazy", devoting himself to destroying as many raiders as possible.
He poisoned water holes and shot bandits on sight. If he captured
one alive he devised his own way of killing with a noose; frequently
merely hanging a raider was not sufficient because Durham
described how on some occasions his methods of torture involved
decapitation. But Sandoval was considered by the men of McNelly's
command as the "best of all our scouts."[9]

William Crump Callicott had learned that, some time before
joining McNelly, Sandoval and a companion had captured four
raiders and hanged the quartet from a single tree. Instead of simply
stringing them up to a tree limb, Sandoval created his "Paint gallows" — forcing the condemned raider to stand on the back of
Sandoval's Paint horse with the noose tight around his neck. Then
the horse was slapped out from under him.[10]

Long scouts resulting in little action, and belatedly catching up
with stolen cattle just after they had been crossed over, proved frus-
trating to McNelly as well as to his men. Durham wrote that the men
knew that when D. R. Smith broke open boxes of ammunition they
expected to see action: "Old Dad Smith issued us two hundred
rounds each." On one such occasion when they felt a fight was imminent, some of the young recruits such as Durham who had never
had cause to shoot at another human being, realized they might be
among the casualties. This time Mrs. McNelly was in camp, a "little
ninety-pound girl that before the war had known only plantation
and college life . . . she was hardly more than twenty; but she was a
woman; and she was the Captain's wife, and until now I hadn't got
in speaking distance of her. But this morning, with all this in the air,
I wanted to talk to a woman." Durham's "talk" consisted of asking
Mrs. McNelly to send the news to his mother in Georgia, if he
should not return, and a note telling who should receive his few

belongings.[11]

By sundown the advance guard, consisting of Horace Maben and H. G. "Deaf" Rector, brought in a captive. Although he denied knowing anything about raiders, he was riding in a Dick Heye saddle, as Durham recalled. Seeing the saddle, McNelly pointed the prisoner to a tree where he was held strangling until he talked. Durham identified this first victim as Rafael Salinas. Early the next day they caught another bandit, identified as Incosnasción García, who was searching for Salinas. After a little "persuasion" García talked as well. McNelly may have had some compunction about torturing prisoners, but he believed that this was the only sensible way to fight the raiders; and Sandoval was enthusiastic about it.[12] Without special knowledge of bandit movements McNelly knew he would not accomplish anything on the border. Learning of the raiders' movements in sufficient time to act with a reasonable chance of breaking up the raids involved the torture and killing of prisoners, and in McNelly's mind the situation demanded such harsh actions. McNelly's treatment of suspected raiders was apparently well-known; Brigadier General E.O.C. Ord, in preparing a lengthy report to the Assistant Adjutant General, Division of the Missouri at St. Louis, dated September 10, 1875, wrote of his methods.

> The success of Captain McNally [sic], of the State troops, in striking the party of Cortina's men in possession of a stolen herd recently, was due to his accidentally capturing two straggling robbers, who, by the use of the only effectual means known in such cases, but not legitimate enough for regulars to apply, were compelled to betray the position and strength of their band.[13]

Callicott also commented on executing prisoners, stating that although he permitted Sandoval to deal with prisoners as he wished, McNelly "didn't like this kind of killing." The captain could stand death better by any other form than he could hanging. In spite of what Durham and Callicott both unhesitatingly expressed in their reminiscences, that McNelly allowed his "scout" to torture prisoners to gain important information, and despite what General Ord had reported to his superior about McNelly's treatment of prisoners, in this case McNelly reported the two prisoners were delivered to

General Edward Otho Cresap Ord, Commander Military Department of Texas. Ord recommended a vigorous and aggressive campaign against the raiders south of the border. From a photo by Brady originally appearing in Frank Leslie's *Illustrated Newspaper*, December 18, 1875. *Courtesy The Library of Congress.*

Cameron County Sheriff James G. Browne.[14]

The first dramatic engagement between the rangers and the banditti would not have occurred had not McNelly had an effective spy organization, in this instance resulting in the capture of the two straggling raiders and then defeating a raiding party consisting of over a dozen of Cortina's band. He had, on Saturday, June 5, "received information of a party of Mexicans, sixteen in number," who had crossed the river eight miles below Brownsville for the purpose of stealing cattle. He immediately ordered Lieutenant Robinson and eighteen men to proceed to the crossing of Arroyo Colorado and send out scouts from there to learn specific details. Three days later Robinson reported he had captured one of the raiders. McNelly later reported that he "at once went to the company and learned from the prisoner, Rafael Salinas, that the party consisted of sixteen men" and was under the command of Camillo Lerma and José María Olguín, alias El Aguja [The Needle], and that they had been sent by General Cortina to La Parra neighborhood to get a drove of cattle for the Cuban market. Salinas "further stated that he had been left behind to remount and act as rear guard." McNelly then sent one of his spies to follow the raiders and stay on their trail until they returned with their stolen cattle. In the meantime McNelly kept his men concealed and guarded all the passes of the Arroyo Colorado for twenty miles up and down the river to prevent the raiders from attempting to cross without his knowledge.

Incosnascíon García, another member of the raiding party, was captured on Friday, June 11. His story agreed with that of Salinas, that the sixteen-man raiding party had about three-hundred head of cattle and intended to cross the Arroyo Colorado that night. A McNelly spy brought in the word that the thieves had passed, so McNelly headed towards the Laguna Madre and caught sight of them about 7:00 a.m., some eight miles distant. The raiders discovered McNelly's group about the same time and started running the cattle. After chasing them three miles McNelly started to gain on them. Then "they drove the herd on a little island in a salt marsh, and took their stand on the opposite side and *waited* our approach for a *half hour*, before we reached the marsh." McNelly saw the raiders drawn up in a line on the south side of the marsh about six-hundred yards wide, filled with mud and water, eighteen or twenty inches deep, and behind a bank four or five feet high. McNelly formed his men in a skirmish line and rode into the marsh, but did not allow his men to unsling their carbines or draw their pistols. As McNelly described it,

> As soon as we struck the water, the raiders commenced firing on us with Spencer and Winchester carbines. We advanced at a walk (a more rapid gait being impossible,) and not firing a shot or speaking a word, our line well dressed. On our nearing the position they held, perhaps within 75 or 100 yards, they wheeled their horses round, and gallopped [sic] off at a slow gait. When we got out on hard ground, we pressed forward and soon brought ourselves, within shooting distance, 50 or 60 yards. The Mexicans then started at a full run, and I found that our horses could not overtake them. So I ordered three of my best mounted men to pass in their right flank, and press them so as to force a stand, [and] as I anticipated, the Mexicans turned to drive my men off, but they held their ground, and I got up with four of five men, when the raiders broke.

The Mexicans, seeing they were about to be cut off, panicked. "After that it was a succession of single hand fights for six miles before we got the last one. No one escaped out of the twelve that were driving the cattle. They were all killed."[15]

Callicott's description is informative and mirrors McNelly's, although written forty-six years later.

Capton Mcnelly wer in command of us all when we
Started a crows the lagoon in line of Battle. while the
mexican Bandits wer fiern [firing] on us all the time the
capton not payen but little heed to thire bullets[.
McNelly] hopend to cast his eyes to the Right and dis-
coverd a long Skirt of timber Runen north and South
in dyrectton of the Reo grand River[.] the capton new
that as soon as we got onto wher the warter and mud
wer Shallo a nuff to a low us to make the Charge it
would Be made[.]

Callicott recalled that when McNelly noticed the raiders'
attempt to reach the timber, he called Jesús Sandoval and five or six
others nearest to him to follow. They rode in water and mud, "nee
deep to belly deep." When the bandits saw they could not make the
timber they rallied and prepared to fight. After the initial exchange
of fire, in which one or two of the bandits were killed, they lit out
with every man for himself. Callicott said "it wer a Runen fight from
wher the capton and his men Killed the first to wher the capton
killed the last one in the dager thicket," a running battle of eight to
ten miles.[16]

Durham recalled that there were about five-hundred head of cattle in the stolen herd, and that most of the raiders had also been in
the raid on Noakes' store. He also recalled that McNelly's order had
been for each man to stay ten paces behind him, to "do exactly as I
say," to hold fire until McNelly opened the fight with his first shot,
and then to shoot only at the target directly in front, not to the right
or left. Prior to the rangers' opening fire, several of their horses were
wounded. William L. Rudd's horse went down; Durham's horse was
wounded as was Rector's. Durham claimed that he downed a raider
with a white scar, the man who had quirted Mrs. Noakes during the
Nuecestown Raid. One raider, after losing his horse, jumped up
behind a companion and rode double until Lieutenant Linton L.
"Lon" Wright fired on them and dropped both, two with one shot.
Durham said Wright used his carbine[17] while Callicott recalled he
used his Colts .45 pistol.[18]

McNelly himself shot the last raider. As Durham recalled, the
captain had pinned down one of the raiders behind a tree but could
not obtain a good shot because of his cover. McNelly resorted to a
ruse, hollering to his men that his pistol was empty and to bring him
shells. At that point the raider jumped out from cover intending to
kill the captain; McNelly fired and killed him.[19] Callicott recalled

this incident slightly differently, that they killed the raider's horse close to a Spanish dagger thicket into which the bandit scampered for cover. McNelly had the thicket surrounded and proceeded in. The bandit and the captain met on foot about eight feet apart. The bandit's pistol was empty and McNelly had but one shot left. Drawing his Bowie knife the raider started towards the captain, with a big grin saying, "Me got a you me got a you now," apparently believing McNelly's pistol was empty as well. McNelly fired a careful shot — the last shot he had — and placed the bullet "Betouen the Bandits teeth as if he had of

Linton Lafayette Wright, a McNelly Ranger who served as Sheriff of Duval County from 1880-1890. Photo by D.P. Barr, San Antonio, Texas. *Courtesy W.W. Meek.*

plast it thire with his fingers" dropping him dead in his tracks."[20]

Callicott placed the number of dead bandits at sixteen Mexicans and one Anglo, Jack Ellis, with only one bandit's escaping. Durham recalled there were sixteen dead bandits. There is indeed some controversy in regards to this question. Herman S. Rock, a mounted inspector of customs and deputy inspector of hides and animals, testified that in capturing two of the bandits, Salinas and García, they learned the names of the raiders who would fight McNelly: Camillo Lerma, Captain; Lieutenant George Ximenes; Pancho Lopes, Manuel García, Juan El Guarachi, Guadalupe Espinosa, Jacinto Ximenes, Cecelio Benavides, Tibutio Fuéntez, Casimiro García, Rafael Salinas, Encarnación García, Telesforo Díaz, José María Olguín, alias El Aguya, Guillermo El Cara Cortado, Dorote de la Garza and Guadalupe Escuval [Esquivel?]. This amounts to seventeen raiders with Hispanic names, and apparently includes the sixteen killed. He also recorded that all the raiders were either killed or wounded and that the state troops recovered 260 head of stolen cattle. Besides the cattle, some of the bandits' horses were taken, at least five of them stolen from Morgan Bavides [Benavides?] and Teodoro

García, Cameron County ranchers. All accounts agree that at least one of the raiders survived the battle, yet there is evidence that one American outlaw was with the group, identified by Callicott as Jack Ellis. Although Rock's identification was limited to men with Hispanic names, Callicott claimed one of the dead was named Jack Ellis. After being killed Robinson took possession of his horse and when in Mexico was riding the same mount, which he now called "Jack Ellis." [21]

Although wounded, at least one of the raiders, José María Olguín, alias El Aguja, did escape. He reportedly sought medical attention in Matamoros. Olguín had earlier managed to escape the Brownsville jail while waiting to be delivered to Huntsville to begin serving a fifteen year term for theft.[22] He then rejoined Cortina's raiders and was among those attacked by McNelly. A June 14 special to the Galveston *News* stated that Olguín had been wounded but feigned death, crawled into high grass, and was not found. Later he crawled into a cart being driven south, where he managed to find medical attention in Matamoros.[23] Ranger N.A. Jennings, who was definitely *not* in the force at this time but learned much of the details later from ranger comrades, wrote that the raider who escaped death, identified as Mario Olguine, "terribly wounded," had been nicknamed the Needle "because he had such a quiet way of slipping into ranch houses, on raids, and murdering the inmates while they slept. [He] was sent to jail, but died there, after lingering several weeks."[24] Cortina was furious when he learned of what McNelly had done to his men, and he claimed that his men had been assassinated while asleep. When McNelly learned of this charge he responded with jocularity that if they were asleep he didn't want to find any of them when awake![25]

McNelly's preliminary report to Governor Coke, hastily prepared on June 12 and with several errors which were later corrected, included this paragraph.

> This morning I came up with a band of twelve raiders. They attacked me when I over took them. It was a running fight. After that I got seven of them engaged and killed all. They fought desperately. I lost one man, Benj. Smith, and two horses killed and two wounded. I captured 250 beeves. To-night I go for another party. Men all trumps.[26]

McNelly further described the engagement as a "succession of single-handed fights for six miles, before we got the last one. Not one escaped out of the twelve [sic] that were driving the cattle. They were *all* killed." And McNelly recognized the intensity of the combat, adding that he had "never seen men fight with such desperation. Many of them, after being shot from their horses and severely wounded three or four times, would rise on their elbows and fire at my men as they passed." McNelly lost one man in his force, young L.B. "Berry" or "Sonny" Smith of Lee County. He further noted that Lieutenant T.C. Robinson and Private J.T. Wofford's horses were killed and two other horses were wounded. None of his men was wounded.[27] The engagement had worn down McNelly's horses so much that they were unable to go after a second party of thieves led by Ricardo Flores.[28]

McNelly's initial calculation was that he captured twelve horses which had belonged to the raiders, numerous guns, pistols and saddles, and 265 head of beef cattle belonging in the neighborhood of King's Ranch. McNelly had somehow notified Cameron County Sheriff Browne that the fight was imminent, because he reported that Browne, with a posse of Mexicans, had been "in sight of the whole affair, but their horses were too much jaded for them to get into the fight."

McNelly was not satisfied with merely recovering a few stolen cattle and killing a few raiders. He turned them over to Sheriff Browne who knew most of them. Browne, or perhaps his posse members, identified all of them as Cortina's men, noting that four of them, Camillo Lerma, George Jimmies [sic, Ximenes], alias the "Coyote," Telesporio [sic] Díaz and Guadalupe Espinosa, were "said to be Cortina's favorite bravos."[29] Rather than leave the dead men on the prairie for the buzzards, McNelly had the bodies taken to Brownsville and had them placed on display after City Marshal Joseph P. O'Shaughnessy, on Saturday June 12, went out with a cavalry detachment to the battleground, about twelve miles northeast from Brownsville, to collect the dead and any wounded. "We arrived on the battle ground after twelve o'clock Sunday morning. We found and placed on two wagons, the bodies of eight dead Mexicans, which were transported to Brownsville. These were all we could find, though not all that were killed."[30] Once in Brownsville McNelly ordered the bodies of the raiders laid out in the city square. Jennings wrote that "Nearly the entire population of Matamoros . . . came over to view their dead countrymen. Many were very angry, and we heard threats that Cortina would come across with his men and kill us all. McNelly sent back word to Cortina that he would wait for him and his men." Fearing what might happen if relatives or friends claimed the bodies, they were all buried in one trench.[31]

By June 14 the press had received word of McNelly's victory from Major H.C. Merriam, of the 24th Infantry stationed at Fort Brown. The San Antonio *Express* headlined their report "Battle near Palo Alto./ Capt. McNalley [sic] Wins a Victory/ Twelve Mexicans Killed!/ One American Killed and one wounded." Merriam reported that besides the twelve raiders killed, one private [Smith] was killed and two wounded. "I sent wagons to bring in the dead Mexicans and have six here already who are recognized as belonging to Matamoras [sic]; the remaining bodies are expected in every hour. I also sent Capt. [J. W.] Clous out later in the night to cut off a party represented to have crossed below him to endeavor to rescue the party disposed of by Capt. McNelly."[32] Strangely, none of the ranger accounts mentions that any of McNelly's men were wounded although Merriam's report states that two were wounded, and a letter from William D. Whipple, Assistant Adjutant General writing to his superior in the absence of General Sherman, mentioned that besides the dozen Mexican cattle thieves and one ranger killed there were *two wounded* as well.[33]

The number of rangers actually engaged in the fight is also contradictory. A report from Brownsville on June 12 stated that the raiders, after being flanked by McNelly and three others, "halted and fought desperately. McNelly's horses were jaded, and but seven men were able to get into the fight. All the raiders, twelve in number, were killed. Berry Smith rushed in the midst of them and was shot by their leader, Camalo [sic] Lerma."[34] Other sources indicate sixteen rangers were actually in the fight.

Durham, in the *West* article, stated there had been some argument about who was in what has become known as the Palo Alto prairie fight and wanted to "clear it up for the first time." He named the following: Captain McNelly, lieutenants T.C. Robinson (who he incorrectly identified as T.J. Robinson) and Lawrence B. Wright; sergeants Linton L. Wright and R.P. Orrell, corporals M.C. "Polly" Williams and William L. Rudd; and privates Spencer J. Adams, George P. Durham, Matt Fleming, Horace Maben, Tom McGovern, H.G. Rector, Jesus Sandoval, L.B. Smith and Jim Wofford, a total of fifteen besides the captain.[35]

Because the Monthly Returns did not identify which men were

on which scout or action, the names of the participants in what has become known as the fight on the Palo Alto prairie can only be reconstructed from incomplete records. Surprisingly Durham did not mention William Crump Callicott who was in the company and who left a valuable record of his experience. He not only was in this bloody engagement but he also was with McNelly — as was Durham — later that year when the Rio Grande was crossed resulting in several days' activity in Mexico. However, with Durham and Callicott's record as well as with McNelly's report written shortly after the fight, the battle can be fairly accurately reconstructed.[36]

The cattle being driven by the raiders must have widely scattered during the running fight. John Jay Smith, Deputy Inspector of Hides and Animals, District of Cameron County, certified that on June 14 he received 216 head of beef cattle captured by McNelly and which were then sold "for the benefit of whom it may concern." Of the 216 head, Smith was able to determine the rightful owner of only one-hundred head belonging to thirty-six different individuals whose brands were legible. Three of the cattle were the property of Captain Richard King and five were the property of T. Hynes Clark, formerly a leader of one of the unauthorized posses which McNelly had forced to disband.[37]

McNelly arrived in Brownsville the evening of June 12 with the body of Ranger L.B. Smith, who had enlisted in the McNelly company with his father, D.R. "Dad" Smith, on July 25, 1874. The father and son were the oldest and the youngest in the company. With "Sonny" Smith's death, George P. Durham became the youngest in the company. Callicott recalled that his horse was used to transport Smith's body, and with several others he delivered Smith's remains to the Brownsville undertaker. Once in Brownsville, Lieutenant Robinson was placed in charge of the men while McNelly went to the hotel where Mrs. McNelly and son Leander Rebel were waiting. McNelly had told the men he wanted to spend as much time as he could with his family. The men were to stay at Captain King's Brownsville house until time for the funeral. The horses were to be left there while the men attended the funeral on foot.[38]

McNelly made Smith's funeral into an elaborate display and had the remains escorted to the city cemetery by a large procession made up of citizens and soldiers, as well as McNelly's men. Colonel H.C. Merriam and Colonel John S. "Rip" Ford were the marshals.[39]

At 3:30 in the afternoon of June 13 Lieutenant Robinson, Jesús Sandoval and the other rangers marched to the Brownsville undertaker where a hearse was waiting, hitched to two big black horses. Two marching bands were also there to provide the appropriate funeral dirges. Two companies of regular U.S. troops and McNelly and his wife and son made up the imposing cortege, which marched to a church where Smith's funeral message was given. Then the mourners proceeded on to the Brownsville cemetery where all paid their last respects to a McNelly ranger. The U.S. regulars fired shots over his grave. This was as great a contrast as possible compared to the disposal of the bodies of the Mexican raiders who were also killed in action.[40] No stone marks the location of young Smith's grave today although the location is known. D. R. Smith remained in the service until being discharged at his own request on November 26, 1876, having served a total of twenty-nine months and seven days. His son had served a total of ten months and eighteen days.[41]

The funeral of Ranger Smith was an opportunity for McNelly to make a statement to all rustlers: he was promising no quarter, and death would be the result if caught in the act. Clearly, the death of a McNelly ranger was the political equivalent to the assassination of a king.

Initially McNelly reported that twelve raiders had been killed in the engagement. His June 14 telegram to General William Steele reported he had killed that number and ended with a "Wish you were here" which suggests he was quite proud of his accomplishment and wished that Steele was there to savor the victory with him.[42] McNelly explained the conflicting numbers of Mexicans killed in his report to Adjutant General Steele, after stating that he turned over Rafael Salinas and Incosnasción García to Sheriff Browne, "I have just learned that we wounded two men in our fight that escaped, and one of them has since died. It seems there were fourteen in the party. As I only counted twelve as the firing commenced, and found twelve bodies after it was over, I supposed we had killed all."[43] Weeks later, on September 30, McNelly corrected the numbers and wrote that fifteen Mexicans had been killed and one wounded in the engagement. He further wrote that in July he had recovered three-hundred head of cattle from a party of Mexicans "who hearing of my approaching pursuit deserted their herd & Succeeded in escaping." He also reported that in June, July and August he had recovered from the other side of the Rio Grande forty horses belonging to parties in Texas. No details were disclosed as to how these actions were accomplished.[44]

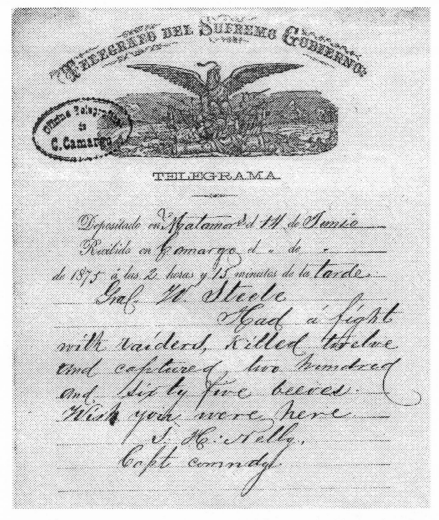

The "Wish you were here" telegram from McNelly to Adjutant General Steele.
Courtesy the Texas State Archives & Library Commission.

Although McNelly could claim an impressive victory after two months on the border, there was still a tremendous amount of work to be done. The *Express* of July 1 called him the "master of the situation," yet it was Cortina who was "king on the other side [of] the river." But in Mexico's volatile political world, Cortina's situation was not secure and was becoming "more perilous every day." The

Mexican government was calling for his presence in the capitol, and he did "not know which way to turn." Cortina had made a large fortune off of robbery, but it appeared his days as border chieftain were numbered.[45]

Many were concerned as to what Cortina might do after losing not only the stolen cattle and horses but a good number of his top men as well. General Philip H. Sheridan in Chicago kept in close communication with the military on the river. On June 16 he telegraphed to General E.D. Townsend in Washington that there was "a well founded fear that Cortina may retaliate for the just punishment administered . . . on the Band of Mexican robbers." Although the garrison at Fort Brown had been increased by three companies of cavalry and one of infantry, "Still I would recommend that the President make his conditional Order about navy

Juan Nepomuceno Cortina, rancher, general, governor, and recognized head of all bandits in the Nueces Strip during McNelly's campaign on the Rio Grande Frontier. *Courtesy The Texas State Library & Archives Commission, Austin.*

Vessels and a tug to the Rio Grande a positive one. . . ."[46] Eventually President Grant did order a vessel and a launch to the Rio Grande. While the telegrams rushed back and forth from South Texas to Washington, the United States military on the Rio Grande became more and more concerned about how Cortina would gain his revenge.[47]

Men in Texas were equally concerned. On June 22 Lieutenant James W. Guynn swore in twenty-five more men in the Washington County Volunteer Militia Company and took up the line of march from Colorado County to Camp Santa Maria on June 30. In some respects Guynn was as much a newspaper correspondent as militia officer; he sent reports and wrote letters for publication in *The Colorado Citizen* of Columbus, Colorado County, although in much fewer numbers and frequency than Lieutenant T.C. "Pidge" Robinson. Guynn's descriptions of the march from Columbus to

Brownsville provide a glimpse into the communities of Oakland, Cuero, Goliad, San Patricio, and the "miserable muddy village" of Banquete. The command arrived at King's on July 9. Guynn wrote,

> Capt. King [was] a gentleman of the highest standard. He came forward and made us every proffer of assistance, furnishing us with food for ourselves and horses, made your humble servant a present of a fine saddle horse for himself, as well as four for the use of the company; besides, changing horses with several of the company for their worn out and jaded ones, giving them the choice of his *caballado*. Too much praise cannot be given Capt. King for his openhearted generosity and kindnesses to us. The Captain has 86,000 acres of land under one fence for pasture grounds. . . . His residence is located upon a high hill, commanding a view of the surrounding country for miles around us.

Guynn and his men left King's Ranch after a resounding "three cheers" for Captain King and continued the march to Brownsville. They passed through sixty miles of sand, finding the grass good but no water except for an occasional salt lake which was of no use. Nothing happened of interest except "the constant bombardment of rattle snakes by the entire company, as their dead carcasses left in our wake will testify." [48] Guynn and his men reported to McNelly at Brownsville on the morning of July 14 and were described by one reporter as "splendid looking scalp hunters."[49]

When McNelly met his new rangers he formed them into line and gave them what Guynn termed a "lecture."

> Gentlemen, I make it a rule to allow no gambling in camps, no cursing, no drunkenness. If there are any here who can not abide by these rules, I will release him at once from his obligations to the State. Whereupon five timid hearted ones wisely concluded to "return to their dwellings, a lonely return."

In contrast, Durham recalled that the five men who quit the service before seeing any combat resigned shortly after McNelly broke up the Clark and Culver mobs, during early May. Guynn's account, written only days after it happened, must be given more credence than Durham's recorded many decades later.

After these five had left, the new recruits "were ordered by him to take up a line of march for our present camp [Santa María], 35 miles from Brownsville, where we met the old company, under command of Lieutenant T.C. Robinson, an officer of fine department and bearing. Our boys were met with the kindest advances by the members of his company and are well pleased with the officers. . . ." Guynn said McNelly and Robinson were considered "the *beau ideal* of officers and gentlemen."

But life in McNelly's ranger camp was not total drudgery as attested by Lieutenant Guynn. Many of the rangers attended the "Spanish Fandangos, given by the Mexicans almost nightly." As Guynn and McNelly were the only married men in camp, they of course did not participate. He ended this first communication to the home newspaper with a positive tone. "We are expecting to have a fight with raiders soon, or as soon as they set foot on Texas soil. The boys are well, in good health and spirits, and anxious for a fight."[50]

Governor Coke was proud of McNelly's accomplishment on the river. On July 9, after due time for reflexion on the Palo Alto prairie battle and the reaction of the press, the following was directed to Captain L.H. McNelly, "Commanding Rangers on Rio Grande:"

> The conduct of yourself and the officers and men under your command in discharge of the arduous duty of defending the Rio Grande border, and especially the skill and gallantry displayed by all in the signal blow struck the freebooters on the 12th day of June last, merit and receive the highest praise from the authorities and people of the State.
>
> The pride of true Texans in the historic fame of the Texas ranger, is fully gratified in the record your command is making and the people of the State are confidently expecting that your combined efforts will contribute greatly towards the restoration of peace, and a sense of security to our long suffering border.
>
> Much was, and is expected of your command; our highest anticipations have to this time been realized — you have done well. Continue the good work.[51]

This statement from the governor should remove all doubt as to whether or not McNelly was a Texas Ranger!

CHAPTER 15

INVADING MEXICO

> If this party that has been making So much preper-
> ations [sic] to cross fail & backs out there will be no fur-
> ther use for my company down here. I have Kept up
> Such an active System of scouting that they are contin-
> ual[l]y reporting my company in fore [sic] or five differ-
> ent places at the Same time & these theives [sic] have
> become disgusted with this country & are moving up
> the river. — L.H. McNelly to Adjutant General William
> Steele, August 13, 1875.

Following the blood bath on the Palo Alto prairie, McNelly and his men experienced quietude for a period of time. On August 12 the captain arrived at Brownsville, having placed his camp a mile above Santa María. Through his spy system he had learned of a contem-plated raid from Camargo and Las Cuevas; in fact he boasted to Adjutant General Steele that due to his spy system he was able to keep himself "posted in all their movements & in fact I know through my Spies all the general movements of the raiding parties on the other side from Matamoris [sic] to Camargo."[1]

Nine days earlier he had received a telegram stating that raiders planned to cross at Las Cuevas on August 6. The intended crossing point was the "Magotee of Don Juan." After dark on the night of August 4, McNelly and a portion of his company left camp and trav-eled at night, hiding in the brush during the day. On the morning of August 6 the rangers reached a point twelve miles from the Magotee. McNelly stationed his men there and remained until the night of August 11 when he learned from one of his spies the reason the raiders had failed to come — the raiders had changed their plans. Their night marches had been for nothing. McNelly had received a note written in Spanish and included it in his communication to Steele.[2] N.A. Jennings wrote that the rangers had "prepared to go to meet them and give them a warm reception; but before we started, a scout came in and told us that the leader of the gang had been assas-sinated by one of his own men on the day they were to start for

Mexico, and that the raid had been abandoned. Investigation showed this to be true."[3]

The document, addressed to "Capitan L H McNeles" and consisting of a few lines, was written at Rancho Davis [Rio Grande City] on August 11, by a correspondent identifying himself only as "Su amigo." It explained that Francisco de León had been killed for thirty pieces of silver given to him "for the expenses" [para los gastos]. The correspondent stated that he was starting for Las Cuevas on that same day, but no further explanation was provided. Apparently "Su amigo" had been the middleman between McNelly and one of Cortina's traitors and had delivered the payment for information about the raid. De León then was killed because the raiders discovered he had been acting in concert with McNelly.[4]

However, McNelly could express some optimism in his letter.

> There has been no determined attempts at driving off cattel [sic] Since you were here & no crossing below my camp. the mexicans won't ride across Palo Alto Prarie [sic] after dark. most all the leading Spirits have gone up to Camargo & above. three crossings were made above Edinboro [sic] one [on] July 20 one [on July] 22ond & one on the 27. [They were in] small parties & but one got back with cattel and they crossed near "Rancho Davis."

McNelly expressed concern that there would be no use for his company to stay unless raiding parties increased their efforts to steal cattle. "I have Kept up Such an active System of scouting that they are continual[l]y reporting my company in fore [sic] or five different places at the Same time & these theives [sic] have become disgusted with this country & are moving up the river."[5]

Lieutenant T.C. Robinson, now contributing his humorous and informative correspondence to the Austin *Gazette* but still using the pseudonym of "Pidge," also wrote of the heavy scouting details. His September 20 letter began,

> I would have written you long before now, but we have kept so constantly on the move that it was impossible. We have rode by day and by night over this whole country, and there is not a ranche, no Mexican or American in four counties who does not know every man in this company as well as he does his own

brother. If we did not keep constantly on the move, we would soon be a broken community, for the Mexicans seem to regard us as their own property, to be cheated, robbed and extorted upon generally, to the fullest.

Robinson explained that one rancher who resided on the road to Rancho Davis "wished to charge fifty cents per head for company horses occupying a corral for two hours, hardly large enough for them all to stand in." Although his letters were intended for publication in the *Gazette*, this particular communication was reprinted in *El Sentinel* of Brownsville and was also reprinted in *La Voz del Pueblo* of Matamoros. In the editor's commentary, worthy of note as it presents a radically different account of a simple event, McNelly and his men spent a night between Rancho Davis and San Luís and in the morning he asked how much the "poor Mexican rancher" wanted for the hay and fodder. The amount was fifty cents per horse. Accordingly the rangers began their insults.

> The very civil and educated Rangers started cussing and shouting obscenities against the poor defenseless rancher. They continued shouting and insulting him, telling him that he and his family had black souls, like the black beans they had just eaten. . . . The Rangers continued to insult and use vulgarity towards the rancher, until they threatened to kill him. The poor Mexican rancher told them if you don't want to pay me, don't pay me, just leave me alone and leave. The Rangers then started to tear his wooden fence down, so that each one of them should take a post with them.

The editor unintentionally provided ironic humor in his additional comment that, with such destructive conduct on the part of McNelly's men, "What is left for the real bandidos. . . ?"

Of further interest is the ironic comment made regarding McNelly's guide, Jesús Sandoval, in this same issue: "To make matters worse, the Rangers['] guide was Sandoval, the hangman, and we are told that he has a kind heart." [Para colmo de desgracias, los Rangers llevan de guia al colgador Sandobal, y este nos cuentan, que tiene un corazon tan hermoso como lo signiente le presenta.][6] One cannot help but wonder if Pidge obtained copies of *El Sentinel* or *La Voz del Pueblo* and thus became aware of how his writings were treated on the other side of the river.

Strangely McNelly himself had difficulties with the custom officials, certainly adding frustration to his work on the river. On
August 11 a wagon, its contents and team were seized by custom
inspectors at Santa María who charged that the wagon had been
driven into Mexico to obtain corn for the company horses and consequently had not properly passed through customs. McNelly wrote
a formal complaint to John L. Haynes, Collector of Customs, on
August 14.

> I hereby file claim for one Wagon two Mules two
> sets of harness, and eighteen bushels of Corn seazed
> [sic] by Inspectors Handy & Guzman August 11th for
> alleged violation of the revenue laws of the United
> States, upon the ground[s] that said Seazure [sic], was
> made on ter[r]itory of the U. Ss. and said articles
> seazed [sic], were all the growth and production of the
> United States, and not smuggled or brought from any
> foreign ter[r]itory, hereby offering bond for same, in
> accordance with law ect.[sic] Said articles Seazed [sic]
> are the property of the State of Texas, and are in my
> charge as Captain of Company of State Troops in serv-
> ice on this frontier and I claim them as agt of the
> State.[7]

The claim was filed on August 14 and McNelly gave $250 in
bond "for cost and expenses of suit in case the State looses [sic],
which is very improbable . . . . I was made the Custodian of the
property so as to give me the use of the transportation."[8] How this
misunderstanding was ultimately resolved is not shown in the existing record.

During this relatively quiet period Sergeant Roe P. Orrell almost
lost his life, not to a raider's bullet but to the captain's son! Leander
Rebel McNelly, about nine years old, occasionally visited the ranger
camps with his mother. When the men were idle they sometimes
gave a pistol to young Rebel to practice shooting. George Durham
thought that he "got to be a pretty durn good shot; that is for a kid
his age." On one occasion some of the men wanted to go bathe in
the river after returning from a long dusty scout, and Rebel started
to go along. Orrell told him to stay in camp, but Rebel followed.
When far enough from camp so that Mrs. McNelly could not hear,
Orrell "reached down and give his seat a good whack and told him

to go back before he got a good paddling."

Rebel did, and the men went on to the river and forgot all about the captain's son. But Rebel resented the "good whack" and managed to get Orrell's pistol, took aim and fired several shots. Fortunately Rebel missed; Jesús Sandoval, who had heard the sounds of gunfire, came up, took in the situation at a glance, and managed to confiscate the pistol before anyone was hurt. Orrell probably saw little humor in this incident although George Durham related that Sandoval found it extremely funny. Durham does not relate if Captain or Mrs. McNelly ever learned that their son might have shot a ranger![9]

During this period McNelly continued to improve his spy system. While on the river he casually inquired into the character of the men who composed the various bands of raiders and "selected those whom I knew to be tricky, and secured interviews with them." He propositioned them to sell out their companions, promising to pay them more for the betrayal than they could make as a raider. McNelly knew that in order to stop the raids he had to know ahead of time where a raid would occur, and when the raiders would cross the river with their stolen animals. McNelly promised that, if information from the traitor resulted in his seeing the raiders on the Texas side in possession of stolen cattle, he would pay ten dollars for each raider in the group. If the raiders escaped, the informant would still receive the ten dollars bounty. If McNelly caught up with the raiders and recovered stolen cattle, so much the better. If the raiding group was large and well-armed, then the bounty would be fifteen dollars, in addition to giving them a regular salary of sixty dollars per month! McNelly noted that all these potential traitors whom he approached readily entered into his plans, and without any exception he found them to be "reliable and trustworthy." Further, McNelly agreed not to "interfere with their own individual stealing at all. I gave them liberty, when I was not there in their neighborhood, to cross over with their friends."[10]

In addition to establishing a group of traitors among the raiders' ranks, McNelly managed to infiltrate Cortina's organization with his own man, Sergeant George A. Hall. McNelly was very proud of this accomplishment, and Durham echoed this sentiment, writing of Hall's being "across the river sitting right in the innermost secret council of the crafty [Cortina], admittedly the brains and the head of the entire bandit organization on the south bank of the Rio Grande."[11] McNelly later testified before the Special Committee on Texas Frontier Troubles that Cortina had contracted with a Cuban firm in June to deliver five or six-hundred head of cattle. The Spanish vessel came to the mouth of the Rio Grande to receive them.

> I sent my first sergeant on board of the lighter that was to carry the cattle from the shore to the steamer, for the purpose of taking down the brands. He went in the character of a spy. His name is G. A. Hall. Cortina was present himself, with a force of probably 150 or 200 men, delivering these cattle. These men are considered his body guard in Matamoros, and are known . . . by the people of both sides of the river. I was informed by some parties on the other side that some ten or twelve of these men . . . were about to cross the river after more cattle, as the boat was able to carry more than Cortina had on hand. I was told that he intended to send into the interior of Texas to get 250 more cattle to put upon the boat. I got my men out. I found that these Mexicans had crossed over, and I learned the course that they were to return on. I stationed my company on the line, put out scouts, and the very day that General Cortina had agreed to deliver the cattle, I intercepted these men, some eighteen miles from the river, coming in with a drove of 250 head of cattle. We had a fight, and they were all killed. . . . They were all identified as men who composed the immediate body guard of Cortina, and who had been down at the mouth of the river helping him to load these cattle.[12]

Further evidence of Cortina's direct involvement in the raiding business was offered by George W. Miller, mounted inspector of Customs at Brownsville, who reported that on June 2 he had gone aboard the schooner *Inez Huston* that had cleared from the port of Bagdad, Mexico. The schooner was loading the cattle, and while on board he saw General Cortina "superintending the shipment, accompanied by a large armed guard." Among the guard he recognized Pancho Lopez, Guadalupe Espinosa, Rafael Salinas and José María Olguín, who were all fighting for their lives on the Palo Alto prairie a little over a week later.[13]

Even with Ranger Hall in Cortina's territory and on boats carrying stolen cattle and hides, and in spite of McNelly's spy system, the success of the Palo Alto prairie engagement was not to be easily duplicated. Durham recalled that McNelly was gone from camp "all the time it seemed like."[14] There were a half-dozen spies across the river while there were three scouts to lead the men whenever McNelly needed them: Lina Saldana, Jesús Sandoval and Herman S. Rock.

The frustration mounted until McNelly gave up trying to catch raiders on the Texas side and did the only thing left — he crossed the river and engaged them on their own soil. His actions in crossing the river to recover stolen cattle resulted in the killing of many men, all alleged Mexican bandits, and the recovery of stolen cattle which were returned to their rightful owners. In so doing, however, McNelly both challenged the authority of the U.S. Secretary of War and brought a great deal of fame to himself and his men, who were outnumbered by at least ten to one.

George Durham, the youngest McNelly ranger after Smith's death, recalled that at one point he felt the captain had abandoned his men because it had been so long since there had been any communication from him. Durham was almost to the point of quitting the service but Sergeant Orrell convinced him to remain until the end of the year. In his absence from camp, however, McNelly was working on a plan.[15]

In late October Lieutenant Commander De Witt Clinton Kells, commander of the U.S. *Rio Bravo*, arrived at the port of Brownsville. The idea of using a sidewheel steamboat on the Rio Grande had its origins with Brigadier General Edward O.C. Ord, commander of the Department of Texas since April 1875, who believed that the U.S. Navy would have to assist if the number of raids from Mexico into Texas were to be reduced. His requests for assistance finally bore fruit when President Grant sent orders to Secretary of the Navy George M. Robeson to station a vessel on the lower Rio Grande. Its captain was to cooperate with the U.S. troops already stationed there. The U.S. *Rio Bravo*, a light draft, sidewheel steamer purchased by the Navy in 1875 for special service on the Rio Grande, was captained by Lieutenant Commander De Witt C. Kells.

Once on the border the *Rio Bravo* was intended to be stationed there for five years, its purpose to protect the frontier against raiders based in Mexico and to discourage smuggling into the United States. Some doubted if the stationing of such a vessel would accomplish much. Commented one editor, "We have no doubt that the vessel [described as having eight officers and a forty-five man crew, four howitzers and one thirteen pound rifle gun] is well adapted to running the Rio Grande, but how about the Cattle-thieves?" In spite of all the great intentions the *Rio Bravo* accomplished little, and Commander Kells did not last as long as McNelly on the river.[16]

Among Kells' first duties was to communicate with the U.S. Consul in Matamoros, Thomas F. Wilson. Kells' major concern was to be kept informed of the movements of armed bands of marauders from the Mexican side. Wilson communicated to Kells on October 26, "I shall always take pleasure in giving you the earliest information in my possession in regards to these marauders, and to co-operate with you So far as in my power to check these depredations." Wilson at that point knew only of "a band of about fifty armed robbers" which had left Mier a week earlier to raid into Texas. Wilson believed that the raiders had left Mier "without any effort at concealment, evidently with the intention of drawing the United States Military forces up the Rio Grande, while they probably intend to recross into Mexico with their booty." It was Wilson's opinion that the best place to intercept the raiders would be by carefully patrolling the mouth of the Rio Grande rather than at any point further up the river. Kells would be unable to move up the river in pursuit of raiders because the level of the Rio Grande "was falling so rapidly" that the *Rio Bravo* could not leave Brownsville. Wilson informed Secretary of State Hamilton Fish in Washington of his concerns in the matters on the border.[17]

But Commander Kells had his own ideas as to how to accomplish his mission, which he believed was to precipitate an armed conflict with Mexico. Thomas Wilson heard a rumor on November 7, while picking up his mail in the Brownsville Post Office, that Kells was ready to move the *Rio Bravo*. To see for himself, Wilson, in company with John L. Haynes, went on board the *Rio Bravo* and made inquiry. Kells informed them that he and McNelly were ready to leave but were delayed because the regular pilot was unavailable and he as yet had not found a replacement. Kells had originally wanted to go *up* the river, but he had been issued orders contrary to his wishes and now was contemplating going *down* the river, which in Kells' mind was not disobeying the letter of his orders. The next day, November 8, the regular pilot was back and Kells and McNelly were preparing to start down the river to join a force of cavalry from Fort Brown. Kells and McNelly were on their way but the launch grounded within sight of Brownsville due to the low water level. By this time additional orders prohibited Kells from going either up or down the river![18]

But Kells was not to give up easily and approached Customs Agent John L. Haynes with a dangerous scheme. Kells wanted

Haynes and others to arrange for someone from the Mexican side of the river to fire upon the *Rio Bravo* so that Kells could justifiably return fire, ostensibly to preserve the integrity of the American flag. Haynes claimed that the arrangement could not be made with Americans, and that Mexicans on the other side would not be interested. Haynes related that Kells felt his purpose in being sent to the Rio Grande was to "precipitate an armed contest with Mexico."[19]

Then, according to Haynes, Kells went to McNelly and proposed that some of the rangers could cross the river and fire upon the *Rio Bravo* so that Kells could "justifiably" return fire. No official record indicates that Kells and McNelly conferred on this idea of a false attack, but one of Pidge Robinson's letters suggested they did. On March 4, 1876, he contributed to the *Gazette* a lengthy letter concerning the problems on the border. "I wish that Captain Kells . . . was here . . . for he has a keen appreciation of such things, and enjoys them to the fullest extent. The first time I ever saw the Captain was on board his ship . . . when he entertained me with a description of the terrible storm experienced by the vessel while crossing the gulf from New Orleans." Pidge described how on one occasion Kells had moored the boat for the night near a Mexican village. Some of the village inhabitants came down, ostensibly out of mere curiosity. From the initial verbal exchange the Mexicans did not believe the captain understood their language and commenced talking of how they could "finish up" the steamer and how they could riddle it with rifle balls and sink it. Kells said nothing until they had finished and then pulled the tarpaulin off the Gatling guns. "Now," said Kells, "suppose you try that on a little; just a little; and by the tail of Jonah's whale, I'll make you think that h-ll has broke loose in Georgia!" When the would-be steamer-destroyers realized Kells knew what they had been contemplating, they "went back somewhat crestfallen at being so taken in." [20]

Officials did have evidence that Kells was plotting to bring about an armed confrontation. Earlier, on October 14, U.S. Consul Wilson had communicated a confidential statement concerning Kells, feeling it was of great urgency because it concerned Wilson's own personal safety. Wilson stated that after Kells had arrived at the mouth of the river, on October 12, he had made semi-confidential statements to several persons that it could be arranged so that a party of Texans could cross the river and fire onto the *Rio Bravo*, "in order that he might have an excuse to return the fire [and] destroy adjacent Mexican Ranches and land and occupy Mexican Soil, ostensibly to avenge the insult to the United States flag; and thus precipitate an armed conflict with Mexico on this frontier." Wilson was convinced that such a project was contemplated and that it had the sanction and perhaps the support of many Texans, some of whom would expect to reap large profits in case there was another war with Mexico, "by furnishing Supplies to the United States Army and employ steam ships and steam boats which are now lying idle on the Texas coast." Wilson was certainly aware that cattleman Richard King had been a steamboat captain and during the Mexican War had transported troops and supplies. Wilson even reported that "it has been given out" that the U.S. wanted another war with Mexico and specifically sent Kells to the mouth of the river "for the express purpose of forcing such a conflict."[21]

Wilson was also aware that the *Rio Bravo* needed repairs and would not be able to travel up the river "for some time." He suggested a full investigation but cautioned against Kells' being relieved of command at that point because it would interfere with the investigation. Kells obviously intended to accomplish his mission, "for the Suppression of irregularities and depredations committed by bands of robbers on the Texas Shore," as he understood his mission to be, but Wilson did not believe his method of accomplishing the mission was suitable at that time. [22]

Because of Wilson's secret communications to his superiors, the Navy decided to take no further chances and relieved Captain Kells. Commander George C. Remey replaced him, arriving at Brownsville on November 16. The military was very much aware of the events involving the raiders and of their potentially destructive consequences. On November 8 Colonel Joseph H. Potter, from Brownsville Headquarters, issued Special Order #156 to 1st Lieutenant Henry Joseph Farnsworth, directing him to take as many men of Company H, 8th Cavalry as could be mounted and armed and proceed the next morning at eight o'clock to Ringgold Barracks. Each man was to be armed with forty rounds of carbine ammunition, twenty-four rounds of pistol ammunition, and sixty rounds per man to be transported on wagons. At the same time Captain James Franklin Randlett of Company D, 8th cavalry, was to proceed to Edinburg to scour the country searching for armed bands of Mexican cattle thieves and marauders. Of particular interest was the statement in the orders that "the utmost endeavors will be used to recover stolen property and bring the thieves to justice."[23]

In addition to the troubles with the customs inspectors, developing the spy system and working to destroy raiding parties, McNelly was again experiencing communication difficulties with

Adjutant General Steele. He may have forgotten about the various reprimands from Adjutant General Davidson during the State Police years, but now the reprimands were happening again. In addition he never knew when he would have to assist a sheriff elsewhere. In mid-July Nueces County Sheriff John McClane had visited with William Steele advising him that many indictments had been found at the recent term of district court and he would need assistance in making arrests. Steele ordered McNelly to go to Corpus Christi "at some convenient time before the middle of September" and indicate to McClane when he could assist him. Steele ordered him to take any prisoners to Galveston for safe keeping if he felt it was warranted.[24] No record of McClane and McNelly's actually communicating about this matter exists. Steele either did not know for sure where his captain was or he himself could not keep track of his own orders, because on July 16 he acknowledged receipt of a scouting report to Loma Blanca after raiders, directed to McNelly, addressed at Brownsville.[25] On the very next day he sent a message to McNelly addressed to him at Burton.[26] McNelly may have purposely avoided keeping his superior informed of his actions as virtually no reports were written or preserved. Possibly his illness contributed to his being lax in reporting. Steele was patient only so long, because on October 9 he sent orders to McNelly at Laredo that he was to notify him every Sunday as to where he was located, his post office address, and any further information which might be of interest.[27] Exactly where McNelly was in the ensuing weeks was uncertain even to Steele; on October 29 he directed a letter addressed to either McNelly or Lieutenant T.C. Robinson at Edinburg. The order was for him to move the company to Columbus "at once" and to keep Steele informed so that new orders for the company would be waiting for him when he arrived at Columbus. Steele added, "You can leave behind an intelligent officer or non-commissioned officer to collect all accounts against the State, who can overtake the command en route." [28] Ten days later on November 8 Steele ordered McNelly to remain in Brownsville until further orders arrived.[29] The next day McNelly telegraphed his response that "the affair has proved a failure. Am ready to start to Columbus. Answer."[30] In his answer on November 9 Steele ordered McNelly to move in the direction of Washington County "with a view to mustering out on the 30th inst." The reason given was that it was time to reduce the company for the winter. Any man who "belongs on the Rio Grande" or who wanted to be discharged at Brownsville could receive their discharge there.[31]

But McNelly was able to avoid going to Columbus to discharge the company; there was the promise of action involving raiders. On November 12 McNelly wrote to Adjutant General Steele that he was going to move up the river the next day. He had met with Major A.J. Alexander, stating in his letter that Alexander had told him he would "instruct his men to follow raiders anywhere I will go." McNelly, eager to catch raiders and knowing his men wanted action as much as he did, hoped to put Alexander "to the test in a few days" because he had learned that "the parties who buy most of the stolen cattel [sic]" had contracted to deliver *eighteen-thousand head of cattle* in Monterrey within the next ninety days. That would mean an average of two-hundred cattle per day for ninety days to be crossed over, stolen from Texas ranchers! McNelly added, perhaps with a glint in his eye, "I should think myself in bad luck if I don't find some one of their parties on this *or the other side of the river*." [italics added][32] Further, McNelly had Adjutant General Steele's order allowing him "in any immediate and close pursuit to cross and recross."[33] With this idea in mind, and having Alexander's tacit blessing to cross over with assistance from the military forces, McNelly must have believed that he was entirely within his rights and that he would have sufficient protection in crossing the river.

Historian Webb, in *The Texas Rangers*, felt there was "little doubt" that McNelly had "some deep scheme in mind" and suggests he wanted to bring on a war with Mexico, citing the evidence of Kells' conspiracy to have the *Rio Bravo* fired upon as well as Alexander's promise. There hardly seems to remain a question that President Grant intended to create a situation which would lead to war, although evidence was not made public until late 1877, after McNelly's death. On December 14 of that year a correspondent of the New York *Herald* reported that the subcommittee of the House Military Affairs Committee had discovered that in 1875 the U.S. "had a very narrow escape from war with Mexico." The Grant administration, or at least the president himself, intended to "precipitate trouble upon the border." The gunboat *Rio Bravo*, the troops under Colonel J.H. Potter and "the volunteer forces under Texan commanders were to begin the work." Although McNelly is not mentioned by name, it is clear the committee was thinking of him in their reference to "Texan commanders." The "latter force" was to cross the Rio Grande and burn certain property that was believed to be the headquarters of Cortina's forces, i.e., Las Cuevas. The gunboat and U.S. infantry were then to provide protection for the Texan invaders. The *Herald* reporter explained the plot did not come to fruition because Secretary Hamilton Fish was "not a party to this plan [and] he at once interposed his offices, and the commander of the Rio Bravo was instructed not to carry out the details of the plan." [34] It is doubtful that such a plot would actually have caused a war between the two countries. If U.S. officials intended to bring about an official military action with Mexico certainly there would have been more substance than a few shots fired on a single vessel on the Rio Grande, or the burning of a few ranches, or the possibility of McNelly's pursuing stolen cattle across the river. Rather than bring about a full scale armed conflict with Mexico, it is more likely that McNelly intended to bring about a change in foreign policy so that United States lawmen, in their "war" with cattle thieves, could cross over in pursuit of marauders. Word came about mid-November, Durham recalled, when one of Captain Randlett's soldiers delivered a telegram to camp ordering Lieutenant Robinson and company to move to Rio Grande City; everyone believed there would finally be action. Durham recalled that Robinson, after reading the order, "went out in the open, threw his hat high in the air, and shot it twice as it came down. He let out a war whoop and told us to catch out a mount and saddle up in five minutes."

Durham explained that the invasion of Mexico had "been told so many times in so many ways by several folks who weren't there that I'd like to get it down straight."[35] This was certainly an honorable intent, but the most reliable versions of McNelly's invasion remain the contemporary reports, the reports of McNelly and of the U.S. Army officers at nearby Fort Brown, the newspaper accounts which were printed within hours of the events, and the writings of

View of Fort Brown, Texas, 1876. The military assistance offered by the U.S. Army came from this fort. *Courtesy The National Archives.*

Lieutenant T.C. Robinson, who was there and wrote of the affair soon after. Also valuable but subject to the weakness of failing memories are those of rangers Jennings and Callicott. Jennings wrote as if he had been among the invading rangers but he was not, although he claimed to have kept in touch with many of the rangers, some of whom may have been involved, and thus might have learned accurate details from them; Durham, whose account was written in 1934, was one of the rangers but his version must have been colored by Wantland; in addition there is considerable conversation which could not have been accurately recorded. Callicott, who wrote his version for Walter Prescott Webb in 1921, was sixty-eight at the time he wrote, and although his eyesight was bad his memory was sharp and his writings are considered dependable. Although some details may be in conflict, the versions are essentially in harmony on the main points. The primary theme which runs through all the accounts is that the men who served with McNelly worshipped him as their leader and would have followed him into any dangerous situation regardless of the consequences. Secondly, none felt that there was any wrong committed in invading a foreign nation or killing innocent Mexicans.

McNelly's men were in camp when not acting on reports of bandits in the area, but if such reports were received, according to Durham, McNelly "would send one of his pilots to get a detail of us; we would make a twenty or thirty mile ride north, south, east, or west, behind the scout. And we were getting them, one or two at a time, but we were not stopping the big raids."[36] McNelly later reiterated this fact, testifying, "I have followed fifty herds of cattle to the bank of the Rio Grande, and I would see the stock on the opposite bank. The Mexicans dare me to cross the river and take them. They would say, 'Here are the cattle, come across and take them if you dare.'"[37] The captain's spy system, although McNelly believed it effective, was not providing information to him in time for a spectacular *coup*, as had been the case on Palo Alto prairie.

The hard riding was especially difficult on the horses, and Durham claimed that during the first fifteen days of November he had ridden four good horses to death.[38] In spite of exhaustion as well as suffering from epizoon, the remuda was kept full by local ranchers, and perhaps in particular Captain Richard King, who supplied the rangers with good mounts.

Word finally arrived of a big raiding party; one of McNelly's spies reported that a herd of seventy-five to one-hundred head was being driven towards the ranch known as Las Cuevas, generally considered by Texans as being the headquarters for all of Cortina's raiding bands. Durham related in the *West* article that Jesús Sandoval came to camp with orders to prepare to leave immediately for Las Cuevas Ranch.[39] Robinson was more specific, writing that orders were received from Captain McNelly at 1:00 p.m. of November 18 "to ride rapidly to *Las Cuevas*, alias Robber's Roost. We obeyed them to the letter; we rode rapidly, fifty-five miles in six hours, each man carrying one hundred rounds of ammunition."[40] Here Pidge was not exaggerating for humorous effect. Durham, in the *West* article, related that after orders were received the men were ready to ride within the space of ten minutes. Durham recalled they faced into a "blowing norther; and them sizzling rain pellets fairly singed your beard." The command made only two brief stops, arriving at their destination only to see the bandits cross over the last of the stolen herd. "Robinson," he complained, "didn't give us a shot."[41] Callicott recalled that their strenuous efforts had been to no avail, as "we got thire a little too late[;] they had beet us to the River and had crost the cattle over in to mexico to the los cuavos Ranch the head cuarters for all the cow Bandits."

Callicott also recalled that it was McNelly himself who led the ranger group, leaving camp on November 18 to make the sixty-mile ride to the anticipated crossing. McNelly, Sandoval, Sullivan and twenty-four volunteers made the ride; the force would have been larger but some rangers were out on scout. Those present were given time to gather forty rounds of pistol and forty rounds of carbine ammunition. With McNelly in the lead the group made the ride in less than five hours, a difficult ride in any weather conditions, but they still missed the raiders and the cattle.

While McNelly was on the move, Captain Randlett was not sitting idle. He had left Fort Brown on November 9 with 1st Lieutenant H.J. Farnsworth and forty men of H Company, and 2nd Lieutenant J.W. Williams with forty-four men of D Company, all 8th Cavalry. The force reached Edinburg, some miles from Fort Brown, on the tenth. Two days later Farnsworth and his command proceeded to Ringgold Barracks while Randlett established camp. The next day, the thirteenth, Randlett sent out small patrols to scour the country, to become familiar with it and with its people. Three nights later a "Mexican Citizen of Texas," who resided thirty miles from the river, came into camp and informed Randlett that a party of fifteen thieves had crossed his place a few days before, coming from Old Mexico, and who would probably re-cross the river the next day.

Randlett telegraphed the commander at Fort Brown that he

believed a party would cross at Las Cuevas the next day and would start at nine o'clock on November 16 to intercept them. He would inform the commander of his movements and the results and requested a party from Ringgold Barracks to be sent to cooperate with him, believing the raiding party would increase in numbers once it reached the river.[42]

Colonel J.H. Potter telegraphed Randlett the same day from Fort Brown, informing Randlett that a scout had been sent towards Las Cuevas to cooperate with him and ordering, "if you catch the thieves hit them hard, if you come up with them while they cross the river follow them into Mexico. McNally [sic] in command of State Troops is near Edinburgh[.] try to connect with him and take a Sheriff or deputy with you, if possible. Keep me advised of result."[43]

Randlett left camp at nine o'clock with Lieutenant Wilkinson and thirty men and then proceeded up the river eighteen miles to "Panyitas Ranche" where he met with John Thompson, the mounted Custom Inspector at Edinburg. Randlett proposed that Thompson, who knew the country and people, go with him, and he at once consented. He sent Thompson to obtain some "suitable Mexicans" to act as scouts and spies. Randlett remembered to keep his superior informed and sent a courier to headquarters to inform him of his plans to apprehend the raiders. When the courier returned Randlett was informed that the scouting party earlier sent out consisted of thirty men of M Company, 8th Cavalry, commanded by Lieutenant O'Connor. Now Randlett was informed that the thieves were making for the river with a herd and would probably cross that night at Las Cuevas. Randlett then informed Thompson that his plan was to move to the rear of the thieves and catch them at the river; he then sent another courier to O'Connor telling him to hit the thieves without mercy on their right flank when they hit the river.

At 2:30 Randlett and his men began to follow the trail of the thieves, galloping towards the river and reaching it at 4:15. Randlett discovered the thieves had driven the cattle off a steep bank in a bend of the river, some four or five miles in length, into a fence earlier built in the shape of a "V" through which the cattle were forced to move onto the opposite bank. Randlett had difficulty in finding a place to cross; some cattle had sunk in the quagmire and on the opposite shore thirty or forty men and boys were pulling them out with ropes attached to their horns. At this point that Randlett opened fire, killing two and wounding another. The thieves then retreated and returned the fire but without effect. Randlett attempted to find a place he could safely cross his men but was unable to do so before darkness settled in with heavy clouds. He was compelled to suspend crossing until the next morning. He sent a communication to the alcalde.

Randlett informed the alcalde that "certain persons citizens of the Republic of Mexico" (identifying ten of the group by name) had that day stolen and driven over the river to Las Cuevas 250 head of horned cattle, property of citizens of the state of Texas. In the name of the government of the United States he was demanding the arrest of all of that party and their delivery to him to be tried by the civil authorities of the state of Texas. In addition the 250 head of cattle were to be "at once

Lieutenant Colonel James F. Randlett who assisted McNelly in the fight against Las Cuevas bandits. *Courtesy The Massachusetts Commandery Military Order of the Loyal Legion and the U.S. Army Military History Institute.*

returned." The message was translated, "without regard to form of law or military etiquette," and sent over by one of the "Mexican Scouts." Randlett, convinced that all the people of Las Cuevas were thieves and surmising both that his communication would be ignored by Mexican officials and that the Mexicans would not suspect he would cross over, began making plans to cross over the next morning, to capture the cattle and "finish up the job."[44] He then sent a dispatch to have Major D.R. Clendenin of the 8th Cavalry, with Farnsworth and his company, join him. When they arrived Randlett informed Clendenin of his plans. Major Clendenin approved of what Randlett had done so far but did not approve of his crossing into Mexico, "declaring such a Course to be [a] warlike invasion of a country with which our own was at peace, and that my orders would not justify such process of recovering the cattle."[45]

At daybreak Randlett received a reply from the alcalde to the effect that shooting had been heard the preceding day and that he had sent the Chief of Police to investigate. The chief and ten men came across the herd being driven by the thieves and they had a skir~ mish. The police did manage to take possession of some of the cat~ tle, but the thieves escaped with the majority of the herd, heading south. A dispatch was sent to the justice at Camargo, notifying him what had happened, with a copy of Randlett's note "for them to resolve whatever they deemed proper, and to answer you as soon as possible." The alcalde concluded by saying that an attempt would be made to follow the thieves the following morning.[46]

While this was transpiring Randlett had learned that yet another herd of cattle was coming in to cross not far above where the previous herd had been crossed. Thompson and a group of the Mexican scouts and spies were sent out to intercept them, and the cattle were driven back to their ranges. There was no fight in this instance.

About noon McNelly arrived, followed by his men later in the afternoon. McNelly "at once declared his determination to cross the river and called upon Major Clendenin to give him assistance when he should call for it."[47]

McNelly now had to make a decision: obey the law and hope that the next time he would be able to engage the raiders on Texas soil, or ignore the law and cross the boundary river between the two countries, paramount to invading a foreign country with resultant serious repercussions between Mexico and the United States. In McNelly's mind, crossing the river was not a violation of interna~ tional law. In later testimony before the House of Representatives committee investigating the troubles on the Texas border, he stated,

> I do not know of any writer on international law who does not agree to the principal that where a nation is unable or unwilling to restrain its turbulent people from depredating on a neighboring territory, the nation so depredated upon has the right to pursue those robbers into their fastnesses across the line, and there to punish them for their offense.[48]

When the word came to prepare to march not all the rangers were in camp. McNelly arrived and of course needed Jesús Sandoval as guide and Tom Sullivan as interpreter. He called for two dozen volunteers, explaining that it would be a hard ride if they were to have a chance of beating the thieves to the river. Their strenuous efforts had been to no avail, as "we got thire a little too late[;] they had beet us to the River and had crost the cattle over in to mexico to the los cuavos Ranch the head cuarters for all the cow Bandits" as Callicott recalled.[49]

McNelly, who as a State Policeman had seemingly refused to communicate with his superiors, was now keeping Adjutant General Steele closely informed of his intended actions. On November 18 he had sent the following telegram: "A party of raiders here crossed two hundred & fifty cattle at Loz Cuevos [sic] they have been firing on Maj. Clendenins men[.] he refuses to cross without further orders. I shall cross tonight if I can get any support." This was signed "L. H. McNelly Capt Comdg Rangers."[50]

A second telegram read, "I commence crossing at one oclock tonight [November 19]. [I] have thirty one men [and] will try & recover our cattle[.] the U. S. troops promise to cover my return[.] Lt Robinson has just arrived making a march of fifty-five miles in six hours." Now he signed the communication simply, "L. H. McNelly Capt Rangers."[51]

McNelly chose to ignore the law and enter Mexico for the express purpose of recovering stolen Texas cattle. He had not been alone in following this group of raiders; Captain James F. Randlett, 8th United States Cavalry, had arrived with two-hundred troops and two Gatling guns which were planted and aimed at Mexican soil. McNelly requested the loan of one-hundred soldiers to assist him in crossing over into Mexico. All was to be ready by midnight for a 1:00 a.m. crossing. Randlett had to refuse McNelly's request, to which McNelly was recorded as saying, "Well if you cant let me hav the men I will Risk the law in mexico with my 26 men[.] they cant get any mo[re] of us than we can of them[.] if we doent get the cattle Back we can Say we had the plesure of Killen a few of them." So recalled Callicott. [52]

McNelly was not known for giving long speeches, but William Callicott remembered the speech he gave the rangers in their ranks before crossing over.

> boys, you hav follerd me as far as I can ask you to do un less you or [are] willin to go with me[.] . . . it is like goen in to the Jaws of deth with only 26 men in a forren cuntry wher we hav no Right accorden to law but as I hav went this far I am Goen to the finish with it[.] . . . Some of us ma[y] get back or part of us or mabey all of us or mabey non of us will get back and if any of you doent want to go over with me Step a Side[.] I doent

want you un less you or willin to go as a vallentier[.] . . .
under Stand thire is no Surrender in this[.] we ask no
canters [quarter] nor giv any[.] If any or you doent want
to go Step a Side.[53]

Callicott recalled the men all said to McNelly, "if you can Risk
your life we can Sertenley Risk ours." McNelly continued, "all Right
boys thats the way to talk it[.] we will lirn them a texas lesen that
they hav forgotten Since the old mexican wargh[.] well boys all of
you get Reddy to go over[.] I will take old casuse[,] tom Sullivan and
my Self over first."[54] It was typical of McNelly to lead his men into
a dangerous situation, a characteristic which undoubtedly endeared
him to his men, who would be willing to die for him and with him.
One cannot help but wonder if McNelly remembered the speech
General Tom Green had given his volunteers prior to the Battle of
Galveston thirteen years before, wanting only men who were willing
to die for their country.

CHAPTER 16

ACROSS THE RIO GRANDE

> Were there forces sufficient on the Rio Grande
> frontier to follow these murderous bandits to their
> secret haunts in Mexico, robbery would soon be too
> precarious a mode of gaining a livelihood; a few more
> such lessons as this one given them by Capt. McNelly
> would teach them that on their own side of the river
> they are not always *perfectly* safe, as they have heretofore
> considered themselves. — Correspondent "Pidge" to
> the *Daily State Gazette*, written from Laguna de los
> Calabaso [sic], 15 January 1876.

McNelly did not leave a list of the rangers who crossed into Mexico with him, but from available sources the names of some have been determined: McNelly, T.C. Robinson, George A. Hall, Roe P. Orrell, George P. Durham, William C. Callicott, Jesús Sandoval, Tom Sullivan, John B. Armstrong, H.G. Rector, Robert Pitts and William L. Rudd. Only a dozen names are identified, but Callicott consistently refers to twenty-six men being with McNelly.

Pidge Robinson wrote his version of the invasion in mid-January 1876, only two months after the event and thus still fresh in his mind in contrast to the memories of Durham and Callicott. Robinson also noted, in typical jovial manner, that he would have given his readers an account of the invasion much earlier except that McNelly had given him special orders to write "a true account of it, which has been awful straining to the mind; I am not accustomed to this, and have scarcely recovered from it yet."

Pidge described the killing ride after the company received orders to march rapidly to Las Cuevas, alias Robber's Roost, and noted that they came across the tracks of Major A.J. Alexander and his men of the 8th Cavalry who were on their way to Las Cuevas as well. In addition to Alexander's tracks, Pidge made note of viewing the swinging body of a raider who had been lynched, possibly by rancheros who had by chance caught a raider, "swung to the tree in full view of the road . . . a hideous object waving in the night breeze, fearful to look upon."

An unidentified artist's rendition of Major A.J. Alexander and troops on their way to assist McNelly during the "Las Cuevas affair." This appeared in Frank Leslie's *Illustrated Newspaper*, January 1, 1876. *Courtesy The Library of Congress.*

Robinson arrived about midnight and met with McNelly. The telegram sent to Steele shows he was confident that if he crossed the U.S. troops would cover him. Robinson recorded this exchange with McNelly, after he had given orders to have the horses ready for a midnight crossing.

> "I suppose you have rations with you."
>
> "No, sir; but we have sixty rounds of carbine ammunition and forty of pistol –."
>
> "You certainly have brought bread?"
>
> "No, sir; but we have lots of car –."
>
> "No salt?"
>
> "None; but just dead loads of cartri –."
>
> "So I suppose the men have nothing but coffee in their haversacks?"
>
> "They haven't got that even, but they've got a hundred rounds of –."
>
> "Well, don't this beat the devil!" said [McNelly]; "there is nothing to eat this side of Ringgold Barracks, and you've come up here without even a grain of coffee; how do you expect to live when you get across?"
>
> "Don't expect to live long Captain, but in these two belts I have a hundred rounds of –."
>
> "Oh, go to h-ll with your cartridges."

"Well," thought I, "that's just where you've ordered me to go."

"Are your horses much fatigued?"

"They've got plenty of metal on them if they haven't in them," I answered; "each saddle has strapped to it a hundred rounds of metalic –."

"If you mention cartridges to me again," said the Captain, "I'll put you in arrest and leave you on this side of the river."

Pidge realized that anything he would say would be inappropriate, but he handed McNelly a box of Winchester cartridges then said a silent prayer that he would be left on the Texas side. He really did not want to be left out of the action, but typically his humor was of the self-deprecating type and thus he naturally would indicate he felt cowardly.

Getting the men across the river took more time than anticipated. Pidge wrote "[i]n single file and leading the horses, we gathered at the beautiful, the beautiful river and in silence commenced the embarkation; on each side of the crossing crouched the men, gun in hand, to protect the passage of the first boat. . . ." Crossing the horses was so dangerous that after three were crossed the decision was made to leave the remainder on the Texas side; the men would attack on foot. The boat was small and leaked, consequently only four men at a time could cross. "What a tub to cross Jordan in!" wrote Pidge, "it kept four men busy bailing to keep the nose of the man who paddled above the water. It only carried four; it might have carried more had there been room enough for them to bail, but there wasn't."[1]

Callicott also wrote about the crossing, but without the humor. He recalled they had started to cross at 1:00 a.m. with a Mexican to take them over in a "little dug out." There was a leak in the dugout so one man did have to bail to keep it from sinking. Callicott remembered that they did have some jerked beef, and that McNelly had ordered the food and their cartridges put in the horses' feed bags so they wouldn't become wet. McNelly, Jesús Sandoval and Tom Sullivan crossed over first; then, according to Callicott, Lieutenant Robinson, Sergeant Armstrong and George Hall crossed with their horses. The remaining horses were left on the Texas side because if they became stuck in the quicksand it would take too long to free them. Five horses were across; the remainder of the men would be on foot. "So we all went 3 at a time one would hav[e] to

dip out the warter to Keep the little dug out from Sinking while the
mexican paddled us over[.] we all got over all OK all 26 to gether."[2]
Callicott placed the time at 4:00 a.m. when the rangers were all
across. Other than the time involved and being without their horses,
there were no problems in crossing the force into Mexico. At dawn
they began the march to Las Cuevas, "said to be one mile distant;
after we had walked about three, we concluded there must be a mistake somewhere, or that the town was marching too" as   Pidge
described it, able to find humor in almost any situation.[3]

The Mexican pilot had informed McNelly that Las Cuevas was
picketed with high posts approached by only a little cow trail so narrow the men would have to march in single file. McNelly's plan was
to drop the bars at the front gate to allow the men with horses —
Robinson, Sandoval, Armstrong, Hall and Orell — to dash through
yelling and shooting. The men on foot would follow as best they
could. The orders were to shoot everyone they saw except old men,
women and children. McNelly "all ways pland his Battles before he
went in and told the boys what to do and he expected them to do as
he Sed" recalled Callicott. McNelly and Sandoval led the way,
through the heavy undergrowth and trees so heavy and thick "you
couldent see a Rabbit 10 steps a way."[4] Callicott wrote that he and
the guide were about fifty yards in the lead, suggesting McNelly was
closer to the main body of men. Three miles into the interior of
Mexico, supposedly at the Las Cuevas ranch, the pilot let down the
fence bars while McNelly told the men to stand aside to allow the
mounted rangers to go through with Sandoval in the lead, the "first
chance old casuse had to Breeth mexican air or to hav a chance to
giv a yell in over 20 years."[5]

A little further and the rangers "fell upon the ranche Las
Ancharvas, which we did not know was on the road." This statement
of Robinson was the first indication that they had entered the wrong
ranch, not Las Cuevas but a ranch called Las Ancharvas by Robinson
and the Cachattus Ranch by Callicott. Most likely the proper
spelling was Las Cucharas, or Ranch of the Spoons. Durham simply
referred to it as Little Las Cuevas. Callicott remembered no resistance. Robinson merely wrote that the men in the ranch, whom he
called the "Cacharassers", "popped it to us pretty lively for a while,"[6]
suggesting there was an exchange of gunfire between the Mexicans
and the rangers. Callicott wrote that the McNelly rangers were the
first rangers these Mexicans had seen since the Mexican War. Many
of the men were at the wood piles cutting wood while their wives and
children were preparing breakfast. Callicott wrote "we Shot them

down on thire wood piles and wher ever we Saw one we Killed him till we Killed all we Saw" which suggests that the wood choppers had no firearms at all and could not return fire.[7] Durham recorded that when the firing ceased McNelly realized that Las Cuevas should have had many more men; this was not Las Cuevas but another ranch. Strange to say, they saw an old woman "calmly putting out her daily portion of *tortillas*. If the shooting had disturbed her, she sure didn't show it."[8] Pidge also wrote of this strange behavior, not only of the woman but of the men as well. "Some of them were smoking ciga- rettes and looking on with *sang froid* while the others fought; they were a cool set sure; the old woman in the *jacale* did not stop pulling *tortillas*."[9] The interpreter, identified as McGovern but elsewhere identified as Sullivan, was sent over to inquire of her what place this was. When he realized they had raided the wrong ranch, McNelly knew there was no longer a chance of a surprise attack at the correct ranch. The pilot, or guide, explained that he had erred because he had not been there for ten years, and the real target, Las Cuevas, was a mile further up the road.

Callicott did not estimate the number of men killed. A lengthy account published in the Galveston *News* gave the number killed at four; Robinson wrote that they afterwards learned seven were killed and nine wounded. Durham wrote that they counted seventeen dead but later learned that they had killed twenty-six.[10] Assuming that some of the wounded may have later died, the exact number killed at the wrong ranch was probably closer to over a dozen. Since the rangers and Texans in general believed that Mexicans on that side of the river, especially this close to Las Cuevas, were all thieves, the question of having killed innocent men was not raised.

McNelly telegraphed to Steele, "I crossed the river on the eigh- teenth[.] on the nineteenth I marched on foot to ranch Las Cuevas[.] Killed four men before reaching the ranch & five afterward."[11] Major D.R. Clendenin heard the gunfire of the "skirmish" after McNelly had crossed and positioned a Gatling gun on the bank of the river to cover McNelly should he return.

To McNelly the idea of having killed innocent men apparently did not enter his mind. His concern at this point was that a surprise attack was no longer possible once they reached the Las Cuevas ranch, a mile up the trail. Robinson wrote that once they arrived at Las Cuevas,

> the alarm had been given, and out from the houses poured the robbers by hundreds; in a strong *corral*

immediately in our front two hundred men, well fortified, awaited our coming; beyond this was another full
to overflowing, from every side they were pouring in on
foot and on horseback, and estimates of their forces
were made by "the boys," according to the view each
had ranging from two hundred to twenty-seven thousand; to the right and outside of the fortifications, I
caught a glimpse of a column of cavalry, in sets of fours,
which seemed to me to stretch to Matamoras [sic].[12]

Callicott wrote that they saw 250 Mexican soldiers on horseback,
150 yards ahead.[13] McNelly's estimate was that a force of three hundred waited to engage the invaders.[14] The soldiers opened fire on the
rangers over the open ground with only an occasional tree between
the two forces. Sandoval, when he saw a soldier clearly enough to
shoot at, would shoot and yell, "Son a bitch kil em."[15] Besides their
numerical superiority, the soldiers had horses which could effectively
be used as cover. It was clear they had reached the Las Cuevas ranch,
the ranch owned by Juan Flores Salinas who also had, according to
Callicott, several pieces of artillery![16] With overwhelming odds
against them, McNelly ordered his men to retreat by the same route
they had come, Robinson leading the way with the mounted men
while McNelly brought up the rear with the rangers on foot. "[A]fter
a few shots," McNelly later telegraphed, "I retreated to the river as
the US [troops] were ordered not to cross[.] The mexicans followed
me to [the] River and charged me[.] they were repulsed & as they
seemed to be in force some forty US Soldiers came over[.]" Reports
indicate that Captain James F. Randlett of the 8th Regiment did
cross with between twenty-five and fifty soldiers. McNelly's telegram
continued, "The Mexicans made several attempts during the evening
to dislodge us but failed[.] United States troops withdrew to left bank
last night[.] I am in temporary earthworks and have refused to leave
until the cattle are returned[.] The Mexicans in my front are about
four hundred[.] What shall I do[?] L H McNelly Capt Rangers."[17]
    Callicott, recalling their return through the Cucharas on the
retreat to the river, wrote that "thire wer nothing thire except the ded
and they lay like they fell on the wood piles and in the Streets or
Roads the wimen and children and old men wer all gon not a liven
Sole to Be Seen."[18]
    Robinson also wrote of the retreat to the river in his usual
humorous way. "I was awfully fatigued, but I scorned to let this interfere with my duty, and stepped up with much alacrity; such fiendish

yells I never heard, but I could see very little; where the smoke came from the guns it hung like a pall, and I was not sorry to leave, for it had a very offensive odor to me. Back to the river we went, and waited further developments."[19]

McNelly's men remained on the Mexican side of the river. About midday an attack was made against the invading Texans, led by General Juan Flores Salinas, an officer of the *rurales*, or Rural Guards. Callicott recalled that the Las Cuevas men probably intended to catch them in the water. Robinson, Armstrong and Hall were all mounted when the group led by Salinas and twenty-five followers started their run to the river, "yelling and shooting." Armstrong's and Hall's horses jumped out from under them, leaving them afoot. The horses were taken up by the Mexicans. Robinson managed to keep his, called "Jack Ellis" because it had belonged to the American raider of that name killed on the Palo Alto prairie. McNelly ordered the men to charge the oncoming Mexicans and to "open up on them boys as fast as you can."[20] Then the Mexican line broke; Salinas fell "with his pistol in his hand with 2 needle gun Bullits through his body Killen him ded."[21] McNelly stooped down and picked up Salinas' pistol, a Smith & Wesson plated with gold and silver.

With the death of General Salinas, McNelly and his rangers returned to the river bank where, with the river's being low, there was a natural shelter for them, "under the Bank of the River" as Callicott expressed it. One guard was placed fifty yards up the river and another placed fifty yards down the river. Lieutenant Robinson was placed in charge of the men while McNelly returned to the Texas side hoping to gather troops of Randlett's command.[22]

The Juan Flores Salinas Monument as it appeared in 1997. George H. Edgerton, grandson of Dr. A.M. Headley who negotiated between McNelly and the raiders, stands in front of the monument. *Photo by Chuck Parsons.*

During McNelly's action on the Mexican side of the river the United States forces were not idle. Colonel Joseph H. Potter, commander at Fort Brown, reported that McNelly requested assistance when he first arrived at the fort. Major Clendenin directed Potter to assist and sent a sergeant and six men a few miles down the river to make a diversion, while Potter with ten soldiers stayed on the bank prepared to assist McNelly if he were attacked. Potter related that it took the rangers three hours to cross the river, "the attempt to cross horses causing great delay." Just before daylight Potter heard the sharp firing and in less than an hour saw the McNelly command back on the river. At this point McNelly had indeed returned to the Texas side, leaving Lieutenant Robinson in command of the rangers who had dug in on the river bank, the lower level of the river leaving a natural breastwork for cover. McNelly reported to Potter that there were at least 250 men against him. About 7:00 p.m. there was additional firing, and Potter stationed some of Farnsworth's and O'Connor's and his own men to open fire on the Mexican bank while McNelly recrossed and joined his men. McNelly, under the mistaken belief that the U.S. troops would come to his aid, called over for help, "Randlett, for God's sake come over and help us." [23]

Captain J.F. Randlett did respond. Believing the rangers were to be annihilated, he sent some forty of his men across the river, leaving Farnsworth in charge of the remainder on the U.S. side to cover McNelly with not only the fire from the individual soldiers, but a Gatling gun! Pidge Robinson wrote, "on the Texas side were some of the Eighth Cavalry, and a Gatling gun, and just here I would like to remark that if there is an inanimate object in this whole world for which I have a pure and unadulterated veneration, respect and love, that object is a Gatling gun; if Mr. Gatling has a daughter I would marry her to-morrow, if she would have me, for the sake of her father — and the gun."[24] Randlett, however, was quickly ordered to return to Texas, leaving McNelly with the river at his back and a huge force of Mexicans facing him.

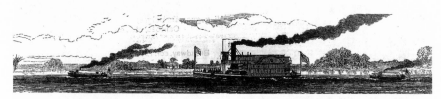

Pictorial representation of the U.S. flotilla steaming up the Rio Grande during the McNelly-created "Las Cuevas affair." From Frank Leslie's *Illustrated Newspaper*, January 1, 1876. *Courtesy The Library of Congress.*

McNelly was dissatisfied with their particular location and
moved his men fifty yards further down the river so that, as recalled
by Callicott, "[w]e can Stand off a thousend or mo[re] with out any
trubble," he explained to his men. There was an open space of 150
yards over which "[w]e can Stand hear and mo[w] them down with
but little danger of ever getten hit with a bullet un less it is in the
hed and if you do the pain woent last long."[25] Was he being serious
or was he being influenced by Pidge Robinson's sense of humor?

During Callicott's turn to stand guard he saw five men approaching with a white flag about a half mile off. McNelly pointed out
there was no danger in white flags, but he didn't want this party to
approach too closely because they would realize how few men he
actually had. Pidge Robinson also wrote of the peace party. "Then a
flag of truce came down and informed us confidently that the party
who . . . charged the Gatling gun and everything else, came down for
the purpose of making peace; we were so much obliged to them for
this information — we would never have known it otherwise." Pidge
said the peace party brought "a lengthy communication from the
Agun - something or other at Camargo, and addressed to the
'Commanding officer of the forces invading Mexico.'"[26] Callicott
identified two members of the party as the governor of the Mexican
state of Tamaulipas and "a white man from arkansaw." The Arkansas
man was Dr. Alexander Manford Headley, although Callicott did
not know that. Callicott recalled that the party wanted to recover the
body of Salinas and that Headley also pointed out there had been
seven men killed during the attack on Las Cucharas and several of
the wounded had since died. McNelly told them he intended to stay
in Mexico until the stolen cattle were recovered, but he did allow
them to recover Salinas' body.[27]

The next day, November 20, found McNelly "and his little Band
of 26 Rangers Still in mexico and all a live."[28] When one of the
guards alerted McNelly that there were Mexicans lining up along the
edge of the woods and along the edge of the thicket, a large group
composed of "Regulers, Bandits and Sittersons," McNelly sent two
men across the river to obtain spades; they returned with two spades
and a shovel.[29] McNelly went down, stepped off a trench forty feet
long, then told three men to dig the trench two feet deep and three
feet wide and pile all the dirt on top of the bank and pack it down.
The men worked an hour and then were relieved. The trench was
completed by 3:00 p.m. McNelly complimented the men by saying
that the old Confederates of 1864 and 1865 could not have dug a
trench any better.

About 4:00 p.m. the five men again approached with a white flag, this time in a boat. Callicott did not identify any of the quintet, which was probably the same group as before. Again they implored McNelly to cross over the river; the "white man from Arkansaw" who was doing the talking feared McNelly and all his men would be killed. Again McNelly informed them he came over to recover the cattle and would stay until he had them.[30]

When it was Callicott's turn to guard, McNelly escorted him to where he wanted him posted. If anyone approached, Callicott was to command "halt" three times; if there was more than one he was to fire into the group. During his guard duty Callicott saw something moving in the thickets. After his third "Halt" he was about to fire when the stranger revealed itself as a cow! Callicott told the captain of this narrow escape, and McNelly replied that he was glad Callicott had not fired because it "might of woak up that US capton on the other Side of the River" who might have thought the Mexicans were firing and begun firing the Gatling guns! McNelly said they would not have lasted twenty minutes, "I am a frader of his gatlin guns than I am of the mexicans."[31]

The citizens of Rio Grande City had learned what was happening and knew McNelly was still on the opposite bank with little food or provisions. The Anglo population therefore sent down a skiff called *The Woman of the Lake*, apparently providing the rangers with sufficient food because Callicott reported having plenty to eat that night.[32]

The peace party approached the third time under the white flag of truce. This time the captain met them with five men, and again the same message was put to McNelly: return to the Texas side of the river or all would be killed. McNelly answered that he would return when he had the cattle. The "Governor," apparently Dr. Headley, the spokesperson on each occasion, said that every boy over fourteen years old along the river had been conscripted and he feared he could not control them any longer. Even though there were now fourteen or fifteen-hundred armed Mexicans lining up to combat the invading Texans, they were ready to negotiate. Headley stated that if McNelly took his men back to Texas he would deliver the cattle, the horses, saddles and bridles of rangers Armstrong and Hall as well as all the thieves he could find.[33] McNelly replied he had killed all the thieves he wanted, but he and the peace party agreed that the cattle and other items could be returned the next morning at Rio Grande City.

The skiff, which would hold from fifteen or twenty men, was

now put to use, and McNelly had thirteen men at a time return across the river, warning them to keep their guns ready. All the rangers were finally safe on the Texas side after three days and nights on the Mexican side of the Rio Grande.[34]

Callicott recorded that the quintet approached three times to negotiate with the rangers. As Callicott's education was minimal and he in all likelihood read little if anything of the affair from newspapers or other sources, he probably recorded what he remembered rather than what he had read. Pidge Robinson wrote as if there had been only one meeting between the peace party and the rangers. N.A. Jennings, who was not there but who may have spoken with men who were, and who certainly could have read a great deal about the invasion, also wrote as if there was but one meeting between the two groups, a quintet with the flag of truce and Sergeant Armstrong with four rangers. Robinson had sent a man across the river to bring back McNelly, who had gone over to the Texas side to "establish direct communication with President Grant . . . certain the President would back him up in his action in crossing."[35]

Jennings described the leader of the group as an American, a

> tall, handsome man, about forty years old, but his hair and long beard were as white as snow, giving him a most patriarchal appearance [when seen] at a little distance. A closer view showed he had a youthful, ruddy complexion and deep, soft blue eyes. He wore a fine, white linen suit and a broad, white *sombrero*. He introduced himself as Dr. Headly.

The description was correct but his name was incorrectly spelled.[36] Jennings described Headley, carrying a carbine with a letter of communication fastened to it under its hammer, as speaking in English concerning the purpose of their visit, but that Armstrong refused to communicate with him other than to say that McNelly was on his way. Here, according to Jennings, Headley placed his hand in his horse's nosebag and brought out a bottle of *mescal*, "which he politely offered to Armstrong." Armstrong and the rangers declined the offer saying they were on duty. Headley then was quoted as saying with a smile, "you gentlemen must be afraid of poison. I am an American myself, and I would not play such a trick as that upon you, and to convince you that the liquor is all right, I here drink to your good health." The men in Headley's group, two of whom were in "officers' uniforms," each drank, and then the doc-

tor became very talkative and asked Armstrong a number of questions. Armstrong continued to refuse to communicate, saying only
that he was under orders not to converse with them.

After McNelly returned, and while reading the communication
of the Mexican delegation, Sergeant Armstrong received a message
from Lieutenant Robinson. There was whispering among the
rangers, and McNelly inquired as to the matter. "Lieutenant
Robinson sends word that the enemy is advancing . . . on our right
. . . he can hear them close by, in large numbers, and he expects firing to begin at any minute." This was said loud enough for Dr.
Headley and his men to hear. McNelly then supposedly responded,
"Very well . . . instruct your men to kill every one of this flag-of-truce
party if there is a shot fired."[37]

Dr. Headley "seemed greatly perturbed" and cried out, "You
don't intend to have us murdered, do you?" McNelly merely replied
that his men would do as they were ordered. Ultimately Dr. Headley
and his group managed to send word to the advancing parties to
refrain from any firing. Dr. Headley inquired if McNelly knew how
many men he had already killed, to which McNelly answered calmly,
"No." Dr. Headley answered "gravely" that twenty-seven had been
killed and accused McNelly of invading his country. Here McNelly
responded with fervor that they had not invaded the country but
were there to recover horses and cattle which had been stolen from
Texas. Finally Headley and McNelly agreed that the stolen livestock
would be returned the next morning at 10:00 a.m. at Rio Grande
City, fifteen miles further up the river. When Dr. Headley had
signed a paper to that effect, the Mexicans were permitted to carry
off their dead.[38]

This version as presented by Jennings in 1899 describes only one
exchange between Dr. Headley's group and the rangers. Callicott
recorded his version of three meetings in 1921, almost certainly without having read Jennings. Certainly the confrontation between Dr.
Headley and a group of Mexicans and some of McNelly's rangers did
take place, but it cannot be determined with certainty if there were
three meetings or two or only one. Over a decade later George
Durham and Clyde Wantland began their versions of the border
experience, almost certainly also using Jennings.

Durham records that McNelly had crossed over to wire President
Grant to inquire about the nature of a message which had been sent
to Fort Brown. Durham claimed to have later seen a message from
Colonel J.H. Potter, Commander of Fort Brown, and recorded it as
saying,

Secretary of War Belknap advises to have McNelly return at once to Texas. Do not support him while he remains in Mexico. Let the secretary know if McNelly acts on these instructions and returns to Texas.[39]

Jennings indeed saw this communication; his version in *A Texas Ranger* was almost an exact copy of the original preserved in the Texas State Archives. The order was directed to "Major Alexander Commdg in the front" dated November 20 at Fort Brown, from Colonel Potter.

William Worth Belknap, Secretary of War during McNelly's invasion of Mexico. *Courtesy The Massachusetts Commandery Military Order of the Loyal Legion and the U.S. Army Military History Institute.*

Advise Capt[.] McNelly to return at once to this side of the river. Inform him that you are directed not to Support him in any way while he remains on Mexican territory. If McNelly is attacked by Mexicans forces on Mexican ground, do not render him any assistance. Keep your forces in the position you hold now and await further orders. Let me Know whether McNelly acts upon your advice and returns.[40]

Durham then noted that McNelly read that message and "began pawing the ground." He continued chomping his dry cigar and then, using his sombrero as a writing table, wrote the following on the reverse of the Potter communication:

At the front
Near Los Cuevos [sic], Mexico
November 20, 1875
I shall remain in Mexico with my rangers . . .
and will cross back at my own discretion . . . Give

my compliments to the Secretary of War and tell
him and the United States Soldiers to go to Hell.

L.H. McNelly,
Commanding.[41]

Jennings' version is nearly identical,

I shall remain in Mexico with my Rangers until
to-morrow morning — perhaps longer, and shall
recross the Rio Grande at my own discretion. Give
my compliments to the Secretary of War and tell
him the United States troops may go to hell.

L.H. McNelly,
Commanding Texas State Troops, Mexico.[42]

If indeed McNelly wrote this response it has not been preserved.
McNelly then went across the river to wire the President to "see what
in the hell they mean sending down that kind of wire." In McNelly's
absence the truce party arrived "holding high a rifle, with a white
flag on it, and a letter held under the hammer." Durham has
Robinson and Armstrong's meeting the truce party and finding the
leader "was Doctor Headly [sic]; an old filibustering American who
looked like a General Washington, but whose name was down in the
book." Durham recalled that Headley "wanted to pass the time of
day" but Robinson told him they were under orders not to talk.
Again the question as to the number of rangers involved was raised,
and Durham quoted McNelly as saying he had enough men to march
from there to the City of Mexico. Jennings had McNelly himself saying they could go to Mexico City. Durham also has McNelly ordering his men to shoot the truce party if a shot was fired, *specifically
ordering that Dr. Headley be shot.* The rangers bickered over who would
get "that purty pistol of his'n" and "that Dick Heye saddle" and his
horse![43]

Certainly the most adverse treatment of this entire river crossing
experience was the representation of Dr. Alexander M. Headley, por-
trayed as a filibuster and a drunken cowardly man, which he was not.
Walter Prescott Webb's *The Texas Rangers*, for decades considered the
classic history of the Texas Rangers, made bare mention of Dr.
Headley, also misspelling his name and at first referring only to the
"flag-of-truce episode" without identifying any of the team. Webb
later indirectly identified two of the Mexican party as Dr. Headley
and Senor Alberretti.[44] McNelly's telegram of November 21 read

simply, "I withdrew my men last night upon the promise of the mexican authorities to deliver the cattle to me at Rio Grande City this morning."[45] Other existing documents testify that there was a truce party and that Dr. Headley was instrumental in setting up terms for the invaders to leave with at least a part of what they wanted.

At Rio Grande City, on November 21, McNelly wrote a communication to Diego Garcia, Chief Magistrate of Camargo, in which there is nothing to suggest the meeting had been anything except friendly, at least outwardly.

> Your communication of this date is received.
>
> The agreement of yesterday with your representatives (Genl Alberretti & Dr Headly [sic]) was that as many of the stolen cattle as you had in your possession, should be delivered to me at 10 ock today — Upon this understanding all troops were withdrawn from the right bank of the river.
>
> This agreement has not been complied with, and as the Commanding Officer of the United States forces is here awaiting your action in this matter I would be glad if you would inform me of the earliest hour at which you can deliver these cattle and any of the theives [sic] you may have apprehended[.]
>
> I have the honor to be Sir
> very respectfully
> Your Obedient Servant
> L.H. McNelly
> Capt Comg
> Texas Rangers[46]

Fortunately Dr. Headley also left a version of the McNelly invasion during an interview on August 21, 1909, with Dr. W.D. Hornaday, who described Headley as a "typical soldier of fortune," a "striking figure. His beard and hair are long and perfectly white," certainly very similar to how he appeared in 1875. Headley gave this version of the events on the border.

> I was making my headquarters at Camargo in the '70s when word was brought to me that Captain McNeeley [sic] of the Texas State Rangers and his men had crossed the Rio Grande in pursuit of Mexican cattle thieves and were holding the town of San Miguel

[Las Cuevas] in a state of siege. McNeely was threatening to burn the town unless the thieves surrendered and
the stolen cattle were given up. He was backed by a force
of 800 United States troops, under Colonel Alexander.
The Federal troops did not cross the river, however, but
were located upon the Texas bank of the Rio Grande,
directly opposite San Miguel, and were ready to enter
Mexico should their services be required in assisting
McNeely and his men. This was the situation that I
found when I entered San Miguel. I had a conference
with Captain McNeely and he reiterated his demands
for the surrender of the thieves and the cattle. I played
for time, and, after seeing Colonel Alexander, I promised to give my answer the following morning. As soon
as it was dark I sent out couriers in every direction and
by daylight next morning I had a force of 600 armed
men at my command in the town of San Miguel. I did
this merely as a matter of protection for the inhabitants
of the place. I could not guarantee to deliver up all the
cattle nor the thieves, and at the conference next morning with McNeely and Colonel Alexander I made them
acquainted with the fact that they would meet with desperate resistance should they make an attack upon the
town. I agreed to have as many of the stolen cattle delivered unto them as I could find. They accepted my terms
and I turned over to them fifty-two head of cattle.
When this had been done Colonel Alexander said to
me:
    "What would you have done if I had crossed the
Rio Grande with my 800 men?"
    "I would have taken my 600 armed men and started
upon a march through Texas," I told him.[47]

Dr. Headley maintained that he would have taken a route down
the valley of the Rio Grande and up the Gulf Coast; he would have
captured Corpus Christi then would have continued marching until
reaching San Antonio. He also related telling Colonel Alexander
that if he (Alexander) had crossed the river it would have brought a
war between Mexico and the United States "that would have been
hard to quell." Dr. Headley reported that in the fighting that
occurred before he arrived on the scene one official of the town had
been killed, Juan Flores Salinas, and *twenty-seven Mexicans*. Two

Mexicans also had been hanged by American citizens.

A question not addressed by the writers who have claimed Dr. Headley was listed in a fugitives book is that, if he indeed was a fugitive and "in the book," why didn't McNelly simply arrest him when he had him covered during the flag of truce parleys? Threatening to kill the quintet was nothing if indeed he believed he could carry it out; and indeed making Dr. Headley a prisoner to use as a hostage certainly would not have been difficult. Quite simply Dr. Headley was not listed in any fugitives book because there was no published list of "fugitives from justice" until 1878, and Headley was not a fugitive wanted by Texas or any other state in 1875.

Alexander Manford Headley, M.D. Dr. Headley practiced medicine on both sides of the Rio Grande during the 1870s and later. He played a key rold in the "Las Cuevas affair." *Courtesy George H. Edgerton.*

That there were meetings between Mexican officials and McNelly is beyond question, but certainly no one passed around a bottle of mescal to drink in such a tense situation. And certainly McNelly's letter to Diego García belies the writings of those who claimed McNelly ordered his men to slaughter the quintet under a white flag of truce if a single shot was fired. McNelly's letter reiterating the agreement included a polite request to inform him when the cattle and any of the thieves would be delivered. McNelly ended his letter in the traditional polite form, "I have the honor to be Sir very Respectfully Your Obedient Servant L H McNelly Capt Comg Texas Rangers."

In fact Dr. Headley's contribution to the whole Las Cuevas affair may have been saving the lives of McNelly and his rangers. The two ranches, Las Cucharas and Las Cuevas, were in Mexico. Even if McNelly and his men crossed over in the dark, the fact that they were there several days certainly gave the Mexicans sufficient time and opportunity to determine fairly accurately just how few there were invading their land.

Dr. Headley was in no sense of the word a filibuster. In fact he was McNelly's fellow Confederate veteran. Alexander Manford Headley was born in England in 1836; he served in the British Navy after prep school then traveled to Louisiana. The title of doctor was not honorary as he attended the Eclectic Medical School of Cincinnati, Ohio from which he was graduated in 1859 and shortly afterward moved to Arkansas. At the age of twenty-five he entered the Confederate Army and served first as assistant surgeon then as senior surgeon. Before the war ended his hair and beard had turned white. Later in Texas and Mexico he was known as *el doctor canoso*, the "gray-haired doctor." When the South surrendered Headley joined Brigadier General Joseph O. Shelby's group of "undefeated rebels" and went to Mexico, their object being to join the French forces under Emperor Maximilian. Crossing into Mexico at Eagle Pass, they reached Mexico City in August 1865. Not long after Headley relocated to Camargo where he established his medical practice and a large mercantile business called *La Casa de Comercio*. When Lerdo de Tejada came to power in 1872 Headley was appointed military commandant of Camargo, located across the river from Rio Grande City. He regained U.S. citizenship in 1880, continued his medical practice on both sides of the border, and became involved in Texas' political struggles. In 1890, Governor John Ireland dispatched sixty rangers to arrest Headley, who had overthrown the Edinburg city government. The rangers instead surrendered their warrant to Headley's allies. Headley continued his practice until his death in February 1912.[48]

What in all likelihood happened was that instead of an offer of *mescal* or a threat to kill all the members of the peace party, Dr. Headley kept control of the citizens, bandits, regulars and any others on the Mexican side so that McNelly and his small force were allowed to live. The number of Mexicans ready to fight the invading force were estimated from several hundred to over a thousand and certainly could have easily overcame McNelly and his rangers, even if there were Gatling guns on the other side of the river. Dr. Headley was no outlaw or fugitive; he was a highly respected citizen in his community and was certainly well known on both sides of the river. In this situation in November of 1875 Headley was the hero and McNelly was the outlaw, having indiscriminately shot down a number of men at Las Cucharas, attacked a second ranch, and established his force illegally in a foreign country. Were some of the dead guilty of plundering on the Texas ranches, as the typical Texan believed they were? Probably. Were some totally innocent of any crime? Certainly. Invading Mexico with such a small force and risking not only his own life but the lives of his men for a herd of cattle was a reckless and extremely dangerous move. McNelly wanted to make a point, and he made it, but the success of his mission owes more perhaps to Dr. Headley and his leadership capabilities than it does to the daring and genuine courage of McNelly which, never-theless has contributed to the Texas Ranger mystique.

***

The next morning McNelly went with ten men to Rio Grande City to claim the cattle. Although they were to be delivered in the morning, no one showed from the Mexican side until 4:00 p.m., at which time a delegation which included twenty-five Mexicans told McNelly the cattle could not cross as they had not been inspected! McNelly recognized this as a needless delay and said, "well boys 25 to 10 that's near a nuff[.] we will go over a gain." They crossed the river on a ferry provided and faced the Mexicans yet again. He instructed Tom Sullivan to tell them that the "Governor" had prom-ised to deliver the cattle and horses. When the Mexican spokesman again said the cattle could not be returned until they were inspected, McNelly told Sullivan to tell him they had been driven from Texas without being inspected and they certainly could be returned with-out being inspected. The spokesman again said no and McNelly ran out of patience. The men were told to fall into ranks, load their guns, and point them at the Mexicans. Callicott recalled that McNelly "told tom to tell him a Son of a bitch if he dident cross them cattle in less than 5 minutes he would Kill the last one of them." The cattle were crossed in much less than five minutes, all except one old cow so near given out it wouldn't enter the water. She was pulled on the boat and returned to Texas, then given to the boat man in payment for his work. Callicott recalled that he had never before heard McNelly utter a cross word, but McNelly "had Got his Red fether Rosed he was a man that Seldom Got mad and never did get exsited he all ways handled his men like a farther would his chil-dren[.] I never did hear him Speak a cross wird to one of them but when ever he gave a command it Sertenly had to be obade . . . when he gave and order it had to be obade to the letter."[49]

McNelly's telegram to Steele revealed none of the dramatics described by the chroniclers. "Mexicans delivered sixty five beeves last evening [and] promise more soon as captured and the delivery of the thieves. Have just received this assurance from the president of Jurisdiction of Camargo in accordance with cartel of twentieth."[50] If McNelly did in fact threaten death to the group responsible for plac-ing the stolen beeves at McNelly's disposal, and if he did in fact threaten to shoot the truce team holding a white flag, he did it in violation of his usual acceptance of the rules of honorable warfare. He was well aware of the futility of killing more men on the Mexican side of the Rio Grande. He could not count on United States troops' crossing over to his assistance in time to rescue him. His chroniclers may have wanted to contribute the success of the mission to bluffing, as McNelly had learned to do so well in the swamps of Louisiana, but in reality it succeeded because of an American doctor.

The bronze plaque on the Salinas Monument,
present day Gustavo Díaz Ordaz, Mexico.

Al Ciudadano
Juan Flores Salinas
Que combatiendo, murió por su patria
el 19 de Noviembre 1875.

Photo by Chuck Parsons.

CHAPTER 17

AFTER THE LAS CUEVAS AFFAIR

> Capt. McNelly, by his real "bull-dog" bravery and
> firmness, has compelled the Mexican authorities to
> accede to his demands, that of returning the sixty-five
> head of stolen cattle, which were driven across the Rio
> Grande a few days since by the Mexican cattle-thieves. -
> *The Brenham Banner*, 26 November 1875.

McNelly thought he had a deal with the Mexicans; the stolen cattle, or at least some of them, were to be returned the morning of November 21 at 10:00 a.m. Pidge described how McNelly and ten men went to receive the cattle, the ranger horses which had been captured, and their equipment.[1] Durham recalled that the ride to Rio Grande City where the cattle were to be crossed was "made virtually in silence so far as I know." They arrived about daylight and were all taken to a restaurant where Captain McNelly gave them all the coffee they could hold and some *pan dulce*, "but nothing more. Which didn't look so good; this was a fighting ration."[2]

While on the Texas side McNelly told Armstrong to pick out ten men and for the others to "retire back from the river with the rest and be ready." They left their horses on the Texas side and crossed down to the ferry to cross the Rio Grande one more time. The ten, dubbed the "Death Squad" by Durham, were McNelly, Pidge Robinson, sergeants Hall and Armstrong, privates Pitts, Rudd, Callicott, Maben, McGovern and himself, nine in addition to McNelly.

According to Durham, McNelly realized that he was being surrounded by a superior force and took the offensive. At a prearranged signal the rangers drew their pistols and covered the head official who was giving excuses that the cattle could not be crossed. Durham described how McNelly kicked "the officer in the belly and sent him sprawling. And then he handed one or two good kicks in his ribs." Then McNelly ordered his interpreter to tell the official that if there was a shot fired from anywhere he would die with ten bullets in him.[3] This is preposterous, perhaps Wantland's efforts to add what he considered "color."

In the later book version of Durham's recollections the incident was taken one step further, as if the incident needed further dramatics. McNelly drew his pistol and crashed it against the side of the official's head then put his knee in the man's belly as he went down. Pitts even shot one of the Mexicans who attempted to draw his own pistol before all of the Mexicans surrendered.[4] Then the "big senor" suddenly remembered he could speak English as well as anybody "and didn't need McGovern or any other interpreter." The Mexican official was forced to order his men to swim the cattle across, spending an hour to do so. The cattle were gathered up on the Texas side where Inspector Rock had their brands identified. Word was sent to the owners to come and retrieve the recovered stock. At first some were reluctant to do so, fearing possible retaliation from the raiders once McNelly had left the country. Orders went back in stronger language for the owners to come and claim their animals.[5]

According to Pidge's version, McNelly was "informed at the hour appointed that they [the Mexicans] were really so very busy with matters of the utmost importance they did not have time to attend to the affair that day, and to call again."[6] Durham recalled that they were initially put off because business could not be transacted on a Sunday. Then McNelly was told that if the beeves were sent to the crossing they would need assistance from the rangers to cross them over. Then the Mexican Customhouse officers wanted a permit for them to be crossed. Robinson wrote that this idea of requiring a permit to recross the cattle was "sublimely cocky — appealingly so. They went over without any permit and it was *surmised* that they might return in the same manner." Captain McNelly exhausted all arguments with the officials, except one which Pidge called the "clincher"; he gave the order to his men to load, and the "ominous 'kerchack' of the carbine levers as the long, murderous looking cartridges were chambered home, satisfied them as to the permit and the cattle were allowed to cross over without one; such is the power of a fifty-calibre argument, such the authority of Sharps on International law."[7]

What exactly happened to the cattle is not known, although Callicott wrote that those recovered were driven out about two miles from Brownsville where those belonging to Captain Richard King bearing the Running W brand were cut out. The others were left to drift back to their accustomed range. McNelly asked for four volun-

An image showing William C. Callicott on his horse "Old Ball" in 1874.
Courtesy the W.P. Webb Collection, University of Texas, Austin.

teers to deliver King's cattle back to the Santa Gertrudis Ranch; the four volunteers were Durham, Callicott, Pitts and Rudd.

Callicott described the journey as uneventful, except during one night Durham experienced a horrible dream and woke up ready to start shooting. The rangers eventually removed his pistols when he was to turn in, fearing he would start shooting during his nightmares. Only seventy-five head had been crossed over, of which thirty-five were King's, so it was a simple chore for four men to drive that few head of cattle. Once at the Santa Gertrudis the rangers were brought up to date; King was surprised that any of McNelly's men had survived as it was feared all had been killed. King, having read the reports that McNelly's men might become a second Alamo, had started gathering one-hundred men to go to his rescue. "[O]ut of the many thousand hed I hav had Stolen and driven to mexico this 35 hed or all I hav ever got back." Then King ordered his hands to saw off the right horn of each of the thirty-five and turn them loose on the range. He ordered that none was to be killed for beef or be sold

Nettie King (left) and Ella Morse King (right), daughters of Richard and
Henrietta Chamberlain King, two of the "King Women." Photos by A.J. Fox,
St. Louis (left) and A.B. Rice, Danville, Kentucky (right). *Courtesy The King
Ranch Archives, Kingsville, Texas.*

as he wanted them all to spend "the ballence of thire days in Piece."
These one-horned cattle came to be known as *los viejos* by King's
vaqueros.[8]

The four rangers were invited to spend the night in the house.
Instead they chose to sleep outside as they had not washed or
changed their clothes for days, but they were brought up to the ranch
house where they met the two daughters of the captain. The girls
had just been graduated from a Kentucky school and had come
home to spend the winter. Two big pound cakes were sent to the
rangers with the message, "Compliments of the 2 Miss Kings to the
McNelly Rangers," as Callicott remembered;[9] Durham recalled the
writing slightly different, "Compliments of the King women to The
McNelly Rangers."[10] The warm reception provided the quartet of
McNelly's men was not the only reward given; not long after Captain
King made a presentation of $500. to the company in appreciation
for its daring accomplishment.[11]

Although Cortina would never be dealt the kind of justice Texas
ranchers would have wanted, his days as ruler of the border were
numbered; President Sebastián Lerdo de Tejada "arrested" him,

although in reality the arrest was nothing more serious than being placed under house arrest. The San Antonio *Express* penned a lengthy article discussing the difficulties with the neighboring nation, in which it was stated that there was no reason to fear a war with Mexico, but warfare with bandits was needed. "[W]e do not consider the border thieves as the Mexican Republic. Against these marauders we entertain a most inveterate hatred, and crave the arrival of that time when every man of them shall have met the ends of justice." The "arrest" of Cortina was a political move on the part of Lerdo de Tejada, according to the *Express*, the idea being that Cortina held the thieving population between the river and the mountains under his control. If Cortina's favor could be counted upon, his influence would assist Lerdo de Tejada politically. But Lerdo de Tejada could not attempt to arrest Cortina's followers, described as "a disaffected class throughout the northern part of Mexico," because if he did the result would be "another civil contest in that god-forsaken and unhappy country." Thus, concluded the *Express*, the only real answer to the thieving problem was not to depend on Mexico. The state of Texas herself should "send a regiment of her fearless rangers to the border, and these troubles would be as dreams of the past." There is no doubt the *Express* had McNelly in mind to solve the dilemma. Furthermore, said the *Express*, wars are terribly expensive not only in money but in lives, it would be cheaper for the United States to purchase the strip of territory below the Rio Grande, resulting in the Sierra Madre's becoming the new border, the mountain line being followed through Tamaulipas, Nuevo León, Chihuahua and Coahuila, and continuing through Sonora and Lower California. The *Express* did not end its comments there, but chose to quote correspondence from an undated New York *Herald*.

> What Texas intends to do for her own protection may be gathered from the recent action of Captain McNally [sic]. She proposes to protect herself if the United States government will not protect her. Governor Davis, a Republican, made application to the President for aid and his appeal was disregarded. Governor Coke, his democratic successor, has made a similar appeal, and it is unheeded. Captain McNally [sic], who is under thirty years of age, energetic, cool, brave and possessed of wonderful physical endurance, was appointed first by Governor Davis and afterward

by Governor Coke, to take charge of a company of rangers and do police duty on the frontier. In the late war he entered the Confederate army as a private, but soon obtained a sort of "free lance command," and won the fame of John Morgan in the Trans-Mississippi department. He has already pursued into Mexico bands of thieves, recovering the stolen property and showing no mercy to the robbers. His last exploit proves of what stuff he is made, and shows that he will not hesitate to "carry the war into Mexico" on every occasion. Captain McNally some time ago visited Washington and had an interview with President Grant; hence it is tolerably certain that the government has been previously advised of the course the Texas ranger chief intended to pursue.[12]

A lengthy editorial of the same tone appeared in the following edition, headlined "Mexico Again." Now, realizing that even though Texas felt herself the aggrieved party, the *Express* editors believed there were two sides to the question. In order to be fair, a lengthy article from a recent *Heraldo de Bravo*, a Matamoros newspaper, was presented. In case the reader might miss it, the *Express* requested the reader "to observe that peculiar spirit of mean pride and insolence characterizing it throughout." The *Heraldo* reminded its readers that "the Rural Police of Camargo fought and defeated the cattle thieves, who are the cause of these difficulties, not without some loss, taking from them, according to some reports, twenty-four head of cattle, according to others, seventy-five head." But in spite of this, "the Rangers had the audacity to cross to this side at a point near Camargo [numbering] fifty men [sic], but in addition to these, three companies of the United States regular army, although on the other bank of the river, are in observation." The *Heraldo* concluded its report by suggesting that the "filibuster invasion should not subject us to serious alarm" and the "miserable pirates" should be punished upon their being taken prisoners, which we confidently believe will be if they remain longer on the Mexican soil." The *Express* could not deny that there had been wrong on both sides and that some people had exaggerated the losses in hopes of a war's being declared between the two countries, but it did "most emphatically deny" there being any truth in the statements that the United States wanted war with her southern neighbor.[13]

McNelly later was interviewed by the editor of the *Ranchero* in which he denied the reports stating his force had backed down; on the contrary, he was always the aggressor and never backed an inch. Only when all the demands were pledged by Mexican authorities did he consider recrossing the river back to the United States. The authorities complied with his demands as much as they possibly could, being compelled to return the stolen stock, "and, as an exchange says, without dimming 'the Lone Star of Texas.'"[14]

In spite of McNelly's accomplishment, little had actually been achieved. Reports of McNelly's activities were occasionally reported, such as in the "Brownsville Items" where the simple statement appeared that "Captain McNelly is in town. He arrived on the steamer I.G. Harris." But the stealing of Texas cattle continued. In the *Express* of December 19 a report itemized the number of cattle being crossed over: at Edinburg, 350 head; at Roma, 180 head; at Ringgold, 150 head; at Las Cuevas, 250 head; 435 head were crossed at Brownsville and 300 head at Los Grullos, a total of 1,620 stolen head of cattle known to have been crossed during the month of November. Reports had reached Austin that a contract had been made at Monterrey for the "prompt delivery of 18,000 beeves." Every Texan undoubtedly assumed that meant eighteen-thousand head of *Texas cattle*. And even though the press could praise McNelly for his accomplishment and his strength of will in forcing the Mexican authorities to yield to his demands, the man himself was losing strength. A report datelined Austin on December 10 concluded with a single line, "McNelly is still at Brownsville, slightly unwell."[15]

By December 20 McNelly was well enough to attend a mass meeting in Brownsville, called for by Major Parker, a meeting which was "largely attended." Colonel John S. "Rip" Ford was selected to act as president over the gathering. The main themes were the questions of how McNelly could be kept on the border and the general problems with Mexico. A committee of eleven was selected to prepare a "memorial" to Governor Coke representing the conditions of affairs along the frontier and to urge the continuance of McNelly's command in the service. Not only was his presence desired, but the gathering of men felt that the company should be increased to two hundred! A mere petition to the governor was not sufficient; delegates were selected to travel to Washington, D.C. to represent the severity of frontier conditions to the national authorities. Colonel John L. Haynes was nominated as chairman with McNelly and Colonel Ford selected as delegates to deliver their concerns. McNelly was called on to make a statement, described as being uttered in "a few terse remarks" in which he said that he was not a speaker, but "if his force were increased to 200 men he would perform all that could be expected of him in ridding the frontier of the presence of cattle thieves." His remarks, which must have been brief in the extreme, were followed with "vociferous applause." Colonel John L. Haynes then spoke, stressing the need for McNelly's command to be retained and increased. He was followed by Judge Ed Dougherty, who bore testimony from experience of the efficacy of McNelly's force on the river and that he "endorsed the action of the meeting heartily." Major Parker said he had recently returned from a trip into the interior and learned that the people generally expressed great sat~ isfaction and that a healthier feeling of safety and relief existed in the cattle interest in the country based upon McNelly's presence. The committee to prepare the memorial to keep McNelly on the border, originally to number five, enthusiastically grew to eleven: Haynes to act as chairman, Honorable Ed Dougherty, Colonel Ford, Ed Downey, William Neale, A. Werbiskie, William H. Russell, R.B. Kingsbury, Mariano Trevino Garza, Stephen Powers and Major Parker. McNelly, because he was soon to visit Austin, was himself chosen to deliver the memorial. Parker and Werbiskie were charged with the responsibility of collecting funds to defray the expenses of the trip to Washington. The committee did not overlook the tech~ nicality of asking Governor Coke to grant McNelly a leave of absence to go to Washington as a delegate.[16] The report of the mass meeting, prepared by secretary L. Cowen, was to be printed in "all the news~ papers published in the Valley of the Rio Grande." The report was published at least as far north as Dallas, allowing desperadoes as well as honest citizens of Texas the knowledge that Captain McNelly would be out of the state for at least a while.[17] By December 23 McNelly was leaving the border for another trip east.

On January 24 and 29 McNelly provided detailed testimony before a House of Representatives committee dealing with Texas border troubles. The committee consisted of Gustav Schleicher, a Texan who had been elected to the House from the 6th District in 1874; A.S. Williams; Nathaniel Prentiss Banks, former Governor of Massachusetts and Union general who had faced McNelly during the war; L.Q.C. Lamar and S.A. Hurlbut. His testimony was recorded for publication in the House of Representatives Report No. 343 of the 1st Session of the 44th Congress of the United States.

McNelly's contribution began with questions from chairman Schleicher, who inquired how long McNelly had been on the Rio Grande and his "occupation" there. McNelly's brief response merely indicated he had been sent there the previous April to "see what could be done in breaking up this raiding of Mexicans on the ranches on the borders of the Rio Grande."

Schleicher's next question elicited a lengthy response concerning his "means and facilities of information" about the raids, suggesting Schleicher knew there was more than mere chance in catching up with a raiding party! McNelly answered in detail describing his spy system, the numbers of men he had which varied considerably, and his efforts at catching raiders. He could brag that the rangers caught up with a raiding party every month and forced them to choose between keeping their stolen cattle or escaping: "We succeeded every month in turning loose from two to four herds of cattle that were driven off — that is, forcing the raiders to turn the cattle loose."

In response to additional questioning McNelly explained to the committee that part of the difficulty was that so many of the "Mexicans" in the area were seemingly related either to Mexicans on the Mexican side of the river or on the Texas side. Many living on the Texas side claimed no citizenship to Texas but were in direct sympathy with the raiders. The raiders were their kinfolk, their cousins, or uncles, or brothers "for it seems to me as if all the Mexicans on both sides of the river are relatives," explained McNelly.

To a question from Mr. Hurlbut, McNelly explained that the only "Mexicans" he could trust were those who actually owned a ranch in Texas. Any "Mexican" owning a ranch McNelly felt was a good citizen because he would want the thieving rings broken up. Although they would not take an active part in fighting the raiders, they still were very brave. McNelly was "willing to take a good many chances" but, he added perhaps cryptically, "I certainly would not live on a stock-ranch west of the Nueces River, at any point from the mouth of the Devil's River to the north of the Rio Grande . . . the risk is too great. My position, in command of a company of troops, I do not consider half so hazardous as that of those men living on ranches."

McNelly explained that if a force of Americans crossed the river to retaliate or recover stolen stock they would probably be annihilated; he further claimed that it would take perhaps a force of four or five or six-hundred strong to cross over and then move rapidly if they hoped to succeed in returning.

Mr. Lamar was incredulous upon hearing that the Mexicans could gather together enough fighting men so quickly as to overpower a force of five- hundred armed men. McNelly reiterated his claim, adding that they could be gathered within twenty-four hours. If five hundred of the best United States troops were to cross the river, go four miles into the interior, and remain twenty-four hours in one place, he doubted they would ever return. "I speak as a soldier. I served four years in the confederate army. I have met some of these Mexicans out there, and they are men who stand killing splendidly."

The Mexicans who could overpower five hundred were of three distinct groups: the "rural police" who could be called together on the word of the *encargados*; the civil officers who would send out word to a ranch, then from there the word would be spread and the appeal of help would travel fifteen miles an hour. The frontiersmen who would respond would be armed with Winchester rifles and carbines, or Spencer rifles. These men would gather rapidly and "are very patriotic." In addition there would be the Mexican Federal troops, men very indifferently armed and mounted. They were armed with all sorts of weapons, and the only similarity was they all wore a uniform cap. And then there were the raiders themselves, who could whip the regulars three to one.

To McNelly the raiders made no secret of their business. It was common knowledge that Cortina was the chieftain, although he himself no longer crossed the river. McNelly described a contract which Cortina had to furnish a Cuban market with five or six-hundred head of cattle. Even though Cortina was overseeing the shipment on the lighter which was receiving the cattle, McNelly was able to send over Sergeant George A. Hall to make note of the American brands. With Cortina were twelve or fifteen men who were going to cross over to steal more cattle, since the lighter had room for 250 more head. It was men of this group who were caught and engaged in battle with McNelly on the Palo Alto prairie, "all identified as men who composed the immediate body-guard of Cortina, and who had been down at the mouth of the river helping him to load these cattle." At the time of this engagement Cortina was the Mayor of Matamoros, or, *el presidente del ayuntamiento*.

The question of crossing over the river to retaliate against bandits was raised by Mr. Hurlbut. He said, "I suppose that you are aware that sending a body of troops, under the flag of the United States, into a country with which we are at peace is a declaration of war." McNelly responded that he hardly thought so, that there was the principle of international law; if a nation was unable or unwilling to restrain its own "turbulent people from depredating on a neighboring territory," then the neighbor so depredated had the right to pursue and punish the offenders.[18]

McNelly's questioning by the committee concluded on Saturday,

January 29; by February 20 he was back in Austin.[19] It is unknown if the entire McNelly family visited Washington at this time, but most likely Carey and the children did accompany him. Mrs. McNelly and son Rebel occasionally visited camp so it would seem probable that the Washington trip was also a family vacation.

During his Washington visit the border unrest continued and vigilante action seemed imminent. At almost the same time as McNelly was leaving Texas, ranchers Strickland and Slaughter complained that they had lost eight-hundred head of cattle and nearly sixty head of horses to thieves. Other reports of loss totaled nearly six-hundred head of cattle. When the *Express* of San Antonio received these reports it added, although not naming sources, that citizens were organizing themselves into companies similar to McNelly's and were threatening to cross the river to recover their stolen stock. The policy of the United States in prohibiting troops from helping citizens who were losing thousands of head of livestock was disgracing the army. Although its editor formerly had stated war was not wanted, now the statement in a supplement had this exhortation, "Push over the river, soldiers and citizens, and destroy the whole nest of thieves, regardless of the consequences."[20]

Although McNelly was absent, his command was not idle. Lieutenant Robinson was in charge and continued McNelly's practice of having scouting parties constantly on patrol. On December 28 one scouting party in charge of an unidentified sergeant, possibly George A. Hall, were on the Rincon de Perro, some forty miles north of Las Rucias, when they found a "perfect Golgotha of stolen hides" as Robinson expressed the grisly scene. He arrested the ranchero nominally in charge who then attempted to bribe him. When the sergeant refused to be bribed, the ranchero attempted to escape and was killed in the attempt. Robinson provided no additional details.[21] Although not identified by name, the ranchero may have been Manuel García because a brief report in the Galveston *Daily News* stated that García had been "lately killed by McNelly's men." He was a companion of Pedro Perales, alias El Cojo, who was killed resisting arrest by the sheriff of Cameron County, James G. Browne, "a few weeks ago."[22]

Major Henry Joseph Farnsworth, who operated against bandits on
the Rio Grande with McNelly during the 1870s. *Photo courtesy The
Civil War Library & Museum, MOLLUS, Philadelphia, Pennsylvania.*

CHAPTER 18

INVADING THE PENDENCIA

On the 4th, arrested King Fisher and nine of his gang.

On 6th, King Fisher and gang released, whilst Capt. McNelly was on his way with witnesses. Seven of the nine could have been indicted for murder in several cases.—*Adjutant-General's Report, for the Year Ending August 31st, 1876.*

McNelly was back in Texas by mid-February. Undoubtedly he spent some time in Austin discussing his trip and experience before the House of Representatives committee with Governor Coke and Adjutant General Steele. Scant information about the congressional testimony or the trip itself appeared in the Texas press, but attention was surprisingly given to the health of Steele! Certainly the travel and testifying before the committee was exhaustive for McNelly, but it may have been equally difficult for Steele, fifty-six years old, a generation older than McNelly. Ironically it was Steele's condition which warranted notice by a reporter of the Austin *Gazette*, who stated that he looked "in fine health, and is none the worse for his trip."[1] McNelly probably spent some time back in Burton, but by early March he was en route to Brownsville.

But on the road to Brownsville he stopped in Cuero, DeWitt County, because Mrs. McNelly was there visiting the J.Y. Bell family.[2] Arriving there on March 2, McNelly found the town "in such a disturbed condition" that he felt it necessary, at the solicitation of a number of prominent citizens, to remain there a few days "so that in case of any serious disturbance I might be of some servis [sic] to the State if not to the local officers."[3] What caused this disturbance was that the Sutton-Taylor Feud had flared up again resulting in another killing a few days before his arrival. On Sunday night February 27, deputy sheriff Goethry of Henderson County requested assistance from Sheriff William J. Weisiger to arrest Joseph Allen, charged with

killing a man in Henderson County. Weisiger sent deputy Joseph
Agee and a posse composed of Sutton followers, according to
McNelly, to arrest Allen. When the posse arrived the men were told
young Allen was not there. Nevertheless they searched the Allen
house and found their suspect, who rose up from a large dry goods
box and fired on the posse. When the shooting stopped young Allen
was severely wounded, Agee had received a load of buckshot in the
leg, and posse member J.E. Lampley was dead. Initial reports from
the scene indicated that members of the Taylor party were guarding
the wounded Allen. On Friday March 3, Sheriff Weisiger summoned a posse of sixty men to assist in arresting those who had resisted his deputy. At the Allen house the posse arrested "old man
Allen" and a younger brother of Joseph and then started for the
home of Mannen Clements, a cousin of John Wesley Hardin and a
sympathizer of the Taylors, where the wounded Allen was reported
to be in hiding. There young Allen was found, but he was so weak
from loss of blood that Weisiger refused to move him. While still
there determining his next move, Weisigner saw a group of men
advancing, "well mounted and armed, evidently intent on mischief."
Weisiger readied his men for an attack, causing the newcomers to
turn and gallop off. Bill Taylor was recognized as one of the group.
Although some of the sheriff's posse wanted to pursue Taylor, others advised caution, fearing an ambush; further, the posse had been
on horseback nearly twenty-four hours and Weisiger wisely returned
to Cuero. The special correspondence from Cuero indicated great
confidence in the county lawmen. The unidentified reporter wrote
in the conclusion of his report, "I am satisfied the present county
officials will be well sustained in their effort to enforce the law by the
majority of the citizens from the promptness with which the huge
posse responded to the Sheriff's call."[4] McNelly's letter to Adjutant
General Steele, written a few days later from Captain King's ranch,
indicated that the confidence was perhaps premature. Wrote
McNelly,

> It seems that a few days previous to my arrival, a
> deputy sheriff of Henderson County had come to
> Clinton with a "writ" for one "Allen" who is said to be
> one of the "Taylor" party and summoned a possee [sic]
> of eight or nine of the "Suttons party" to aid him in
> making the arrest. (it seems that no one but some of the
> "Suttons Party" can be found to attempt to arrest "a
> Taylor" and visa versa .... Young Allen & another man

was badly wounded & the Henderson county officer &
party left in "double quick" time without waiting to see
whether their friends or the party they went to arrest
was killed or not.

McNelly explained that a few days later some of the Taylor party
from Gonzales County arrived and sent word to the Sutton party,

> that if they wanted a fight to come up and try it.
> Accordingly the Sutton party organized and as I came
> through were ready to start so I waited until they
> returned. They found young Allen in a dieing [sic] con-
> dition & left him (as some of them told me on their
> return) as they had no ammunition to waist [sic] on
> behalf [of a] dead man when they were in the "Taylors
> jurisdiction."[5]

Although John Wesley Hardin had been out of the state since
mid-1874, rumors continually reached the ears of lawmen that he
was in their area. McNelly was as alert to such rumors as other lawmen, and in March he contemplated going after Hardin again. There
were rumors the noted gunfighter and members of his gang were in
the Devil's River area, probably the small community in southeast-
ern Val Verde County. McNelly wrote to Steele that if the rumor was
true, "we may have an opportunity of ridding the State of these pests
for good and all for I shall deal with them without mercy," but
McNelly concluded it was a false report and abandoned the idea of
scouting in Val Verde County for the elusive outlaw, worth a $4,000
reward dead or alive.[6] By the end of April the company was still stationed in the Brownsville area, but events would soon draw it westward towards Laredo in Maverick County. Due to McNelly's success
against the raiders in the Brownsville region, raiders had taken their
thieving further up the river.

Occasionally natural events wrought havoc for the rangers. On
May 8 a heavy storm struck the camp area and severely damaged the
company's tents. Even though the weather was hard on the men, the
rains had improved the grass and their horses were "getting in fine
condition."[7]

On May 17 the company broke camp at Santa María, some forty
miles from Brownsville, with orders to report to Laredo two-hundred
miles distant. That evening, near Edinburg (present day Hidalgo)
McNelly and a squad came upon a group of cattle thieves in the act

of crossing a herd of stolen cattle. Although few details are extant, McNelly went on the offensive and his rangers killed two raiders and wounded a third in the ensuing gunbattle. McNelly crossed the river again and recovered some of the stolen stock.

Strangely, this time the act of crossing and engaging cattle thieves on their own ground received very little coverage in the press of the day. McNelly's first telegram to Steele merely reported he had attacked the thieves, killing and wounding some and recovering stolen stock. His second telegram dated May 19 was more informa~ tive. The rangers were following the trail of the rustlers but lost it in the darkness at ten o'clock in the evening. By the time they caught up with the thieves, most had already crossed over and only four were still on the Texas side. In addition to repeating that he killed two and wounded a third, McNelly now detailed that he had recov~ ered six horses, saddles, bridles and camp equipment, coffee pots, cups, blankets, ropes and other miscellaneous items.[8] McNelly and his men possibly enjoyed a good laugh when they learned that, while they were engaging the bandits on the river, Mexican General Escobedo and some U.S. Army officers were dining and enjoying the musical strains of Escobedo's twenty~piece band all within view of the gun fight on the river bank!

After the initial engagement resulting in the deaths of two raiders, McNelly needed more men to cross into Mexico to recover more of the cattle and asked for assistance from Captain H.J. Farnsworth, 8th U.S. Cavalry. Farnsworth, realizing it was too late for "hot pursuit," declined. His offer to provide fifty men to assist on the Texas side was useless because McNelly needed help in recover~ ing the stolen cattle on the Mexico side. After Farnsworth refused to allow any soldiers to cross, McNelly with only three men crossed over to within one and a half~miles of Escobedo's lines but failed to recover the cattle that had been crossed. McNelly summoned Reynosa's *alcalde*, Desiderio Rodríguez, and ordered him to recover the remaining cattle and to deliver the thieves; the alcalde promised both and did nothing. It was generally understood, at least in McNelly's view, that the stolen cattle were destined to feed Escobedo's troops.[9]

A fascinating detail which appeared in the contemporary press reveals McNelly's participative style of leadership. On May 18 McNelly obtained the services of newspaper correspondent "Ojo" to act as interpreter during a meeting between McNelly and alcalde Desiderio Rodríguez, President of the *Ayuntamiento* of Reynosa. McNelly demanded of Rodríguez the return of the cattle, numbering about two dozen head, and the surrender of the thieves who had escaped, identified by McNelly as Abundo Mungia, Lino Pérez, Candelario, Garza, Escobia Mancías, Andrés Cavazos and others. The greatly agitated *alcalde* wanted to know why McNelly was sending armed men into Mexico; McNelly replied "that he hadn't sent armed men into Mexico but went and took them with him." The alcalde promised to return the cattle as well as the thieves, but while the cattle were being rounded up he sent a message to Escobedo that the Mexican territory had been invaded by Americans! Fifty men were sent to protect him. The delay provided time for the identified thieves to escape deeper into Mexico. Ojo pointed out that they had received a warning to "make themselves scarce. It is well known that the parties concerned in this cattle stealing reside at this ranch with their families and have all their interest there." McNelly and three men obtained a good view of the holding corrals and their trail heading to the Sabinito Ranch four miles from Reynosa, and why he didn't force the issue further than he did is unknown. Perhaps he was satisfied in having recovered part of the stolen herd as well as killing two and wounding one of the thieves.[10] A month spent in the nation's capital had not altered the leader's attitude towards international law.

Perhaps Adjutant General Steele heard complaints against his captain, possibly Farnsworth communicated to Austin, or possibly General Escobedo himself expressed displeasure at McNelly's tactics of ignoring the Rio Grande boundary, because McNelly found it necessary to write an explanatory letter to Steele. His letter, written from Laredo on May 31, read in part, "You may depend on my not doing anything that will not be justifiable legally, and I shall have a duly authorized civil officer accompany each of my squads." By now McNelly had decided to establish camp at Fort Ewell in La Salle County.[11] Future operations would start from that point, located on the south side of the Nueces River less than thirty miles from Laredo. The fort had been abandoned since 1853, but there was still a small civilian community and a post office.

Although the requirement that he have a county officer or someone acting in an official capacity accompany him when he made an arrest or challenged raiders, which was not always possible, and the necessity of honoring international law may have caused McNelly some frustration, capturing outlaws did bring some satisfaction. Killing an occasional cattle thief crossing stolen cattle would not drastically reduce crime along the river, but the arrest of a noted outlaw might cause outlaws to relocate elsewhere. The arrest of King

Fisher, for example, ultimately did reduce lawlessness. Although he never earned the statewide notoriety as did John Wesley Hardin, during his violent life King Fisher earned great notoriety in South Texas. John King Fisher was born in Texas in 1854 and as a teenager began his criminal career by breaking into a storehouse in Goliad County and stealing some trifling items. On October 5, 1870, he was arrested by State Policeman C.C. Simmons in Goliad County and charged with "theft & robbery."[12] He was sent to Huntsville for a two-year term, beginning on October 30, 1870, but was pardoned after serving only four months. On April 6, 1876, he married Sarah Vivian. Although some accounts have him killing dozens of men — and even McNelly believed he had killed at least nine — he probably killed less than half a dozen. His reputation originated from the influence he held over the area around the Pendencia Creek, an intermittent stream rising in northwestern Dimmit County and flowing into southwestern Zavala County. The range lands which depended on the Pendencia became known as "King Fisher's Territory." King Fisher was leader to many young men, some of whom were outlaws and hardened fugitives. He was intelligent, and his ability to manipulate the court system and avoid prison for his alleged crimes — after the brief Huntsville experience — proved it. When McNelly arrested him, he knew fighting was senseless and that he would probably be acquitted of any crime charged to his door.[13]

The anticipation of capturing King Fisher, and the potential excitement of a gunfight, may have been greater than the arrest itself. The actual arrest became anticlimactic when Fisher surrendered without a struggle. KING FISHER AND SEVEN OF HIS GANG CAP-TURED headlined the San Antonio *Express*, followed in smaller type with, "Captain McNelly Did It" and "His Men Scouring the Country for More of Them." McNelly had "charged upon Pendencia" on June 3 at six o'clock in the evening. No resistance was offered "as it would have been useless." The prisoners were left with authorities at Eagle Pass while McNelly proceeded on to Oakville in search of more outlaws. Arrested on Saturday, the prisoners were released on bond almost immediately.[14] Reports varied the number from seven to nine, but McNelly's telegram to Steele identified nine by name: King Fisher, Burd Oberchain alias Frank Porter, Warren Allen, Bill Templeton, Al Roberts, Bill Wainwright, Jim Honeycutt, Wes and Bill Bruton. William R. Templeton had once been a McNelly ranger although he served but a short time and never rose above the rank of private.[15] Although the arrest of King Fisher brought considerable publicity to McNelly and the rangers, the fact that King could so quickly obtain his freedom was galling to the captain. He notified Steele that Fisher and his men were released while he was bringing in witnesses to testify against them. "There were seven out of nine that could have been convicted of murder in several cases," he wrote. Believing the situation would probably be repeated, he informed Steele that it is "useless to bring prisoners here [because] the authorities are two much alarmed to try them." McNelly was not about to give up and proposed obtaining warrants from other counties further away from King Fisher's influence. He had recovered between six and eight-hundred head of stolen cattle and horses, presumably from Fisher's control, but the brand inspector refused to inspect them. The sheriff would not do the inspecting and no one could be found to serve subpoenas. Frustrated, McNelly turned the livestock loose, assuming they would drift back to their natural ranges.

N.A. Jennings, who had just joined on May 26 and who handled McNelly's paper work after the violent death of Lieutenant T.C. "Pidge" Robinson in early April in his home state of Virginia,[16] devoted an entire chapter to the arrest of King Fisher and thus was writing from personal experience. The company had arrived in Laredo on May 25, 1876, and camped for three days. From there they continued on towards the Nueces River and established a camp for several days, ostensibly to rest their horses. At this camp, "we learned first about the desperado, King Fisher, and his notorious gang of horse thieves, cattle thieves, and murderers." Jennings suggests the company "learned" of Fisher at this time although it is difficult to believe the rangers were not already very familiar with the man, at least by reputation. He further wrote that Fisher had about forty or fifty of his followers always with him, who "preyed upon the substance of the toiling settlers. They stole the ranchers' horses and cattle and robbed their corn cribs, and they did not stop at murder to further their ends."

Jennings theorized on how the rangers were able to accomplish what they did against the thousands of outlaws. McNelly had less than fifty men against their thousands, but "we were backed by the law and the good-will of all the honest frontiers-men — a big factor in our favor. And then we made up in self-confidence and reckless disregard of danger what we lacked in numbers. Our success on the lower Rio Grande gave us the feeling that we were invincible. We not only did not fear the result of a conflict with the desperadoes; we were eager to try conclusions with them."

Jennings described how McNelly divided his force into two squads about two miles apart and traveled to King Fisher's "stronghold" in parallel lines. Scouts were sent out a mile in advance, riding a half mile apart and picking up any man they met. These were turned over to the main force. Hoping to approach as close as possible, the ranger force managed to ride within a quarter-mile of the stronghold unseen by Fisher or his men. McNelly, no doubt mindful of Adjutant General Steele's order to be accompanied always by civil authorities, possibly had with him Webb County Sheriff Darío Gonzales. A later rumor that Gonzales had been killed was obviously just one of several false reports dealing with the King Fisher arrest.[17]

When both squads reunited before the final move, McNelly again divided them into two squads, one going through the chaparral to the other side of the house. At a prearranged signal all converged full speed with pistols in hand. The rangers managed to reach the house before the outlaws could prepare a defense. McNelly demanded their surrender or they would be killed. All surrendered.[18]

When her husband was in irons Mrs. Fisher came out to inquire of McNelly just why her husband had been arrested. Possibly she did not know who McNelly was, because she asked him who he was and then asked what had her husband done to be arrested. McNelly simply answered, "Plenty." To Mrs. Fisher and the others on Pendencia Creek, King Fisher was far from being an outlaw, "Not a one of them had ever seen him mad; not a one of them had ever seen him whip out them pistols. All they knowed was they was safe and not molested on Pendencia after he came across the Nueces and took charge." George Durham recorded the exchange between McNelly and Mrs. Fisher, although Jennings made no mention of any women being present.

After the King Fisher group had been ironed, McNelly called out to Mrs. Fisher and told her they were taking her husband to Eagle Pass, but that if any of his gang attempted to rescue him he would be shot, "the prisoners will all be killed on the spot. That's our rule." This was *La Ley de Fuga*, or the Law of Flight, "the harshest law ever devised by man" as Durham perceived it. If a prisoner attempted to escape he was shot. If his friends attempted to take him from the officers, he was shot.[19] This was one of those acts for which many had condemned the State Police only a few years before; now the former State Police Captain was supporting its legitimacy.

After Fisher and his outlaw gang had been turned over to authorities at Eagle Pass, Jennings wrote that they did make more arrests but, while delivering them to Eagle Pass, "we met King Fisher and his men going home . . . out on bail, although charged with murder and many other serious crimes." Jennings quotes Fisher as telling McNelly they were out under $20,000 bond and that any member of his gang could get out on bail, but the amount of Fisher's bond was probably only $5,500 according to the *Express* of June 10.[20] At this point McNelly uncharacteristically gave up, saying, "[N]o use in working my men night and day for such a farce as this" and ordered his prisoners turned loose. Jennings then observed McNelly speak to Fisher, "If we ever come up here again, we'll come to kill . . . and if you keep up your system of robbery and murder, you'll be hearing from us." Supposedly some of Fisher's men had gone to various merchants in Eagle Pass requesting them to put up the bail money, implying that if they refused the merchants would be harmed so that a "scared justice of the peace and a timorous sheriff made the arrangements for providing the bonds."[21]

Authorities in the Eagle Pass area were gravely concerned about the lawless conditions. A special dated June 8, printed in the *Express*, informed readers that McNelly had arrived that very morning and then itemized a list of grievances: There was no security "in all this country" for either life or property and one hundred head of horses had been stolen within the last fourteen days from various parties; shooting through the doors of houses had become a common practice almost every night.[22] Two days later the *Express* published a lengthy article, headlined THE STATE ON THE ROAD TO RUIN, which stated that McNelly had been in Austin when word reached there that a band of robbers had stolen some property in Webb County. Steele had consulted with the governor and then ordered McNelly and his command to Laredo. After arresting King Fisher a number of people telegraphed the governor complaining that nobody could be found to testify against Fisher and his gang, because if they did so their lives would be forfeited. Telegrams supposedly had been sent to parties in Eagle Pass asking the question "Can the law be executed in Maverick [County]? If not, why?" Answers came explaining that the law could not be enforced because of the "very large element of lawless characters on both sides of the river, and the facility with which the river may be crossed, but particularly because very many reckless men, probably refugees from justice elsewhere, have made rendezvous in the county and set the laws at defiance." Another said that lawlessness prevailed because the number of desperadoes was so great as to intimidate the officers from serving writs.[23]

McNelly arrived in San Antonio and checked into the Menger

Hotel with his family on the evening of June 15. An *Express* reporter visited him there, "the first occasion of our meeting this distinguished soldier, than whom no other man ever labored more wisely or effectually in the interior of our frontier." The reporter promised an interview in the next issue. McNelly now was showing obvious weakness due to his disease. Durham noted, "You could see that. His cheek bones was sunk in. His straight shoulders drooped. And he was breathing in them short gasps like consumptives do. Only his eyes had any life about them now."[24]

The *Express* reporter followed through and provided an interview with the captain. It must have been rather brief but McNelly said this about his command:

> My men are mostly from the interior of the State, many of them from Washington county, near my home. I prefer men from the interior, because of their greater steadiness. I find that they can ride longer, stand more hardships, eat less, and are most obedient to my commands. I enforce the very strictest discipline, and would not hesitate to compare my company with a similar number of men anywhere, in any respect, regarding their qualifications as soldiers. I allow no whiskey in camp, — there has not been a drop of liquor in my camp for many months. No man who wears a Mexican hat with snakes around it can belong to my company. I allow no obscene language to be used by my men. When any of them violate these rules they are dismissed. I can bring my men to your city, and they would be so quiet you never would know they were about. They know better than to get drunk, shout, run their horses through a town or past a house in the country. I can rely upon my men.

McNelly told a "rough story" about the condition of affairs at Eagle Pass, where the country was completely overawed by outlaws. When he had arrested King Fisher and his men and taken them to Eagle Pass, he had turned them over to the authorities with a list of names of witnesses who would testify against them, some of whom lived forty miles distant. As no one could be found to summon these witnesses, McNelly himself volunteered. The morning after his departure to bring in the witnesses, a body of armed men appeared and demanded a trial of the prisoners. On entering the room where the justice's office was, they were told the prisoners would be tried, but they must remove their arms. This the men did, laying them on the floor beside them. The prisoners were arraigned, but as no witnesses were present, and it was dangerous to his life for the Judge to tell the men they must wait, he dismissed the charges against the accused, with the exception of Fisher, for whom a bond was taken, which the Capt. says is not worth five dollars. When McNelly returned and learned the fruitless result of his arrest it disheartened him.

Certainly McNelly was closer to anger than merely being "disheartened!"[25]

Although McNelly's efforts to keep King Fisher and his men in custody were for naught, he at least derived some satisfaction from the capture of two of Fisher's confederates, John and Pink Smith, alias Burns, fugitives guilty of theft and murder in McLennan County. After escaping from the county jail, the pair fled to south Texas where, according to McNelly's statement, they became members of Hardin's gang in DeWitt County before joining up with King Fisher.[26] McNelly's men were scouring the country in pursuit of fugitives and, with the assistance of a Lieutenant Hassan, captured the pair without firing a shot. Several of McNelly's men delivered them to San Antonio's Bexar County jail while arrangements were made to deliver them to McLennan County authorities. Although McNelly bragged about how quiet his men could be when visiting a city, the rangers still attracted attention. The *Express* reporter noted that "several of Capt. McNelly's boys were in the city yesterday [June 16]. They are well mounted men, and armed to the teeth."[27]

Although McNelly provided no report on how his men were involved in the arrest of the notorious Smiths, a Frio County correspondent contributed a lengthy letter dated June 20 to the *Express*. "Frio" reported that Lieutenant Hassan and an eleven man detachment had been "scouting and scouring this section of our western domain, in search of all desperadoes and lawless characters generally." Frio's report contains confusing statements; no "Lieutenant Hassan" is listed in McNelly's company. If Hassan belonged to the U.S. Army he ought not to have been working as a member of a posse in assisting civilian authorities. Yet Frio writes of "Lieutenant

Hassan, with a detachment of eleven men." Frio realized that common citizens could not be expected to become and remain a standing posse comitatus. He later states that "These men were detailed from the command of Captain McNelly, and have thoroughly caught the spirit of their commander, who is noted, even in the discharge of the roughest duty, as being polite and humane to the very limit of forbearance, being a man 'sans peur et sans reproache.'"

Sans peur et sans reproche! Fearless and above reproach! Although Frio's report is confusing as to just how McNelly's men captured the Smith brothers, his endorsement could only reinforce the reputation of McNelly and his rangers. Correspondent Frio concluded that he had learned of McNelly's command arresting "about three hundred outlaws at sundry points on and near the Rio Grande since it has been detailed on this duty."[28] Statements such as this, although certainly subject to exaggeration, could create the idea in the minds of some that McNelly was invincible!

McNelly could spare only two men to deliver the Smith brothers from the Bexar County jail to McLennan County and assigned Charles B. McKinney and Thomas J. Evans to the task, both young men from Washington County who had enlisted on the first of February. The pair delivered their prisoners without incident to Waco and assisted the local authorities in arresting a would-be murderer before returning to the McNelly command.[29]

Although few writers have described King Fisher as a cold-blooded and ruthless killer and marauder, accounts in the contemporary press treated him differently. The *Express* advocated the governor's increasing McNelly's command to two-hundred men then sending him to assist civil officers in all lawless portions of the West, and "to either capture or kill King Fisher and his gang, and all men of like character." McNelly had telegraphed Austin that the condition of the country between Castroville and Eagle Pass as "critical." There were more than a hundred outlaws from different sections there and were holding "the reins of power." The *Express* openly charged Fisher with murder, as well as stealing horses and cattle. Some citizens of Carrizo Springs who had assisted McNelly as guides were promised protection, but after the arrest and release of the prisoners Fisher "swore he would not leave a house standing at Carrizo, nor a man alive." McNelly therefore left a detachment at Carrizo Springs for their protection.[30]

In spite of the reputation which McNelly and his men had, King Fisher was an equally effective leader, although of lawless men. McNelly feared that after his men were withdrawn the settlement of

Carrizo Springs would be wiped out. The *Express* warned its readers that the "reign of lawlessness and terror is not confined to one county. It is spreading. Fisher's band is reinforced by cut-throats almost daily."[31]

The reputation of both Fisher and McNelly were now linked together, especially when an article describing Fisher's arrest appeared in an issue of a major St. Louis newspaper. The *Republican*, printing the report in its issue of June 15, gave no indication as to its source and made no commentary. Two weeks later the San Antonio *Herald* reprinted it verbatim, also with no editorial comment.

The noted John King Fisher who created his own "outlaw empire" in the Nueces Strip. *Courtesy Ed Bartholomew.*

KING FISHER is the suggestive name of the chief of a band of robbers who have long been the terror of the people of the western border of Texas. This king fishes for plunder and generally succeeds well in the catch. But he was threatened with bad luck recently. Capt. McNelly, commander of the Texas State Guards, had been looking for him, and succeeded in "corraling" and capturing the king and seven of his men at Eagle Pass, on the Rio Grande. The prisoners were turned over to the civil authorities to be dealt with according to law. The king sent word to a number of the "best citizens" of the country that he wanted bondsmen to go bail for him. The aforesaid "best citizens" responded with alacrity to the request, the robbers were carried before a judicial tribunal and held to answer, the bonds being fixed at five hundred dollars in each case. The "best citizens" signed the bonds, and King Fisher and his merry men rode away. The prospect for exterminating brigandage on the Texas border is not brilliant. It is due to say in behalf of the "best citizens" that they excused themselves on the ground of their mortal dread of the

king in case they refused to sign for him and his
band.[32]

Following the brief visit to San Antonio with his family in mid-
June, McNelly reported to Austin where he appeared before the
Senate Committee on Indian Affairs and Frontier Protection, giving
general details on the condition of affairs along the Rio Grande. On
June 21 McNelly further described the tumult in Dimmit, Maverick
and the adjacent counties for the committee. McNelly explained
that King Fisher's men "had inclosed pastures of two or three thousand acres; that they robbed citizens, shot into dwelling houses, and
killed whoever interfered. Fisher himself has killed nine men within
less than a year." When arrested Fisher had between seven and eight-
hundred head of stolen cattle in his possession, McNelly testified.
Although McNelly had taken possession of them, the hide inspector
would not receive them; citizens were afraid to take possession of
them and the stolen cattle were turned loose, hopefully to drift back
to their rightful owners. The result of McNelly's testimony was the
creation of a bill entitled "An Act to Suppress Lawlessness and
Crime in Certain Portions of the State."
    In the initial form, prepared by the Committee on Indian Affairs
and Frontier Protection chaired by famed frontiersman John S.
"Rip" Ford, the bill specifically identified the two counties of
Dimmit and Maverick "and some adjacent counties" as the area
which would benefit from the bill's passage. It was there that existed
the "combinations of men which impede the execution of the laws,
and also organized bands of lawless men who have committed murders, and robberies, and have intimidated the inhabitants to such an
extent that they passively submit to acts of violence and rapine."
There were more than one hundred of these men who had murdered and "kept women and children in constant dread of outrage,"
and thus the bill was to authorize and require the governor to issue
an order immediately for the organization of a company to be captained by L.H. McNelly.
    This McNelly company was to have an aggregate of fifty-three
men: one captain, one first lieutenant, one second lieutenant, four
sergeants, four corporals and forty-two privates. If McNelly refused
to lead the company then the governor was to select another person
for the role. The company was to be mustered into the service of the
state for a period of six calendar months, each man furnishing his
own horse, saddle, bridle, rope, clothing and other personal items
while the state would furnish arms and ammunition, camp and gar-

rison equipage, and rations and sustenance for men and horses as well as transportation necessary to move men and supplies. Arms issued would become the responsibility of the man. If a man lost his arms by disobedience of orders or neglect he would be charged for the cost, but if the item was lost in the discharge of his duty he would not be charged.

For pay the captain was to receive $166 per month; the first lieutenant $133 per month while the second lieutenant was to receive $125 per month. Sergeants would receive $50 while corporals and privates would receive $40 per month. The company would be governed by the rules and regulations of the army and the articles of war. Each man would be "clothed with the powers of peace officers, and shall aid the civil authorities in the execution of the laws." Each one was to take an oath to perform faithfully his duties in accordance with the law. The men of the company could also call on private citizens to assist them. Their expenses while transporting prisoners would be reimbursed by the state.

The original appropriation called for $23,814 but, among other changes, in its final form the amount appropriated was $40,000. Other essential differences were the elimination of McNelly's name and of the names of the two specific counties. A key element which McNelly perhaps found not to his liking was that it remained illegal for the rangers to cross the Rio Grande in pursuit of desperadoes.[33]

While McNelly was in Austin, W.W. Lawhon, a resident of Pleasanton in Atascosa County, visited the *Express* office in San Antonio and stated that a group of McNelly's men had met a "detachment" of King Fisher's desperadoes on the Nueces, about ten miles from Fort Ewell, and in the fight *seven of McNelly's men had been killed*. McNelly did not believe the report was accurate, and indeed it was not. Apparently the rumor was kept alive for some time, because McNelly was still being asked about it as late as October! The Galveston *News* finally resolved to get to the bottom of it, perhaps due to the concern of editor Belo himself. The *News* repeated McNelly's claim that such a disaster could not have happened without his knowledge. The alleged facts, now not only seven men killed but also the burning of Oakville, had been met with skepticism by the *News*. "The extraordinary nature of the story suggested at once that it was a hoax, but it was related in such a manner . . . as to cause some anxiety and lead to investigation. We are glad to find our first suspicion sustained." As with all rumors, one is left to wonder what incident inspired its creation. In truth, during all the years McNelly served the state as both police and ranger captain, he lost only one man while in the line of duty, young L.B. "Sonny" Smith, on the

Palo Alto prairie in June of 1875.[34]

On Tuesday August 15 the banking firm of E. & H. Seeligson & Company in Goliad was robbed. Cashier Mitchell was alone when eight disguised men rode up to the back door of the bank at two o'clock in the afternoon. Searching for bank robbers was a new responsibility for McNelly and his men; prior to this it had been primarily cattle and horse thieves who received their attention.[35]

McNelly was needed with a portion of his company at Oakville, but he stationed Lieutenant Jesse Leigh "Red" Hall at Goliad, presumably to focus on identifying the bank robbers and capturing them. Hall had joined the Special Force on August 10, 1876, with the rank of second lieutenant, no doubt due to the quality work he had performed as City Marshal of Sherman, Texas, and as deputy sheriff of Grayson County, Texas. Goliad viewed the rangers as "sober, determined, straight-forward men."[36]

While the authorities were attempting to arrest the Goliad bank robbers, a report from Brownsville stated that on Saturday, August 19, General Revueltas, commanding at Matamoros, delivered José María Olguín to Texas authorities. He was the raider who had escaped from the law back in July 1872 while under a sentence of fifteen years. He had then joined cattle thieves, raided into Texas, and had escaped, although badly wounded, from the gunfire on the Palo Alto prairie in June 1875. The fact that Mexican officials honored a Texas requisition was unusual, and McNelly certainly saw the report in the San Antonio *Express*.[37]

By the end of August McNelly was thoroughly established in Oakville, intending to end the stock troubles there, and requested the sheriffs of surrounding counties to send him a descriptive list of all persons who had committed crimes and who had evaded arrest. He indicated he would give the matter his "special attention." Perhaps he was contemplating preparing his own list of fugitives from justice! Oakville could not have been more pleased with McNelly's presence, lauding the man. The *Tribune* advocated the idea that McNelly "should be the next United States Senator, Governor or the like. It sounds McNelly's praises quite lustily and as justly. He keeps Oakville 'straight' and the country quiet." [38]

Lieutenant Hall and fifteen men remained at Goliad. By mid-October the Goliad reporter wrote that the "profoundest peace and quiet exists in our community. Your correspondent saw quite a number of McNelly's men at church last Sunday night."

The reporter had conversed with Hall and quoted the lieutenant as saying "things shall be straightened up here," even if it took two years to "fight it out on that line." The "disturbed" elements were "scattering rapidly," causing the reporter to wax poetically upon the tranquillity established by Hall. "Daylight breaks, but the evil spirits of lawlessness and crime must be exercised by the power of the gospel and the sentiments of purity and justice as well as by the smell of gunpowder." Since "peaceful days are beginning to come upon us again," more of McNelly's men would probably not be necessary.[39]

Even though McNelly was still captain he was finding it necessary to spend more and more time in San Antonio due to his failing health. He was no longer able to be in the saddle as before, and some suspected he stationed himself at San Antonio with more accessible telegraph lines in order to direct the movements of his men better. If his location was only a matter of being better able to direct the actions of his men, his continued presence in San Antonio would be acceptable to his superiors, if the results warranted. He did not forget about his responsibilities to the State and to law-abiding citizens; fortunately he had capable lieutenants in the form of Jesse L. Hall and John Barclay Armstrong.[40]

John B. Armstrong had proved his effectiveness in late September 1876 when rumors had reached the ears of the rangers that a band of outlaws were camped on the shores of Espantosa Lake in Dimmit County. Some thought the Goliad bank robbers might be there. King Fisher was still on the loose and it was hoped that he might be caught and would resist arrest. Jennings recorded that the squad sent to investigate at Lake Espantosa included Armstrong and privates Thomas N. Devine, Thomas J. Evans, George P. Durham, George W. Boyd, A.L. Parrott and himself.

On the way to Espantosa Lake the rangers arrested young Noley Key, suspected of horse theft and of being a member of the King Fisher gang. Key was convinced, either through words or some form of torture, to lead the rangers to the desperadoes' camp. Within sight of the outlaw camp Armstrong assigned rangers Devine and Evans to guard Key and the horses while the rest of the squad advanced on foot. Armstrong and his men were anxious for a fight. According to his version, within twenty feet of the outlaw campfires they were fired upon with six-shooters and "responded promptly & a lively little fight ensued." When the little fight was over there were three dead outlaws in camp: John Martin, Jim Roberts and George Mullen. Jim McAllister, shot by Jennings, was nearly dead. The rangers left guarding the horses had their own little fight; Noley Key attempted to escape when the firing broke out between the rangers and his companions but covered only twenty paces or so before the gunfire of Devine and Evans cut him down.

In addition to the men with him at Espantosa Lake, Armstrong had sent a detachment with private citizens under the command of Corporal M.C. "Polly" Williams to arrest a party at the Pendencia. Williams learned their suspect had fled but went on to the Whaley *rancho* to arrest "a bad Mexican," as Armstrong described him. The suspect refused to surrender and was killed, according to Armstrong's report. Assuming the badly wounded McAllister expired, the rangers had killed six suspected outlaws during the night of September 30-October 1, 1876.

The rangers may have been sorely disappointed that King Fisher had not been one of those "rounded-up." Armstrong's lengthy telegram to McNelly sent from Carrizo on October 1 concluded, "King Fisher left about a week ago with a large drove of cattle. Porter [Burd Oberchain] is supposed to be with him. The parties that we killed had about fifty head of stolen horses and twenty-two yoke of work oxen in Thompson's pasture, taken from Mexicans on the Rio Grande. We will round-up the pasture tomorrow."[41]

An *Express* reporter met with McNelly on Monday, October 2, and learned that the "bad Mexican" killed was named Cortina, no relation to the notorious Cortina from across the river, described as "a mean, low-lived villain, noted only for his dark crimes and damnable treachery." McNelly predicted that this "blow of Sergeant Armstrong," the first effectual effort since the re-organization of the company in July, would do more good work in restoring peace to the "outraged frontier than any previous work of anyone." McNelly said he would keep on pressing the bad men troubling the border until they disappeared due to his vigilance and the bravery and activity "of the gentlemanly men under his command."[42]

Sergeant John Barclay Armstrong who earned state wide fame for his capture of John Wesley Hardin in August 1877.
Courtesy John M. Bennett.

Although McNelly and his

men were praised for their conduct as well as for driving out the lawless, the mother of the dead Noley Key felt they were no more than
common murderers and did not intend to let the matter rest. Upon
learning of the death of her son, Mrs. Key wrote to Adjutant General
Steele asking for a copy of the orders under which the rangers were
acting when the gunfight took place. Presumably she intended to
take some form of legal action. Although the entire correspondence
between Mrs. Key and Steele has not survived, her second letter in
response to Steele's answer to her initial letter, is informative.

> Your letter of Jan 31st at hand. It does not give the
> desired information. What I want is the Instructions
> McNally [sic] was acting under when he murdered those
> boys in Espanosa [sic] Lake on the night of the 31st of
> Sept 1876. They are or were on file in the Adjt Gens
> Office[.] McNally's men murdered my Son And
> Armstrong's only justification at an inquest held was
> that his Instructions covered his case.
>
> The only excuse rendered at the Inquest was that
> He attempted to escape — And who was there but his
> two Murderers to see that He even attempted that[?]
> And what Man is there living —after committing mur-
> der — but would have Some excuse[?]
>
> And we learn that they had no Authority even to
> arrest him.

Mrs. Key stated again to Steele that she wanted a certified copy
of McNelly's instructions with the seal of the state attached. She further wanted to know the names of the two men who were in charge
of the horses and the prisoner, her son. She claimed he was taken
from the supper table in the little village of Carriza. Mrs. Key was
well aware of the praises that McNelly received, but her feelings were
radically different.

> McNally [sic] & his Troop have been lauded &
> praised by the Authorities of the State - for what? For
> taking one nearly deaf Boy seven or eight miles
> unarmed - in the dark hours of night, shooting him all
> alone. Then killing three other Boys sleeping quietly in
> their Camp. Their only Arms six-shooters — wounding
> one badly — leaving him for dead "as they thought." at
> Whaly's ranch killing one poor Mexican in "Self

defence." Does this seem like "Desperadoes, a Terror to
the Country[?]"

Why did not the "gallant" Band follow King Fisher
who had only been gone a few days with a Drove of
Texas Cattle? How many Indian Scalps have they taken?
Also when King Fisher was in question [custody?] Their
Cowardly hearts failed them, they dared not. But when
it was only a few Boys asleep in their Camp — who most
of them had been in the employment of the best
Citizens for near two years — why they were very
brave.[43]

Angelina B. Key was not alone in challenging the rangers' methods of dealing with real or suspected desperadoes of the brush. From
Bolivar Landing in Mississippi, Daniel Mullen, the brother of the
slain George Henry Mullen killed in the gunfight with Armstrong's
men the same night as Noley Key was killed, wrote Adjutant General
Steele. His question was simple: what crime was George charged
with and why was the McNelly company allowed "to murder him in
cold blood sum where [sic] in the vicinity of Eagle Pass Maverick Co
Texas."[44] For Daniel Mullen to learn of his brother George's death
so quickly, someone in Texas must have notified him by telegram.
The single correspondence in the Adjutant General's files does not
give any indication as to how Steele responded to the grieving family members. Perhaps he merely ignored both the Key and Mullen
families, since his rangers had been exonerated by a Dimmit County
jury so there would be no legal ramifications, but the complaints
reached Governor Hubbard and ultimately the President of the
United States! The order to investigate then went to General E.O.C.
Ord, and second lieutenant T.W. Jones, 10th Cavalry, conducted an
investigation of the affair. Jones' report basically reflected what
Armstrong had reported to McNelly, which had also appeared in the
press. Armstrong's party had gone to the house of rancher Silas Hay
where they arrested Noley Key. Armstrong divided his troop, taking
about ten or twelve men with him and Key as a prisoner. Two citizens were taken with him as guide, Levi English, Sr., probably always
glad to cooperate with McNelly's rangers, and I.C. Smith. English
later reported that, about seventy-five yards from the outlaw camp on
Espantosa Lake, shots were fired towards them. The result was the
death or wounding of the outlaws and the death of Key while
attempting to escape. Lieutenant Jones did learn that John Martin
had said several times and to different persons that he would never

be taken alive by the state troops. Further, English had testified that Armstrong had ordered his men, "Don't shoot any man unless he attempts to resist or escape, but don't give any desperado the first shot at you, if you can help it." The investigation clearly proved that Armstrong's men fired either in self defense or to prevent the escape of prisoner Key. Except for the grieving family members, the matter was no longer a concern for the authorities at any level.

To Armstrong and McNelly and the rangers, the biggest disappointment may have been that there were only minor players present during the raid on the outlaw camp. Ideally King Fisher would have been there as well as Bob Callison and Alf Day, the latter a Taylor sympathizer run out of DeWitt County but now running with King Fisher. All were considered suspects in the Goliad Bank robbery as well as having stolen cattle and horses from ranchers in the area.[45]

McNelly's name was not always associated with violence and lawlessness. An item in the Granbury *Vidette*, reported by the Austin *Statesman* in the popular "Texas Facts and Fancies" column, pointed out an apparent increase of husbands' abandoning their wives and children. The article cited an unidentified woman who had learned the whereabouts of her husband and was "coming across the Mississippi, with the children, to claim support, etc., at his hands." There was a "rapid depreciation of farms and town lots everywhere in and around Granbury. Every old reprobate in these parts is crazy to sell out and get away and join McNelly."[46]

There were even weightier problems on Steele's desk; he had to decide what to do with Captain L.H. McNelly, whose medical bills were becoming prohibitive. Possibly the complaints from grieving parents made his decision a little bit easier. It also appeared the Sutton-Taylor Feud in DeWitt County had flared up again, and the gunplay in DeWitt County would help Steele forget about the young victims at Espantosa Lake.

A view of McNelly and his rangers in camp. McNelly is seated on the camp
stool to right of center. On the original his widow wrote: "Picture of Capt. L.H.
McNelly's Company Texas Rangers taken in 1877. Mrs. W.T. Wroe." *Courtesy*
The W.P. Webb Collection, University of Texas, Austin.

CHAPTER 19

DYING EMBERS

In DeWitt county, the knife and the pistol seem never to be idle. Fathers of families are butchered almost in the arms of their loved ones, and their offspring are trained to deeds of blood and death with the lisp of childhood still upon their lips." — The San Antonio *Daily Herald*, February 15, 1876.

If McNelly considered his accomplishments as the centennial year of 1876 ended, he left no record of his thoughts. In the fall his praises in the newspapers, although undoubtedly sincere, were approaching the ludicrous. Popular and respected as he may have been, McNelly entertained no thoughts towards seeking a political office; it was more important for him to know that honest citizens of various communities in South Texas felt more secure due to his work. In the opinion of many, McNelly had accomplished great things in the two-and-one-half years of service under Governor Richard Coke. He had prevented additional battles between the Sutton and Taylor forces in DeWitt County; he had recovered stolen stock from the Las Cuevas stronghold; he had arrested the notorious John King Fisher and his gang as well as dozens of other desperate but lesser known outlaws. These actions, with which only the desperadoes could find fault, had resulted in both statewide and national attention.

But, as McNelly had predicted, the DeWitt County hostilities did flare up again. On September 11 Jake Ryan shot and killed Joe DeMoss following an argument over a cattle deal. Witness William D. Meador testified that DeMoss had approached Ryan with an upraised quirt. Ryan fired four revolver shots, "three taking effect at equal distance in a line from the shirt collar to the waistband, producing death almost instantly."[1]

Prior to this argument and resultant killing, DeMoss, Ryan and Meador had all been followers of the Sutton banner. In August of 1874 DeMoss and Meador had been among the men charged with murdering Senator Bolivar Pridgen's ex-slave, Abraham. With former Suttonites now shooting one another, it appeared former close associations were crumbling.

Jake Ryan and Bill Meador again joined forces with deadly results a few weeks after the DeMoss killing when Dr. Phillip H. Brassell and his son George T. Brassell were killed by a group of assassins. This double homicide, which caused a great cry of outrage from law-abiding citizens, kept the rangers and the courts busy transporting the prisoners back and forth from jails to court rooms until nearly the turn of the century.

On the evening of September 19, 1876, between ten and eleven o'clock, a mob had aroused the sleeping Brassell family. The widow Brassell later testified that her young sons Theodore and Sylvanus were removed and placed under guard while their house was searched. Her twenty-two-year old son George recognized three mob members and immediately gave their names to his mother: Bill Meador, Jake Ryan and Joe Sitterlie. Mrs. Brassell did not recognize anyone but said that eight or ten were involved. She claimed she initially took little notice of the incident because she knew her menfolk had done nothing for which to be killed. Dr. Brassell and sons George, Sylvanus and Theodore were led away. Ten minutes later Mrs. Brassell heard shooting. She still could not believe her men had been killed and only later had to accept the fact that her husband and son George were dead. Her husband's body lay sprawled 150 yards away from the house and George's body some thirty-five yards distant.[2] Many questioned why they were killed; Dr. Brassell was a respected member of the community and was described as "a good and peaceful citizen," although son George "did not bear a good name in the community and his death is not regretted" according to one report.[3] Public opinion condemned the murder of the tubercular doctor, taken from what was expected to be his death bed, marched away from his home without hat or shoes or coat, and murdered with his son. On September 30 a Clinton correspondent of the Galveston News called the "killing of the doctor by the midnight mob" as "one of the blackest deeds that has ever been committed in the State."[4]

Ranger N.A. Jennings, who indeed may have been involved in the subsequent arrest of the accused murderers, noted, "Shortly after our arrival in the county, a despicable murder was committed by members of the Sutton party. They went at midnight to the residence of Dr. Brazell [sic], an educated, refined old gentleman, dragged him from a sick bed in the presence of his wife and daughter, and murdered him in cold blood. At the same time, they killed his son."[5] Some believed the mob intended to kill only George, but the doctor may have recognized some of them so he too had to be eliminated.

Based on the testimony of family members who managed to elude the mob in the darkness, the grand jury of DeWitt County handed down two indictments against seven men: David Augustine, James Hester, William Cox, William D. Meador, Joseph V. "Jake" Ryan, Charles H. Heissig and Joseph Sitterlie. They were charged with shooting George Brassell "upon the head and near the right eye" causing his death, and shooting Phillip H. Brassell with leaden bullets which "did penetrate and wound . . . the right breast . . ." causing a wound four inches in depth and one half inch in breadth.[6]

Those who could not accept the grand jury's decision believed the witnesses were merely mistaken in the darkness concerning their recognition of the seven men. The Clinton correspondent, doubting the guilt of the accused, stated that the killing party had no ill-feeling against the Brassells, some of them in fact were "very intimate with the family."[7]

Although McNelly's strength did not permit him regular activity, he had a fine subordinate in Lieutenant J. L. Hall. When the indictments were handed down on December 20, Hall went to work immediately and made plans to arrest all seven of the indicted men. Only a month earlier on November 22, the indicted William D. Meador had married Amanda Augustine, the daughter of the indicted David Augustine.[8] On December 20, the day of the indictments, the indicted Joseph Sitterlie married Melissa O. Cox, a sister of the indicted William Cox, and Lieutenant Hall surmised all the men for whom he had indictments would be at the wedding dance.

Hall and sixteen rangers left their camp at night in a drizzling rain. Two-hundred yards from the house the rangers dismounted; Hall told them there would probably be a "pretty hot fight" within minutes. According to Jennings, Hall produced a bottle of whiskey and each man took a drink "to the success of the undertaking." They then surrounded the house.

Hall led, entering the doorway with a carbine in his hands. His sudden presence caused the music to cease abruptly. Jennings recalled seeing many six-shooters being flourished and hearing women scream. Groom Sitterlie called out, "Do you want anyone here, Hall?" Hall called out the names of the men he sought.

When Meador, learning Hall had only sixteen men besides himself, announced they were ready to fight, Hall ordered his rangers to prepare to sweep the porches with shotgun blasts and to fire

Jesse Leigh "Lee" Hall who had served as City Marshal of Sherman, Texas and deputy sheriff of Denison, Texas prior to joining McNelly's rangers on August 10, 1876. He replaced McNelly less than six months later. *From Scribner's Magazine, 1873.*

through the windows with their Winchesters. He wanted the women and children moved out first, however, saying, "We don't want to kill them, but it is as much as I can do to restrain my men. We came down here for a fight and we want it."

When Hall showed his eagerness for combat, the "fighting men" of the wedding party chose to surrender. Meador gave up first, the others followed, and within minutes "the entire Sutton gang" had been disarmed. Hall allowed the party to continue, his men taking turns standing guard, but made it clear anyone who attempted to escape would be shot down. Although guarding the exits, the rangers partook of the wedding food and drinks and some even danced with those of the ladies willing to dance with a ranger so cruel as to take away a groom from his wedding dance. Jennings wrote that the only one who attempted to "escape" was the minister who had married the couple; he wrote, "[O]ne fat old fellow came plunging out of the house wildly in the dark and ran as hard as he could straight for me. I punched him in the stomach with the end of my carbine, and he doubled up and turned like a hare back to the house."[9]

George P. Durham also recorded his version of the arrest of the men indicted for the Brassell killings. Contrary to Jennings, however, he made no mention of Hall's producing a bottle of whiskey or drinking to the toast of the mission. McNelly had a rule disallowing whiskey in camp, so if indeed Hall did encourage the toast it was certainly contrary to what McNelly would have wanted.

Durham also differed from Jennings in that he placed McNelly in Clinton during the arrest and subsequent hearing. This is doubtful because McNelly would have personally led the detachment to make the arrest if he had been in Clinton. In other doubtful variances, Durham wrote that McNelly became the personal guard of Judge Pleasants during the subsequent hearings and that visitors to the court room were allowed to keep their weapons.[10]

At dawn the prisoners were delivered to the Clinton jail; two of the rangers went inside with the prisoners and four others remained outside. During the habeas corpus hearings the court room was crowded with members of both the Taylor and Sutton parties, but every man who entered the building was disarmed. Judge Henry Clay Pleasants, who had resolved to bring an end to the feuding, presided.

In contrast to Durham's account, Jennings recalled that six rangers stood up by the bench, three on each side of the judge. Jennings stood next to Pleasants. "Like the other five men" he wrote, "I had my carbine in my hand and, like the others, I threw a cartridge into the breech and cocked the gun in plain sight of all in the court-room. Then we stood at 'ready' while Judge Pleasants addressed the crowd of men in the room. With supreme dignity he stood and looked at them for a full minute before he spoke."[11]

Jennings never forgot how the judge's eyes flashed and how his voice rang as he made his speech. Although Jennings had his hands full with a carbine then, he may have later made notes on what Pleasants said and, if not exactly the speech Pleasants delivered to the packed courtroom, he wrote what he remembered.

> The time has come for me to announce my decision in this case. I shall do so without fear or favor, solely upon the evidence as it has been presented. This county is and has been for years a reproach to the fair name of the State of Texas. Over it have roamed bands of lawless men, committing awful outrages, murdering whom they pleased, shooting down men from ambush in the most cowardly manner possible. Here in this very room, listening to me now, are murderers who long ago should have been hanged. I do not speak of the prisoners at the bar, but of you who are free. You are murderers, bushwhackers, midnight assassins.
>
> Some of you have dared to threaten me with cowardly anonymous letters, and I have had to bring State soldiers into this court of justice. I learn that you have blamed the Sheriff of this county for calling upon the

Rangers to assist in restoring order. No, it was not the Sheriff who had the Rangers sent here; it was I. I called for them and I am going to see that they remain here in this county until it is as peaceful and law-abiding as any in the State — as quiet and orderly as any in the Union. I tell you now, beware! The day of reckoning is surely coming. It is close at hand. When you deal with the Texas Rangers, you deal with men who are fearless in the discharge of their duty and who will surely conquer you.

I shall send these men at the bar to jail to await trial for as wicked and cowardly a murder as ever disgraced this State. It is but the beginning. Others will soon follow them. The reign of the lawless in DeWitt County is at an end![12]

McNelly's monthly return for December merely records that Joe Sitterlie, Jake Ryan, William Meador, Jim Hester, William Cox, Dave Augustine and C.H. Heissig were arrested on December 22 and delivered to the jail in Clinton.[13] There is no mention of the arrest's taking place at a wedding dance or of any of the heroics recorded by Jennings or Durham. Years later famed western artist Frederic Remington interviewed Lieutenant Hall who gave his version of the event. Nothing was done to punish the men who committed the murders, related Hall, "as the lynchers were men of property and influence in the country. No man dared speak above his breath about the affair [of the murders]." Hall related to

Judge Henry Clay Pleasants. Pleasants deserved the credit for bringing an end to the Sutton-Taylor Feud through the judicial system. McNelly's last official act brought indicted murderers before Pleasants' bench in DeWitt County. *Courtesy The Western History Collections, University of Oklahoma Library.*

Remington how he had his men surround the house and then demanded the surrender of the indicted, saying that he did not want to kill women and children, who then were allowed to depart. He then gave his ultimatum, "Now, gentlemen, you can go to killing Rangers; but if you don't surrender, the Rangers will go to killing you." Hall stated that this was "too frank a willingness for midnight assassins" and they surrendered.[14]

Judge Pleasants did not allow bail and directed that the men were to be delivered to the Galveston County jail because Clinton's jail was insecure. Pleasants' commitment order, dated January 2, noted that as "the jail of DeWitt county is an insecure prison and that there is no secure jail within the limits of this judicial district" it was therefore ordered that the prisoners, denied bail by himself, be delivered to Galveston. Pleasants did not want a repeat of the lynching which had taken the lives of Taylor, Tuggle and White back in June 1874, nor did he want the many friends of the accused to liberate them from the jail. Captain McNelly did take charge of the prisoners' transfer to Galveston, traveling by rail. Stopping at Flatonia, Lieutenant Hall telegraphed to Steele that "The agony is over [I] am here with Capt McNelly." By the use of the term "agony" did he wish to confirm that the arrest of the Brassell murderers was an exceptional event? Or did he mean that the Sutton-Taylor Feud — the agony of families' killing their neighbors and the long-lasting hatreds — was finally over? In the same telegram Hall requested five days leave to visit Austin. Captain McNelly, Lieutenant Hall, Sergeant R.P. Orrell and Privates G.H. Allen, E.R. Jenson and T.M. Quesenberry arrived at Galveston on the morning train, January 5, 1877. The trip had been uneventful. Strangely McNelly himself was paying the expenses of the guards as well as the prisoners! Once the prisoners were safely in the Galveston jail, McNelly was left in charge while Hall proceeded on to Austin for both personal reasons and to settle expenses as ordered by Steele.[15]

Sheriff Christian Jordan accepted the prisoners for one night but officially told McNelly that the jail was full and they could stay only until another commitment order arrived. McNelly requested another from Judge Pleasants which ordered him to deliver the prisoners to the Travis County jail in Austin. While in Galveston a *News* reporter interviewed McNelly, recognizing that he always made "good copy." The lengthy article was headlined "Capt. McNelly in the City" and said the ranger company was then stationed at Clinton and would be next sent to Goliad. McNelly expressed concerns over the continued support of his company. The appropriation was about expended, and the company's enlistment would expire at the end of the month. McNelly feared it would have to be disbanded. McNelly "referred warmly" to the efforts of the *News* in behalf of its preservation of law and order throughout the state, saying, "the good effect of its endeavors were to be noted as daily becoming more evident." The newspaper had taken a "high stand" and had given law officers moral support in desperado-ridden sections of the state. McNelly felt the "prompt publication of names of horse thieves, murderers and pillagers" resulted in making them "shy"; some had averred that no act of theirs could escape being reported in the *News*! As soon as the "dark deeds" were committed their names were published and "bandied about the State" which put officers on the alert for them, "defeating their schemes by directing public vigilance toward them."[16]

The Travis County jail accepted the prisoners, described by the *Statesman* as "desperate characters," on Tuesday, January 9, delivered there by Hall.[17] Austin had a fine new facility, far more reliable than the insecure box in Clinton. During the following months other desperate characters would also be incarcerated as the rangers thinned out the worst of Texas' bad men. Bill Taylor, a leader of the Taylor forces and who had killed Gabe Slaughter while cousin Jim Taylor killed Bill Sutton, would be brought in; John Ringo, who would later achieve great notoriety in Arizona was delivered; Pipes and Hearndon of the Sam Bass Gang and George Gladden from the Mason County War were there; later in the fall, Brown Bowen and John Wesley Hardin were brought in from Florida, captured by McNelly's sergeant, John B. Armstrong. For William Cox it must have been a time to gloat; the man who had led the ambush which killed his father was now behind bars, facing one of many murder charges.

The killings of Dr. Brassell and his son marked the end of the shooting phase of the Taylor-Sutton Feud, but the court battles continued for decades. The case against Charles H. Heissig was dismissed on insufficient evidence. Dave Augustine and James Hester were eventually acquitted. Cox, Ryan and Sitterlie were convicted of murder in the first degree, but then through various legal maneuverings the decision was reversed and remanded and all charges were eventually dropped. The case against William D. Meador was dismissed in 1894. Augustine was then re-indicted for the murder of Dr. Brassell and in 1896 was found guilty and sentenced to twenty-five years; Governor J.S. Hogg, however, did not consider it to be just that, of all the men indicted, only Augustine should serve time.

Hogg pardoned him before he ever arrived at Huntsville.[18]

As McNelly grew weaker from the effects of his disease, it became more and more difficult to serve in the field. He spent more and more time away from his camps and his men and directed operations from San Antonio as best he could. Writing to Adjutant General Steele on October 9 from San Antonio, he apologized for being "compelled to write you from this place again" and enclosed a certificate of disability from George Cupples, M.D., who feared that further exposure "just now would doubtless result fatally." McNelly requested Steele to allow him to move his camp to some point ten or twenty miles from San Antonio so that mail facilities would be better. He suggested that detachments could be kept at such "centers" as Goliad, Oakville, Carizzo Springs or Frio City from which scouts could move towards the neighboring villages. Thus, with a man or two kept in the centers, citizens would know at any time just how to contact the rangers when needed. In addition, such a plan would allow a ranger in pursuit of a fugitive to have easy access to fresh horses.[19] A report from an unidentified source stated that in order for McNelly "to move quickly and directly" upon any outlaw band he needed to be near the telegraph lines, thus the reason for his making San Antonio or its "vicinage" his headquarters.[20]

While in San Antonio a correspondent from the Houston *Daily Telegraph*, identified only as "Prickly Pear," sought out McNelly to interview him regarding the rangers' recent emphasis on the capture of Anglo outlaws. Prickly Pear met him while McNelly was dining with his family in the Menger Hotel and provided a valuable description of the man-hunter.

> [McNelly] is of medium stature, and physically seems the very reverse of robust, and is certainly not more than forty years of age. He has a high forehead, and his head and face create the impression of great intellectuality. His hair and whiskers are brown, nose of medium size and somewhat curved, with steel gray glittering eyes under closely knit eyebrows. The careless observer would note nothing extraordinary about them or their owner, but those who study men and faces find no difficulty behind the quiet address and modest demeanor the indications of inflexible determination and untiring activity that make him the terror of the frontier outlaws. I must regret to add that he is in failing health, brought on by over-exertion and exposure.[21]

In October some of the stock raisers in Bee County and the sur~
rounding areas, approximately one-hundred miles southeast of San
Antonio, looked to McNelly for help. A group gathered at the court
house in county seat Beeville on October 7 intending to devise a
plan by which assistance could be given to McNelly in "ferreting out,
hunting down and bringing to punishment murderers, horse and
cattle thieves in general, and particularly that large class of criminals
engaged in changing and blotching brands on stock." The resolu~
tions from the meeting included four essential points: (1) raising a
fund to be placed at McNelly's disposal to be used by him to employ
guides, detectives or spies to carry out the stated objectives; (2) cir~
culating a subscription to raise a portion of the said fund; (3) having
every law~abiding citizen present pledge himself to assist McNelly or
any other peace officer in enforcing the laws and bringing criminals
to justice; (4) appointing a committee in each county represented to
raise additional money by subscription. By the end of this gathering
the stockmen had raised a total of $960 in amounts ranging from $5
to $250.[22]

Even Live Oak County's vote on the prohibition of whiskey
evoked the specter of McNelly. The only one vote against total pro~
hibition inspired the *Statesman* editor to comment, "Was the county
*molly*fied by the presence of Nelly ~ the McNelly we read about?"[23]

The *Statesman* reported the result of another action when two of
McNelly's men, Rangers T.W. Deggs and T.J. Quesenberry, pursued
five men who had robbed Jackson's Store near Harwood in Gonzales
County. Ed and Frank Wingate, Howell Little and G.W. Keith and
two other "bloody scoundrels" were captured, but they all proved to
have an alibi and the *Statesman* had to print a correction.[24]

On November 18 McNelly reported from San Antonio that he
had nothing of importance to relate but had kept his men busy, mak~
ing it "lively for the thieves who make this and the neighboring coun~
ties a place of refuge." He complained of not having "had so much
success as might have been expected but we can always catch a thief
easier when he gets out of his own locality than in it as he is gener~
ally off his guard when he is in a strange place."[25]

Possibly anticipating troubles again in DeWitt County, McNelly
reported that he had ordered Lieutenant J.L. Hall from Oakville
with nine men and Sergeant George A. Hall with six men to
Clinton. He had written to Judge Pleasants asking if the condition
of affairs was bad enough that his presence was necessary. Any such
trip, however, also depended on what Dr. Cupples advised.[26]

Hall arrived at Clinton by November 23 with his seven men,

Lawrence Baker Wright, brother of
L.L. Wright who participated in the
Palo Alto Prairie battle. He was later
a physician in Duval County.
Courtesy P.T. Wright, Jr.

George Cupples, M.D., whose
diagnosis sealed McNelly's fate
with General Steele. *From The
Encyclopedia of the New West.*

meeting sergeants George A. Hall, R.P. Orrell and L.B. Wright on
his arrival. Although he gave no details on the affair in his report to
Adjutant General Steele, he did come close to capturing Alf Day and
Tom Callison, or Kalleson, who was a suspect in the Goliad bank
robbery and who unfortunately had not been at Lake Espantosa
when Armstrong raided that outlaw camp.[27]

The Austin *Statesman*, which seemingly could not give enough
column space to McNelly, reported in its issue of December 3 that
McNelly, described as "the terror of evil-doers" was needed in
Brenham because six desperadoes led by "a diabolical woman" had
assailed a house at night and fired at the fleeing inhabitants.
Reportedly the assailants had robbed the helpless wife, taken her
children and then fled towards the west.[28]

On the first day in December McNelly participated in an
unusual experience for him by attending a reception for Governor
Coke and Governor-elect Richard B. Hubbard at the popular
Raymond House in Austin. Sixty to seventy Austin citizens were
present, some making "speeches and other wise asserting their per-

sonal respect and friendship for the out-going and incoming governors of Texas." Among the dignitaries were Attorney Major Charles West, land agent Major Clement R. Johns, and banker James H. Raymond. McNelly, possibly in jest but possibly making a valid claim that he had brought greater security to the frontier, said that "the thieves and bandits of the frontier were unusually quiet just now."[29] A later news item stated that McNelly represented "a feeling of safety for life and property in the frontier counties where he and his men have been operating for the past few months." The *Statesman* added that McNelly claimed that he had arrested and killed about seventy-five of the worst men that had ever disgraced Texas, and quite likely that many more had been frightened out of the country.[30]

While McNelly was enjoying the comforts of the Raymond House amid governors and other dignitaries, his men captured Mark Tiner in Blanco County, a fugitive wanted for the killing of Austin policeman Cornelius Fahey on March 7, 1875. He was delivered to authorities in Austin.[31]

McNelly's concerns expressed in the Galveston *News* interview almost a year earlier were now being realized; not only would his company be reduced to twenty men but he himself would be honorably discharged and replaced by Lieutenant J. L. Hall. At Victoria on January 20, 1877, McNelly surrendered all state property including such camp necessities as seven tents and flags, eighty-seven skillets and six water buckets. Also inventoried were forty-two pistols, thirty-two carbines and four shotguns. What was once a company of over four dozen men had been reduced to twenty.[32]

As one of his final acts McNelly delivered to Judge Pleasants a letter dated at Clinton, January 16. The note accused Pleasants of having sent the "rong men" to prison for the Brassell killings. The real murderers were not identified by name, but were "the Jermans that done it and the reason why they kill[ed] them was because the old man and his sons [had] riten a hole lot of black gard and put it all over the shillow [Shiloh] church a bout women, and the Jermans said they intended to have revenge for it." The letter writer promised to kill Pleasants if Ryan and Cox were not given bail. So far as known, McNelly, who gave a "full copy of the original" to the *News*, never determined who had composed the letter. The Galveston *News* commented that the threatening letter revealed the necessity of maintaining the military organizations under McNelly's control.[33]

The San Antonio *Daily Express* also reported that the assassination threat in the letter emanated from a "band of desperate villains who have for the last ten years held sway in a little monarchy of theirs in DeWitt county." Pleasants had recognized the risk necessary to do his duty as a judge, and the outlaws threatening his life now "tremble for their power." The *Express* supported the *News*, saying that a force of state rangers "amply sufficient to bring the outlaws to grief and justice" was necessary. Governor Hubbard needed only to provide adequate protection.[34]

McNelly's adventurous career was now behind him. He had fought as a Confederate in the New Mexico Territory, at Galveston Bay and in Louisiana. He had held the rank of captain with the State Police, responsible for nearly a quarter of the civilized state. He had commanded the Special Force in DeWitt County and led his men into their bloody work on the Rio Grande frontier. In stark contrast were his trips to the Eastern coast, one in pursuit of absconding Adjutant General Davidson, the others to testify in the nation's capital about the problems on the Texas-Mexico border. He could contemplate all these accomplishments as he pondered his honorable discharge dated January 31, 1877. He was due $498 in pay from November 1, 1876, to the present; less his indebtedness to the state of $108 he had $390 to take home to Burton where Carey, Irene and Leander R. awaited.[35]

McNelly arrived in San Antonio on Sunday, January 28, where the *Express* visited with him and reported that his health was "improving, though since he was here last, he has been very unwell." McNelly was on his way home to Washington County but indicated he would reside in West Texas. Wherever McNelly decided to locate, stated the *Express*, he would "find the doors of every house, where honesty abides, open to welcome him, in Western Texas."[36] He then traveled to Boerne in Kendall County, perhaps to seek treatment from the noted Dr. Ferdinand Herff.[37] By August he was back in his home near Burton, "without having received any benefit to his health."[38]

Adjutant General William Steele received considerable criticism for dropping McNelly from the ranger force. To explain his decision Steele provided a lengthy response for the press. His statement was a reaction to newspaper "articles" which gave "an erroneous impression" as to the action taken relieving McNelly of his command. Steele, well aware that many Texans believed McNelly had been improperly released from the new organization, explained his decision.

First, McNelly had organized his company on July 25, 1876, with thirty-three men and sent it to Oakville, where McNelly joined it on August 27. Steele did not offer an explanation as to why McNelly was away from his command for a month.

Secondly, on September 29, 1876, McNelly reported being at San Antonio, and on October 9 sent to General Steele a certificate of disability from Dr. George Cupples, explaining that he was "under treatment for an affliction of the wind pipe and lungs, which disables him from service in the field." McNelly could not, according to Dr. Cupples' professional opinion, "bear the exposure without a great and manifest risk." Then McNelly had asked if his company could be brought to within ten or twenty miles of San Antonio. He intended to continue to direct the actions of his company from San Antonio, where he remained until November 20.

Thirdly, McNelly, on November 20, asked and received permission to visit Austin. He spent a few days there and then went home to Washington County where he remained until the end of December. Steele reported McNelly's only accomplishment was "visiting Galveston with a guard to take a few prisoners to that city, which duty should have been performed by a subordinate."

Steele did not make his decision solely on McNelly's performance record but had also communicated with Dr. Cupples who had indicated on January 21, 1877, that McNelly "would not be fit for active service at any time during the winter. His situation when I last saw him was a very grave one." Medical costs had also entered into Steele's decision; the cost for medical attention and medicine showed McNelly was under treatment in July, September, October, November, December 1876 and January 1877. The expense for McNelly alone was nearly one-third of the medical allotment for his company.

Steele asked rhetorically whether he would have been justified in recommending, or the governor in appointing, McNelly to continue with his command when "there was at hand an officer [Hall] who had already been represented by the people amongst whom he had been serving, in command of a portion of McNelly's company, as the right man in the right place, and who was in the full vigor of early manhood and health."[39] To Steele it was not a difficult decision. McNelly was incompetent and needed to be released, no matter his previous record. The present command under Hall, purportedly selected from the best of McNelly's old company, was costing less than half as much as the old one.

Governor Hubbard also questioned Adjutant General Steele regarding McNelly's termination. On March 8 Steele responded with a three page letter, "delayed for the want of Some data necessary to a correct answer." Steele revealed matters withheld in his report to the press. McNelly was "extremely negligent in making his reports" and "he appeared to Know but little as to the outstanding accounts." McNelly, Steele complained, "appeared to pay no attention to the directions given him to have all debts reported for Settlement at the end of every month, and bills have been coming in that date back to the first month of Service." Because of this, when the company was reorganized in late January it was impossible to do more than estimate the amount paid and due out of the appropriation of $40,000. Once all accounts were settled Steele estimated he had a balance of $13,278 which would have maintained the entire company in service for three months.

In addition, Steele pointed out that reducing the company to twenty men had not made it less effective. Comparing the reports of arrests during the previous six months with the one month of February under Hall, since reorganization, Steele noted fifty-five arrests reported during the six-month period, of which Lieutenant Hall and others in the new company had made thirty-five, and nineteen arrests for whom no one individual was credited. But in the month of February the reorganized company made twenty-six arrests, had scouted twenty-five counties, and recovered and returned to the proper owners $6,000 worth of stolen property.

To Steele the arrest records were not the only examples of the former captain's incompetence. McNelly, "was physically incapacitated for active work, & I have nothing to indicate that 1st Lieut. L B Wright ever did any valuable Service," Steele wrote. Not only that but there were several men with the company "unknown to other members of it. Captain McNelly states that they were detectives. If anything was done by them, it is unknown to me." Steele believed the cost for transporting prisoners, always an unknown in estimating company expenses, would be drastically reduced because he had arranged with railroad and steam boat companies to provide reduced rates for Hall and his men. Apparently Steele's explanation to Hubbard for dismissing McNelly was deemed adequate. McNelly, aware he could not continue as a company commander anyway, was probably too weak to protest the decision.[40]

Adjutant General Steele experienced not only the dissatisfaction of the ordinary citizens of Texas but also that of some of McNelly's men. A group signing themselves simply "Ex-Rangers" expressed their reaction and sent it to the *Express*. They suggested there was not a "very strong tie of friendship" between Steele and McNelly and interpreted Steele's remarks as wanting to give the public a bad impression of McNelly's reputation "as a gentleman and a soldier, and for why?"

Further, McNelly's health had been in "a critical condition" for the last six months, not through living in luxury and ease in Austin, but through "hardships and real duty" on the Rio Grande. McNelly had exposed himself to dangers that few others would subject themselves to. The rangers had seen him in action at Palo Alto, at Las Cuevas and at Sabinitas, encouraging his men, not with the command "Go ahead men!" but with the request, "Come on boys." Now instead of thanks for being a brave soldier he received insults from the state.

The ex-rangers accused Steele of making untrue statements and that the rangers of Hall's command were "not the pick of the best men," as Steele stated, but those who remained "because they could not better themselves in pecuniary matters outside of the company." Several of the ex-rangers would have stayed "under any circumstances" had McNelly himself remained as captain.[41]

Over the next few months McNelly's condition weakened further. While he approached death the men remained active under Lieutenant Hall. Ranger Davis and several men from Dripping Springs in Hays County had "a lively chase" about daylight on Friday, February 2, after two men charged with having a herd of stolen cattle in their possession. Shots were exchanged but both men escaped; one of them was Charley Cannon.[42] Later that month Lieutenant Hall received praise in the *Statesman* for his "cleaning out the crop of knaves and bloody-handed scoundrels about Goliad."[43]

In April the *Statesman* commented on the "several terrible fellows" in the Austin jail, identifying DeWitt County's William D. Meador as "a hard nut." Meador was "the sweet boy that took an old man off his dying bed and shot and then hanged him and his son. There are five and should be fifty representatives of Cuero devils in the jail." Later the *Statesman* apologized, claiming an injustice had been done Meador and the others. "They are not murderers, but only charged with the crime. It has not been proven, and they have not been executed." The *Statesman* pointed out the "great wrong" which had been committed in printing the article. It then stressed that Cuero, the people and the town, were "now as law-abiding a place as any in Texas, having as good and orderly population as any other."

The Taylor-Sutton Feud, which had been "the cause of many of these false impressions" had ended. The Suttons remained, while "the other parties to the strife have left the country." The Suttons "are an honest, law-abiding people. They were the first to attack the desperadoes and robbers, West. [sic] Hardin and the rest, who once frequented the county." The *Statesman* was "well pleased to announce the fact."[44]

Through the spring and summer of 1877 McNelly's health condition remained newsworthy. He was reported as "quite sick" in late May; after his stay at the American House in Boerne he was "in a very precarious condition."[45] By the end of July, with no physical improvement, he chose to leave Austin for Burton. By mid-August the McNellys knew there was only a short time remaining. On Saturday, August 11, Mrs. McNelly wrote A.H. Cook, Jr., son of the noted Texas architect in Austin, to send ice regularly to the captain, who, she said, was "gradually sinking." The following day she telegraphed Cook to send a priest. That evening Father Daniel J. Spillard left Austin by the Central train; his friends in Austin feared McNelly would be dead within hours.[46]

With such negative statements in the press, it was probably inevitable that a premature report of his death would appear. The Galveston *News* reported in its issue of August 24 that McNelly had died at his farm near Burton "a few days ago" citing a telegram from Burton dated August 23.[47] On August 31 *The Western Chronicle* of Sutherland Springs in Wilson County wrote a lengthy and equally bogus obituary for McNelly. Editor E.R. Tarver reminded his readers of McNelly's contribution for "conspicuous gallantry" during the late war, making for himself a "brilliant reputation." In spite of McNelly's being a "strong Democrat," Governor Davis had appointed him to command a company of State Police. He was such an effective leader that Governor Coke appointed him to again command a force. McNelly's ability to recruit good men was now paying off. Due to his "unerring judgment" Texas was indebted for his providing such men as Hall, Armstrong and Watson, under whose command the "State Police" continued to be a "terror to evil-doers."[48] The Brenham *Banner*, Washington County's only newspaper, not yet advised of the premature report of his death, said he was in his usual health "though in the last stages of consumption."[49]

Death did come to Leander Harvey McNelly on Tuesday, September 4, 1877, with wife and children and other family members around him. Ranger John McNelly had taken a leave of absence from the service when he knew his uncle's death was imminent. A.H. Belo, editor of the Galveston *News*, wrote a brief obituary in the issue of September 7, correcting the earlier report. Belo explained death came "from the effects of the insidious disease which necessitated his retirement from the State service several

Alfred Horatio Belo, friend to McNelly from the war's end through his ranger career. He caused a great expansion of the Galveston *Daily News* and in 1885 established the Dallas *Morning News*. *Courtesy The Rosenberg Library, Galveston, Texas.*

months ago." He praised Captain McNelly, saying he had "enacted a conspicuous part in the recent history of the State, not less in the internal police than in the military defense of the frontier." Belo reminded his readers that the greatest problem of the times was the "suppression of lawlessness and crime, particularly in the frontier counties." A few perhaps could rival McNelly, Belo stated, but "no officer contributed better service toward its solution." McNelly was able, gallant and faithful "in all his enterprises against the enemies of a young and struggling society and civilization." His name would long be remembered and cherished with affection by the thousands of beneficiaries of his skill and bravery.[50]

Belo was not satisfied with this ode of praise to the deceased commander. Over a month later he provided an obituary tribute which described Captain McNelly's last days. He had pondered over what he would say, as he had been close to McNelly for many years and had, during the last five weeks, tried to write, "for the gratification of many kind friends in Texas, something of the closing life of this brave man." Belo utilized many of the flowery tributes of the times relevant to death, but he also stated that McNelly had "died as he had lived, bravely and without fear of that 'unknown future.'" During McNelly's period of extreme illness he had "manifested patience and fortude [sic] that were heroic." At times his suffering was agonizing, but no word of complaint or injustice was wrung from his lips. With "strict obedience to the directions of his attending physicians" Drs. Cupples and Herff, he was "very hopeful until even a few weeks before his death." Belo quoted McNelly as saying on his death bed, no doubt to his family, when he could not speak above a whisper, "I will never give up the fight as long as one feeble breath is left me, for your dear sakes. I have so much to live for, surely God does not expect me to welcome death; but if it is His will, then all is for the best, and I am perfectly resigned." Belo reported McNelly had "prayed earnestly and fervently to God for many months for Christian fortitude to bear all He saw fit to send upon him, and was prepared for death."

More realistically Belo reported that for several weeks McNelly was at times compelled to take opiates to relieve the pain, and at such times he was more or less delirious. Then he imagined himself back in the service, sometimes marching, sometimes looking for a camping place, at other times conducting a court martial, that aspect of the military which troubled him most of all. At times he imagined himself upon the battlefield, surrounded or cut off from reinforcements. A great look of distress would then cross his face. Unknowingly perhaps, Belo provided a bit of humor as he wrote that at other times in his delirium McNelly was "busy with making out his reports."

Shortly before his death McNelly gazed "with the greatest astonishment" at something on the opposite wall, as if he was viewing something which was beyond his comprehension. A beautiful expression beamed from his dying eyes just before the last fleeting breath. His death was as painless, seemingly, "as the slumber of a tired child." Besides his friends, and the state, who would mourn him, "few can have any conception of the desolation that reigns in that once happy home, since his departure from it."[51]

The monument erected at the grave of Captain McNelly by
Richard King in appreciation of his services. Adjacent to
McNelly's is that of his daughter Mary Irene.
Photo by Gary P. Fitterer, 4 July 1987.

CHAPTER 20

CAREY ALONE

One of the greatest, perhaps the greatest, problem of
the times during which he figured, in this State, was
the suppression of lawlessness and crime, particularly
in the frontier communities. While a few have rivaled
him, no officer contributed better service toward its
solution. Able, gallant, faithful in all his enterprises
against the enemies of a young and struggling society
and civilization, long will his name be remembered and
cherished with affection by thousands of beneficiaries
of his skill and bravery, and by all Texans who desire
the well-being and development of the State. — A.H.
Belo, Galveston *Daily News*, September 7, 1877.

Many people felt the state treated McNelly unjustly by dropping
him from the force because of his health. Some also felt concern
over the welfare of his widow and children and considered it to be a
"sacred" duty of the legislature to provide a suitable income for Mrs.
McNelly and her two children.[1] This notion was ridiculed by others,
pointing out that the "proposition to make the widow . . . a pen-
sioner of the State seems to have been made with unadvised haste"
as she was left in "independent circumstances" and thus did not
need assistance. Certainly she did not want for financial support,
but she perhaps needed emotional support to assist her during her
period of mourning.[2]

Leander Harvey McNelly was laid to rest in the Mount Zion
Cemetery, several miles from Burton, on what is now farm to market road #1948. The Baptist Church adjacent to this cemetery was
the first in the immediate Burton area. It is not known if Carey
McNelly herself had any type of marker erected at his grave; perhaps
not, but it was not long before someone did feel the last resting place
of a Texas hero required a monument — Captain Richard King, cattleman.

King must have taken action almost immediately after learning of the death of his friend. By January 1878 a "very handsome mon~ument" had been erected which cost King $3,000. The large granite stone was placed as a token of respect and admiration for the mem~ory of McNelly and his contribution to the establishment of law and order in southwestern Texas.[3]

The nearly fifteen~foot tall, obelisk~style monument carries a Masonic insignia on the north side and a cannon representing his war service on the west side. The inscription is on the south side.

LEANDER HARVEY McNELLY
BORN IN
BROOK COUNTY, VIRGINIA
MARCH 12, 1844
DIED AT OAKLAND, TEXAS
SEPTEMBER 4, 1877
AGED 33 YEARS AND 7 MONTHS
How sleep the brave who sink to rest,
by all their country's wishes blest.

Presumably Carey had the final determination as to what was inscribed on the monument, but it indicates McNelly died at Oakland when all the contemporary reports indicate he died at his home near Burton. If Richard King chose the inscription it is under~standable why this mistake could have been made.

Carey McNelly's letter of appreciation, addressed to "Capt. Richard King" was shared with the press of the day; the Brenham *Banner* published the letter in its issue of February 5, 1878. Other newspapers such as the San Antonio *Daily Express* and the Dallas *Daily Herald* published it as well. In the letter she thanked King for the "handsome monument you so generously presented to mark the last resting place of my departed husband." She informed him that it had been erected, suggesting that King did not oversee its actual installation. Carey stated that it was with feeling of "deep emotion and eternal gratitude" that she thanked him for the tribute of his appreciation of McNelly's "patriotism and personal friendship." She continued with unabashed praise, "It will stand a fitting emblem to mark his grave for ages, unchanged by the rough storms and tem~pestuous rains that may sweep over it, even as he was unchanging in his patriotism and devotion to Texas during his life." She promised King that when she visited the "sacred spot," she would breathe a prayer for him, his friend, constant to McNelly's memory in death as he was faithful to McNelly while he was alive.[4]

Shortly before his death, McNelly had attempted to be reimbursed for the expenses he had incurred while delivering the DeWitt County prisoners from Clinton to Galveston and then to Austin for safekeeping. McNelly's own account has not survived, but after his death Mrs. McNelly attempted to recover those expenses. She wrote to Colonel Jeremiah Y. Dashiell, a Civil War veteran and one-time editor of the San Antonio *Daily Herald*, hoping Dashiell could exert some influence on Governor Hubbard. "Pardon me for asking a favor of a comparative stranger, except by reputation," she began. "Only the high esteem in which my deceased husband held you and his advice to pursue this course could prompt me to take such a liberty. She pointed out that the last duty her husband had performed in the service of the state was the conveyance of the prisoners to Galveston and thence to Austin, "where they are still confined." McNelly had paid all the expenses for the prisoners and guards "out of his own private funds," but when the accounts were forwarded to Steele, "he refused to settle them, saying they could not be paid out of the appropriation for the company. He had repeatedly paid similar accounts unhesitatingly." She reminded Dashiell of how her husband had been treated,

> You are aware of some of the ill treatment Capt. McNelly received at his [Steele's] hands and can understand what prompted this refusal of a debt that should have been paid at once. He never asked Gov. Hubbard to pay it, but always believed he would do so if he could see and talk with him. But as General Steele promised the last time he visited him in Austin to pay it, he left without seeing the Governor, and when, two days afterwards, he received a letter from his officer declining to pay the same, he was not well enough to return. And, as you know, continued declining. A few days before his death, he told me to write to you and ask you to write to Gov. Hubbard in regard to it. Will you be kind enough to do so? I need it very much — although a small amount compared to what my husband spent in the service of the State out of his own private fortune.

The amount was $318. As a last thought she added "I hope you will be successful. This is private." Dashiell's reply has not been preserved.

The request from Mrs. McNelly reached the desk of Governor Hubbard who referred it to Adjutant General Steele. On October 8 Steele explained to Hubbard that the expenses of transporting pris~ oners and transfer was not the responsibility of the state but of the county where the offense was committed, thus it was the responsi~ bility of DeWitt County to reimburse whatever expenses McNelly could justifiably claim. Steele pointed out that this "fact was stated to Capt. McNelly . . . and when I last saw Capt[.] McNelly he apolo~ gized to me for intemperate expressions which he had used . . . and left with apparently the kindest feelings to me." Hubbard then responded to Colonel Dashiell four days later, reiterating Steele's recommendation that the county of DeWitt reimburse Mrs. McNelly. "I am certainly anxious to see justice done by the State in this case" he added, "and more especially to this widow of a gallant soldier."[5]

Horace Rowe, a young ranger interested in writing and publish~ ing, saw an opportunity for his creative talents and contemplated preparing a biography of the late ranger captain. An item in the Houston *Daily Post* announced his intention and stated that Carey was "assisting" Rowe in "compiling a memoir" by furnishing him articles clipped from newspapers relating to his experiences. She had dutifully saved the clippings "up through seven years before his death" suggesting that as early as 1870 Mrs. McNelly may have started gathering news items about her husband, possibly with the intent of someday writing his biography. It is not known today if the biography ever proceeded past the planning stages; if a biography ever did become a reality no copy is known to exist. Mrs. McNelly may have intended such a biography as a means to preserve her hus~ band's memory as much as a source of income.[6]

Carey McNelly, not yet thirty years old, was left alone with two children, Irene, then less than ten years of age, and Leander R., a year younger. When the 1880 census was made on June 11 she was listed as "Carrie McAnally" a thirty~one year old widow keeping house. How enumerator W.C. Braische [Broesche?] could misspell the name of such a noted individual is difficult to understand, but he revealed his inability to spell again when he identified the daugh~ ter as "Irine McAnnelly" and the son as "L R McAnally." Living with the McNelly family at the time was a twenty~year~old single female friend, "Manerva Cain" a native of Arkansas.[7]

As if the death of her husband at a relatively young age was not enough, another tragedy entered into Carey McNelly's life when daughter Irene suffered an accident while attending classes at Old Baylor College in Washington County. In early May 1884 a class-mate pulled out the chair, on which she was standing, from under her. Irene fell and died a few days later of the injuries suffered in this tragic prank. A large white stone was erected, to the left of her father's, to mark the grave of Irene. The simple inscription reads:

SACRED TO THE
MEMORY OF
MY BELOVED DAUGHTER
IRENE
APRIL 29, 1868
PASSED TO HIGHER LIFE
MAY 8, 1884.

It is not known what Mrs. McNelly did over the next several years . She was still residing at Burton as late as December 1895, but then she relocated to Austin when she was offered meaningful employment with the State of Texas in January 1896. The 1900 census shows her boarding on Brazos Street, a forty-nine-year old widow born in June 1850, having given birth to two children only one of whom was living. She indicated she could read and write English.[8]

Son Rebel was to give her many worries. He found it easy to get into difficulties, and on one occasion committed an assault upon one Frank Broesche. McNelly and Broesche had been raised together and were close friends. Some argument arose and Rebel McNelly and Frank Broesche fought; Rebel was charged with assault to murder. There were no witnesses to the difficulty. McNelly was induced to plead guilty by his friends, as the best course out of his trouble, and received a two-year sentence on March 27, 1893, the term to be served in the Texas State Penitentiary at Huntsville. McNelly's certificate of prison conduct shows he entered as Number 9223 for a term of two years and was received on April 24, 1893. He was twenty-six years of age, five feet eight inches tall, weighed 136 pounds and not married. His habits were "Temperate." Although he had received only a limited education his occupation was given as clerk, suggesting his education was above average. Throughout his sentence he had only two offenses on his record, both smoking vio-lations; he was punished on September 21, 1893, and February 11, 1894, by spending twelve hours in "D.C." presumably dark confinement or isolation. A certificate of prison conduct prepared at Huntsville on October 5, 1894, and signed by L.A. Whatley, Superintendent of State Prisons, prepared at the request of Mrs. McNelly indicated that if he were to serve his full term he would be eligible for release on March 27, 1895. He had earned a commutation of one month and eight days, thus with full commutation his sentence would expire on February 1, 1895. In an accompanying letter Whatley indicated to Mrs. McNelly that Rebel was "an excellent prisoner" since he had entered Huntsville, was trusted by officials and was working as a clerk in the Financial Agent's department. Another document, directed to Governor J.S. Hogg and signed by S.L. McCulloch, W.B. Blalock and R.W. Brahan, specified that during the time he had been employed in prison "he has conducted himself in such a manner as to convince us that he is entirely trustworthy and reliable; doing his work promptly and effeciently [sic]." Many Washington County citizens signed the petition to have Rebel McNelly pardoned. The petition stated "Mr. McNelly is a son of the gallant and noble Capt. McNelly, and the only living child of his widowed mother, who is a most estimable lady and has the deepest sympathy of her many friends." The petitioners prayed for the pardon so that Rebel might reside with his mother.

Another document prepared by a penitentiary agent, name indecipherable, states that McNelly had been working as a stenographer and was "very faithful and trust worthy." Perhaps the agent had encouraged McNelly to discuss what brought on the troubles which resulted in his being incarcerated because the document states that "the trouble he got into was brought on by drinking and keeping bad company." McNelly assured the agent that "if he can get out he will go to work and be a man." Governor Hogg responded positively to the petitioners, granting Leander R. McNelly a full pardon and restoration of full citizenship and right of suffrage on December 4, 1894. He had served approximately twenty months of the two-year sentence.[9] Earlier that year on February 17, 1894, John Wesley Hardin had walked out of Huntsville, also pardoned by Governor Hogg. Undoubtedly Hardin and McNelly became somewhat acquainted while in prison, and one wonders if Hardin ever spoke of eluding Captain McNelly's efforts to capture him years before in DeWitt County.

Rebel did spend time at home with his mother, not only in Burton but in Austin as well. After his release from prison it is apparent he had difficulty in finding useful employment, but at least one of the rangers who had served under his father attempted to assist him. Spencer J. Adams who began service under McNelly in July 1874, and served to 1877, petitioned Governor Charles Allen Culberson in early 1898 for special consideration. His letter first spoke of a request from Mrs. McNelly, the "Widow of that noted Texas Ranger, Capt. McNelly" who had been employed in the Land Office for several years. Adams continued in admitting he knew little of Rebel McNelly "except that he is her only Son and Child. The boy, I have been informed, has been rather wild but his Mother has faith in him yet." Adams informed the governor that his mother "is very anxious that he should become a member of the 'Governors Guards' as it seems to be the boy[']s ambition to become a soldier like his father." No record has been found that young McNelly was able to attain his goal of becoming a soldier of any degree, in spite of the efforts of Adams.[10]

The next known location of Rebel McNelly is in Arizona Territory. His efforts to find some relief from the disease which was destroying his health prompted him to locate there, and the change in climate may have lengthened his life somewhat; but on January 1, 1907, Leander R. McNelly died from "the dread destroyer, tuberculosis" in Tombstone, Cochise County, Arizona. He had been admitted the day before to a hospital. The brief, two-line obituary in the Tombstone *Prospector* gave no reference to his famous father and merely stated that his relatives at Austin had been notified and that the remains were to be shipped there for burial. His unpretentious grave stone in Austin's Oakwood Cemetery provides only his name and the years of his life, 1866-1907.[11]

Mrs. McNelly, still only in her late forties and not one to rest on the laurels of her husband, had begun searching for employment in Austin shortly after her son was released from prison. She applied for a position as a clerk in the State Department. On September 6, 1895, former Ranger John Barclay Armstrong, writing from his office at his Chicago Ranch, Cameron County, penned a letter to Governor C.A. Culberson, requesting his assistance in the matter.

> The widow of the late Captain L.H. McNelly is an applicant for a clerkship in some of the State Departments, and as I had the honor of serving under her husband, as a member of the "Special State Troops," I can truly say that he did more to suppress

lawlessness & crime in this section of the State than
any other man. He caught cold & died from exposure
in the service. I have lived to see & appreciate the good
results of his labors, Peace and prosperity are now in
the land where terror once reigned supreme. Justice
demands that the widow of such an officer receive
some consideration from the state. Mrs. McNelly is an
accomplished lady, competent to fill a position in any
of the Departments. As a plain, law-abiding citizen (and
an admirer of our Governor) I respectfully ask that your
Excellency give this case some attention, & if possible
assist Mrs. McNelly in securing a permanent position
should she call upon you to do so.

Your Obedient Servant Jno. B. Armstrong.[12]

Armstrong was but one of many who felt she deserved a special
position with the state; Land Commissioner Andrew Jackson Baker
received petitions from nearly every county in Southwest Texas.
From Live Oak County came a petition containing forty-eight names
of stockmen, farmers and county officials, asking Governor
Culberson to consider her "condition" and to her application for a
clerkship, urging him to accept her claim and right to earn an honest living by working for the state her husband served so well "in the
trying days of the six-shooter rule." In case the governor did not realize the contribution McNelly had made in those days the petitioners
reviewed his work.

Capt. McNelly was a brave and efficient officer who
was sent into this section when it was terror-stricken,
run over and imposed upon by reckless American desperadoes and bands of Mexican raiders. He restored
law and order in Counties where good citizens dared
not open their mouths against the oppressions they
lived under; where men were shot down on the high-
ways in the broad light of day, and taken from their
homes and families at night and hung to trees and left
to strangle to death. The History of Gonzales, DeWitt,
Karnes, Live Oak, Nueces, Cameron, Hidalgo, Starr
and many other Counties during these turbulent days
is written in the blood of their citizens, and to no man
are we so much indebted for the peace and prosperity

we now enjoy as we are to the memory of Captain
McNelly.[13]

In early January 1896 the governor responded affirmatively to
the many petitions and offered Mrs. McNelly a position; she was at
her home in Burton when the offer came but her letter of acceptance reached Commissioner Baker on January 18. The news release
from Austin pointed out that she was the "widow of the gallant
ranger captain, who did so much toward suppressing lawlessness in
Southwest Texas in other years." Carey McNelly became the first
salaried female employee of a Texas state governmental branch,
becoming a clerk in the State Land Office.[14]

She was not to spend the rest of her life alone. During her stay
in Austin she met widower William Thomas Wroe, a successful
Austin businessman, who had come to Texas with his parents in
1859. He possibly became acquainted with McNelly because both
were in the New Mexico campaigns of 1862 and both saw action in
Louisiana.

Although it is not known when and where Mr. Wroe and Mrs.
McNelly met, likely it was in Austin where her work and his business
might have caused them to meet. They were married on April 15,
1909, in San Antonio. In her application for a widow's pension she
stated her marriage date as April 15, 1909; the license was indeed
issued that day but was not returned to be recorded. Two witnesses
to the marriage, Mrs. P.H. Swearingen and S.J. Brooks, both of San
Antonio, made affidavit that Mrs. McNelly and W.T. Wroe were
indeed married on that date. The couple enjoyed about twenty-four
years of married life together; William Thomas Wroe died in Austin
on January 3, 1933. The cause of death, according to F.T.
McLaughlin, M.D., was "senility and disease of bladder, prostate
gland."[15]

Due to her education and status, Carey McNelly Wroe became
deeply involved in the Texas Daughters of the Confederacy, William
Sidney Johnston Chapter 105, which she had joined in 1901. In that
organization she held many chapter and district offices, serving with
distinction and loyalty. She also served on legislative committees
and on the Board of Regents of the Texas Confederate Museum. In
1925 she was made an honorary member of the Texas Division,
United Daughters of the Confederacy. For a number of years she
was the oldest living student who had attended "Old Baylor"
University. On September 28, 1937, she was admitted to the Texas

Women's Confederate Home in Austin, where death claimed her at age ninety on October 29, 1938, of pneumonia. Her funeral was held at St. David's Episcopal Church in Austin, and she was laid to final rest beside Rebel in Oakwood Cemetery[16], her stone simply reading:

Carey McNelly Wroe
1848-1938.

ENDNOTES

AUTHORS' FOREWORD

1.George Durham as told to Clyde Wantland, *Taming the Nueces Strip: The Story of McNelly's Rangers* (Austin: University of Texas Press, 1962), 178. George P. Durham's recollections were written in 1934 and published first in the monthly magazine *West* in 1937, entitled "On the Trail of 5100 Outlaws: The Inside Story of McNelly's Rangers" then with slight revisions in book form entitled *Taming the Nueces Strip: The Story of McNelly's Rangers in 1962*. Both were written with the assistance of Clyde Wantland. To distinguish between the two the magazine version is noted as Durham, "5100 Outlaws," and the book version as Durham, *Nueces Strip*.

2. Ramon F. Adams, *Six-Guns and Saddle Leather: A Bibliography of Books and Pamphlets on Western Outlaws and Gunmen*. New Edition, Revised and Greatly Enlarged (Cleveland, Ohio: John T. Zubal, Inc. 1982), 196-97.

3. Durham, *Nueces Strip*, 136.

CHAPTER 1
GENESIS OF A FIGHTING MAN

1.N.A. Jennings, *A Texas Ranger* (1899. Reprint. Norman: University of Oklahoma Press, 1977), 82-85. Jennings was born in Philadelphia on January 10, 1856. After years of adventure in the American West as well as other countries, he returned to the East where he died December 15, 1918. After two years in business with his father he went to Texas, reportedly to purchase a ranch, and joined up with McNelly on May 26, 1876, serving until he was honorably discharged on February 1, 1877. His book describes many events in which he did not participate, but he felt justified in such creative writing for the sake of the reader. After his book was published in 1899 he wrote to McNelly's widow, "In the book I made myself a member of the company a year before I actually joined. I did this to add interest to the recital and to avoid too much of a hear-say character." Quoted in John H. Jenkins, *Basic Texas Books* (Austin: Texas State Historical Association, 1988 Revised edition), 282.

2. Durham, *Nueces Strip*, 45.
3. Durham, "5100 Outlaws, 110.
4. Durham, *Nueces Strip*, 5.
5. Durham, *Nueces Strip*, 142.
6. The historical marker reads as follows:

Leander H. McNelly/ (March 12, 1844-Sept. 4, 1877)/ Born in Virginia, was valiant/ Confederate soldier./ In 1870, appointed one of four/ State Police Captains by Gov. E. J./ Davis, then with Texas Rangers,/ McNelly was assigned a special/ force, "The Washington County/ Volunteer Militia", to mediate the/ Sutton-Taylor Feud. Company then/ assigned to Rio Grande border/ to control international cattle/ thieves in "Las Cuevas War."/ His men always proudly called/ themselves "Little McNellys."/ Recorded-1967.

7. *Population Schedule of the Seventh Census of the United States, 1850.* Brooke County, Virginia, 256B & 257A. "The name Owen is used for John in Ireland (often spelled in the Irish way: Eoin) so it could be interchangeable." Correspondence from Elizabeth McNelly Shannon to authors, 21 March 1996.

8. Mrs. Robert A. Newman spelled the name of Leander's mother as Katherine Killian in her chapter "Peter J. McNelly Volunteer 1838-1864" in *Who's Who of the Confederacy*, Compiled by Susan Merle Dotson (San Antonio: The Naylor Company, 1966), 171. The 1850 Brooke County census spells the name Catherine, 256B. In "Leander Harvey McNelly" F. R. Avis wrote that the parents of Leander were Owen and Mary Katherine and had migrated from Ireland in 1832. Annie Maud Knittel Avis, compiler, *History of Burton*, Vol. 1 (1974), 266.

9. *Population Schedule of the Sixth Census of the United States, 1840.* Brooke County, Virginia, 217B.

10. When the State of Virginia seceded from the United States in 1861, fifty western counties, including Brooke, objected and refused to secede. These counties united to form "The Restored Government of Virginia" and petitioned to Congress for re-admittance to the Union. This land, which became the State of West Virginia, became part of the Union in 1863. *The Handy Book for Genealogists* 8th Edition (Logan, Utah: The Everton Publishers, Inc. 1991), 277.

11. Avis, *History of Burton*, 268.

12. *Population Schedule of the Seventh Census of the United States*, 1850. Brooke County, Virginia, 256B & 257A. The daughter identified on the census as "Clarinda" is identified by Mrs. Newman as "Clorinda." Nor did Mrs. Newman list a son James, who is listed on the census as the younger brother of Leander by two years. The census does not show a daughter named Jennie.

13. Mary Ellen McNelly, "The McNelly Family From Ireland to Virginia to Texas." Genealogical data courtesy Mary Ellen McNelly, Sister Clared. Transcript copy in possession of authors, 8.

14. Mary Ellen McNelly, 8.

15. Chauncey B. Shepard was born October 15, 1812 in Virginia. By the time of the 1870 census he was quite successful as he claimed $51,000 worth of real estate and $7,000 personal estate. Within his household were eight people, five children and three others identified as "Hostler" or "domestic servant." *Population Schedule of the Ninth Census of the United States, 1870.* Washington County, Texas, enumerated September 7, 112A. Chauncey Berkeley Shepard had moved to Texas early in the Republic of Texas period and developed a successful law practice. He served in the Texas Senate from 1856 to 1864. Shepard was a volunteer in the Battle of Galveston on January 1, 1863, as was McNelly. Shepard died at Brenham on December 30, 1892. Paul Gervais Bell, "Chauncey Berkeley Shepard" in *The New Handbook of Texas*, Vol. 5, 1014. Newman, 172.

16. Newman, 172. Correspondence from Mrs. W.T. Wroe to E.D. McNelly, 2 January 1937. Original in Texas Ranger Hall of Fame and Museum, Waco, Texas.

17. Newman, 172.

18. Bert McNelly, "Thomas H. McNelly" in *A Proud Heritage: A History of Uvalde County, Texas written by the people of Uvalde County* (El Progreso Club, 1975), 397.

19. "Mementoes of Charles B. McNelly" in Avis, *History of Burton*, 268.

20. "John McNelly" obituary, *The San Antonio Daily Express* (23 April 1919).

21. Avis, *History of Burton*, 14-15.

22. *Flake's Daily Bulletin*, Galveston (15 June 1870), and *The Daily Banner*, Brenham, (7 June 1870).

CHAPTER 2
FIRST TASTE OF WAR

1. *Population Schedule of the Ninth Census of the United States, 1870.* Washington County, Texas, 151B. Campbell's post office was Longpoint where he was identified as a deputy sheriff. He held real estate valued at $4,000 and personal estate valued at $3,000; he and his wife had five children.

2. Civil War Muster Record for L. H. McNelly, National Archives, Washington, D.C. The date of August 21 as well as August 27 is recorded as the date of McNelly's enrollment in Campbell's company.

3. Jerry Thompson, "Henry Hopkins Sibley", 1039 and "Sibley's Brigade", 1041 in *The New Handbook of Texas* Vol. 5; Jerry Thompson, *Confederate General of the West: Henry Hopkins Sibley* (1987. Reprint. College Station: Texas A&M University Press, 1996).

4. McLeary had relocated in Texas as a teenager in the late 1850s, studied at Soule University in Chappell Hill, Washington County, and then joined Sibley's army. Following the war he earned a law degree from Washington and Lee University, was elected to the Texas Legislature in 1873 and then became State Attorney General in 1880. He died in Washington, D.C. and is buried in Arlington Cemetery. J.H. McLeary, "History of Green's Brigade" in *A Comprehensive History of Texas 1685-1897* edited by Dudley Goodall Wooten (1898. Reprint. Austin: The Texas State Historical Association, 1986). "James Harvey McLeary" by Claudia Hazlewood in *The New Handbook of Texas*, Vol. 4, 428.

5. McLeary, 695.

6. *The Texas State Gazette*, Austin, 14 September 1861.

7. Alwyn Barr, "Thomas Green" in *The New Handbook of Texas*, Vol. 3, 316-17.

8. McLeary, 696. From 1879-81 Sayers served as lieutenant governor; his nomination was by E.G. Bower and the second was by J.H. McLeary.

9. *The San Antonio Daily Herald*, 19 October 1861.

10. *The Texas State Gazette*, Austin, 9 November 1861.

11. William H. Smith, "With Sibley in New Mexico; the Journal of William Henry Smith" contributed by Walter A. Faulkner in the *West Texas Historical Association Year Book*, Vol. 27 (October 1951), 115.

12. McLeary, 697.

13. *The Houston Telegraph*, 5 February 1862 printing a letter dated 13 January 1862.

14. McLeary, 698.

15. Joseph G. Dawson III, "Edward Richard Sprigg Canby" in *The New Handbook of Texas*, Vol. 1, 955-56.

16. John Taylor, *Bloody Valverde: A Civil War Battle on the Rio Grande, February 21, 1862.* (Albuquerque: University of New Mexico Press, 1995), 67-70.

17. *The Texas State Gazette*, Austin, 19 March 1862.

18. McLeary, 699.

19. Thomas Green, "Report of Thomas Green Fifth Texas Cavalry" written at Camp Valverde, New Mexico, February 22, 1862 in *The War of the Rebellion: A Compilation of the Official Records of the Union and Confederate Armies,* Series I, Vol. 9, (Washington: Government Printing Office, 1883), 520-21, hereafter cited as *O.R.*

20. Jennings, *A Texas Ranger*, 58.

CHAPTER 3
BACK TO TEXAS AND GALVESTON

1. McLeary, 700.
2. Taylor, 107.
3. McLeary, 700-701.
4. Taylor, 108.
5. Ibid.
6. McLeary, 706.
7. T.T. Teel, "Sibley's New Mexican Campaign—Its Objects and the Causes of Its Failures" in *Battles and Leaders of the Civil War* Vol. 2. Part 2 (New York: The Century Company, 1888), 700.
8. [Harold V. Hunter] "Civil War Diary: Dr. Harold V. Hunter. Co. I, 7th Regiment, Texas Mounted Volunteers." Transcript copy in Martin Hardwick Hall Papers, Texas State Archives, 17.
9. *The Texas State Gazette*, Austin. 7 June 1862. Charles Magill Conrad (1804-1878) also served as a member of the Confederate Provisional Congress representing Louisiana in the 1st and 2nd Confederate Congress. He rose to the rank of brigadier general in the Confederate Army.
10. *The State Gazette*, Austin. 7 June 1862.
11. William Randolph Howell, *Westward the Texans. The Civil War Journal of Private William Randolph Howell* edited with an introduction by Jerry D. Thompson (El Paso: The Texas Western Press, 1990), 104-109.
12. McLeary, 706.
13. Thomas W. Cutrer, "John Bankhead Magruder" in *The New Handbook of Texas*, Vol. 4 (Austin: Texas State Historical Association, 1996), 464-65.
14. J. Thomas Scharf, *History of the Confederate States Navy from its Organization to the Surrender of its Last Vessel* (Albany, New York: Joseph McDonough. 1886), 504-506. J. Bankhead Magruder gives this information in greater detail in his report of 26 February 1863, written from Galveston to Samuel Cooper, Adjutant and Inspector General, Richmond, Virginia. *Official Records of the Union and Confederate Navies in the War of the Rebellion,* Series I, Vol. 15 (Washington: Government Printing Office, 1905), 213.
15. This is how correspondent "Sioux" recalled the speech which he included in his "Reminiscences of the War" No. 4, Battle of Galveston, January 1, 1863, appearing in *The Galveston Daily News*, August 6, 1876. It is slightly different in McLeary, 707. "Sioux" was the pen name of William P. Doran, a Rochester, New York native who became the war correspondent for the Galveston *News* for forty-one years. Apparently he came to Texas not long before the war began, because in 1860 he resided in Lynchburg, Harris County, where he worked as a "machinist." The census lists his age as twenty-five and from New York. *Population Schedule of the Eighth Census of the United States, 1860,* Harris County, Texas, 365B. His headstone in the Hempstead Cemetery, Waller County, gives his life as March 3, 1836, to November 25, 1901, and adds that he was "A Confederate Soldier in the Battles of Shiloh, Vicksburg and Galveston." Thus he may indeed have heard the pre-battle speech offered by Thomas Green.
16. McLeary, 709.
17. Ralph A. Wooster, *Texas and Texans in the Civil War* (Austin: Eakin Press. 1995), 64-67. According to Captain Lubbock's report "Col. Tom Green, Major Leon Smith and Capt. James Martin, were among the first, followed closely by the men, cutting the nettings down with their knives." *The Galveston Weekly News*, 7 January 1863,
18. McLeary, 709.

19. *The Galveston News*, 5 January 1863.

20. Magruder to Samuel Cooper, Galveston, February 26, 1863 in *Official Records of the Union and Confederate Navies in the War of the Rebellion*. Series I. Vol. 15, (Washington: Government Printing Office), 215. Hereafter cited as *O. R., Navies*.

21. Statement of M. McCormick, *Bayou City* Pilot, in *The Houston Weekly Telegraph*, 7 January 1863.

22. Statement of Commodore Henry Lubbock of the *Bayou City*, in *The Houston Weekly Telegraph*, 7 January 1863.

23. Robert Morris Franklin, *Battle of Galveston January 1, 1863*. Publication of a speech delivered to the Magruder Camp of the United Confederate Veterans in Galveston. (Galveston: San Luis Press, 1975).

24. Charles B. McNelly, "Mementoes of Charles B. McNelly" in *History of Burton*, compiled by Annie Maud Knittel Avis (Wolfe City, Texas: Henington Publishing Company, 1974), 268

25. Jennings, *A Texas Ranger*, 58.

26. Charles B. McNelly, "Mementoes of Charles B. McNelly," 268.

27. Byron A. Johnson, Director of the Texas Ranger Hall of Fame and Museum, Waco, to authors, 8 April 1997.

28. Reprint of an undated item from *The Houston Telegraph*, printed in *O. R., Navies, Series* I. Vol. 19 (Washington: Government Printing Office, 1905), 470.

29. *The Galveston News*, 5 January 1863.

30. Thomas N. Penrose, "Report of Casualties occurring on board of the U.S.S. *Harriet Lane*, in Galveston Bay, January 1, 1863", prepared for Fleet Surgeon J.M. Foltz, U.S. Navy. *O.R., Navies,* Series I, Vol. 19 (Washington: Government Printing Office, 1905), 443.

31. *The New York Herald*, November 30, 1864.

32. *The New York Herald*, 19 December 1864. Letter of Captain Leon Smith "of the Rebel Navy" to the Editor, written 8 December from Havana, Cuba.

33. Captain Leon Smith to *The New York Herald*, 19 December 1864.

34. J. Bankhead Magruder to General S. Cooper, Galveston, Texas January 2, 1863 in *O.R.*, Series I, Vol. 15 (Washington: Government Printing Office, 1886), 211.

35. Interview and authors' notes with Dan Alger, Curatorial Technician, Texas Ranger Hall of Fame and Museum, Waco, 21 August 1998.

CHAPTER 4
IN THE SWAMPS OF LOUISIANA

1. Jennings, *A Texas Ranger*, 58.

2. Durham, *Nueces Strip*, 45. Durham's count of one-hundred guerrilla scouts seems high. Following the Galveston victory when Green's army was still in Texas, a cavalry brigade report prepared by Green at Columbia, Brazoria County, for the month of February, showed McNelly was stationed near La Grange; he had four officers and twenty-eight men present for duty with forty-one absent, being an aggregate of only seventy-three. In *O.R.*, Series I, Vol. 34, Part II, 1010.

3. Theophilus Noel, *A Campaign from Santa Fe to the Mississippi: Being a history of the Old Sibley Brigade from its First Organization to the present time,* newly edited and with an introduction by Martin Hardwick Hall and Edwin Adams Davis (Houston, Texas: The Stagecoach Press. 1961), 67.

4. Noel, 70-78.

5. Brigadier General Alfred Mouton, C.S.A., Report of Operations, 22 June-4 July, 1863. *O.R.,* Series I, Vol. 26, Part I, 215.

6. Mouton, Report of Operations, 22 June-4 July, 1863. *O.R.,* Series I, Vol. 26, Part I, 215-16.

7. Noel, 134.

8. Jennings, *A Texas Ranger,* 58-59.

9. Charles B. McNelly, "Mementoes of Charles B. McNelly," 268.

10. E.J. Davis to Frederic Speed, June 5, 1864. Colonel Davis at this time was commander of the First Texas Cavalry (Union). *O.R.,* Series I, Vol. 34, Part I, 964.

11. Alwyn Barr, "Thomas Green" in *The New Handbook of Texas,* Vol. 3 (Austin: The Texas State Historical Association), 316-17.

12. Thomas Green to Major Louis Bush, written in camp on July 3, 1863 on Lafourche near Paincourtville, Louisiana. *O.R.,* Series I, Vol. 26, Part I, 228-29.

13. Thomas Green, "To any Confederate Officer. . ." 5 July 1863. *O.R.,* Series I, Vol. 26, Part I, 183.

14. Green to Major Louis Bush, written July 14, 1863 at Assumption Church on LaFourche, *O.R.,* Series I, Vol. 26, Part I, 231.

15. McLeary, 720.

16. Green to Bush, written October 2, 1863, headquarters on Atchafalaya, Camp McBride, Louisiana. *O.R.,* Series I, Vol. 26, Part I, 331.

17. *O.R.,* Series I, Vol. 26, Part I, 330.

18. *O.R.,* Series I, Vol. 26, Part I, 331-32.

19. Noel, 101.

20. E. Kirby Smith, Special Orders 126, Shreveport, Louisiana written September 1, 1863. Original document in Center for American History (hereafter cited as CAH), Austin, Texas.

21. Green to Colonel S.S. Anderson, Vermillionville, Louisiana, written November 25, 1863. Original document in CAH, Austin, Texas.

22. E. Kirby Smith, Special Order No. 221, December 19, 1863 at Shreveport, Louisiana. Original document in CAH.

23. J. Bankhead Magruder. Special Order No. 21. January 21, 1864 written at Houston, Texas. Original in CAH.

24. McLeary, 724.

25. Noel, 134.

26. Charles B. McNelly, "Mementoes of Charles B. McNelly," 268.

27. Noel, quoting General Orders of Major General Richard Taylor, April 13, 1864, 122. Headquarters, Mansfield, District of Western Louisiana.

28. *The Weekly State Gazette,* Austin, 20 April, 1864.

29. *The Weekly State Gazette,* Austin, May 4, 1864. By an odd coincidence Shepard and Sayers were both mentioned in Green's report on the battle of Valverde, written February 22, 1862. In praising certain men, he noted, "Sergt. Maj. C.B. Sheppard [*sic*] shouldered his gun and fought gallantly in the ranks of Captain McPhaill's company in the charge. Lieut. Joseph D. Sayers, adjutant of the Fifth, during the whole day, reminded me of a hero of the days of chivalry. He is a gallant, daring, and dashing soldier, and is as cool in a storm of grape, shell, canister, and musketry as a veteran. I recommend him, through the general, to the President for promotion." *O.R.,* Series I, Vol. 9, 521.

30. Noel, 133.

31. *The Daily Banner,* Brenham, Texas, 15 February 1879.

32. Ibid.

33. Noel, 136.

34. Alabama native Joseph Doss, judging from the concern showed his surviving family members, must have been a popular soldier. Before the war he was a thirty-year-old farmer, living in Milam County, Texas, with wife Mary and children Wash, Mary, Jackson, ages five, four and two years old respectively. Doss' per-

sonal estate was evaluated at $400. *The Population Schedule of the Eighth United States Census, 1860.* Western District of Milam County, Texas, enumerated June 30, 37A.

35. Edmund J. Davis to Captain Frederic Speed, June 5, 1864. *O.R.,* Series I, Vol. 34, Part I, 964.

36. *The Galveston Weekly News*, Galveston, Texas. 5 July 1864. "N." correspondence dated June 7 at West Baton Rouge, Louisiana.

37. Noel, 135-36.

38. B.F. Weems, Acting Adjutant General, to Captain McNelly, commanding scout company, written at Hempstead, Texas 26 April 1865. Original document in CAH.

39. John E. Walker to McNelly, 3 May 1865. Original document in CAH.

40. John E. Walker to McNelly, 5 May 1865. Original document in CAH.

41. John G. Walker Special Order from Hempstead, Texas 23 May 1864. Original document in CAH.

42. James P. Major, Major General C.S. Army, at Houston, 28 May 1865 to "Know all persons that McNally [*sic*] captain of Cavalry. . . ." Original document in CAH.

CHAPTER 5

CAPTAIN - TEXAS STATE POLICE

1. *The American-Statesman*, Austin, Texas. 30 October 1938. F.R. Avis, "Leander Harvey McNelly" in *History of Burton*, Annie Maud Knittel Avis, compiler, Vol. 1 (Wolfe City, Texas, Henington Publishing Company, 1974), 267.

2. *Population Schedule of the Eighth Census of the United States, 1860.* Washington County, 167A, enumerated 20 June. Their post office was Union Hill. Two dwellings later, the enumerator John C. Harris visited the Alfred C. and Anna Hall residence. Mrs. Hall was the sister of Sarah Matson. Their son George, twelve years old in 1860, would later serve under McNelly as a Texas Ranger. Memorial stone, Mt. Zion Cemetery, Burton, Texas.

3. Marriage License, County Clerk's Office, Washington County, Texas. *The American-Statesman*, Austin, 30 October 1938. *Population Schedule of the Ninth Census of the United States, 1870*, Washington County, Post Office Brenham, 256A.

4. Avis, *History of Burton*, Vol. 1, 271. Mrs. Virginia Van Ness and Mrs. Eunice Wooster, "Burials in Mt. Zion Cemetery" in *History of Burton*, Vol. 1, 262-63.

5. F.R. Avis, "Leander Harvey McNelly" in *History of Burton*, Vol. 1, 267.

6. *The Brenham Banner*, 9 May 1884.

7. *The Austin Statesman*, 4 and 7 January 1907, *The Tombstone Prospector* (Tombstone, Arizona), 2 January 1907.

8. *Agriculture Census of Washington County, Texas, 1870.* 10 October, 37. Although the actual agriculture census was made in October the amounts of crops, products and livestock and so on were to be counted as of June 1 of that year.

9. *Agriculture Census of Washington County, Texas, 1870.* 10 October, 37.

10. *Population Schedule of the Ninth Census of the United States, 1870*, Washington County. Enumerated 8 September, their post office was Brenham, 116A. *Roster 3rd District State Police*, Ledger Book 401-1059, 106-107. Original in Texas State Archives, Austin.

11. *Population Schedule of the Ninth Census of the United States, 1870*, Washington County, post office Brenham, 116A.

12. Jennings, *A Texas Ranger*, 59. Commission date from State Police Roster, 2. Ledger Book 401-1059.

13. This item originally appeared in the Brenham *Enquirer* and was reprinted in the Hempstead *Reporter* of 5 August 1870. In *Flake's Daily Bulletin* of Galveston, 21 July, the officers were identified: M.P. Hunnicutt, E.M. Alexander, L.H. McNelly and J. Helm as captains. Lieutenants were Thomas Williams, E. Kellner, A.H. French, L.J. Gallant, N.W. Cuney and Winn Bower, "colored," and Asa P. Lacey. Sergeants were George E. Haynie, Frank D. Fuller, Thomas Sheriff, S.D. Harn, William Gannon, William C. Slade, E.Z. Jones, V.A. Bond, John Hennieman, B.F. Boldridge and A. Lieck.

14. *The San Antonio Daily Express*, Texas. 23 June 1870.

15. *Flake's Semi-Weekly Bulletin*, Galveston, Texas. 2 July 1870.

16. *An Act to Establish a State Police and Provide the Regulation and Government of the Same* (Austin: 4 July 1870), 1. The existing pay vouchers for state policemen are in the Texas State Archives. The item on badges appeared in *The Daily Houston Telegraph*, 18 January 1871, citing an undated article from *The Waco Register*.

17. Carl H. Moneyhon. "James Davidson" in *The New Handbook of Texas*, Vol. 2. (Austin: The Texas State Historical Association, 1996), 522.

18. *An Act to Establish a State Police and Provide the Regulation and Government of the Same* (Austin: 4 July 1870), 2.

19. Blank oath is among the Adjutant General's files, Texas State Archives, Austin. McNelly was commissioned on July 12 and took the oath on July 18.

20. *An Act to Establish a State Police and Provide the Regulation and Government of the Same* (Austin: 4 July 1870), 4.

21. *State Police Ledger Book*. Original in Texas State Archives, Austin. Ledger 401-1001, 32-33. Sammy Tise, *Texas County Sheriffs* (Hallettsville: Tise Genealogical Research, 1989), 30.

22. *Flake's Daily Bulletin*, Galveston, Texas, 25 August 1870; *The Daily State Journal*, 19 July 1870.

23. *The Daily Austin Republican*, 12 July 1870.

24. Ibid.

25. Adjutant General James Davidson to L.H. McNelly, 21 July 1870. Adjutant General Letter Press Book, 401-1030.

26. *The Daily Austin Republican*, 19 July 1870; *The Daily State Journal*, 19 July 1870.

27. *An Act to Establish a State Police and Provide for the Regulation and Government of the Same* (Austin, Texas: 4 July 1870), 4.

28. W.S. Wright to Davidson, 3 August 1870. *State Police Ledger* 401-985, *Index to Letters Received, 1870*, 27, hereafter referred to as *Letters Received*. Davidson to L.H. McNelly, 4 August 1870. Adjutant General Letter Press Book, 401-1030.

29. *The Daily State Journal*, Austin, 26 July 1870 and report to the Bastrop *Advertiser* reprinted in *Flake's Daily Bulletin*, 3 August 1870.

30. *The Houston Daily Telegraph* reprinted in *Flake's Daily Bulletin*, Galveston, Texas, 26 August 1870.

31. The reward was printed in the *Daily State Journal*, 18 August 1870.

32. Pleasant M. Yell to Davidson, 6 August 1870. *Letters Received*. State Police Ledger 401-985, 29.

33. William Green to Davidson, 8 August 1870. *Letters Received*. State Police Ledger 401-985, 31.

34. George W. Farrow to Davidson, 18 August 1870. *Letters Received*. State Police Ledger, 401-985, 44.

35. A. Womack to Davidson, 25 August 1870. *Letters Received*. State Police Ledger, 401-985, 52.

36. McNelly to Davidson. Telegram from Hempstead, 16 August 1870. *Letters Received,* State Police Ledger 401-985, 98.

37. *The Weekly State Journal,* 1 September 1870, citing Dodd's report from Brenham, dated 23 August 1870.

38. McNelly to Davidson. Telegram from Galveston, 20 August 1870. *Letters Received,* State Police Ledger 401-985, 98.

39. McNelly to Davidson, 30 August 1870. *Letters Received,* State Police Ledger, 401-985, 99.

40. *The Daily State Journal,* 1 September 1870.

41. McNelly to Davidson, 30 August 1870. *Letters Received,* State Police Ledger, 401-985, 101; Davidson to McNelly, 22 September 1870. *Letter Press Book,* 401-1030, 290.

42. *The Daily State Journal,* 1 September 1870.

43. Ibid., 21 August 1870.

44. Charles S. Gillespie to Davidson, 4 September 1870. *Letters Received,* State Police Ledger, 401-985, 99. The Stephens name comes from Davidson's letter to Navasota's Policeman S.D. Harn "to arrest Ed. Pearce, John Pearce and Bob Stephens and others of the gang," an order Harn was totally unable to carry out.

45. Chris Emmett, *Shanghai Pierce: A Fair Likeness* (Norman: University of Oklahoma Press, 1953), 68-69. This unlikely account was (perhaps unintentionally) continued by Mrs. Tom Whitehed, writing a "Special" to *The Houston Post* from Brenham in which she wrote, following the description similar to Emmett's, "[Shanghai Pierce] joined McNelly's outfit and was instrumental in the later capture of his five brothers. And McNelly kept his promise never to shoot a Pierce—all were captured alive. That was the kind of man Leander H. McNelly was." Mrs. Whitehed dates the incident as late 1874. *The Houston Post,* 29 October 1961, "Obscure Plot Holds Famed Ranger's Grave," copy in McNelly Vertical File, CAH, Austin.

46. *The Daily State Journal,* 23 August 1870.

47. J.S. Lane, Sheriff Caldwell County. "Return of Crimes Committed" in Caldwell County. Original in Texas State Archives, Box 407-864, #23.

48. John Wesley Hardin, *The Life of John Wesley Hardin, As Written By Himself,* with an introduction by Robert G. McCubbin (1896. Reprint. Norman: University of Oklahoma Press, 1961), 25-26.

49. Rick Miller, *Bloody Bill Longley* (Wolfe City, Texas: Henington Publishing Company, 1996), 26-27.

50. *The Daily Republican,* Austin, 25 August 1870.

51. *The Houston Daily Times,* 20 September 1870.

52. *The Daily Republican,* Austin, 10 September 1870.

53. *The Daily State Journal,* 16 August 1870.

54. *The Daily Houston Telegraph,* 27 November 1870.

55. *The Daily Republican,* Austin, 10 September 1870; 10 October 1870.

56. *The Daily State Journal,* Austin, 5 November 1870.

57. *The Galveston Daily News,* 7 December 1870.

58. *The Galveston Daily News,* 15 December 1870; report of his promotion from the *Daily Houston Telegram,* 10 December 1870. The correct spelling "Robert F. Haskins" is given in the *Report of Arrests,* 401-1001.

59. Adjutant General James A. Davidson to L.H. McNelly, — September 1870. Letter Press Book 401-1030, 217..

60. Davidson to McNelly, 17 September 1870. Letter Press Book 401-1030, 233.

61. Davidson to McNelly, 18 September 1870. Letter Press Book 401-1030, 241-42.

62. Davidson to McNelly, 19 September 1870. Letter Press Book 401-1030, 261.

63. Davidson to McNelly, 20 September 1870. Letter Press Book 401-1030, 266-67.

64. Davidson to McNelly, 22 September 1870. Letter Press Book 401-1030, 300.

65. Davidson to McNelly, 27 September 1870. Letter Press Book, 401-1030, 317. The victim was probably A.D. Kiels because the only Kiels family enumerated in 1860 was that of A.D. and Mahale Kiels, residing at Eagle Valley. Kidd's Mill had a post office during the Confederacy period. *Population Schedule of the Eighth Census of the United States, 1860*, Leon County, Texas, 200B.

66. Davidson to McNelly, 28 September 1870, 329; 29 September 1870, 325-26; 30 September 1870, 359. Letter Press Book, 401-1030.

67. *The Calvert Tribune*, report printed in *The Daily State Journal*, 28 October 1870. Tise, 381.

68. *Population Schedule of the Eighth Census of the United States, 1860*, Montgomery County, Texas, 91B and 1870, 389A. At the time of the Montgomery County census, Womack was identified as the sheriff, a forty-seven-year-old Alabama native who must have been considered among the wealthiest men in the county. He listed his real estate at $4,000 and personal estate at $1,500. His family consisted of his wife Virginia and three children, all in their teens. In 1851 he had married Virginia Johnson in Washington County, Alabama, and their first son, Joseph, was born there about 1853 before they migrated to Texas. Fannie followed in 1855 and Abner in 1856. Before the war he claimed real estate valued at $8,000 and personal estate at $18,000. For help on his farm he had a teenage black boy identified as Dave Womack, undoubtedly a former slave.

69. Davidson to McNelly, 27 October 1870. Letter Press Book 401-1030, 433-34.

70. Davidson to McNelly, 5 November 1870. Letter Press Book 401-1030, 499.

71. *Flake's Daily Bulletin*, Galveston, Texas, 19 November 1870, reprinting an article from the Brazos *Eagle* of 16 November 1870. See Also W.C. Nunn, *Texas Under the Carpetbagger* (Austin: University of Texas Press, 1962), 50-51.

72. Davidson to McNelly, 11 November 1870, 522.

73. Davidson to McNelly, 5 and 7 December 1870, 608 and 622.

74. Davidson to McNelly, 12 December 1870, 654; 13 December 1870, 659.

75. *The Daily Houston Telegraph*, 13 December 1870.

76. Davidson to McNelly, 13 December 1870, 660.

77. *The Daily State Journal*, Austin, 27 January 1871.

CHAPTER 6
GUNFIRE IN WALKER COUNTY

1. *The Galveston Daily News*, 19 November 1870. See also W.C. Nunn, *Texas Under the Carpetbaggers* (Austin: University of Texas Press, 1962), 53-54. *State Police Roster*, 3rd District, 106. Ledger 401-1059, original in Texas State Archives. *The San Antonio Daily Herald*, 20 December 1870.

2. *The Galveston Daily News*, 15 December 1870.

3. *Flake's Semi-Weekly Bulletin*, Galveston, 24 December 1870.

4. *The Galveston Daily News*, 15 December 1870.

5. Ibid.

6. Ibid. George B. Dealy, "Alfred Horatio Belo" in *The New Handbook of Texas*. Vol. 1, 479-80.

7. *The Galveston Daily News*, 15 December 1870.

8. *The Galveston Daily News*, 15-16 December 1870. Adjutant General James A. Davidson to L.H. McNelly, 16 December, 17 December 1870. Letter Press Book 401-1030, 678, 681-82. *The Houston Daily Telegram*, 14 December 1870.

9. *The Houston Daily Telegraph*, 14 December 1870.

10. Davidson to McNelly, 26 December 1870. Letter Press Book 401-1030, 769.

11. *Report of Arrests* [State Police] Ledger Book 401-1001, 98-99. Original ledger in Texas State Archives, Austin.

12. Davidson to McNelly, 21 December 1870, Letter Press Book 401-1030, 710.

13. *The Houston Daily Telegraph*, 18 December 1870.

14. The reward notice is in *Records of the Executive Office. E. J. Davis - Richard Coke, January 8, 1870 - February 9, 1874.* Microfilm: Texas State Archives. The reward was also published in the *State Journal*, 20 December, stating the murder was on or about 9 December.

15. *The Daily State Journal*, Austin, Texas 27 January 1871. Charles Taylor Rather, "Around The Square In 1862 With A Barefoot Boy" in *Huntsville And Walker County, Texas: A Bicentennial History*, compiled and edited by D'Anne McAdams Crews (Huntsville: Sam Houston State University Press, 1976), 139. Charles Rather was the son of George W. Rather and witnessed a portion of the subsequent difficulties.

16. Henry W. Graber, *A Terry Texas Ranger: The Life Record of H.W. Graber.* 1916. Reprint. Facsimile reproduction of original with new introduction by Thomas W. Cutrer (Austin: State House Press, 1987), 333-34.

17. Davidson to McNelly, 26 December 1870. Letter Press Book 401-1030, 761.

18. J.R. Burnett, *Message of Gov. Edmund J. Davis with Documents in Relation to Lawlessness and Crime in Hill and Walker Counties* (Austin: J.G. Tracy, State Printer, 1871). J.R. Burnett to Governor Davis from Huntsville, 12 January 1871, 22.

19. J.R. Burnett to Governor Davis from Huntsville, 12 January 1871, 22.

20. Statement of Captain McNelly in "Proceedings of G.C.M. [General Courts Martial] for the Trial of Cyrus Hess & Others." Huntsville, Texas 26 February 1871, 1. Original in Adjutant General's Files, Texas State Archives.

21. Statement of Thomas Keesee in "Proceedings of G.C.M. for the trial of Cyrus Hess & Others." Huntsville, Texas 26 February 1871, 4. Original in Adjutant General's Files, Texas State Archives.

22. *The Daily State Journal* (Austin) 27 January 1871. Statement of Captain McNelly in "Proceedings of G.C.M. for the Trial of Cyrus Hess & Others." Huntsville, Texas 26 February 1871, 1.

23. Correspondence of W.E. Horne to Adjutant General James A. Davidson. 24 February 1871. Original document in Texas State Archives. Sammy Tise, *Texas County Sheriffs*, 518. The position of county sheriff was indeed tenuous in the 1870s. *The Galveston Daily News* of 20 December reported that W.H. Stewart, "elected by the Loyal League at the last election" had been removed from office on 19 December by order of the governor. Michael Butler, a thirty-year old native of Ireland and Collector of Customs residing in Brazoria County in 1870, was appointed sheriff on 21 December 1870 but served only until April 1871. Tise, 518. *Population Schedule of the Ninth Census of the United States, 1870.* Brazoria County, Texas, 581B.

24. Correspondence of W.E. Horne to Adjutant General James A. Davidson. 24 February 1871. Original document in Texas State Archives.

25. McNelly interview, "The Huntsville Affair Once More" in *The Galveston Daily News*, 8 March 1871.

26. Statement of Thomas Keesee in "Proceedings of G.C.M. for the Trial of Cyrus Hess & Others." Huntsville, Texas 26 February 1871, 4, original in Adjutant

General's Files, Texas State Archives. J.R. Burnett to Governor Davis from Huntsville, 12 January 1871, 22.

27. Special Order No. — "In the Trial of Nat Outlaw, Citizen" of James A. Davidson, from Huntsville, 6 March 1871..

28. *The Galveston Daily News*, 9 March 1871, citing dispatches from Huntsville, 4 March 1871 and "General Court Martial Convened Huntsville Walker county for the trial of Thomas Walker." Original document in Texas State Archives.

29. Charles Taylor Rather, 139.

30. Court Martial Order No. 4, Huntsville, Texas. 2 March 1871. Adjutant General's Files, Texas State Archives.

31. Edmund J. Davis, 22 March 1871. Original document in Adjutant General's Files, Texas State Archives.

32. Correspondence of J.H. Banton and Others to Adjutant General James A. Davidson, Huntsville, Texas 4 March 1871. Original document in Adjutant General's Files, Texas State Archives.

33. Charles Taylor Rather, 140.

34. *The Galveston Daily News*, 8 March 1871. Although McNelly was frequently ordered to provide delinquent reports of his actions, in this case what he says is true. Davidson's record of letters received show that McNelly on 11 January wrote a report relating to the escape and his attempt to recapture the prisoners, and also inquiring about the reward; on 13 January his report related to the shooting affray in the court room; then on 4 February he wrote indicating Wright and Parrish had gone to Arkansas, and finally on 19 February his report again dealt with the shooting affray and escape of prisoners.

35. *The Galveston Daily News,* 8 March 1871.

36. *The Galveston Daily News*, 11 March 1871.

37. *The Daily Houston Telegraph*, 15 March 1871, and *The Daily State Journal*, 17 March 1871.

38. *The Galveston Daily News*, 14 March 1871. Martial law in Walker County was revoked on 20 March 1871. Singletary, Otis A., "The Texas Militia During Reconstruction" in *The Southwestern Historical Quarterly*, Vol. 60, No. 1 (July 1956).

CHAPTER 7
AFTER THE WALKER COUNTY AFFAIR

1. *Message of Gov. Edmund J. Davis, with Documents in Relation to Lawlessness and Crime in Hill and Walker Counties* (Austin: J.G. Tracy, State Printer, 1871), 4-5.

2. *The State Journal*, Austin, 22 January 1871, noted in *The San Antonio Daily Herald*, 24 January. This report is from Navasota and states that McNelly and Attorney Horne had just arrived the night of 19 January from Huntsville.

3. Sammy Tise, *Texas County Sheriffs* (Tise Genealogical Research, Hallettsville, Texas 1989), 518.

4. [William Steele] *A List of Fugitives from Justice* (Austin, 1878), 150. Facsimile edition entitled *Fugitives from Justice: The Notebook of Texas Ranger Sergeant James B. Gillett* (Austin: State House Press, 1997).

5. *Message of Gov. Edmund J. Davis, with Documents in Relation to Lawlessness and Crime in Hill and Walker Counties* (Austin: J.G. Tracy, State Printer, 1871), 21. Frequently Parrish is identified as McParrish, although the "Mc" was only part of his middle name, the correct surname being Parrish. Before the war the head of the Parrish household was North Carolinian W.A. Parrish, a farmer

who claimed $8,600 in real estate and personal estate of $15,582. He was 54-years old. His wife Catherine E. was only 35-years old, hailing from Tennessee. At the time they had five children: Joel, E. Lee, John Mc., nine years old, William G., seven years old, and Lucinda E., all born in Texas. No doubt John was better known as "Mac." *Population Schedule of the Eighth Census of the United States, 1860*, Walker County, enumerated July 9. 116.

6. Governor E.J. Davis to Adjutant General James Davidson, 15 February 1871.

7. Graber, 334. On 4 February, while in Harrison County, McNelly wrote to Davidson that Wright and Parrish had gone into Arkansas. Ledger, *Letters Received*, 4 February 1871, 401-701, 348.

8. James A. Davidson to L.H. McNelly, 21 February 1871. Letter Press Book 401-1031. McNelly to Davidson, 15 March 1871. *Letters Received*, Adjutant General's Files. 401-701.

9. James A. Davidson to R. Green, Esq., Secretary, Houston Direct Naval Company, 27 February 1871. Letter Press Book 401-1031, 493.

10. *The San Antonio Daily Herald,* 12 January 1871, citing a report from the Galveston *News*.

11. James A. Davidson to Captains State Police, circular dated 20 March 1871. Letter Press Book 401-1031.

12. *The San Antonio Daily Herald,* 25 January 1871.

13. Ibid., 1 March 1871.

14. James A. Davidson to L. H. McNelly, 10 March 1871. Letter Press Book 401-1031.

15. *The Galveston Daily News*, 8 March 1871.

16. James A. Davidson to L.H. McNelly, 17 April 1871.

17. James A. Davidson to L.H. McNelly, 18 April 1871.

18. *The Galveston Weekly News*, 3 April 1871.

19. James A. Davidson to L.H. McNelly, 26 April 1871. Letter Press Book 401-1031. McNelly to Davidson, *Letters Received* - Adjutant General's File, File 401-701.

20. Davidson to Captain G.S. Whitmore, April 28, 1871. Letter Press Book 401-1031.

21. *The Galveston Weekly News*, 24 April and 1 May, 1871; McNelly to Davidson, 3 May 1871; Davidson to McNelly, 29 May 1871. The Roster 3rd District shows Steen was commissioned July 8 but not accepted until August 10; his oath is also dated August 10, 1870. He had been dismissed on November 30, 1870, then reinstated on December 1. The date of his death in the record shows April 27, 1871. *The Population Schedule of the Ninth Census of the United States, 1870,* Freestone County, shows a "Robin" Steen family, which probably is the state policeman. His age in 1870 shows he was forty-one years old and was born in Arkansas. Enumerated 27 August, 56A. *Population Schedule of the Eighth Census of the United States, 1860*. Robertson County, Texas, 178A. The Browns' post office was Sterling, enumerated 18 July 1860. The census shows Green Brown, a forty-six-year-old farmer from North Carolina as head of household with no real estate and personal estate of $1,935. There is no woman listed in the household; of the six Browns besides Green Brown in the family there is a two-year-old son and a six-year-old daughter. There is an eight-year-old named "T.C. Brown" who is probably Code. The 1870 census of Robertson County clarifies things somewhat: Greenwood Brown's first name appears to be "Gaun" age fifty-eight year old. The three others in the household are John, Calvin — now an eighteen-year-old laborer — and twelve-year-old Sarah, 271B. Following their service as members of the state police the Trammells became desperadoes themselves. Merrick Trammel was

killed on June 13, 1875 near Groesbeck, Limestone County, by M.D.L. Harkraw. Trammell, who had "long been a terror to this county, defying the law" was suspected of having killed five or six men and having burned down the court house. There was a $300 reward for his capture. . *The Daily Democratic Statesman*, 18 June 1875 and *The Galveston Daily News*, 18 June 1875.

22. Davidson to McNelly, 1 May 1871. Letter Press Book 401-1032, 42.

23. Davidson to McNelly, 10 May 1871. Letter Press Book 401-1032, 143.

24. Davidson to McNelly, 17 May 1871. Letter Press Book 401-1032, 212.

25. Davidson to McNelly, 29 May 1871. Letter Press Book 401-1032, 284.

26. Davidson to McNelly, 30 May 1871. Letter Press Book 401-1032, 289.

27. Davidson to George W. Farrow, 6 June 1871. Letter Press Book 401-1032, 351-352.

28. Davidson to McNelly, 12 June 1871. Letter Press Book 401-1032, 407.

29. Letter of Joseph Lancaster published in *The New York Tribune*, 10 July 1871, headlined "Ku-Klux in Texas."

30. *The Galveston Daily News*, 23 September 1868. A lengthy description by Lancaster of his son's final hours appeared in *The Clarksville Standard*, 14 November 1868, from *The Navasota Ranger*.

31. J.W. McCown, Sr., "Reports of Crimes — Washington County," 11 July 1870. Original in Texas State Archives, 401-864, folder # 41..

32. *The New York Tribune*, 10 July 1871.

33. *Flake's Daily Bulletin*, Galveston. 18 July 1871.

34. Davidson to Farrow, 14 June 1871. Letter Press Book 410-1032, 430-35. Adolph Cramer was a 34-year-old Prussian native living in Houston's 3rd Ward. Although he claimed $5,700 worth of real estate and $800 in personal estate no occupation was given. At the time of the census he had a 24-year-old wife, Louisiana born Sarah, and two children age seven and two years, both Texas born. *Population Schedule of the Ninth Census of the United States, 1870,* Harris County, 1870, 582A. Their post office was Houston. Census enumeration by William S. Clayton.

35. Davidson to Farrow, 14 June 1871. A.B. Cunningham was a 26-year-old Louisiana native, living in Bryan, Brazos County, practicing law. He had a wife, 20-year-old Jane, also from Louisiana, and one child, one-year-old Mary, Texas born. *Population Schedule of the Ninth Census of the United States, 1870*, Brazos County, 114B. Enumeration by W.B. Foreman.

36. Davidson to Farrow, 15 June 1871.

37. Davidson to J. Lancaster, Esq., 28 June 1871. Letter Press Book 401-1032 and Letter Press Book 401-614, 19 June 1872, 460. The 1860 census show William Lancaster as twelve-years old and older brother Frank as fifteen, both working as printers. Their father is listed as editor with real estate valued at $10,000 and personal estate at $2,000. *Population Schedule of the Eighth Census of the United States, 1860*, Washington County, 28 July, 187B. See also "Joseph Lancaster" by Hobart Huson in *The New Handbook of Texas*. Vol. 4, 52.

38. Davidson to McNelly, 30 June 1871. Letter Press Book 401-1032, 666.

39. Davidson to McNelly, 30 June 1871. Letter Press Book 401-1032, 668.

40. Davidson to McNelly, 5 July 1871. Letter Press Book 401-1032, 669.

41. Davidson to McNelly, 8 August 1871. Letter Press Book 401-1032, 921.

42. Davidson to McNelly, 9 August 1871. Letter Press Book 401-1032, 932.

43. Davidson to McNelly, 14 August 1871. Letter Press Book 401-1032, 967.

44. Joseph Jung was appointed by General J.J. Reynolds to the office of Bastrop County Sheriff on August 5, 1869 by Special Order # 183; he was then elected sheriff on December 3, 1869 and served until November 11, 1871 when he resigned. Sammy Tise, *Texas County Sheriffs* (Hallettsville, Texas, Tise

Genealogical Research,1989), 31.

45. *The Weekly Democratic Statesman*, 15 and 17 August, 1871.

46. *The San Antonio Daily Herald*, 24 August 1871. German born August Werner was a farmer prior to becoming a member of the State Police, was married and had children. He had been commissioned as a private in the police force on November 12, 1870 in the 3rd District. He was then transferred to the 4th District to work out of Bastrop. He had resigned on February 11, 1871, was reinstated and then dismissed on June 22. He was reinstated on August 7 only to be killed in the line of duty a week later. The police record of August Werner is in *State Police Ledger* 401-1059, 108-09, 290, 300-01. Original in Texas State Archives, Austin. *Population Schedule of the 8th Census of the United States, 1860*. Austin County, post office Industry, enumerated 20 July 1860, 202A & B.

47. *The Bastrop Advertiser*, 12 August 1871; *The Galveston Daily News*, 15 and 16 August 1871.

48. McNelly to Davidson, 1 September 1871. *Letters Received*, Adjutant General's File, 401-702.

49. *Court Record [Book] E District Court*, Bastrop, Texas, 3 April 1872, 572.

50. *Court Record [Book] E District Court*, Bastrop, Texas, 7 August 1872, 684.

51. *Court Record [Book] E District Court*, Bastrop, Texas, 14 August 1872, 445.

52. *Court Record [Book] E District Court*, Bastrop, Texas, 18 August 1872, 462.

53. *Report of Arrests*. Ledger Book 401-1002, 2-3.

54. *The Brenham Banner*, 2 November 1871.

55. *The Brenham Banner*, 26 October 1871.

56. *Flakes Daily Bulletin*, 22 September 22, 1870, reprinting an article from the *Brenham Banner*, 20 September 1870.

57. [Frank L. Britton] *Report of the Adjutant General of the State of Texas, for the year 1872* (Austin: James P. Newcomb and Company, 1872), 12; Hardin, John Wesley, *The Life of John Wesley Hardin, As Written by Himself* (Norman: University of Oklahoma Press, 1961) with introduction by Robert G. McCubbin. *The Houston Daily Telegraph,* 25 October 1871, citing a report from *The Gonzales Inquirer* of 21 October. *The San Antonio Daily Herald*, 31 October 1871. The spelling of Green Paramore's name has varied greatly in differing accounts. Hardin used the "Paramoor" version; the name is "Perrymore" in the 1872 *Adjutant General's Report*; the 1870 Gonzales County census, shows Green "Paramore" as a 25-year-old black male with occupation given as "Laborer." He was born in Georgia and had but $100 in personal estate. He and his wife Lucinda, age thirty, a native of Mississippi, are shown to have three children, Cory, Rena and James, all Texas born. The census was enumerated 3 October 1870 by M. H. Beaty. 471A & B. The San Antonio *Herald* and the 1870 census use the "Paramore" spelling which has been used throughout.

In addition to Hardin's autobiography two excellent biographies are Richard C. Marohn's *The Last Gunfighter: John Wesley Hardin* (College Station: The Early West, 1995) and Leon Metz's *John Wesley Hardin: Dark Angel of Texas* (El Paso: Mangan Books, 1996; reprint Norman: University of Oklahoma Press, 1997).

CHAPTER 8
A DEATH WARRANT AND A TRIP TO THE RIO GRANDE

1. Merline Pitre, "Matthew Gaines" in *The New Handbook of Texas*, Vol. 3 (Austin: Texas State Historical Association, 1996), 43.

2. *The Galveston Daily News*, 16 February 1872.

3. Alwyn Barr and Robert A. Calvert, Editors. *Black Leaders For Their Times* (Austin: Texas State Historical Association, 1981), 68-72. And *Cases Argued and*

Decided in The Supreme Court of the State of Texas. "Gaines v. The State."
Reported by Terrell & Walker. (St. Louis: The Gilbert Book Company, 1882) originally printed in 1875. Vol. 39, 528-614.

4. Merline Pitre, "Matthew Gaines" in *The New Handbook of Texas*, Vol. 3, 43.

5. *The Galveston Daily News*, 25 April 1872. Article contributed by "D. R."
Special telegram from Corsicana, dated 24 April.

6. Original reward document is in the Texas State Archives, Austin. Also
printed in *The Galveston Daily News*, 27 April 1872.

7. E.J. Davis to James A. Nelms, 15 January 1871. Letter Press Book of E. J.
Davis. Box 301-89, 28. Tise, Sammy, *Texas County Sheriffs* (Hallettsville, Texas:
Tise Genealogical Research, 1989), 389.

8. *The Galveston Daily News*, 30 April 1872.

9. *The Galveston Daily News*, 4 June 1872, reprinting item from the *Daily
Democratic Statesman*.

10. *The Galveston Daily News*, 4 June 1872.

11. *The Galveston Daily News*, 17 August 1872.

12. *The Daily State Journal*, 12 June 1872.

13. Ibid. Tise, *Texas County Sheriffs*, 389; and W.P. Murchison & William
Polk, "James A. Nelms" in *Navarro County History*, 1978, Vol. 2, (Navarro
County Historical Society, Dallas, Texas, Taylor Publishing Co.), 156. *The
Democratic Statesman*, 6 June 1872. *The Galveston Daily News*, 6 June 1872.

14. *The Galveston Daily News*, 6 June 1872.

15. *The Galveston Daily News*, 6 June 1872. Special from Hearne dated June 5.

16. Ibid.

17. Ibid.

18. *The Galveston Daily News*, 7 June 1872. Reports from Austin and
Hempstead, June 6.

19. *The Daily State Journal* (Austin), 7 June 1872.

20. *The San Antonio Daily Herald*, 13 and 18 June 1872

21. *The Galveston Daily News*, 7 June 1872. Report from Hempstead, June 6.

22. *The Galveston Daily News*, 7 June 1872. Report from "P." at Houston,
June 6.

23. *The Galveston Daily News*, 14 June 1872.

24. Testimony of Levi English, House Representatives Report, 43rd Congress,
1st Session, Executive Document #257, Deposition #572, *Depredations on the
Frontiers of Texas,* 11. This so-called "Robb Report" prepared by committee members Thomas P. Robb, Richard H. Savage and Thomas O. Osborn, was the result of
their inquiry into the depredations on the Texas frontier, examining reports of
losses from Mexicans as well as Indians.

25. Davidson to McNelly, 9 July 1872. Letter Press Book 401-615. This also
appeared in *The Galveston Daily News*, 14 July 1872.

26. *The Galveston Daily News*, 16 July 1872.

27. Original Muster Roll in Adjutant General Papers, Texas State Archives.
"Escamino" may be "Escamillo." Apparently McNelly had more applicants than
allowed. Four young men from Crockett, Houston County, on July 3, "leave today with Captain McNelly for the West, to operate against the Indians, Mexicans
and white renegades, who are committing depredations on the frontier." They were
unable to join the force. *Flakes Semi-Weekly Bulletin*, 10 July 1872, citing
Crockett's *East Texas Herald* of 3 July.

28. *The Daily State Journal* (Austin), 10 July 1872.

29. *The Daily State Journal*, 11 July 1872. An "official" version of the talk
appeared in the 12 July issue of the *Daily State Journal*.

30. Davidson Special Order, 13 July 1872. Letter Press Book 401-615, 151.

31. E.J. Davis to "Commanding Officer of United States Troops," 13 July 1872. Letter Press Book 401-615, 155.

32. *The San Antonio Daily Herald*, reprinted in *The Daily State Journal* of 23 July 1872.

33. *The San Antonio Daily Herald*, 17 July 1872.

34. Ruben E. Ochoa, "Maverick County," in *The New Handbook of Texas*, Vol. 4, 577.

35. Reward dated August 12 appeared in the *Daily State Journal* 19 September 1872. See also Tom Lea, *The King Ranch* (Boston: Little Brown & Co., 1957) and *The San Antonio Daily Herald*, 15 and 16 August 1872, and *The Galveston Daily News*, 12 October 1872.

36. Davidson to McNelly, 12 August 1872. Letter Press Book. 401-616, 20.

37. Davidson to McNelly, 27 September 1872. Letter Press Book. 401-616, 335.

38. Davidson to McNelly, 30 August 1872. Letter Press Book. 401-616, 145.

39. Davidson to McNelly, 31 August 1872. Letter Press Book. 401-616, 153. *Flake's Semi-Weekly*, 25 May 1872. J.M. Brock was suspected by some to have instigated the riot in Tyler which resulted in the deaths of attorneys Reuben E. House and Fred A. Godley, allegedly at the hands of a State Policeman. Brock shortly thereafter disappeared, but on April 27 his body was discovered in a Wood County creek by young boys fishing. It was learned that Brock, a week before, had been taken into the woods and shot by a "posse" of about a dozen men. Freedman Shed Riley claimed to have killed some of the men guilty of Brock's murder.

40. Davidson to McNelly, [undated] September 1872. Letter Press Book. 401-616, 176.

41. *The Galveston Daily News*, 28 September 1872, reprinting article from the Canton *News*, 12 September 1872.

42. Davidson to Sheriff J.T. Holbert, 23 August 1872. Letter Press Book. 401-616, 99.

43. *The Daily Democratic Statesman*, 28 November 1872, summarizing an article from *The Quitman News*.

44. Davidson to McNelly, 27 September 1872. Letter Press Book 401-616, 335.

45. Davidson to McNelly, 27 September 1872. Letter Press Book 401-616, 326.

46. Davidson to McNelly, 3 October 1872. Letter Press Book 401-616, 399. Knittel is found in the *Population Schedule of the Tenth Census of the United States, 1880*, Washington County, 14 June, 225A.

47. McNelly to Davidson, 3 October 1872. Letters Received. Book 401-703. Adjutant General's Papers. Additional details in *The Daily Democratic Statesman*, 12 October 1872, reprinting article from the Brenham *Times*. Joelyn Spencer, "Adolph Neese" in *Fayette County Heritage,* Vol. 2 (Dallas: Curtis Media, Inc. 1996), 486.

48. *The Brenham Times*, reprinted in *The Galveston Daily News*, 12 October 1872.

49. *The Lone Star Ranger* (Austin), reprinted in *The Galveston Daily News*, 21 November 1872.

50. Davidson to McNelly, 8 October 1872. Letter Press Book. 401-616, 444. Leon Metz, *John Wesley Hardin: Dark Angel of Texas* (El Paso: Mangan Books, 1996), 83-86.

51. *The Galveston Daily News*, 17, 20 and 24 October 1872. Report from Anderson, 10 October 1872. The census of Grimes County, Texas, 1870, shows Paul Sante, a 58-year-old freedman and farm laborer. Anderson was the family's

post office, 237.

52. *The Galveston Daily News*, 20 October 1872, and *The San Antonio Daily Herald*, 24 October 1872.

53. *The Daily Democratic Statesman*, 19 December 1872. Carl H. Moneyhon, "James Davidson" in *The New Handbook of Texas*, Vol. 2, 522.

54. The amount of money missing is in "James Davidson," *The New Handbook of Texas*, Vol. 2, 522. Further details in Letter Press Book 401-618. Adjutant General F.L. Britton to McNelly, 20 January 1873.

55. E.J. Davis to S.M. Swanson, 24 December 1872. Letter Press Book, Box 301-91, 207. This would be the Marine National Bank, 79 & 80 Wall Street. H. Wilson, compiler, *The New York City Register* (New York: John F. Trow, 1871), 16.

56. *The Galveston Daily News*, 1 January 1873. Britton's letter to Davis of 26 December 1872 appeared first in the *Daily State Journal* and reprinted in the *News*, 1 January 1873.

57. *The Galveston Daily News*, 1 January 1873.

58. *The Daily Democratic Statesman*, 31 December 1872.

59. Britton to McNelly, 20 January 1873. Letter Press Book, 401-618. 231.

60. The original is now in the Texas Ranger Hall of Fame & Museum, Waco, Texas. Information on Inglis from *Lovell's Montreal Directory, for 1875-76*, 83.

61. Davis to Hunnicutt, 5 February 1873. Letter Press Book, Box 301-91, 467.

62. McNelly to Britton, 12 February 1873. Letters Received, 401-703, 565. W.D. Wood, *Reminiscences of Reconstruction in Texas and Reminiscences of Texas and Texans Fifty Years Ago* (Privately printed, [San Marcos, Texas?] 1902.), 19.

63. F.L. Britton to Mrs. L.H. McNelly, 11, 14 and 15 January 1873. Letter Press Book 401-618, 62, 99, 117, Adjutant General Files.

CHAPTER 9
1873— FOLLOWING THE STATE POLICE EXPERIENCE

1. Britton to McNelly, 12 February (497), 20 February (555), 5 March (622). Letter Press Book 401-618, Adjutant General's Files.

2. *The Brenham Banner*, 22 February 1873.

3. *The Daily State Journal*, 11 October 1872.

4. *The Democratic Statesman*, 14 November 1872. Letter from Bastrop dated 1 November 1872.

5. *The Daily State Journal*, 20 November 1872; "Frank L. Britton" in *The New Handbook of Texas*, Vol. 1 (Austin: The Texas State Historical Association), 744.

6. McNelly to Britton, 24 November 1872. *Letters Received*, Adjutant General's Files 401-703.

7. F.L. Britton, *Report of the Adjutant General of the State of Texas for the Year 1873* (Austin: Cardwell & Walker, Printers, 1874), 118.

8. Green Harris to F.L. Britton, April 14, 1873, 363. *Letters Received*, Adjutant General's Files, 401-703.

9. Ed Bartholomew, *The Encyclopedia of Texas Ghost Towns* (Fort Davis, Texas. 1982), 48.

10. McNelly to Britton, no date or place but received 1 December 1870. *Letters Received* Adjutant General's Files, 401-703, 562.

11. *Population Schedule of the Eighth Census of the United States, 1860; Slave Inhabitants of the County of Washington*. 267A-B. *Free Inhabitants of Washington County, 1860* shows the A.C. Hall family, post office Union Hill, enumerated 20 June by John C. Harris, 167A. By 1870 George is no longer with his

parents, but his location has not been determined. A.C. Hall by 1870 resided in neighboring Fayette County. His pre-Civil War real and personal estate had been drastically altered, now claiming but $4,500 in real estate and $1,000 in personal estate. Within the household are listed A.C., his wife A.E. [Anna Elizabeth?], Clara E. and Thomas. They are shown to reside "West of Caldwell Road." *Population Schedule of the Ninth Census of the United States, 1870* Fayette County Texas, 486B.

12. Mary Ellen McNelly, "The McNelly Family From Ireland to Virginia to Texas." Genealogical data courtesy Mary Ellen McNelly, Sister Clared. Transcript copy in possession of authors, 8.

13. Frederick Nolan, *Bad Blood: The Life and Times of the Horrell Brothers* (Stillwater, Oklahoma, Barbed Wire Press, 1994), 24-26. *Report of the Adjutant General of the State of Texas for the Year 1873*, 127.

14. Shepherd to F. L. Britton 18 March 1873. Letter Press Book Adjutant General's Files, 144.

15. Nolan, 27. *The San Antonio Daily Herald*, 25 March 1873. *Report of the Adjutant General of the State of Texas for the Year 1873*, 128.

16. Britton to McNelly, 10 March 1873. Letter Press Book. Adjutant General's Letters 401-619, 41.

17. Britton to McNelly, 13 March 1873. Letter Press Book, 401-619, 106.

18. Britton to McNelly, 15 March 1873. Letter Press Book, 401-619, 141.

19. Britton to McNelly, 18 March 1873. Letter Press Book, 401-619, 152.

20. Britton to McNelly, 25 March 1873. Letter Press Book, 401-619, 183. Harn was commissioned as surgeon of the Eighth Regiment of the Texas State Guard, 23 September 1870. Frank L. Britton, *Report of the Adjutant General of the State of Texas for the Year 1872* (Austin: James P. Newcomb and Company, 1873), 45.

21. Britton to McNelly, 31 March 1873. Letter Press Book. Adjutant General Files. 401-619, 287.

22. Britton to McNelly, 4 April 1873. Letter Press Book. Adjutant General Files 401-619, 343.

23. Britton to McNelly, 17 April 1873. Letter Press Book. Adjutant General Files 401-619, 439.

24. Britton to McNelly, 2 May 1873. Letter Press Book. Adjutant General Files 401-619, 588.

25. Correspondence: Fred J. Romanski, Archivist at National Archives to authors, 21 June 1996. Record Group 217.

26. *The Weekly Democratic Statesman*, 1 and 8 May 1873.

27. *The Daily Democratic Statesman*, 26 September 1872.

28. [Frank L. Britton], *Report of the Adjutant General of the State of Texas for the Year 1873* (Austin: Cardwell & Walker Printers), 1874, 5.

29. *The Daily State Journal*, 21 January 1873.

30. *The Daily State Journal*, 11 April 1873. The "Roll of Honor" listed the following policemen "who have fallen in the line of duty": Jim Smalley, killed 22 January 1871; G. Bell, killed February, 1871; Robert Stein, killed 21 April 1871; Ed. W. Briggs, killed 22 May 1871; August Werner, killed 11 August 1871; Wm. Grigg, killed 11 October 1871; Green Perrymore [*sic*], killed 19 October 1871; J.A. Stewart, killed 16 May 1871; Captain Thomas Williams, Wesley Cherry, James N. Daniels and Andrew Melville, killed 11 March 1873; the article concluded by stating that a list of wounded, who "also deserve their country's notice" was available in the adjutant general's office.

31. *The Daily Democratic Statesman,* 15 April 1873. The "Roll of Horror" listed the following "quiet and peaceable citizens . . . who have been murdered":

D.C. Applewhite and Josiah Bradshaw in Limestone County; James Flanigan in Harrison County; F.A. Godley and R.E. House in Smith County; Jack Roach in Anderson County; Birdwell in Nacogdoches County; T.J. Smith and William Fly in Guadalupe County; Martin Taylor and William Morrison [*sic*, Morris] in McMullen County; Henry and William Kelley in DeWitt County; John Mitchell in Ellis County; Westfall in Wilson County; John Thompson in Grayson County and Ebenezer Davis in Hopkins County. Prendergast added that the "list might be greatly extended with but little trouble."

32. *The Daily Democratic Statesman*, 23 April 1873.
33. John M. Redmon to F.L. Britton, 1 May 1873, from Denton, Texas. Adjutant General Files.
34. *The Union Intelligencer*, Dallas 3 May 1873.
35. *The Dallas Weekly Herald*, 26 April 1873.

CHAPTER 10
AN INTERLUDE FOR MCNELLY

1. Tax Rolls, Washington County, Texas, 1872 and 1873. Microfilm Collection, Texas State Library.
2. *The Weekly Democratic Statesman*, 31 July 1873.
3. Victor M. Rose, *The Texas Vendetta; or, The Sutton Taylor Feud* (New York: J.J. Little & Co., 1880), facsimile edition by Frontier Press of Houston, Texas, 1956, 29-30. The names of Wells and Ragland appear in *The Galveston Daily News* of 27 September 1874 presenting a brief history of the feud.
4. Marriage License, #680, Marriage License Book C, 221. Records of the County Clerk, DeWitt County. J.W. Cox and William Mitchell were the only two witnesses recorded.
5. Both James W. Cox, age forty-seven and Tumlinson, age fifty-eight, took their oaths on 13 July 1870. Cox was stationed at Clinton while Tumlinson was stationed at Yorktown, DeWitt County. *State Police Roster*, Texas State Library.
6. *Report of Arrests*, State Police Ledger Book, 401-1001, 278-79.
7. *Hardin*, 81.
8. *The Weekly Democratic Statesman*, 31 July 1873.
9. *Report of Arrests*, State Police Ledger Book, 401-1001, 34-35. Victor M. Rose devoted an entire chapter to the killing of the Kelly brothers, reprinting the lengthy articles which had appeared in the *Daily Austin Republican* of 1 November 1870.
10. For a thorough overview of the feud see C.L. Sonnichsen's *I'll Die Before I'll Run: The Story of the Great Feuds of Texas* (New York: Harper & Brothers, 1951). A more recent overview is Chuck Parsons' "The DeWitt County Feud" in *The History of DeWitt County, Texas*, (Dallas: Curtis Media Corporation, 1991), 30-45. Versions focusing on the Taylor side include Jack Hays Day's *The Sutton-Taylor Feud* (San Antonio: Sid Murray and Son, 1937) and *The Taylor Party* by Eddie Day Truitt (Wortham, Texas: privately printed, 1992). For the Sutton side see *The Sutton-Taylor Feud* by Robert C. Sutton, Jr., (Quanah, Texas: Nortex Press, 1974).
11. *The Dallas Daily Commercial*, 13 March 1874.
12. *The Galveston Daily News*, article reprinted in *The San Antonio Daily Express*, 12 April 1874.
13. *The San Antonio Daily Express*, 12 April 1874.
14. Ibid., 9 June 1874.
15. *The Galveston Daily News*, 6 July 1874.
16. Ibid., 1 July 1874. DeWitt's letter, written from Cuero, was dated 28 June.
17. *The New York Times*, 30 June 1873.

CHAPTER 11
MCNELLY AND THE SUTTON-TAYLOR FEUD

1. *The Daily Democratic Statesman*, 14 July 1874.
2. Ibid., 25 July 1874. For the complete collection of the Pidge letters see Chuck Parsons, *"Pidge" A Texas Ranger from Virginia. The Life and Letters of Lieutenant T. C. Robinson, Washington County Volunteer Militia Company "A."* (Wolfe City, Texas: Henington Publishing Co., 1985).
3. *The Daily Democratic Statesman*, 19 July 1874.
4. Ibid., 22 July 1874.
5. *The Cuero Weekly Star*, Cuero, 4 July 1874.
6. Ibid., 27 June 1874.
7. *The Galveston Daily News*, 26 June and 1 July 1874.
8. Ibid., 1 July 1874.
9. *The Cuero Weekly Star*, 4 July 1874.
10. Steele to Governor Richard Coke, 10 July 1874. Letter Press Book, 401-621, 297.
11. John Morgan was killed by Hardin, using the alias of Fred Johnson, in Cuero on April 4, 1873, as reported in *The Report of the Adjutant General of the State of Texas for the Year 1873*, 116. Hardin described the killing of J.B. Morgan as an act of self-defense in his *Life*, 79-80. He later pled guilty to this killing and was sentenced to two years in the penitentiary, to be served concurrently with the sentence for the Charles Webb killing.
12. Steele to Coke, 10 July 1874, Letter Press Book, 401-621, 297. The exact date of Abram Bryant's murder — "to which there was not less than forty witnesses" — has not been determined because the case file containing such details is missing from the DeWitt County District Clerk's records. However, it probably occurred in late 1872 or early 1873. The Taylor adherents were convinced that Joseph Tumlinson and his followers were guilty of the gruesome murder; Bryant was disemboweled and his body filled with rocks and placed in the Guadalupe River between Clinton and Cuero. The twenty-seven followers were identified as Joseph Tumlinson, Joseph DeMoss, William Meador, Gus Tumlinson, John Tumlinson, Peter Tumlinson, John Meador, Addison Patterson, James E. Smith, W.W. Peavy, Zan Peavy, W.C. Wallace, John Powers, Buck Powers, Ed Parkinson, Addison Kilgore, Christopher T. Hunter, J.W. Ferguson, William Cox, Andrew Newman, Joseph I. Sitterlie, David Holderman, William T. Petit, Andrew Jordan, Jeff White, W.H. Lackie and James Mason. Who arrested these men and brought them into court in August of 1874 is not shown, although it is known that Deputy United States Marshal E.S. Roberts requested assistance from McNelly in serving writs on these men. McNelly and possibly Sheriff William J. Weisiger were probably involved in bringing in the accused, although McNelly made no mention of it in his infrequent reports. McNelly explained to Steele, "These writs include all of the leading spirits of the Tumlinson party and I think have been issued just in time for old 'Joe' has just joined church and I think must be meditating the death of some preacher or some kindred amusement. I have been on the alert more than ever." Ultimately no one was found guilty of the charge; by the court date a year later on August 9, 1875, the accused, Joe Tumlinson and two others later charged, John F. Cummings and John Gowens, were dead. Joe Tumlinson had died of natural causes on November 23, 1874, and Gowens, according to Jack Hays Day, had been tracked down and killed by B.J. Pridgen in the Indian Territory of modern day Oklahoma. Jack Hays Day, , *The Sutton Taylor Feud*, (San Antonio: Sid Murray & Sons, no date), 39. *Civil Minutes Book F* DeWitt County, Cuero, Texas, final trial and judgment 9 August 1875, cause # 899, 564. J.B. Heard was foreman of the

jury. The remaining men accused of Abraham Bryan's murder stood trial and were found not guilty as charged in the indictment.

13. Steele to McNelly, Special Order No. 2, 14 July 1874. *Special Orders Adjutant General Orders Augt. 1870 to April 2, 1897.* Adjutant General Records, Book 401-1012, 73-74.

14. Steele to McNelly, 14 July 1874. Letter Press Book 401-621, 303-05.

15. Steele to McNelly, 18 July 1874. Letter Press Book 401-621, 312.

16. Steele to McNelly, 22 July 1874. Letter Press Book, 401-621, 318.

17. Steele to Captain J.H. Wells, 24 July 1874. Letter Press Book, 401-621, 326.

18. McNelly to Steele, 3 August 1874, written from Clinton. Adjutant General Papers, *Letters Received.*

19. McNelly to Steele, 31 August 1874. "Report of L.H. McNelly Capt Washington Co V[olunteer] M[ilitia] Co."

20. Victor M. Rose, *The Texas Vendetta; or, The Sutton-Taylor Feud* (New York: J.J. Little & Co., 1880. Facsimile reprint by The Frontier Press of Texas, Houston 1956), 31. Craig H. Roell, "Victor Marion Rose" in *The New Handbook of Texas.* Vol. 5, (Austin: The Texas State Historical Association), 678-79.

21. McNelly to Steele, 31 August 1874. "Report of L.H. McNelly Capt Washington Co V[olunteer] M[ilitia] Co."

22. McNelly to Steele, 2 September 1874.

23. *The Daily Democratic Statesman,* 24 September 1874; letter from Pidge written at Clinton, 18 September.

24. Ibid.

25. McNelly to Steele, 31 August 1874. "Report of L.H. McNelly Capt Washington Co V[olunteer] M[ilitia] Co."

26. *The Daily Democratic Statesman,* 8 August 1874; letter from Pidge written at Clinton, 4 August.

27. Ibid., 24 September 1874; letter from Pidge written at Clinton, 18 September.

28. McNelly to Steele, 31 August 1874. "Report of L.H. McNelly Capt Washington Co V[olunteer] M[ilitia] Co."

29. McNelly to Steele, 7 and 31 August 1874. The original letter dated August 7 has not been located, but both Walter Prescott Webb and C.L. Sonnichsen refer to it in their works, and both quote the expression of surprise when the rangers were challenged by Tumlinson. Only the Adjutant General's secretary's summary of the McNelly letter of August 7 remains in the Texas State Archives. The 31 August letter is a lengthy seven page report of operations written from Clinton.

30. *The Daily Democratic Statesman,* 11 August 1874; letters from Pidge and E.A. Northington, both written at Clinton, 7 August.

31. *The Daily Democratic Statesman,* 11 August 1874; letter from Pidge written at Clinton, 7 August.

32. McNelly to Steele, 7 August 1874; Sonnichsen, 62; Webb, *The Texas Rangers,* 235-36.

33. Samuel H. Tumlinson, "Joseph Tumlinson" in *The New Handbook of Texas,* Vol. 6 (Austin: The Texas State Historical Association, 1996), 587. An obituary for Tumlinson appeared in the Cuero *Star,* reprinted in *The Herald and Planter,* Hallettsville, Lavaca County, 10 December 1874. According to this Tumlinson was buried on 24 November with Masonic honors, "mourned by his family and his many friends to whom his aged arm was still a strong protection."

34. McNelly to Steele, 8 August 1874.

35. Nellie Murphree, compiler, *History DeWitt County,* edited by Robert W. Shook (Victoria: Rose International Press Imprints, 1962), 101, identified him as Abraham Pickens who was killed for "refusing to reveal the whereabouts of his

master." C.L. Sonnichsen, *I'll Die Before I'll Run*, 52, identifies him as merely the "old Negro, Abraham" who was killed by "prowlers, supposedly because he would not give any information about his master's whereabouts." Sutton, Jr., *The Sutton-Taylor Feud*, 51, indicates the killing probably occurred between the treaty of peace signed on August 12, 1873, and the killing of Sutton and Slaughter on March 11, 1874. Sutton identifies the ex-slave as Abraham Pickins. According to Murphree, when B.J. Pridgen was married on his twenty-first birthday he was given two-hundred acres of land as well as some slaves. Abram was one of those slaves who, after emancipation, chose to stay with his former master, considered a trusted and faithful servant of Senator Pridgen. In 1870 when Willis Fawcett enumerated the citizens of DeWitt County he found Abram Bryant as a sixty-one-year-old black man with occupation given as "Farmer on Shares." In the same household were a nineteen-year-old female, Leah, and an eighteen-year-old male, Zac, both working as farm hands. Abram Bryant was a native of North Carolina while Leah and Zac were native born Texans, all illiterate. Senator Pridgen was a North Carolina native who had come to Texas in 1839. *Population Schedule of the Ninth Census of the United States, 1870*, DeWitt County, Precinct No. 5, enumeration made July, post office Clinton, 285A.

36. *The Daily Democratic Statesman*, 2 September; letter from Pidge written at Clinton 28 August 1874.

37. Rose, *The Texas Vendetta*, 31. Here former coeditor and historian Rose is quoting an undated article form the Victoria *Advocate*.

38. McNelly to Steele, 31 August 1874. "Report of L.H. McNelly Capt Washington Co. V[olunteer] M[ilitia] Co."

39. Jack S. Pridgen, untitled and unpublished history of the Pridgen Family, 12. Mrs. G.C. Mayfield in *The San Antonio Daily Express* and reprinted in Hunter's *Frontier Times*, September 1932 (in part) and in full in December 1932, "Interesting Narrative of Capt. W.L. Rudd, Ex-Ranger," 124. Rudd related to Mrs. Mayfield that Governor Coke said to McNelly, "Of course I don't want your company to go down there and fight and kill. No doubt there are good men on both sides. Make friends and help them make friends."

40. Steele to McNelly, 10 and 13 September 1874.

41. McNelly to Steele, 30 September 1874.

42. *The Galveston Weekly News*, 28 September, citing a report from Indianola, 24 September 1874.

43. *The Galveston Daily News*, 27 September, citing a report from Indianola, 24 September 1874.

44. McNelly to Steele, 30 September 1874.

45. Steele to Captain J.H. Wells, 18 September 1874. Letter Press Book, 401-621, 446.

46. Steele to McNelly and to O.F. Nash, 28 September 1874. Letter Press Book, 401-621, 455-56.

47. McNelly to Steele, 20 October 1874.

48. McNelly to Steele, 30 September 1874.

49. The details of Taylor's being released by Crain and rescuing his hat are from C.L. Sonnichsen's *I'll Die Before I'll Run*, 67; the version of Taylor rescuing Crain from the water is from Mrs. Lelia Seelingson, Historian for the Indianola Historical Association and compiler of *A History of Indianola*, published by *The Cuero Record* (no date), 12,

50. The killing of Taylor, Arnold and Hendricks is found in Chuck Parsons' "Mason Arnold - 'He Came From Schulenburg'" in the *Quarterly* of the National Association for Outlaw and Lawman History, Inc. (NOLA), October-December 1997, Vol. 21, No. 4.

51. *The Galveston Daily News*, 27 September 1874. This is a lengthy article written at Indianola on 24 September. The reporter presents a brief but somewhat garbled history of the "much regretted feud between the families of Sutton and Taylor" and surprisingly states that the feud "originated in Alabama, about eighteen years ago." The reporter learned of the background of the feud from two gentlemen who supposedly resided in the DeWitt County area. He identified Taylor's defense attorneys as Judge Lackey, Colonel Staton and General Woodward, all well-known criminal lawyers. He praised District Attorney Crain who, even though realizing the reputation of the defense attorneys, "promptly and boldly announced the State ready for trial." He was described as "but a young attorney, yet faltered not, and would have proved ready to meet them, or others, on any question." The reporter apparently accepted whatever his informants told him, because he stated that the feud had drawn so many people that if a general fight should at any time begin, "there would be ten or twelve hundred involved."

52. McNelly to Steele, 31 August 1874.

53. McNelly to Steele, 18 October 1874.

54. McNelly to Steele, 31 August 1874.

55. McNelly to Steele, 8 October 1874. *The Daily Democratic Statesman*, 14 October; letter from Pidge, October 13, 1874, written at Clinton.

56. McNelly to Steele, 7 September 1874.

57. McNelly to Steele, 19 October 1874.

58. McNelly to Steele, 10 August 1874.

59. McNelly to Steele, 20 August 1874.

60. Steele to McNelly, 17 November 1874. Adjutant General Letter Press Book, 401-621, 562.

61. *The Intelligencer-Echo*, Austin, 18 January 1875.

62. *The Cuero Star*, 19 December 1874, reprinted in *The Herald and Planter*, Hallettsville, Texas, 31 December 1874.

63. *The San Antonio Daily Express*, 30 March 1875.

CHAPTER 12
MCNELLY—ON THE BORDER

1. *The Brenham Banner*, 3 September 1874.

2. McNelly to Steele, 8 January 1875.

3. McNelly to Steele, 10 January 1875.

4. Steele to McNelly, 7 January 1875.

5. Steele to McNelly, 9 March 1875.

6. Steele to McNelly, 17 March 1875.

7. *The San Antonio Daily Express*, 26 March 1875.

8. *The Daily Democratic Statesman*, Austin, 5 May 1877. According to the 1870 DeWitt County census Hudson was a forty-year old farmer from Tennessee. His wife, Mary S., was from North Carolina; their one child was thirteen-year-old R.A., born in Texas. In 1875 she married W.C. Wallace who had served in the posse which killed ex-McNelly Ranger A.R. Hendricks.

9. Jerry Thompson, "Juan Nepomuceno Cortina" in *The New Handbook of Texas*, Vol. 2 (Austin: The Texas Historical Association, 1996), 343-44.

10. *The San Antonio Daily Express*, 11 August 1871.

11. *Texas Frontier Troubles*. House of Representatives Report #343 to the 44th Congress, 1st Session. (Washington: Government Printing Office, 1876) Vol. 1709, Congressional Serial Set, v.

12. *The Brownsville Sentinel* article summarized in the Austin *Daily Democratic Statesman*, 9 September 1874.

13. The article from *The New Orleans Republican* was reprinted in the Austin *Daily State Journal*, 11 October 1872.

14. *The Daily Democratic Statesman*, 14 October 1874. Telegraphic Associated Press dispatch from Galveston of 13 October, citing a dispatch from Brownsville.

15. *The Galveston Daily News*, 13 November 1874, citing a Brownsville special of 12 November.

16. *The Daily Democratic Statesman*, 3 December 1874, and 23 March 1875, citing an undated report from *The Brownsville Sentinel. The Corpus Christi Weekly Gazette,* 22 August 1874, reported that Flores, having been arrested for murdering a man "a few miles beyond Santa Gertrudes [*sic*]" had escaped from the Brownsville jail. Commented the *Gazette*, "As usual." The victim was Vidal La Haille, robbed and murdered by Flores and others on 16 March 1874, according to *Texas Frontier Troubles*, 53.

17. Alexander J. Leo to Governor Richard Coke, 4 March 1875. Governor's Papers, Texas State Archives.

18. Steele to Richard Coke, 30 March 1875. Governor's Papers, Texas State Archives.

19. William H. Hager, "The Nuecestown Raid of 1875: A Border Incident." *Arizona and the West*. Vol. 1, No. 3 (Autumn 1959), 261.

20. *The San Antonio Daily Herald*, 3 April 1875. The lady who reported the gruesome details was identified as Miss Lizzie Joy, according to *Texas Frontier Troubles*, 53.

21. New Noakes, "Thomas John Noakes" in *The New Encyclopedia of Texas*. Compiled and edited by Ellis A. Davis and Edwin H. Grobe (Dallas: Texas Development Bureau, 1925), 2134.

22. Coleman McCampbell, *Saga of a Frontier Seaport* (Dallas: South-West Press, 1934), 34. See also Leopold Morris, "The Mexican Raid on Corpus Christi" in *The Quarterly of the Texas State Historical Association*, Vol. 4, No. 1 (July 1900). Herein is printed entirely T.J. Noakes' account of the raiders' attack and subsequent events. It was written 13 May 1875 so was quite fresh in his mind. Noakes' account appears on pages 131-36.

23. Cynthia E. Orozco, "Nuecestown Raid of 1875" in *The New Handbook of Texas*, Vol. 4, 1059. See also the testimony of John S. McCampbell, 24 January 1876 in *Texas Frontier Troubles*, 3-4.

24. Dee Woods, "Difficulties Encountered In Finding Hanging Site" in *The Corpus Christi Caller*, 26 August 1939. See also Ruth Dodson. "The Noakes Raid" in *Frontier Times*, Vol. 23, No. 10, 184-86.

25. *The San Antonio Daily Herald*, 3 April 1875.

26. B.J. Pridgen to Governor Richard Coke, 19 February 1875; McNelly to Pridgen, 3 March 1875 and McNelly to Steele, 3 March 1875.

27. Muster and Pay Rolls Texas Ranger Records, Adjutant Generals Files. Texas State Archives.

28. Durham, *Nueces Strip*, 17.

29. Durham, *Nueces Strip*, 18.

30. Durham, *Nueces Strip*, 19.

31. Durham, "5100 Outlaws", I, 113.

32. *Mooney & Morrison's Directory of the City of San Antonio for 1877-78* (Galveston: The Galveston News, 1877), 117. An account ledger sheet of Heye advertises him as a "Carriage Trimmer and Manufacturer of Harness and Saddlery" at 111 West Commerce Street in San Antonio. His business was established in 1867. C.L. "Chet" Downs, "Yonder's A Noakes" in *The Texas Gun Collector Journal* (Spring 1993), 12.

33. Coleman McCampbell, *Saga of a Frontier Seaport* (Dallas: South-West Press, 1934), 35.

34. Ruth Dodson, "The Noakes Raid" in *Frontier Times*, Vol. 23, No. 10 (July 1946), 177 and 182.

35. Jennings, *A Texas Ranger*, 1899. Reprint (Norman: University of Oklahoma Press, 1997).

36. William C. Callicott Memoirs in Walter Prescott Webb Papers and Service Record. Adjutant General Files, Texas State Archives. Callicott first appears in the Texas census in 1860 living in Austin County, post office as Pine Grove. He is listed as the six-year-old son of James "Calicut," one of four children, with no mother listed in the household, 215B. In 1870 he is again listed in Austin County as a farmer and attending school. *Population Schedule of the Eighth and Ninth Census of the United States,* Austin County, Texas, 1860 and 1870.

CHAPTER 13
THE LAW WEST OF THE NUECES

1. William H. Russell to Governor Richard Coke, 3 April 1875. Governor's Papers, Texas State Archives.

2. Steele to McNelly, 5[?] April 1875. Adjutant General Letter Press Book 401-622, 149-50.

3. *The San Antonio Daily Express*, 15 April 1875, stating the company started for the Rio Grande "last Saturday" which was 10 April. The 24 April issue reported McNelly had arrived in Corpus Christi.

4. Neal Coldwell to Major John B. Jones, 28 February 1875. Adjutant General Records. Box 410-393.

5. Coldwell to Jones, 30 April 1875. Box 401-393.

6. Cynthia E. Orozco, "Nuecestown Raid of 1875" in *The New Handbook of Texas*. Vol. 4 (Austin: Texas State Historical Association, 1986), 1059.

7. *The San Antonio Daily Express*, 21 April 1875.

8. Sheriff John McClane to Steele, received 18 April 1875. Letters received Adjutant General Files, Box 401-704.

9. Steele to McClane, 19 April 1875. McNelly reported he had left on 10 April while Steele stated he left on the 9th. Adjutant General Letter Press Book 401-622. Beginning with W.P. Webb and various followers this man's name has appeared as "McClure" when in reality it was "McClane." (Webb, *The Texas Rangers*, 238). The original telegram shows it clearly as "McClane" as well as Steele's response directed to *McClane*. Further the 1870 and 1880 census of Nueces County both enumerate him as John McClane; in 1870 he is shown as a forty-two-year-old clerk in the custom house (159B) and in 1880 as a sheep raiser, residing in the dwelling adjacent to the county jail (9B).

10. Neal Coldwell to Major John B. Jones, 4 May 1875, "Reports Operations."

11. Coldwell to Jones, 17 May 1875, "Reports Operations."

12. McNelly to Steele, 4 May 1875, written from Edinburg.

13. [William Steele] *Report of the Adjutant General of the State of Texas, for the Year 1875* (Houston: A.C. Gray, State Printer, 1875), 8-12.

14. Joseph E. Dwyer report to General E.O.C. Ord, 5 July 1875, printed in Ord's report in *Report of the Secretary of War,* Vol. 1, 44th Congress, 1st Session House of Representatives Report Ex. Doc. 1, Part 2, (Washington: Government Printing Office, 1875), 97.

15. Durham, "5100 Outlaws", I, 112.

16. Steele to Coke, 31 May 1875. Original in Texas State Archives, Austin, Box 301-94.

17. Durham, "5100 Outlaws", I, 112.

18. Ibid., I, 112

19. *Population Schedule of the Ninth Census of the United States, 1870.*
Nueces County, Texas, 198A. For a complete biography of King see Tom Lea, *The King Ranch*, two volumes (Boston: Little, Brown, 1957) and Bruce S. Cheeseman, "Richard King" in *The New Handbook of Texas*, Vol. 3 (Austin: Texas State Historical Association, 1986), 1107-108.

20. Durham, "5100 Outlaws", I, 112.

21. Ibid., 113.

22. *Population Schedule of the Ninth Census of the United States, 1870.*
Nueces County, Texas. Culver is enumerated on page 178A and Clark is enumerated on page 192A.

23. Durham, "5100 Outlaws", I, 113.

24. *The Galveston Daily News*, 4 May 1875. Reprinted from *The Daily Valley Times*. This in part was also printed in *The San Antonio Daily Herald*, 6 May 1875.

25. *The Galveston Daily News*, 4 May 1875; this also appeared in *The San Antonio Daily Herald*, 6 May 1875.

26. *The San Antonio Daily Express*, 8 May 1875.

27. *The Brenham Daily Banner*, 7 May 1875.

28. *The Galveston Daily News*, 20 April 1875.

29. *The San Antonio Daily Herald*, 12 May 1875.

30. *The Galveston Daily News*, 14 May 1875, summarizing "State News" from Nueces County.

31. *Norton's Union Intelligencer*, 15 May 1875, reprinting article from an undated *The Corpus Christi Times*.

32. Durham, "5100 Outlaws", I, 113.

Chapter 14
A Challenge to Cortina

1. *The Galveston Daily News*, 4 May 1875.

2. Durham, "5100 Outlaws", II, 108-109. George P. Durham was born in March 1857 in Georgia, according to the 1900 Cameron County census. Thus he had only recently celebrated his eighteenth birthday the month prior to joining McNelly. Durham only mentioned Callicott in his writings, but this is what Callicott had to say about Durham, without corrections: "George was only 17 years of age at that time But a truer or Braver Ranger never lived[.] He was with us in the Palowalto fight with us in Mexico[.] when ever the capton called for voluntiers George was all ways Redy and willen to go to the front . . . ." [Callicott to Webb 29 December 1921, 2-3]. The five men who chose to leave McNelly at this point had been enlisted by Lieutenant James W. Guynn on June 22 in Colorado County and thus were not part of McNelly's company until after the battle on the Palo Alto prairie. They were V. Byars, J.B. Carter and L.R. Carter, E.D. Howland and C. Perry. The reason given for their dismissal was "not complying with company regulations," according to the Muster and Pay Roll "from reorganization to August 31, 1875."

3. The *Express* spelled the name "Doddrige" but according to the 1870 census it was Doddridge. *Population Schedule of the Ninth Census of the United States, 1870*, Nueces County, Texas, enumerated 16 June, 159. He was a thirty-five-year-old retired wholesale merchant from Pennsylvania and an acting Custom House Clerk. In the 1880 Nueces County census he was in Corpus Christi and listed as a banker, 27B.

4. *The San Antonio Daily Express*, 10 May 1875.

5. Ibid., 11 May 1875. At this point Hatch was temporary commander at Fort Ringgold.

6. Ibid., 20 May 1875.

7. *The Galveston Daily News*, 20 May 1875, citing telegrams from Brownsville of 19 May.

8. Durham, "5100 Outlaws", II, 113. Durham, in preparing his memoir with Clyde Wantland, may have had some documents from the 1870s for reference although some names were recorded inaccurately. However, the names of several spies not mentioned by Durham, Callicott or Jennings appear in the work *Century of Conflict 1821-1913: Incidents in the Lives of William Neale and William A. Neale Early Settlers in South Texas*, edited by John C. Rayburn and Virginia Kemp Rayburn (Waco: The Texian Press, 1966), 120-21. Here McNelly is described as arriving in Brownsville with twenty-two men, and as he and most of his men were "total strangers" McNelly "wisely" enlisted men who "worked actively towards suppressing bandits and cattle thieves" who he identifies as James Kenedy, Thomas McGovern, H.S. Rock and George More, although the latter is identified as Moore on the muster rolls and only served from 1 May to 2 August 1875 when he was dishonorably discharged. Also "a squad of both American and native Mexicans who knew the lay of the country as well as some of the worst characters" were enlisted: Bill Burke, Macedonia Longorio, Lino Saldana, Timoteo Solis, Jesus Sandoval and Matias Serata. The existing muster and pay rolls do not carry the names of Burke, Longorio, Saldana, Solis or Serata, although one man on the muster roll is identified simply as "Mex spy name unknown" (Muster and Pay Roll prepared at Tio Cano Ranch, 30 November 1875.) Presumably there were others whose name never were listed as well.

9. Ibid. Durham writes authoritatively of Sandoval's experiences and personal loss at the hands of the raiders. Sandoval's wife and daughter, only fourteen at the time and "ruined for life," had both been "treated something awful." Sandoval's affidavit of 3 May 1875 is less tragic: on 21 April 1875, three armed Mexicans came to his ranch asking for him, threatening to kill his wife if she did not reveal Sandoval's whereabouts. Sandoval said "I was luckily not at home." This statement certainly does not appear to be made by a man who had lost his wife and daughter to those raiders! It is possible his tragedy postdated his affidavit of 3 May. His affidavit appears in *Texas Frontier Troubles*, page 84, House of Representatives Report No. 343, 44th Congress, 1st Session, printed in Vol. 1709, Congressional Serial Set. N.A. Jennings related in great detail how Sandoval's ranch was destroyed and his wife and daughter ravished and delivered to a convent. Jennings' work was published in 1899 and it is possible Durham simply followed Jennings' narrative. Jennings, *A Texas Ranger*, 75-77.

10. William C. Callicott to Walter Prescott Webb, 11 April 1921. This particular letter in Callicott's handwriting is missing from the W.P. Webb Files, but there is a typed transcript dated 11 April 1921. In it Callicott refers to Sandoval and an unidentified white man "some years before" having caught four Mexican cattle thieves and "hung all four of them from one tree." Following this Sandoval had "to hide out a lot, hadn't slept in his house for ten years." In Austin's *Daily Democratic Statesman* of 31 December 1874 appeared a letter signed "Old Texan," written from Brownsville on 18 December, which described how on the day previous the bodies of two raiders had been brought into town, having "been hung for cattle stealing; the animals were in their possession." One Mexican "made oath" identifying the parties who did the hanging. On the night of 17 December warrants were issued for William Burke, deputy sheriff, Lino Saldana and Jesus Sandoval. Later the trio were cleared, but reports then indicated that only two raiders had been lynched, not four as Callicott remembered. *The San Antonio Daily Herald*, 3

February 1873, citing an undated item from *The Nueces Valley Times*.

11. Durham, "5100 Outlaws", II, 115.

12. Ibid.

13. General E.O.C. Ord to Assistant Adjutant General, 10 September 1875. This document is printed in full in *Texas Frontier Troubles*, 39-43.

14. *The Colorado Citizen*, published in Columbus, Colorado County, Texas, 1 July 1875, printing "Official Report of Capt. L.H. McNelly" from Brownsville, — June 1875. The original document written by McNelly to Adjutant General Steele has not been located in the Adjutant General's papers, although W.P. Webb in *The Texas Rangers* quotes from it extensively although admitting he had "slightly amended" it, 239-41. Webb omits the statement that McNelly made of turning Salinas and Garcia over to Cameron County Sheriff James G. Browne with no explanation as to why. Cameron County Sheriff Browne's name has been given with various spellings in different sources. The spelling of *James G. Browne* has been used throughout as that is from Comptroller Stephen H. Darden's letter to Secretary of State A.W. DeBerry of 24 March stating he had qualified as Collector of State Taxes on 3 January 1874, showing his own signature.

15. *The Colorado Citizen*, 1 July 1875.

16. William C. Callicott to Walter Prescott Webb, 2 May 1921, 4-7.

17. Durham, "5100 Outlaws", II, 117. Linton Lafayette Wright was elected Sheriff of Duval County, Texas on 2 November 1880 and served five consecutive terms until 4 November 1890. Tise, *Texas County Sheriffs*, 163.

18. Callicott to Webb, 29 December 1921, 8.

19. Durham, "5100 Outlaws", II, 117.

20. From Callicott's detailed map, drawn probably 29 December 1921. Original in the Walter Prescott Webb Papers, CAH, University of Texas, Austin.

21. Herman S. Rock, affidavit sworn to and subscribed 17 June 1875 before J.F. Parker, Clerk, United States District Court, Eastern District of Texas at Brownsville. *Texas Frontier Troubles*, 84-85; Webb, 248-49; Callicott to Webb, undated account of the invasion, 36. A Jack Ellis was charged with theft of a gelding in Bastrop County, committed 23 April and indicted 28 July, 1871. He was still in the *List of Fugitives from Justice*, 41.

22. *The Daily Democratic Statesman*, 3 December 1874; and *The San Antonio Daily Express*, 26 August 1876.

23. *The San Antonio Daily Express*, 17 June 1875. Contradicting this report, Harbert Davenport, a Brownsville attorney-at-law who corresponded with Dr. Webb in his preparation of *The Texas Rangers*, wrote that the one raider who escaped was Joaquin Trevino. According to Davenport the raider "fell from his horse in the course of the fight and was left for dead, but succeeded in crawling to the road and was brought, hidden, into Brownsville by some Mexican cart men. He was later a member of the Brownsville police force." He was still alive in 1936. Davenport to Webb, 17 January 1936. Original in W.P. Webb Papers, CAH, Austin.

24. Jennings, *A Texas Ranger*, 69. Olguin did not die as Jennings wrote. On 19 August 1876 Matamoros commander General Revueltas delivered Olguin to Texas authorities on a requisition made by Hidalgo County Judge W.P. Dougherty, according to the Galveston *Daily News* of 24 August. Commented the *News*, "Probably he will now go to the penitentiary." Jose Maria Olguin's ultimate fate is unknown but he was in Huntsville prison in 1880 when the prisoners were enumerated on 30 June. He is identified as J.M. Alguin, a thirty-two-year-old male, unmarried and a native of Mexico. His occupation was given as "Laborer." *Population Schedule of the Tenth United States Census, 1880*, Walker County, Texas, 254B.

25. *The Galveston Daily News*, 15 June 1875.

26. McNelly to Governor Coke, 12 June 1875. Telegram cited in *The Galveston Daily News*, 13 June 1875.

27. *The Colorado Citizen*, 1 July 1875.

28. *The Galveston Daily News*, 15 June 1875.

29. *The Colorado Citizen*, 1 July 1875.

30. Joseph P. O'Shaughnessy, affidavit sworn to and subscribed before J.F. Parker, Clerk, United States District Court, Eastern District of Texas at Brownsville, 16 June 1875. Original document in Texas State Archives.

31. Jennings, *A Texas Ranger*, 70. Curiously the contemporary press made no mention as to the disposal of the bodies of the dead Mexicans, although the *News* of June 16 reported that on June 14 two "defunct raiders were found . . . and brought to town and buried. A Mexican found the body of his brother on the battle field and buried it there."

32. *The San Antonio Daily Express*, 14 June 1875.

33. William D. Whipple to Adjutant-General, United States Army, 14 June 1875. Report printed in *Texas Frontier Troubles*, 79.

34. *The Galveston Daily News*, 13 June 1875.

35. Durham, "5100 Outlaws", II, 117.

36. The Callicott documents, numerous lengthy letters to Dr. Webb as well as a large hand drawn map approximately 16 x 27 inches in size depicting in detail the fight on the Palo Alto prairie, and several relevant photographs, are among the W.P. Webb Papers in the CAH, Austin. Dr. Webb excerpted much of Callicott's reminiscences for his *The Texas Rangers: A Century of Frontier Defense*.

37. John Jay Smith, Deputy Inspector of Hides and Animals, District of Cameron County. Affidavit sworn 17 June 1875 at Brownsville, printed in *Texas Frontier Troubles*, 85-86.

38. Callicott to Webb, 11 April 1921.

39. *The Galveston Daily News*, 15 June 1875.

40. Callicott to Webb, 11 April 1921.

41. Muster and Pay Rolls, Washington County Volunteer Militia Company A. Originals in the Texas State Archives, Austin. When killed L.B. Smith was owed $74.99 by the State of Texas. His grave is Lot 10, Block 6 Brownsville City Cemetery. The interment record shows he was killed in battle, occupation given as "Ranger" and was seventeen-years-old. Chula T. and Sam S. Griffin, *Record of Interments in the City Cemetery from May 7, 1854 to December 31, 1880 and a Brief History of Brownsville* Vol. 1 (Brownsville: privately printed, March 1987), 40.

42. McNelly to Steele, 14 June 1875. Telegram sent from Camargo, Mexico. Original in the Texas State Archives.

43. *The Colorado Citizen*, 1 July 1875.

44. McNelly to Steele, 30 September 1875, written on letterhead of William Steele. Original in the Texas State Archives.

45. *The San Antonio Daily Express*, 1 July 1875.

46. General P.H. Sheridan to General E.D. Townsend, 16 June 1875. Letter printed in *Texas Frontier Troubles*, 81.

47. General E.O.C. Ord to W.W. Belknap, 15 June 1875. Letter printed in *Texas Frontier Troubles*, 80.

48. James W. Guynn, "Lieutenant of Rangers," written 25 July to editor, *Colorado Citizen*, 5 August 1875. Guynn resigned from McNelly's command on 27 August 1875 "as the continued bad health of my family would not admit of my remaining longer" as he explained in his letter to Steele dated 8 September 1875. Guynn has attracted virtually no recognition among ranger historians, although Dudley G. Wooten wrote highly of him. "[I]n July,1874, one company of volunteer

militia from Washington County was mustered in for active service in DeWitt and other counties in Southwest Texas, and latterly on the Rio Grande River. This company was commanded by Captain L.H. McNelly, with T.C. Robinson first and J.W. Guyon [*sic*] second lieutenant. . . ." Dudley G. Wooten, editor, *A Comprehensive History of Texas 1685 to 1897*, Vol. 2 (Dallas: William G. Scarff, 1898), 350. This chapter is by W.H. King, "The Texas Ranger Service and History." By 1880 Guynn was residing in Colorado County, Texas, enumerated as a thirty-nine-year-old "Drummer Dry Goods" and an Alabama native. He then had a wife and two children. *Population Schedule of the Tenth United States Census, 1880,* Colorado County, Texas, enumerated 3-4 June, 332B.

49. *The Daily Democratic Statesman*, 28 July 1875.

50. Guynn to editor, *The Colorado Citizen*, 5 August 1875. Lieutenant James William Guynn did not long survive his experience as a ranger with McNelly. On July 27, 1882, while hunting deer with friends near Columbus, he was accidentally shot by J.J. Harrison. Guynn died from the wound on 2 July. He is buried in the Columbus Odd Fellows Rest Cemetery.

51. Coke to McNelly, 9 July 1875. Records of the Governor. File 301-97, pp. 309-10.

CHAPTER 15
INVADING MEXICO

1. L.H. McNelly to Adjutant General Steele, 13 August 1875. Adjutant General Files. Texas State Archives. Ciudad Camargo is directly across the Rio Grande from Rio Grande City, Starr County, Texas; Las Cuevas is today known as Ciudad Gustavo Diaz Ordaz, some twelve miles down the river.

2. The spelling "Magotee" is McNelly's; it was more likely the "Amargosa Don Juan" because Durham uses that term in both "5100 Outlaws" as well as *Taming the Nueces Strip* version. On page 95 of the former he wrote of how in the daylight the camping place was recognized as "being on Amargosa Don Juan; . . . We was bunched in a motte landed high and dry out in this desert; the motte covering maybe an acre of ground." McNelly to Steele, 13 August 1875. Adjutant General Files. Texas State Archives.

3. Jennings, *A Texas Ranger*, 80.

4. "Su amigo" to L.H. McNelly, 11 August 1875. Adjutant General Files, Texas State Archives. The history of "Rancho Davis" reached back over a century. In time it belonged to Henry Clay Davis, a survivor of the Mier expedition. When Fort Ringgold was established adjacent to the small community in 1848, its growth and permanence was assured. It is now the county seat of Starr County. Garna L. Christian. "Rio Grande City, Texas" in *The New Handbook of Texas*, Vol. 5 (Austin: The Texas State Historical Association, 1996), 584-85.

5. McNelly to Steele, 13 August 1875.

6. "Pidge" to Editor John D. Elliott, *Daily State Gazette*, Austin, 16 October 1875. Letter written on "Rio Grande Frontier" 20 September. This also appeared in *El Sentinel* of Brownsville and again reprinted in *La Voz del Pueblo* of Matamoros with considerable editorial comment condemning the rangers, 11 November 1875. Translation courtesy Florentino Gonzales.

7. McNelly to J.L. Haynes, Collector of Customs, District of Brazos Santiago. 14 August 1875. Adjutant General Files, Texas State Archives.

8. McNelly to Steele, 15 August 1875.

9. Durham, "5100 Outlaws", IV, 71-72. Orrell survived his ranger experiences and in 1877 married Betsy A. Nichols, the daughter of a DeWitt County resident whom he undoubtedly met and courted when McNelly was assigned there to end

the Sutton-Taylor Feud. The couple had eight children of which six survived infancy. DeWitt County, Texas Marriage Record Book, License No. 1573, 191. The license was issued on 15 February and the marriage was performed on that date. *Population Schedule of the Twelfth Census of the United States, 1900*. Edwards County, Texas. E.D. 16, Sheet 11, line 22.

10. Testimony of L.H. McNelly before the Special Committee on Texas Frontier Troubles in Washington, D.C., 24 January 1876, 8-9. Reproduced in *Texas Frontier Troubles*, House of Representatives Report No. 343, 44th Congress, 1st Session, printed in Volume 1709, Congressional Serial Set.

11. Durham, "5100 Outlaws", IV, 72.

12. Testimony of L.H. McNelly, 29 January 1875, 14-15, *Texas Frontier Troubles*.

13. Statement of George W. Miller, certified before J.L. Haynes, Collector of Customs, Brownsville. Haynes' statement dated 21 June 1875, printed in *Texas Frontier Troubles*, 136-37.

14. Durham, "5100 Outlaws", IV, 73.

15. Durham, *Nueces Strip*, 96-97. George Durham here quotes the sergeant, whose name he spelled "Orrill," as having known the captain since he was no older than Durham, i.e., a teenager. He further claimed that McNelly suffered from consumption "when he came to Texas before the war. If he hadn't had it he'd have been a preacher in Virginia. He left preaching school to come to Texas to cure his consumption." Although some modern writers have claimed McNelly at one time had studied to become a preacher, Charles B. McNelly denied that was ever the case.

16. A New York native, Kells received his appointment on December 24, 1861, and entered into the service as an acting volunteer officer and first experienced action during the Civil War. By 1867 he had attained the rank of master, was commissioned a lieutenant December 18, 1868, was on special duty in New Orleans in 1869, and commander of the iron-clad *Dictator* in the North Atlantic Fleet by 1870. That same year he was commissioned as Lieutenant Commander; he then commanded the *Pawnee* at Key West from 1871-72, then again was on special duty at New Orleans from 1873-74 and finally commanded the *Canonicus*, an iron-clad, off Pensacola, Florida, until he reported to the port of Brownsville with the U.S. *Rio Bravo*. Lewis R. Hamersly, compiler, *The Records - Living Officers of the U. S. Navy and Marine Corps* (Philadelphia: J.B. Lippincott & Co., 1878), 203. Corpus Christi *Weekly Gazette*, 7 August 1875.

17. Thomas F. Wilson, United States Consulate, Matamoros, Mexico, to Lieutenant Commander D.C. Kells, 26 October 1875 and Wilson to Hamilton Fish, Secretary of State, 27 October 1875. "Dispatches from U.S. Consulate in Matamoros March 19, 1874, to April 18, 1879." Record Group 59, National Archives, Washington, D. C. Copies made available through Dr. Jerry Thompson.

18. Thomas F. Wilson to Hamilton Fish. "Confidential Statement - 207" accompanying letter of 14 October 1875. Record Group 59.

19. Wilson to Fish, 14 October 1875.

20. "Pidge" to Editor John D. Elliott, *Daily State Gazette*, 18 March 1876, written from "Camp Texas Rangers" Cameron County, Texas, 4 March 1876.

21. "Confidential Statement - 207" accompanying letter of Thomas F. Wilson to Hamilton Fish, 14 October 1875. Record Group 59.

22. D.C. Kells to Thomas F. Wilson, 26 October 1875. Record Group 59.

23. Colonel Joseph H. Potter, Special Orders No. 156, 8 November 1875. Original in Adjutant General Correspondence, Texas State Library.

24. Steele to McNelly, 10 July 1875, in Letter Press Book 401-622, *Wm Steele Adj-General January 1st 1875 to November 30*, 1875, 297.

25. Ibid., 16 July 1875, 302.

26. Ibid., 17 July 1875, 307.

27. Ibid., 9 October 1875, 422.

28. Ibid., 29 October 1875, 454.

29. Ibid., 8 November 1875, 461.

30. McNelly to Steele, 9 November 1875, telegram from Brownsville.

31. Steele to McNelly, 9 November 1875, 464.

32. McNelly to Steele, from Brownsville, 12 November 1875. Adjutant General Correspondence, Texas State Library, 401-393-14.

33. Testimony of William Steele, 9 February 1876. Printed in *Texas Frontier Troubles*, 28.

34. Walter Prescott Webb, *The Texas Rangers*, 256; *The New York Herald*, 15 December 1877. News report "From Our Regular Correspondent" dated Washington, 14 December 1877.

35. Durham, *Nueces Strip*, 102.

36. Durham, "5100 Outlaws", IV, 73.

37. Testimony of L.H. McNelly, 29 January 1876, *Texas Frontier Troubles*, 17.

38. Durham, "5100 Outlaws", IV, 73.

39. Durham, "5100 Outlaws", IV, 73.

40. "Pidge" to Editor John D. Elliott, *Daily State Gazette*, 19 January 1876, written from Camp Texas Rangers, Laguna de los Calabaso [*sic, calabaza*, pumpkin, gourd], 15 January 1876.

41. Durham, "5100 Outlaws", IV, 75.

42. Captain James F. Randlett to Helenus Dodt, Acting Assistant Adjutant General, District of the Rio Grande, 1 December 1875, 1-2. Original in Texas State Archives.

43. Colonel J.H. Potter, via Helenus Dodt to Randlett, 16 November 1875, 3.

44. Captain James F. Randlett to Helenus Dodt, 1 December 1875, 3-8.

45. Randlett to Dodt, 1 December 1875, 8.

46. Randlett to Dodt, 1 December 1875, 9.

47. Randlett to Dodt, 1 December 1875, 10.

48. Testimony of L.H. McNelly, 29 January 1876, *Texas Frontier Troubles*, 16.

49. William C. Callicott to W.P. Webb. Undated account of Las Cuevas Raid, 7. Original in CAH, Austin.

50. McNelly to Steele, telegram, Loz Cueves [*sic*] dated 18 November 1875, via Brownsville. Original in Texas State Archives.

51. McNelly to Steele, telegram, Los Cueves [*sic*] dated 18 November, via Ringgold Barracks, 19 November. Original in Texas State Archives.

52. William C. Callicott to W.P. Webb. Undated account of Las Cuevas Raid, 12-13.

53. William C. Callicott to W.P. Webb. Undated account of Las Cuevas Raid, 14-15.

54. William C. Callicott to W.P. Webb. Undated account of Las Cuevas Raid, 15-16.

CHAPTER 16
ACROSS THE RIO GRANDE

1. Pidge to Editor John D. Elliott, 15 January 1876, from Camp Texas Rangers, Laguna de los Calabaso [*sic*], printed in the *Daily State Gazette*, 19 January 1876.

2. William C. Callicott to W.P. Webb, undated document of Las Cuevas Raid. W.P. Webb Collection, 20-21.

3. Pidge, 15 January 1876.

4. William C. Callicott to W.P. Webb, undated document of Las Cuevas Raid. W.P. Webb Collection, 23.

5. William C. Callicott to W.P. Webb, undated document, 25.

6. Pidge, 15 January 1876.

7. William C. Callicott, 27.

8. Durham, "5100 Outlaws", IV, 77.

9. Pidge, 15 January 1876.

10. The death tally: *The Galveston Daily News*, 12 December 1876; Pidge, 15 January 1876; Durham, "5100 Outlaws", IV, 77,

11. L.H. McNelly, Captain Rangers, telegram to Adjutant General William Steele, 20 November, 1875, "Mexico near Las Cuevas."

12. Pidge, 15 January 1876.

13. William C. Callicott, 29.

14. L.H. McNelly. Telegram to Adjutant General William Steele, 20 November 1875, "Mexico near Las Cuevas."

15. William C. Callicott, 31.

16. William C. Callicott, 32.

17. L.H. McNelly, telegram to Adjutant General William Steele, 20 November 1875. "Mexico near Las Cuevas."

18. William C. Callicott, 35.

19. Pidge, 15 January 1876.

20. William C. Callicott, 39.

21. William C. Callicott, 40-41.

22. William C. Callicott, 42-43.

23. James F. Randlett, Captain 8th Cavalry. "Report of Operations" to Acting Assistant Adjutant General Helenus Dodt, 1 December 1875, 11-12. Original in Adjutant General's Files, Texas State Archives.

24. Pidge, 15 January 1876.

25. William C. Callicott, 55-56.

26. Pidge, 15 January, 1876.

27. William C. Callicott, 58.

28. William C. Callicott, 61-62.

29. William C. Callicott, 62.

30. William C. Callicott, 69.

31. William C. Callicott, 75-76.

32. William C. Callicott, 77.

33. William C. Callicott, 80-81.

34. William C. Callicott, 83-85.

35. Jennings, *A Texas Ranger*, 93.

36. Jennings, *A Texas Ranger*, 94.

37. Jennings, *A Texas Ranger*, 95.

38. Jennings, *A Texas Ranger*, 96.

39. Durham, "5100 Outlaws", IV, 80.

40. Jennings, 91-92. J.H. Potter to Major Alexander, 20 November 1875. Original in Adjutant General Files, Teas State Archives.

41. Durham, "5100 Outlaws", IV, 80-81.

42. Jennings, *A Texas Ranger*, 92.

43. Durham, "5100 Outlaws", IV, 81.

44. Webb, *The Texas Rangers*, 268, 272.

45. McNelly to Steele from Ringgold Barracks, 21 November 1875. Original in Adjutant General Files, Texas State Archives.

46. McNelly to Diego Garcia, Chief Magistrate, Camargo, Mexico, 21

November 1875. Original in Adjutant General Files, Texas State Archives.

47. Interview with Dr. Alexander M. Headley by W.D. Hornaday, printed in *The San Antonio Daily Express*, 22 August 1909. General Salinas was killed at Las Cuevas; by the time of the Dr. Headley interview, the community was known as San Miguel. Today the community is known as Gustavo Diaz Ordaz.

48. George H. Edgerton, "Dr. Alexander Manford Headley" in *The New Handbook of Texas*, Vol. 3, (Austin: The Texas State Historical Association, 1996). 523-24. In 1880 Dr. Headley was in the community identified as "Nuevo Rancho," a farmer as well as a practicing physician, 42-years-old with wife Ramona A., a son, a daughter and a step-son. *Population Schedule of the Tenth United States Census, 1880*, Hidalgo County, Texas. 236B.

49. William C. Callicott, 89.

50. McNelly to Steele, Telegram from Rio Grande City, 22 November 1875. Original in Adjutant General Files, Texas State Archives.

CHAPTER 17
AFTER THE LAS CUEVAS AFFAIR

1. Pidge to Editor John D. Elliott, 15 January 1876, from Camp Texas Rangers, Laguna de los Calabaso [*sic*]. Printed in *The Daily State Gazette*, 19 January 1876.

2. Durham, "5100 Outlaws", V, 80.

3. Durham, "5100 Outlaws", V, 81.

4. Durham, *Nueces Strip*, 124. Durham wrote, "Bob Pitts shot the first one to clear leather before the man could bring his pistol up to firing level. Bob's shot was good, as were all his shots, and the fellow dropped like a polled shoat. The others dropped their pistols and reached."

5. Durham, "5100 Outlaws", V, 82.

6. Pidge to Editor John D. Elliott, 15 January 1876, from Camp Texas Rangers, Laguna de los Calabaso [*sic*]. Printed in *The Daily State Gazette*, 19 January 1876.

7. Pidge, 15 January 1876. The question of utilizing the Sharps carbine or the Winchester may have been resolved as much by economics as by effectiveness. The Sharps were standard issue in 1874, but the Winchester Model 1873 was not in standard use until 1877. Further, the Winchester cost about twice as much as the Sharps. With the constant concern for funding for the Texas Rangers it is not surprising that the Winchester was somewhat of a rare item at this time, although a few rangers undoubtedly managed to purchase with their own funds their personal Winchester. Courtesy Lee A. Silva, correspondence 30 September 1998.

8. William C. Callicott to W.P. Webb, undated document of Las Cuevas Raid. W.P. Webb Collection, 114-16. R. Henderson Shuffler, "'Tell the U.S. soldiers to go to hell . . .'" Sunday *Texas Magazine*, 10 October 1965. Clipping in McNelly Vertical File in CAH.

9. William C. Callicott to W.P. Webb, undated document of Las Cuevas Raid. W.P. Webb Collection, 122.

10. Durham, *Nueces Strip*, 127. The two Miss Kings were Ella Morse King, seventeen years old, and Henrietta Maria King, nineteen years old. They had been enrolled in the Henderson Female Institute, a Presbyterian girls' school in Danville, Kentucky. Nettie had been enrolled first, then in 1871 or 1872 Ella was enrolled. Younger sister Alice joined them in 1874. The Miss Kings were home for the holidays when the rangers brought home the cattle. Presumably the entire family was there and, if so, then the rangers met Mrs. King, the former Henrietta M. Chamberlain, and the other children: Alice Gertrudis King, thirteen years old;

Robert E. Lee King, eleven years old. Tom Lea, *The King Ranch* (Boston: Little, Brown and Company, 1957), 195, 214, 324.

11. *The San Antonio Daily Express*, Supplement, 1 December 1875.

12. Ibid., 1 December 1875. Unfortunately no details of this "interview with President Grant" have yet surfaced.

13. Ibid., 2 December 1875.

14. Ibid., 9 December 1875.

15. Ibid., 10 December 1875.

16. Ibid., 1 January 1876.

17. *The Dallas Herald*, 25 December 1875.

18. *Texas Frontier Troubles*. House of Representatives Report No. 343, 44th Congress, 1st Session, printed in Vol. 1709, Congressional Serial Set. McNelly, incorrectly identified as "S.H. McNally" in the printed report, testified on 24 and 29 January 1876. His testimony appears on pages 8-17.

19. *The Daily State Gazette*, Austin, 20 February 1877. McNelly's testimony carried "great weight" with the congressmen, for he was "direct from the seat of war."

20. *The San Antonio Daily Express*, Supplement, 22 December 1875.

21. Lieutenant T.C. Robinson to Steele, 30 December 1875. This appears although in slightly different form in Steele's *Report of the Adjutant General of the State of Texas for the Year Ending August 31st 1876* (Galveston: Shaw & Blaylock, State Printers, 1876), 9.

22. *The Galveston Daily News*, 21 January 1876. In addition to the *News* article is the notation on Robinson's December 5 report of November operations, "Shf Cameron Co [James G. Browne] Killed *Pedro Parales*.

CHAPTER 18
INVADING THE PENDENCIA

1. *The Daily State Gazette*, 20 January 1876.

2. *The Galveston Daily News*, 8 March 1876, citing a report from Cuero of 4 March.

3. McNelly to Steele, 8 March 1876. The original has not been located in the Texas State Archives but a transcript is among the Walter Prescott Webb Papers, CAH, Austin.

4. *The Galveston Daily News*, 8 March 1876, citing a report from Cuero of 4 March, the DeWitt County deputy was identified as both Agee and Agu in the *News*. *The Galveston Weekly News*, 13 March 1876, citing a report from Cuero of 29 February 1876. *The Galveston Weekly News* of 27 March carried a lengthy report from Gonzales, dated 21 which concluded, "Your correspondent was asked several times why the Governor could not send McNelly back. Has he not the same authority now as he had then? The good people have no fears of an abuse of power placed in his hands, even if done so by the re-enactment of the Davis police law."

5. McNelly to Steele, 8 March 1876.

6. McNelly to Steele, 19 March 1876. *Office of the Adjutant General of Texas. Correspondence Concerning the Texas Rangers, 1876*. Vol. III. Texas State Archives.

7. McNelly to Steele, 8 May 1876. *Adjutant General Correspondence*, Vol. III.

8. McNelly to Steele, telegrams of 18 and 19 May 1876. [William Steele], *Report of the Adjutant-General of the State of Texas for the Year Ending August 31st, 1876* (Galveston: Shaw & Blalock, State Printers, 1876), 9. See also *The San Antonio Daily Express*, 19, 20 and 21 May 1876. Alicia A. Garza, "Hidalgo, Texas" in *The New Handbook of Texas*, Vol. 3, 589.

9. *The San Antonio Daily Herald*, 1 June 1876, correspondence from "Ojo."

10. Ibid., 1 June 1876. *The Corpus Christi Daily Gazette*, 26 May 1876.

11. McNelly to Steele, 31 May 1876. *Adjutant General Correspondence*, Vol. III.

12. [State Police] *Record of Arrests*, 54-55. Ledger Book #401-1001. Original in the Texas State Archives.

13. Paul Adams, "John King Fisher" in *The New Handbook of Texas*, Vol. 2, 1011. Larry Shaver, *This Is King Fisher's Road*, unpublished manuscript, copy in authors' possession.

14. [William Steele], *Report of the Adjutant-General of the State of Texas for the Year Ending August 31st, 1876*, 9. *The San Antonio Daily Express*, 6 June 1876. McNelly to Steele, telegram of June 4, 1876. *The San Antonio Daily Express*, 6 June 1876.

15. McNelly to Steele, 4 June 1876. Durham, "5100 Outlaws", VI, 108-109. Templeton served with McNelly from 6 April to 31 August 1875. Ranger Service Records, Texas State Archives.

16. T.C. Robinson took a leave of absence from McNelly's company in March, 1876 to return to his home in Virginia. In his letter written on March 16 and published in the *Daily State Gazette* of 31 March, he indicated he was "going home to spend my pay" but in reality he intended to kill an old protagonist, Jesse E. Mitchell, the brother of a young lady Robinson loved. The extent of the problems with Jesse Mitchell caused Robinson to leave home and relocate in Texas. After working as a cowboy for a short time he found employment in the printing offices of the Austin *Daily Democratic Statesman*. He found success in writing because numerous letters were published in the *Statesman* prior to his joining McNelly's company. Then while serving in DeWitt County more letters were published describing conditions in that feud-wracked county, and the letters continued while in the Nueces Strip, but now published in the *Daily State Gazette*. The newspaper reports describing the gunfight with Mitchell are conflicting; some termed the confrontation a duel while others termed it an ambush by Robinson. Mitchell was wounded and survived; Robinson did not. His headstone carries the dates of his life and his pen-name, "In Memory of 'Pidge.'/ Lieut. Co. A, Texas Rangers/ Born Novr. 27, 1847/ Died April 3, 1876/ A devoted Son and Brother/ A True Friend and brave/ Soldier rests here./ Green be the turf above thee/ Friend of my better days/ None knew thee but to love thee/ None named thee but in praise." At the top of the headstone is engraved a hand holding a pistol. McNelly's monthly return dated 30 April merely states that Lieutenant T.C. Robinson died at Campbell County, Virginia, on April 4, "while absent with leave." It is believed that the shooting took place on April 3 and Robinson died the next day. Robinson's father and sister survived him and they no doubt chose the inscription for the stone. The young woman Robinson loved was Pidgie E. Mitchell, the brother of the man who killed him.

17. Jennings, *A Texas Ranger*, 108-15; *The San Antonio Daily Express*, 6 and 9 June 1876.

18. Jennings, 111-12.

19. Durham, "5100 Outlaws", VI, 109.

20. Jennings, 115. *The San Antonio Daily Express*, 10 June 1876.

21. Jennings, 115.

22. *The San Antonio Daily Express*, 9 June 1876.

23. Ibid., 10 June 1876.

24. Durham, "5100 Outlaws", VI, 109.

25. *The San Antonio Daily Express*, 17 June 1876.

26. McNelly to Steele, 4 June 1876, telegram from Eagle Pass; *The Daily*

State Gazette, 20 June 1876; *The Daily Democratic Statesman,* 20 June 1876.

27. *The San Antonio Daily Express,* 17 June 1876.

28. Ibid., 28 June 1876.

29. *The San Antonio Daily Express,* 24-25 June 1876; *the Waco Examiner,* 22 June 1876; *The Daily Democratic Statesman,* 20 June 1876.

30. *The San Antonio Daily Express,* 23 June 1876.

31. *The San Antonio Daily Express,* 24 June 1876.

32. *The St. Louis* (Missouri) *Republican,* 15 June 1876; *The San Antonio Daily Herald,* 24 June 1876.

33. *General Laws of the State of Texas Passed at the Session of the Fifteenth Legislature, Approved July 22, 1876* (Galveston: 1876).

34. *The San Antonio Daily Express,* 13 July 1876; *The Daily Democratic Statesman,* Austin, 3 October 1876; *The Galveston Daily News,* 22 October 1876.

35. *The Advocate,* Victoria, Texas, 17 August 1876.

36. Muster and Pay Roll, Special State Troops, 25 January 1877. *The Daily Democratic Statesman,* 17 August 1876, refers to Hall as being the "late Sergeant of Arms of the House."

37. *The San Antonio Daily Express,* 26 August 1876.

38. *The Daily Democratic Statesman,* 26 September 1876, citing an undated item from the Oakville *Tribune.*

39. *The Advocate,* Victoria, Texas, 19 October 1876, citing an undated item from the Goliad correspondent.

40. Ibid., 31 August 1876.

41. Armstrong to McNelly, 1 October 1876, published in *The Daily Democratic Statesman,* Austin, *The Galveston Daily News* and *The San Antonio Daily Express,* all of 3 October 1876.

42. *The San Antonio Daily Express,* 3 October 1876.

43. The 1850 Chambers County, Alabama census shows the James C. Key family consisting of the father, wife Angelina, twenty-two, two-year-old Benjamin and daughter, Ally. The family has not been located on any 1860 census but in 1870 the Keys were in Navarro County, Texas; son Benjamin, J.A. and L.N. [Noley] have now a younger sister Leta, six-years-old. Presumably by then daughter Ally had married and was living elsewhere. The 1870 Texas census shows Angelina B. and husband J.C. Key, both from Georgia, as farming and keeping house. Mr. Key claimed $17,000 real estate and $600 worth of personal estate. L.N. "Noley" Key was then ten years of age. The three children then living at home were born in Alabama. *Population Schedule of the Seventh and Ninth Census of the United States,* Chambers County, Alabama, 345A and Navarro County, Texas census, 107B, respectively, 1850 and 1870.

44. Dan Mullen to Steele, 3 September 1876. Correspondence in Adjutant General's Files, Texas State Archives.

45. T.W. Jones, 2nd Lieutenant, 10th Cavalry, to Acting Assistant Adjutant General, District of the Nueces, Fort Clark, Texas, 22 August 1877. Original in Records of Governor Richard B. Hubbard, Texas State Archives.

46. *The Daily Democratic Statesman,* 14 October 1876, in the "Texas-Facts and Fancies" column, citing an undated item from the Granbury *Vidette.*

CHAPTER 19
DYING EMBERS

1. *The Daily Democratic Statesman,* 19 September 1876.

2. Dr. Phillip H. Brassell and his wife Mary Ann were both born in Fayette County, Georgia, he on 13 October 1827, and she on 16 July 1829. Their son

George T. was born there 15 September 1854. In Georgia Dr. Brassell served as a member of the Constitutional Convention of 1866 and the Georgia Legislature in 1868, 1869 and 1870. The family, perhaps hoping the climate would improve the doctor's health, moved to Texas in 1870, settling in December in Shiloh, a little community near Yorktown. Their choice of a residence placed them in the center of the feuding families. The birth dates for the Brassells are from the grave stones in the "Upper" Yorktown Cemetery, DeWitt County. The doctor had been in poor health for the previous few years, in the last stages of consumption, and he knew he had little time left. The day prior to his murder, Monday, 18 September, he had made a "disposition of his property, gave money to his wife to defray funeral expenses" and selected his burial place in a Yorktown cemetery. *The Galveston Daily News*, 4 October 1876. *Population Schedule of the Ninth Census of the United States, 1870*, DeWitt County, Texas, enumerated by Willis Fawcett, — June, 252B. *Cases Argued and Adjudged in the Court of Appeals of the State of Texas.* Vol. 8 (St. Louis: F.H. Thomas & Co. 1880), "W. Cox, J. Ryan, and Joe Sitterlie *v.* The State," 260.

3. *The Galveston Daily News*, 22 September 1876. This article was headlined "Kuklux Law at Cuero."

4. *The Galveston Daily News*, 4 October 1876.

5. Jennings, *A Texas Ranger*, 139.

6. *Cases Argued and Adjudged in the Court of Appeals of the State of Texas.* Vol. 8 (St. Louis: F.H. Thomas & Co. 1880), 278.

7. *The Galveston Daily News*, 4 October 1876.

8. The Sitterlie-Cox marriage is recorded in Marriage Record Book "D," DeWitt County, license No. 1548, page 182. The Meador-Augustine marriage record is license No. 1527, issued 21 November 1876, page 175. Ironically on the same page is recorded license No. 1528, recording the marriage of Oscar F. Pridgen and Miss Mary A. Lowe, united by W.H.H. Biggs. Pridgen had formerly served under McNelly and was the son of Senator Bolivar J. Pridgen.

9. Jennings, *A Texas Ranger*, 140-42. Both the Meador-Augustine and Sitterlie-Cox weddings were performed by S.L. Bradley, Minister of the Gospel. Muster rolls do not identify those rangers with Hall but William Warren Sterling, a Texas Ranger of the 20th Century, wrote that "of the actual participants in the wedding festival arrest" he knew personally Corporal W.L. Rudd, George W. Talley and George Durham; he later saw John B. Armstrong suggesting he was present also. Jennings could have been present. If so Hall had under his command Rudd, Talley, Durham, Armstrong, Jennings and eleven others. William W. Sterling, *Trails and Trials of a Texas Ranger* (Norman: University of Oklahoma Press, 1959), 405.

10. Durham, "5100 Outlaws", VII, 112.

11. Jennings, *A Texas Ranger*, 143.

12. Jennings, *A Texas Ranger*, 143-44. Although differing with Durham on many points, Durham did remember that Judge Pleasants made an impassioned speech, McNelly placing four rangers on either side of the bench and then he — McNelly himself — opened court. "Rangers! Ready ! Load! Aim! This court is now opened. At the first sign of any disturbance from the audience, you Rangers will shoot, and shoot to kill." Then Pleasants made a speech similar in tone to that recalled by Jennings, but considerably shorter. Durham recalled that Pleasants pointed out that as long as Captain McNelly and his rangers were there, "the lawless cannot conquer." Durham, "5100 Outlaws", VII, 112.2.

13. Monthly Return of L.H. McNelly, 31 December 1876 at Clinton. Original in Texas State archives.

14. Frederic Remington, *How the Law Got Into the Chaparral. Conversations*

With Old Texas Rangers, edited by John H. Jenkins (Austin: Jenkins Publishing Company. 1987), 25. This had originally appeared in *Harper's Magazine*, December 1896.

15. J.L. Hall to Adjutant General William Steele, 4 January 1877. Original telegram in Adjutant General Correspondence, Texas State Archives. *The Galveston Daily News*, 6 January 1877.

16. *The Galveston Daily News*. 6 January 1877.

17. *The Daily Democratic Statesman*, 10 January 1877.

18. C.L. Sonnichsen, *I'll Die Before I'll Run: The Story of the Great Feuds of Texas* (New York: The Devin-Adair Company, 1961 edition), 114-15.

19. L.H. McNelly to Adjutant General William Steele, 9 October 1876. Original in Texas State Archives.

20. *The Daily Democratic Statesman*, 24 October 1876

21. *The Houston Daily Telegraph*, 19 October 1876. Correspondence from "Prickly Pear." This description of McNelly's appearing "not more than forty years of age" suggests that McNelly's disease made him look considerably older than he actually was. Born in March 1844, he was only thirty-one when interviewed by Prickly Pear.

22. *The Advocate*, Victoria, Texas, 19 October 1876; *The San Antonio Daily Express*, 20 October 1876.

23. *The Daily Democratic Statesman*, 24 October 1876 and 7 November 1876 Supplement.

24. *The Daily Democratic Statesman*, 15 November 1876 Supplement and 3 December 1876 Supplement.

25. McNelly to Steele, 18 November 1876, from San Antonio. From the typed transcript in the W.P. Webb Papers, CAH, Austin.

26. McNelly to Steele, 18 November 1876.

27. J.L. Hall to Steele, 23 November 1876, from Clinton. The Goliad Bank Robbery has never been completely examined. In Hall's letter to Steele of 4 November he stated that Frank Callison had made a full confession and implicated eleven others besides himself: brother Tom Callison, William Cavitt, James T. Trimble, Lark Ferguson, Alfred Day, John Grun, alias John Cabler and a "fmc" one Thomas Jasper. These were "aided and abetted in different ways" by John King Fisher, William Taylor, "Dock" [Brack?] Cornett and William Brooking.

28. *The Daily Democratic Statesman*, 3 December 1876 Supplement.

29. Ibid., 3 December 1876 Supplement.

30. Ibid., 5 December 1876 Supplement.

31. Ibid., 6 November 1876. Monthly Return, November 1876.

32. Report of J.L. Hall, 20 January 1877. "Received of Captain McNelly the following described government property." Original in Texas State Archives.

33. *The Galveston Daily News*, 26 January 1877.

34. *The San Antonio Daily Express*, 30 January 1877.

35. McNelly Service Record, Texas State Library.

36. *The San Antonio Daily Express*, 30 January 1877.

37. *The Daily Democratic Statesman*, 22 July 1877.

38. *The San Antonio Daily Express*, 27 July 1877.

39. *The Galveston Daily News*, 6 February 1877; *The San Antonio Daily Express*, 9 February 1877.

40. Steele to Governor Richard Hubbard, 8 March 1877.

41. *The San Antonio Daily Express*, 11 February 1877.

42. *The Daily Democratic Statesman*, 3 February 1877.

43. Ibid., 18 February 1877.

44. Ibid., 5 May 1877.

45. *The San Antonio Daily Express*, 27 May 1877; *The Daily Democratic Statesman*, 22 July 1877.

46. *The Daily Democratic Statesman*, 14 August 1877.

47. *The Galveston Daily News*, 24 August 1877.

48. *The Western Chronicle*, Sutherland Springs, Wilson County, Texas, 31 August 1877.

49. *The Brenham Daily Banner*, 25 August 1877.

50. John McNelly to Adjutant General William Steele. 4 September 1877. John McNelly telegraphed for a leave of absence, pointing out that he was in Hall's company. Original in Adjutant General Correspondence. Texas State Archives. *The Galveston Daily News*, 7 September 1877.

51. *The Galveston Daily News*, 17 October 1877.

CHAPTER 20
CAREY ALONE

1. *The Dallas Weekly Herald*, 15 September 1877.

2. *The Victoria Advocate*, 22 September 1877.

3. *The Victoria Advocate*, 26 January 1878.

4. *The Dallas Daily Herald*, 1 February 1878; *The Brenham Daily Banner*, 5 February 1878. *The Dallas Daily Herald* reprinted the article from *The San Antonio Daily Express*. Oakland, located in the northwest portion of Colorado County, south of Washington County, began as a store erected on the stage line between Columbus, Colorado County, and Gonzales, Gonzales County. The population never exceeded three hundred.

5. Mrs. L.H. McNelly to Colonel J.Y. Dashiell, 14 September 1877. Steele to Hubbard, 8 October and Hubbard to Dashiell, 12 October. Records of Governor Hubbard, File 301-99 #18 and Letter Press Book 24 September 1877 to 8 December 1877, 205-206. Originals in the Texas State Archives.

6. *The Houston Daily Post*, 29 October and 12 November 1880.

7. *Population Schedule of the Tenth Census of the United States, 1880*, Washington County, Texas, 11 June, 195A-B.

8. *Population Schedule of the Twelfth Census of the United States, 1900*, Travis County, Texas. 6 June, E.D. 96, Precinct No. 3, 166A.

9. *Application for Pardon*: "Reb McNelly." Original documents in Texas State Archives.

10. S.J. Adams to Governor C.A. Culberson, 21 April 1898, in Records of the Governor, 301-160-109. Adams joined McNelly's Volunteer Militia Company on 25 July 1874 and served until 1 February 1877.

11. *The Tombstone Prospector*, Tombstone, Cochise County, Arizona. 2 January 1907; and *The Austin Statesman*, 4 January 1907.

12. John B. Armstrong to Governor C.A. Culberson, 6 September 1895. Original document in Governor's Records, Texas State Archives.

13. Undated petition for Governor C.A. Culberson from "Taxpayers of Southwest Texas." Governor Culberson Papers, Texas State Archives.

14. *The San Antonio Daily Express*, 20 January 1896.

15. The Wroe family settled in Fayette County near La Grange. On 11 October 1861, at the age of nineteen, he enlisted in Company I, 5th Regiment Texas Mounted Volunteers of the H.H. Sibley Brigade and was sworn in the following month. He rose to the rank of corporal and served throughout the war. He was surrendered by General E. Kirby Smith to General E.R.S. Canby at Columbus, Colorado County on 29 July 1865. Following the war's end he engaged in the sawmill business until 1870 with his father-in-law. He was in the saddlery business

in Giddings, Lee County, for thirteen years, then established himself in Austin on Congress Avenue, between Third and Fourth Streets. By 1900 his firm was the leading saddlery business in Austin. Wroe first married on 21 December 1865 to Miss Bursheba Jane Kennedy, and the couple had five children. In November 1906 Mrs. Wroe died. Ellis A. Davis and Edwin H. Grobe, compilers and editors, *The New Encyclopedia of Texas* (Dallas: Texas Development Bureau, 1922 [?]), 782-83. *Soldier's Application for A Pension*: W.T. Wroe. No. 47594. *Widow's Application for A Pension*: Mrs. W.T. Wroe. No. 51100. Originals in the Texas State Archives.

16. *The American-Statesman*, Austin, 30 October 1938. Mrs. Wroe's burial was on 30 October following a funeral service held in the St. David's Episcopal Church of Austin, clergyman James S. Allen presiding. *Archives of the Episcopal Church at Austin*, Burials, 394-95, in *Parish Registers*, Vol. 4, 1928-41 microfilm reel #5.

BIBLIOGRAPHY

OFFICIAL RECORDS

UNITED STATES

The War of the Rebellion: A Compilation of the Official Records of the Union and Confederate Armies. Washington: Government Printing Office.

McNelly, Leander H. Civil War Muster Record. National Archives, Washington, D. C.

Official Records of the Union and Confederate Navies of the War of the Rebellion. Washington: Government Printing Office, 1905.

Texas Frontier Troubles in House of Representatives Report # 343, 44th Congress, 1st Session, Volume 1709 Serial Set.

Executive Document 1. Part 2. House of Representatives Report Volume I, 44th Congress, 1st Session.

Soldier's Application for Pension, No. 47594. William Thomas Wroe.

Widow's Application for A Pension, No. 51100. Mrs. W. T. Wroe.

TEXAS

Records of the State Police, Texas State Archives.

Records of the Texas State Police. Adjutant-General Papers, Texas State Library, Austin.

Records of the Adjutant-General, Texas State Library, Austin.

Court Record Book E. District Court, Bastrop County, Texas.

Civil Minutes Book F. District Court, DeWitt County, Texas

Cases Argued and Decided in the Supreme Court of the State of Texas. Gaines v. The State. St. Louis, The Gilbert Book Co., 1875, 1882. Terrell & Walker.

Cases Argued and Adjudged in the Court of Appeals of the State of Texas. Vol. 8. St. Louis: F.H. Thomas & Co. 1880.

Marriage Record Books. DeWitt County, Texas

General Laws of the State of Texas Passed at the Session of the Fifteenth Legislature Approved July 22, 1876. Galveston: 1876.

Application for Pardon: "Reb McNelly" Original petition in Texas State Library, Austin, Texas.

Tax Rolls, 1872-1873. Washington County, Texas. Microfilm in Texas State Library.

CENSUS RECORDS

Austin County, Texas 1860
Brazos County, Texas 1870
Brooke County, Virginia 1840, 1850
Chambers County, Alabama 1850, 1870
DeWitt County, Texas 1870

CENSUS RECORDS (CONTINUED)

Edwards County, Texas 1900
Freestone County, Texas 1870
Gonzales County, Texas 1870
Grimes County, Texas 1870
Harris County, Texas 1860
Milam County, Texas 1860
Montgomery County, Texas 1860
Navarro County, Texas 1870
Nueces County, Texas 1870
Robertson County, Texas 1860
Travis County, Texas 1900
Washington County, Texas 1860, 1870, 1880
Wood County, Texas 1870
Agriculture Census of Washington County, Texas 1870

UNPUBLISHED SOURCES

Archives of the Episcopal Church at Austin, Texas. *Parish Registers*, Vol. 4.
Brice, Donaly E. "The Good, the Bad, and the Ugly: A Comparison of Three
    State Police Captains" [L. H. McNelly, Thomas Williams and Jack Helm].
    Paper presented at the 101st Annual Meeting of the Texas State Historical
    Association, 7 March 1997. Copy in authors' files.
Callicott, William C. Papers in Center for American History, Austin, Texas.
Hunter, Harold V. "Civil War Diary: Dr. Harold V. Hunter Co. I, 7th Regiment,
    Texas Mounted Volunteers." Transcript copy in Martin Hardwick Hall
    Papers, 1982/14-5. Texas State Archives, Austin, Texas.
McNelly, Leander H. Papers in Center for American History, Austin, Texas.
McNelly, Mary Ellen, Sister Clared: "The McNelly Family From Ireland to
    Virginia to Texas." Typed transcript in authors' collection.
Pridgen, Jack S. *History of the Pridgen Family*. Manuscript in authors' files.
Shaver, Larry. *This Is King Fisher's Road*. Unpublished biography of John King
    Fisher.
Webb, Walter Prescott Papers. Files re: *The Texas Rangers*, letters, drafts, etc.
    Center for American History, Austin, Texas.

SECONDARY SOURCES

The Handy Book for Genealogists. Logan, Utah. Everton Publishing Company. 8th
    edition. 1991.
Adams, Ramon F. *Six-Guns and Saddle Leather: A Bibliography of Books and
    Pamphlets on Western Outlaws and Gunmen*. New edition, revised. Cleveland,
    Ohio: John T. Zubal, Inc., 1982.
Adams, S.J. "Texas Frontier Reminiscences. L.H. McNelly, Our Captain." in
    Railway Carmen's Journal, Vol. 16, No. 10 (October 1911), 556-57.
Barr, Alwyn and Robert A. Calvert. *Black Leaders: Texans for Their Times*. Austin:
    Texas State Historical Association, 1981.
Bartholomew, Ed *The Encyclopedia of Texas Ghost Towns*. Fort Davis, 1982.
    Privately printed.

SECONDARY SOURCES (CONTINUED)

Davis, Edmund J. *Message of Gov. Edmund J. Davis with Documents in Relation to Lawlessness and Crime in Hill and Walker Counties.* Austin: J.G. Tracy, State Printer, 1871.

Davis, Ellis A. and Edwin H. Grobe (compilers & editors) *The New Encyclopedia of Texas.* Dallas: Texas Development Bureau, 1922 [?]

Day, Jack Hays. *The Sutton-Taylor Feud.* San Antonio: Sid Murray and Son, 1937.

Dodson, Ruth. "The Noakes Raid" in *Frontier Times*, Vol. 23, No. 10, (July 1946).

Dotson, Susan Merle (compiler) *Who's Who of the Confederacy.* San Antonio: The Naylor Company. 1966.

Durham, George (as told to Clyde Wantland). *Taming the Nueces Strip: The Story of McNelly's Rangers.* Austin: University of Texas Press, 1962.

Durham, George (as told to Clyde Wantland). "On the Trail of 5100 Outlaws." *West Magazine*, 1937.

Emmett, Chris. *Shanghai Pierce: A Fair Likeness.* Norman: University of Oklahoma Press, 1953.

Fayette County History. Dallas: The Curtis Media Company, 1996.

Farrow, Marion Humphreys. *Troublesome Times in Texas.* San Antonio: The Naylor Company, 1959, 1960.

Fitterer, Gary P. "Let Justice Be Done Our Western Citizens." *The Quarterly* of The National Association for Outlaw and Lawman History (NOLA) (July-September 1992).

Franklin, Robert Morris, *Battle of Galveston January 1, 1863.* Publication of speech by Robert Morris Franklin, Galveston: San Luis Press, 1975.

Goebel, Patsy and Rosemary Sheppard, compilers, DeWitt County Historical Committee, *The History of DeWitt County, Texas.* Dallas: Curtis Media Company, 1991.

Graber, Henry W. *A Terry Texas Ranger: The Life Record of H. W. Graber.* 1916. Facsimile edition. Austin: State House Press, 1987

Hagen, William H. "The Nuecestown Raid of 1875: A Border Incident." *Arizona and the West*, Vol. I, No. 3, (Autumn 1959).

Hamersly, Lewis R. (compiler) *The Records: Living Officers of the U. S. Navy and Marine Corps.* Philadelphia: J.P. Lippincott & Co., 1878.

Hardin, John Wesley. *The Life of John Wesley Hardin, as Written by Himself.* Introduction by Robert G. McCubbin. 1896. Reprint. Norman: University of Oklahoma Press, 1961.

Howell, William Randolph. *Westward the Texans. The Civil War Journal of Private William Randolph Howell.* Edited with an introduction by Dr. Jerry Thompson. El Paso: The Texas Western Press, 1990.

Jennings, N.A. *A Texas Ranger.* 1899. Reprint. Norman: University of Oklahoma Press, 1997.

Lea, Tom. *The King Ranch.* Boston: Little, Brown and Company, 1957.

McCampbell, Coleman. *Saga of a Frontier Seaport.* Dallas: South-West Press, 1934.

McDonald, Archie P. "Secession, War, and Reconstruction in Texas" in *Journal of Confederate History*, Southern Heritage Press, Vol. 7, (1991).

SECONDARY SOURCES (CONTINUED)

McNelly, Bert. "Thomas H. McNelly." A Proud Heritage: A History of Uvalde County, Texas, written by the people of Uvalde County. Uvalde, Texas: El Progreso Club, 1975.

McNelly, Charles B. "Mementoes of Charles B. McNelly." Avis, Annie Maud Knittel (compiler) History of Burton. Vols. 1-2. Wolfe City, Texas: Henington Publishing Co., Vols. 1-2, 1974.

Mayfield, Mrs. G.C. "Interesting Narrative of Capt. W.L. Rudd Texas Ranger" in Frontier Times, (September and December 1932).

Metz, Leon C. John Wesley Hardin: Dark Angel of Texas. El Paso: Mangan Books, 1996.

Miller, Rick. Bloody Bill Longley. Wolfe City, Tex.: Henington Publishing Company, 1996.

Morris, Leopold. "The Mexican Raid of 1875 on Corpus Christi" in The Quarterly of the Texas State Historical Association, Volume IV, No. 1, (July, 1900).

Murphree, Nellie (compiler) History of DeWitt County. Edited by Robert W. Shook. Victoria: The Rose International Imprints, 1962.

Navarro County History. Navarro County Historical Society. Dallas: Taylor Publishing Co., 1978. W.P. Murchison and William Polk.

Noel, Theophilus. A Campaign from Santa Fe to the Mississippi: Being A History of the Old Sibley Brigade from the First Organization to the present time. (Editor Martin Hardwick Hall). Houston: The Stagecoach Press, 1961.

Nolan, Frederick. Bad Blood: The Life and Times of the Horrell Brothers. Stillwater, Oklahoma: Barbed Wire Press, 1994.

Nunn, William C. Texas Under the Carpetbaggers. Austin: University of Texas Press, 1962

Parsons, Chuck. "Mason Arnold - 'He Came from Schulenberg'" in The Quarterly of The National Association for Outlaw and Lawman History (NOLA) (October-December 1997).

Parsons, Chuck. "The DeWitt County Feud." History of DeWitt County, Texas. Dallas: Curtis Media Company, 1991.

Parsons, Chuck. "Pidge" A Texas Ranger from Virginia: The Life and Letters of T.C. Robinson, Washington County Volunteer Militia Company "A". Wolfe City, Texas: Henington Publishing Company, 1985.

Rather, Charles Taylor. "Around The Square In 1862 With A Barefoot Boy" in Huntsville and Walker County, Texas: A Bicentennial History. Crews, D'Anne McAdams (Editor and Compiler) Huntsville: Sam Houston State University Press, 1976.

Remington, Frederic. How the Law Got Into the Chaparral. Conversations with Old Texas Rangers. Edited by John H. Jenkins. Austin: Jenkins Publishing Company, 1987.

Rose, Victor M. The Texas Vendetta; or, The Sutton-Taylor Feud. New York: J.J. Little & Co., 1880. Facsimile reprint. The Frontier Press of Texas, 1956.

Scharf, J. Thomas. History of the Confederate States Navy from its Organization to the Surrender of its Last Vessel. Albany, New York: Joseph McDonough, 1886.

Seelingson, Lelia. A History of Indianola. Cuero: The Cuero Record, n.d.

Singletary, Otis A. "The Texas Militia During Reconstruction." The Southwestern Historical Quarterly, Vol. 60, No. 1, (July 1956).

SECONDARY SOURCES (CONTINUED)

Smith, William H. "With Sibley in New Mexico, the Journal of William
    Henry Smith." Diary contributed and edited by Walter A. Faulkner in
    West Texas Historical Association Year Book, Vol. 27 (October 1951).
Sonnichsen, C.L. I'll Die Before I'll Run: The Story of the Great Feuds of Texas.
    New York: The Devin-Adair Co., 1962.
Spenser, Joelyn. "Adolph Neese." Fayette County Heritage, Vol. 2, Dallas:
    Curtis Media, Inc., 1996
[Steele, William] A List of Fugitives from Justice. 1878. Facsimile reprint.
    Austin: State House Press, 1997.
Sterling, William Warren. Trails and Trials of A Texas Ranger. Norman:
    University ofOklahoma Press, 1959, 1979.
Sutton, Robert C. Jr., The Sutton-Taylor Feud. Quanah, Texas: Nortex Press,
    1974.
Taylor, John. Bloody Valverde: A Civil War Battle on the Rio Grande, February
    21, 1862. Albuquerque: University of New Mexico Press, 1995.
Teel, T.T. "Sibley's New Mexico Campaign - Its Objects and the Causes of
    Its Failures." in Battles and Leaders of the Civil War. New York: The
    Century Company. 1888.
Thompson, Jerry. Confederate General of the West: Henry Hopkins Sibley. 1987.
    Reprint. College Station: Texas A&M Press, 1996.
Tise, Sammy. Texas County Sheriffs. Tise Genealogical Research, Hallettsville,
    Texas 1989.
Truitt, Eddie Day. The Taylor Party. Wortham, Texas 1992. Privately printed.
Tyler, Ron, Editor in Chief. The New Handbook of Texas. Vols. 1-6. Austin:
    The State   Historical Association, 1996.
Webb, Walter Prescott. The Texas Rangers: A Century of Frontier Defense. New
    York: Houghton, Mifflin Company, 1935.
Wood, W.D. Reminiscences of Reconstruction in Texas and Reminiscences of
    Texas and Texans Fifty Years Ago. San Marcos[?], Texas, 1902.
Wooten, Dudley Goodall (editor) A Comprehensive History of Texas: 1685-
    1897. Dallas: William G. Scarff (1898) and Austin: Texas State
    Historical Association, 1986.
Wooster, Ralph A. Texas and Texans in the Civil War. Austin: Eakin Press,
    1995.

INTERVIEWS & CORRESPONDENCE

Dan Alger, Curatorial Technician. Interview at Texas Ranger Hall of Fame,
    21 August 1998.
Annie Maud Avis, Burton historian. Interview at her home 15 March
    1996.
Byron A. Johnson, Director, Texas Ranger Hall of Fame and Museum to
    authors, 8 April 1997.
Fred J. Romanski, Archivist, National Archives, to authors, 24 June 1996.
Eliza McNelly Shannon to authors, 21 March 1996.
Mrs. W.T. Wroe to E.D. McNelly, 2 January 1937.

NEWSPAPERS

The Intelligencer-Echo, Austin, Texas
The Herald and Planter, Hallettsville, Texas
The Weekly Gazette, Corpus Christi, Texas
The Daily Republican, St. Louis, Missouri
The Burnet Bulletin, Burnet, Texas
The Weekly Herald, Dallas, Texas
Norton's Union Intelligencer, Dallas, Texas
The Daily Commercial, Dallas, Texas
The Daily Express, San Antonio, Texas
Flake's Daily Bulletin, Galveston, Texas
Flake's Semi-Weekly Bulletin, Galveston, Texas
The Daily Banner, Brenham, Texas
The Daily Herald, San Antonio, Texas
The Daily Telegraph, Houston, Texas
The Houston Daily Times, Houston, Texas
The Galveston Daily News, Galveston, Texas
The Galveston Weekly News, Galveston, Texas
The New York Herald, New York, New York
The Weekly State Gazette, Austin, Texas
The American-Statesman, Austin, Texas
The Daily Democratic Statesman, Austin, Texas
The Weekly Democratic Statesman, Austin, Texas
The Tombstone Prospector, Tombstone, Arizona
The Hempstead Reporter, Hempstead, Texas
The Daily Austin Republican, Austin, Texas
The Daily State Journal, Austin, Texas
The Bastrop Advertiser, Bastrop, Texas
The Weekly State Journal, Austin, Texas
The Advocate, Victoria, Texas
The Houston Daily Post, Houston, Texas
The Western Chronicle, Sutherland Springs, Texas
The Weekly Star, Cuero, Texas

INDEX

McPhail, J.R., 12
Meador, Amanda Augustine, 283
Meador, John, 63, 131
Meador, William D., 281-88, 296
Melville, Andrew, 122
Merriam, H.C., 200, 201
Merrick (policeman), 89
Meyer, Taylor, 57
Middleton, C.M., 148-49
Milam Co., Tex., 56, 89, 123
Miller, George W., 212
Miller, Goodloe, 57
Miller, Rick, 62
Millican, Tex., 113
Mitchell, Mr., 274
Monell, Mr., 87
Montgomery Co., Tex., 56
Moore, John H., 12
Moore, Mr., 87
Moore, R.J., 44
Moreland, Isaac N., 12
Morgan, J.B., 142
Mouton, Alfred, 34-35, 36
Mullen, Daniel, 278
Mullen, George H., 275, 278
Mungia, Abundo, 263
Myers (state policeman), 113

Nacogdoches Co., Tex., 56
Nash, Oscar F., 154
Navarro Co., Tex., 100
Navasota, Tex., 77, 79, 84, 85-86, 88, 90, 123
Neale, William, 254
Neese, William, 114-15
Nelms, James A., 100-104
Newcomb, James P., 116, 125
Newman, Mrs. Robert A., 5
Newton Co., Tex., 56
Newton, Mr., 121
Nichols, W.H., 34
Noakes, Thomas John, 167-69, 173, 179, 96
Noel, Mr., 101
Northington, E.A., 137, 149
Norton, A.B., 127
Nueces Co., Tex., 55
Nuecestown, Tex., 167-71, 179

O'Connor, Lt., 222
O'Shaughnessy, Joseph P., 199
Oakland, Tex., 302
Oakville, Tex., 264, 273-74, 289
Oberchain, Burd, 264, 276
Olguin, Jose Maria, 166, 194, 197, 198, 212, 274
Orange Co., Tex., 56
Ord, E.O.C., 177, 193-94, 213, 278
Orrell, Roe P., 157, 200, 210-11, 227, 230, 287, 291

Outlaw, Nathanial A., 73-79, 84, 87-88

Page, Samuel H., 167, 173
Palestine, Tex., 68
Paramore, Green, 97, 115
Parker, Maj., 253-54
Parker, Mr., 56
Parks, Fred, 73
Parrish, Jonathan, 73-79, 84, 85
Parrish, William G. "Willie", 75, 76
Parrott, A.L., 275
Parsons, William H., 55-56
Patrick, J.H., 69
Pearce, Benjamin, 57
Pearce, Ed, 57-60, 66
Pearce, John, 57-60, 66
Pennington, Hugh, 73-75
Penrose, Thomas N., 30
Perales, Pedro, 257
Perez, Lino, 263
Perryville, Tex., 120
Pierce, Abel Head "Shanghai", 60-61
Pipes, Mr., 288
Pitts, Robert, 227, 247-51
Pitts, T.T., 42, 44
Pleasanton, Tex., 273
Pleasants, Henry Clay, 285-87, 292
Polk Co., Tex., 56
Porter, Frank, 190
Potter, Joseph H., 177, 216, 218, 233-34, 238-39
Powers, Stephen, 254
Prendergast, Davis M., 125-27
Pridgen, Bolivar J., 151, 152, 170-71
Pridgen, Oscar F., 171
Pridgen, Wiley, 170
Priestly, Joseph L., 109
Procop, Mr., 94
Pyron, Charles L., 19-20, 27

Quesenberry, T.J., 290
Quesenberry, T.M., 287
Quitman, Tex., 113-14

Ragland, H., 130
Randlett, James Franklin, 216, 219, 221-25, 232, 234
Rather, Charles Taylor, 76-77
Rather, George W., 75, 76-77
Raymond, James H., 292
Reagan, Richard, 115
Rector, H.G., "Deaf," 137, 193, 196, 200, 227
Red River Co., Tex., 54
Redmon, John M., 126-27
Refugio Co., Tex., 55
Reiley, James, 11
Rellas, Rafael, 107
Remey, George C., 216
Remington, Frederic, 286